THE FAIRCLOTH FAMILY HISTORY

A Compilation of
Resources and Genealogy Records

Coat of Arms

Faircloth

Joyce Christine Faircloth Judah, M. Ed.

HERITAGE BOOKS
2007

HERITAGE BOOKS
AN IMPRINT OF HERITAGE BOOKS, INC.

Books, CDs, and more—Worldwide

For our listing of thousands of titles see our website
at
www.HeritageBooks.com

Published 2007 by
HERITAGE BOOKS, INC.
Publishing Division
65 East Main Street
Westminster, Maryland 21157-5026

International Standard Book Number: 978-0-7884-4472-2

DEDICATION

This book is dedicated to my loving daughter,
Jennifer Heather Brooke Judah Fisher, my grandson, Isaih Dale Fisher, my son-in-law,
Jonathan Fisher, and my dear, dear parents, Herman Remus and Erika Else Kreisler
Faircloth. I love them all from the depths of my heart. We are all looking forward to the birth
of my second grandson, Jacob Allen Fisher, sometime in April 2007.

About the Author

Joyce Christine Faircloth Judah earned her B. S. Degree from Pembroke State University and her M. Ed. Degree from Campbell University, Buies Creek, NC. She recently retired from the NC Public Schools system where she worked the past 18 years as a Middle School Counselor, working a total of thirty years in education. She spends her retirement tending to her beloved English Springer Spaniels and her volunteer work with the Brunswick Search and Rescue Team, NC, as the Chief and lead canine trainer.

Christy began this work about 1978. Christy is the daughter of Herman R. and Erika E. Faircloth. She has one daughter, Jennifer Heather Brooke Judah Fisher. She is also the author of An Ancient History of Dogs: Spaniels through the Ages, and K9 SAR 101: Building a Basic Foundation for Search and Rescue Dog Training.

Table of Contents

Essay by Herman R. Faircloth
Holden Beach, N. C.

One morning my wife and I were walking on the beach and God's presence was with us so strong that I saw a lot of Him in the things I saw and found.

I saw the stars and the sun rising which reminded me of the birth and crucifixion of Christ. We saw the waves and thought of the storm when Jesus said "Peace Be Still", and baptism...what it means. I found a pair of old sandals that reminded me of the sandals Jesus wore on the dusty roads and paths in His ministry. I found some old rags that reminded me of the story of the man begot by demons and how Jesus cast the demons out. I saw fish in the water and this reminded me of the time Jesus fed the multitude with just a few fish.

An old fishing net reminded me when Jesus told the fishermen to case their nets to the other side and they caught so many fish they almost sunk the boat, and, also, when Jesus told the apostles, "I will make you fishers of men". An old pair of glasses caught my eye and I wondered if during Jesus' time, the people wore glasses. Some old wood that I found brought my attention to a shipwreck off shore that reminded me of Paul when he was shipwrecked.

I found some seaweed and it reminded me of the manna God provided for His people in the desert and wilderness. Out of the surf, I saw porpoise playing which reminded me of Noah and the ark and Jonah and the whale or great fish. I was reminded of the fact that Jesus gives Life when I found some conch eggs and I thought long and hard about the everlasting life Jesus can and will give if one will accept Him.

My delight and joy was shattered when I found a dead bird and some fish washing up on the shore, but my joy was restored when I thought again about how Jesus can return us back to life if we just believe in Him. Remembering that life is sort of like the waves coming in and going out—Life is our choice to make.

I was again reminded of the love of Jesus when I saw a mother bird and her little ones. What brought all of this together was when I found an old piece of wood with rusty nails sticking out of it. This reminded me of the cross and how Jesus was tacked to the cross with three rusty nails. I truly felt God through the Holy Spirit and knew His presence was with us. I truly thank Him for allowing and showing these treasures to us.

As the many grains of sand, we walked on, so is God's strength and knowledge. Thank you, Lord, for helping me to know Life.

Essay by Herman R. Faircloth, 2005

Great-Grandfather Poppa (Herman) with Isaih Dale Fisher, 2005

Preface

The Faircloth Family Data has been compiled as a resource for all those searching for their family history. When resources were in doubt, a note is made as to the accuracy. Over 1500 individuals are listed in this compilation of our family history. It is with love and a respect for our ancestors that this project began. This is a dedication of the importance of family to whom we are all thankful. I hope our descendents continue to document the expansion of our family.

Note: All records listed are not guaranteed for accuracy or data input errors. All information is presumed accurate, but no liability exists for its accuracy. When doubts of accuracy or documentation to prove accuracy is known, that information is noted. It is well known that others may interpret data differently or re-assign children to different parents. Every courtesy has been taken to present other known views.

This work was compiled from 1985 – 2006 by Joyce Christine Faircloth Judah, daughter of Herman R. and Erika E. Faircloth, with the help of her daughter, Jennifer Heather Brooke Judah Fisher, and other noted Faircloth historians, such as Robert June Faircloth, Robert Earl Woodham, and James Starling. Without the sharing of data, this history would not have been possible. Many thousands of hours have been spent scrolling through microfilm, reviewing documents throughout North Carolina and Virginia, and consulting with family members. It is with a happy heart that I set this work to print.

May God bless all souls who read this book, and shine upon all Faircloth's, their families and their descendents.

Joyce Christine Faircloth Judah, 2007

Part I – Resource Data

The Faircloth Family Name

The Faircloth family name originated in England. The common English spelling of the name is FAIRCLOUGH. The name FAIRCLOTH is very rarely found in England. Instead, one finds the name FAIRCLOUGH. The reverse is true in the United States.

L. G. Penes' The Story of Surnames, states "FAIRCLOUGH means fair cliff". Surnames of the United Kingdom, by Henry Harrison, suggest the meaning "Fair: old English fearr, a bull (later a roebuck); old English fear (h), a boar; or Old Norse faer, a sheep. Clough: Middle English clough: old English sloh, a hollow cleft. This would seem to indicate a caver or cleft in a valley wall where boars and deer are found. Such a place in ancient times would surely be a good source of wild game and excellent food. Thus, P. H. Reaney, in a Dictionary of British Surnames, states "dweller in a fair hollow or cliff".

It is also believed to be associated with the English meaning, "one who made or sold light, and beautiful fabrics". Our name can be spelled in many ways including:

Ffairclough	Fearclough	Faircloth	Ffairclogh
Fairclough	Fayrecloth	Fairlough	Faircliff
Fayreclothe	Faircloe	Fairlose	Fayrecloght
Fayreclose	and many more.		

Quite by accident, my favorite picture of my father is one where he is kneeling beside a wild boar which he had killed on a hunting trip in Germany. My youngest brother, Phillip, loves to hunt; this is interesting in light of our family name.

Faircloth Coat Of Arms

Coat of Arms

Faircloth

The Faircloth Coat of Arms was drawn by a heraldic archives artist from information officially recorded in ancient heraldic archives. Documentation for the Faircloth Coat of Arms design can be found in Burke's General Armory. Heraldic artists of old developed their own unique language to describe an individual Coat of Arms. In their language, the Arms (shield) is as follows: "Or, a lion ramp. Sa. Betw. Two fleurs-de-lis ax". Above the shield and helmet is a crest, which is described as: "a demi lion ramp. Sa. Holding betw. The paws a fleur-de-lis ax". When translated, the blazone also describes the original colors of the Faircloth Arms and Crest as it appeared centuries ago. Family mottos are believed to have originated as battle cries in medieval times. A motto was not recorded with this Faircloth Coat of Arms.

A Coat of Arms was granted by the king to the FAIRCLOUGH family of Hertfordshire, Lancashire, Lincolnshire, and London on 3 November 1583. No family arms for the earliest FAIRCLOUGH knights of the 1300's through 1500's is yet known. Since all knights had a Coat of Arms, there may be an earlier one than that which is known.

The etching of SAMUEL FAIRCLOUGH, who lived approximately 1656, includes a small replica of the FAIRCLOUGH Coat of Arms. A description of the history of Samuel Fairclough is provided later in this work.

One additional replica of the Faircloth Coat of Arms is known and described in the brass in Surry England. The inscription and picture is shown below:

A LIST OF MONUMENTAL BRASSES IN SURREY.

Inscription. *Faith, daughter of Hugh Fairclough, gent., of London, and wife of John Sutton the younger, gent., 1603, aged 24, "she left two daughters and never had more children," with shield. Now on wall of north aisle.*

HERE LIETH BVRIED VNDER THIS STONE FAYTH
SVTTON THE WIFE OF IOHN SVTTON Y YONG'
GENT & DAVGHTER TO HEWGH FEARCLOVGH
OF LONDON GENT: HER AGE AT DEATH WAS 24
YERES SHE DEPARTED THIS LIFE THE 23 OF
AVGVST IN ANNO DÑI 1603. SHE LEFT TWO
DAVGHTERS & NEVER HAD MORE CHILDREN.
GENTLE READER DEFACE NOT THIS STONE.

FAITH SUTTON, 1603. HORSELL, SURREY.

Ancient Beginnings

Our family probably had its beginnings in Lancashire, England, which lies just to the north of Liverpool, a city on the Mersey River, where it flows into Liverpool Bay of the Irish Sea. The family, some members, migrated to the adjoining shires (counties), eastward to Lincolnshire on the North Sea, and then, southward to Hertfordshire, just to the north of London. 1300'S – 1400's

SIR RALPH FAIRCLOUGH

TRANSACTIONS OF THE HARLEIAN SOCIETY, written by an English historian, devote several pages to SIR RALPH (RAWFF) FAIRCLOTH, who lived in Hertfordshire, England was a knight who lived in the 1300's.

LAWRENCE FAIRCLOUGH

The earliest known member of the family in Hertford was Lawrence Fairclough who probably lived in the 14th century. He was the first cousin of Hugh FAIRCLOUGH. It is unknown when he was born. He married Mary Cole, whose father was John Cole, the chief Lord of Haverill. Lawrence had one son, SAMUEL FAIRCLOUGH. Lawrence left his son, Samuel, an orphan at the age of nine. It is uncertain who raised Samuel from that time. (1603)

Having preached a thanksgiving sermon for the coming in of King James in 1603, caught so great a cold by it that he died the next day on 25 March 1603.

SAMUEL FAIRCLOUGH

The Reverend and Learned Divine Samuel Fairclough resided in Haverill, an ancient market town of Suffolk, England. Children of Samuel included:

1. RICHARD FAIRCLOUGH, born 1621. He was a minister, who delivered the Assize Sermon at Somerset. He was the rector of Melis in 1643 and was then ejected by the Act of uniformity in 1643. He died in 1682.

2. SAMUEL FAIRCLOUGH, JR., a minister who was born in 1625.

His first wife was Susan. The children listed below are by his first wife Susan. He married Frances Folke, his fathers' stepdaughter, by his second wife, in 1665.

3. Female – who married George Jones, an Essex gentleman.

4. Female – who married Richard Shute, the minister of Stowmarket, Suffolk.

5. Female – who also married a minister.

6. Male –

7. Male –

8. Stillborn (Susan died during the stillborn death of their eighth child).

SAMUEL married second, Mrs. Folke, widow of William Folke of Cambridge. She had one daughter by William Folke, named Frances. This marriage lasted for only a short time. Because of his failing health and his need for a nurse, he married a third time to Mrs. Sorrell, of Essex. He lived his twilight years with his children and his in-laws, having no proper place to call home. He died the 14th of December 1677 while living in the home of his son-in-law, Richard Shute. Samuel was buried near the vestry door of the church of Stowmarket. Noted on his burial place is the description:

"If any person shall desire to have an account of his bodily shape and form, let them know this: He was pretty fat and a corpulent man, full faced, of a grave majestic aspect, and had a very quick and piercing eye."

SAMUEL was cited by the Bishop of Norwich for omitting the sign of the Cross in Baptism. He was named Rector of Barnardiston in 1623 and published his most notable work entitled "The Pastor's Legacy" in 1663. He was described as a nonconformist and Divine. Samuel lived a disciplined life and had a steady attachment to moderate puritan principles. He was so steadfast in his beliefs that he refused to play the part of a woman in the comedy Ignoramus which was to be presented to King James I. During the English Civil Wars, he showed little active sympathy with the Presbyterians. In 1622 he refused to take the oat of conformity and left a valuable living behind for his family and himself. His lectures were much admired by all ministers for miles around. Often ten to twenty scholars and fellows of the colleges from Cambridge came to hear his lectures.

Samuel Fairclough, Jr.

SIMON deFFAIRCLOGH

Simon is one of the earliest known recorded Faircloghs' listed on the subsidy rolls of Lancashire in 1332. Note the Norman or French use of the word "de" meaning "of or from".

Notes:

JOHN FAIRCLOUGH

WESTON
PARISH CHURCH

men and mortar

In the Weston Parish Church Chancel, is a monument on the wall to JOHN FAIRCLOUGH, 1630. The chancel was rebuilt in red brick in 1840. The construction is lighter than the rest of the church. The walls are 14 inches thick. The bosses of the roof principals are modeled in cement and colored to imitate oak.

In 1902, the beautiful three light windows made by Messrs. Powell and White friars were inserted. The window represents the "Adoration of the ascended Christ by saints and angels". This is the location of the Monument on the wall to JOHN FAIRCLOUGH. The FAIRCLOUGH family lived at Halls Green, Weston, for a considerable time during the late middle ages. The inscription is in Latin: from a translation of which the following passages are quoted:

"Epitaph on the most esteemed JOHN FAIRCLOUGH, esquire, of Fairclough Hall. Virtue outlines the grave. Thou wert worthy of a better site, a better sepulcher. Thou wert unwilling to sound forth grandly they titles. This is thy praise, to have lived for God, for Country, and for Kin, and to be able so to close they last day of December in the year of human salvation 1630, of his age 86, from this transitory to an everlasting life. By his most beloved and refined wife, illustrious as much by her virtues as by birth, Anne Spencer, daughter of Thomas Spencer, of Cophull, in the County of Bedford, esquire, he had two sons and eleven daughters. THOMAS, the first born, married Maria Harvey, daughter of John Harvey of Thurleigh, in the aforesaid county, esquire; by her he had two sons, viz. JOHN and LYTTON, now surviving, and one daughter, deceased. The elder son, JOHN, married Margaret Horne of Tibenham, in the county of Norfold, gentleman."

The well-kept registers date from 1539 and even include some made during the time of Oliver Cromwell. The original nave has disappeared without a trace and the existing one was built sometime before 1400.

John was born approximately 1544 and died 31 December 1630 at the age of 86. He married Anne Spencer, who was the daughter of Thomas Spencer of Cophull, in the county of Bedford, England. JOHN had 13 children, two males and 11 females. Nothing is known about the females. The males were THOMAS and JOHN.

THOMAS FAIRCLOUGH

Thomas was the son of JOHN FAIRCLOTH (who has a monument at Weston Parish). Thomas married Maria Harvey, the daughter of John Harvey of Hurleigh and had three known children: JOHN< LYTTON, and one female. John married Margaret Horne of Tibenham, County of Norfolk

JOHN FAIRCLOUGH

John was the second son of JOHN FAIRCLOUGH (Weston Parish monument). He the child of John and Anne Spencer FAIRCLOUTH. He married Margaret Horne. John was born in 1605 and died in 1666. He was a chorister of All Souls College in Oxford in 1623. He was regarded as the "first preacher of the Gospel" at St. Christopher and was named Chaplain Extraordinary to the King in 1626. He was Precentor of Lincoln and Prebendary in 1660.

JOHN FAIRCLOUGH

John was born in 1524 and married Marian Thrift. He had one unknown male child and one male child named DANIEL FEATLEY-FAIRCLOUGH. Daniel was born the 15th of March 1582 at Charlton-upon-Otmoor in Oxfordshire, England. He died 17 April 1645 and is buried in Surry, England. Daniel married Mrs. Joyce Halloway in 1622. She was older than he and twice married before. Daniel was educated at the age of 12 as a chorister of Magdalene College and was applauded by his teachers for the witty and elegant Latin and Greek exercised which he composed. This scholar and clergyman was further educated at Corpus Christi College at Oxford and received his M. A. in 1635. He was named the Archbishop of Canterbury in 1625. He published a report of the conference between FEATLEY and several Jesuit Priests and composed the devotional manual "Ancella Pietautric" which was used extensively by Charles. I.

DR. DANIEL FEATLEY FAIRCLOUGH

(Daniel Fairclough - Photo from a rare book he wrote.)

After Dr. Daniel Featley received his degrees, he began preaching, and became well known across the country as a renowned orator and disputant. Such was his fame that the King was graciously pleased to engage him in a "scholastic duel". In 1604, Daniel was among those chosen from the Church of England to be commissioned for the translation of the Bishop's Bible in the reign of King James I. He was one of the "oxford Seven" who was responsible for translating the four Greater Prophets, the Lamentations, and the twelve Lesser Prophets. He produced many voluminous writings and devotionals, many of which are classical in their rhetoric and message. It is rather gratifying to learn that one of our ancestors, chosen by King James I of England for extraordinary knowledge of Greek and Latin, was one of the few who wrote the King James Version of the Bible, the most beloved and widely read book of all time.

Daniel was imprisoned in 1643 as a spy and intelligencer. While incarcerated, his health became bad and he was moved to Chelsea College to recuperate; however, while there he died of asthma and dropsy on the 17th of April 1645 and was buried in the chancel of Lambeth Church, Surrey, England.

Daniel lived most of his married life in the home of his wife, Mrs. Joyce Halloway Fairclough at the end of Kensington Lane, in Surrey, England. They had no children.

THOMAS FAYERCLOUGH

Thomas was known to be the Mayor of Liverpool in 1554. No other information is known about him at this time.

HEWGH (HUGH) FEARCLOUGH

Father of FAYTH FEARCLOUGH SUTTON. He lived in London Gent, circa 1579 when his daughter, FAYTH, was born. (Based upon her recorded death date). He was the first cousin of LAWRENCE FAIRCLOUGH. Hugh Was a citizen and grocer in London, England who officially recorded the family Coat of Arms on 2 November 1563 in London. Little is known about him except he had one daughter, FAYTH FAIRCLOUGH, who was born c. 1579 and died on 23 August 1603. She married John Sutton and had two daughters. FAYTH has a

11

monumental stone marking her burial place in surrey, England. The monument lists her husband, John Sutton, and his father, John Sutton, Sr. FAYTH died at the age of 24. John Sutton, Sr. had a second son named Thomas Sutton, who never married.

FAYTH FEARCLOUGH SUTTON

See the Coat of Arms for copies of the arms listed with her name. FAYTH FAIRCLOTH SUTTON was the wife of John Sutton, young gent, and daughter to HEWGH FEARCLOUGH, of London Gent: her age at death was 24 years old. She died on the 23 of August in 1603. She had two daughters and no other children.

FAIRCLOUGH FAMILY HALL

FAIRCLOUGH HALL is a 16th Century farmhouse set in gently rolling countryside on a modern farm of 820 acres.

The farm is mainly arable with herd of pedigree South Devon cattle. The house has been modernized for comfort with central heating throughout, but retains its traditional character with the old oak beams, large walk-in fireplace in the drawing room, and a comfortable sense of history. It is located 35 miles to the south of London and 35 miles north of Cambridge. It is locate din the hamlet of Halls Green, 1.5 miles from the village of WESTON and 4.5 miles from the Letchworth/Baldock exit of the A1 (M), the motorway of London.

JOSEPH FAIRCLOUGH

JOSEPH FAIRCLOUGH was the owner of FAIRCLOUGH HALL in 1635 and called it the Bell Inn of Hatfield. Fairclough Hall is now an Inn, which offers bed and breakfast. JOHN FAIRCLOUGH sold the ancient Hall in the 1600's. This particular family spread from Hertford to several other counties, including London, by the late 1500's. At Hatfield, also in Hertford County, the family's name was more often spelled FAIRCLOTH.

John Fearchew

Of Virginia, mariner, 14 Feb 1657; Margery Rogers of Penhow, Monmouth, spinster, bound to John of Bristol, mariner, to serve 4 years in Barbados; leaving from London. Additional individuals bound to John Fearclew on 21 Oct 1657, 1659, 1660. Various spellings of names include Fearchew, Fareclew, Fearclew, Fairclew, Farclue and Faircly. John married Margery by 1659. Seems our name was evolving....

John ffearclough

There is also another known John, c. 25 Feb 1687, named John ffearclough of Weston in Com. Hertford, who married Jane Spencer whose father was Robert Spencer and married a Rhose, daughter of Elizabeth and William Pavis of Ellington in Com. Huntington.

Notes:

The following are known Faircloth's who were among the first to settle in America.

WILLIAM FAIRCLOTH

William came to America as a Headright with Colonel John Carter, Esquire, circa 1662. John Carter, Councellor of State, was granted 4000 acres being a neck of land on the north side of Rappahannock River in Virginia. The tract was bounded on the westward side by the Cassatta Woman Creek which runs north and east northeast towards the head of Wiccocomica River. This tract was originally granted to Captain Samuel Mathews on August 1, 1643 but was deserted by him. Upon petition of Col. Carter, the land was granted to him by order of the General Court bearing the date October 12, 1665 and further due for transportation of 80 persons, among whom was William Faircloth. This William was born in England, circa 1640.

On March 17, 1674, an inventory of the estate of Ambrose Fielding of Wickocomoca Hall was made after this death, for the Northumberland County Court. Among the inventory is a list of servants including:

1 servt man	William Farecloth	3 years to serve
1 Do	Thos. Holmes	2 do
1 Servt. Boy	Jno. Sonpin	7 years
2 Do Maide	Jane Farecloth	3 do Do.
1 Do Maide	Jane Cooper	2 do

A Court Record in Northumberland County, VA, on 9 May 1660, shows "Wm. Farlowe, adjudged 12 years of age". From these scant records, we can deduct that William was brought to America at a very early age and he was among a group of 80 indentured servants for whom the wealthy John Carter, a member of the Council of State, had paid the costs of transportation for and apparently Carter later sold William to Ambrose Fielding. No records of his parents have yet been found. The Jane listed in the Fielding estate is apparently his wife.

WILLIAM FAIRCLOUGH

A WILLIAM Fairclough came to VA with his family in 1699. This William was born about 1687 in Chorly, Lancashire. He, his mother, Ann (born 1662), and sisters, Margaret (born 1683) and Margery (born 1685) were transported from Liverpool, England, aboard the ship, Elizabeth, in 1699. Their passage was paid for by Gilbert Leivsay, to whom they were bound as servants. Ann was bound for 4 years, and William for 10 years. This means that William would become a free man about 1709. On November 13, 1713, a William Faircloth received a patent for 275 acres of land in the Isle of Wight County, VA. (References: Cavaliers and Pioneers- Abstracts of Virginia Land Patents and Grants 1623-1666). By Neil Marion Nugent, VA Land Office, Richmond, VA. Genealogical Publishing Company, Inc. 1963, p. 536.
Ref: The Planters of Colonial Virginia by Thomas S. Weertenbaker, Princeton University Press, 1922, p. 212.
Ref: English Duplicates of Lost Virginia Records by Louis des Cognets, Jr.

Ref: <u>Virginia Wills and Administrations</u>, 1632-1800. by Clayton Torrence, Genealogical Publishing Co., 1965.

WILLIAM FARECLOTH WILL OF 1728

A WILL WAS FILED ON 27 May 1728 in the Isle of Wight County, VA which was written the 9th of January 1829 by William Farecloth. Listed in the will were the following heirs:

Father: William Farecloth
Mother: not listed
Children:

Benjamin Farecloth	Moses Farecloth
Elizabeth Farecloth Merser	Sarah Farecloth Revell
William Farecloth	Sam Farecloth
Hannah Farecloth	Granddaughter:Martha

Farecloth, daughter of Sam Farecloth

The Will reads:

I, William Farecloth of the Isle of Wight County in Virginia being very sick and weak of body but of sound and perfect mind and memory, thanks to God therefore but knowing the uncertainty of this life and that it is appointed for all men to die I do make and ordain this my last will and testament in the manner and form following principally and first of all I recommend my soul into the hands of Almighty God that gave it to me and my body to the earth to be buried after a Christian manner and for such worldly goods and estates as it hath pleased God to bless me withal in this life after all my lawful debts and dues are paid I give and bequeath to my loving son, Benjamin Farecloth, my feather bed and furniture that I lie on myself and also my water mill and all appurtenances thereunto belonging and two hundred acres of land joining my plantation whereon I live on the south side of the mill to him and his heirs forever and if he dies without heirs to fall to his brother Moses Farecloth and his heirs. I give and bequeath to my loving son, Moses Farecloth, one feather bed and bolster and also one dish and one basin of pewter and I also give and bequeath to my son Moses Faircloth the plantation on the north side of the mill with one hundred acres of land thereunto belonging to him and his heirs forever. I give and bequeath to my daughter Hannah Farecloth one cow and yearling and heifers that are called hers and also one feather bed and furniture the bed having a cotton tick and one gilded trunk. I give and bequeath to my daughter Elizabeth Mercer one cow and yearling. I give and bequeath to my daughter Sarah Revell five shillings. I give and bequeath to my son William Farecloth five shillings. I give and bequeath to my grand-daughter, Martha Farecloth, daughter of Sam Farecloth, five shillings. I give and bequeath to my son, Benjamin Farecloth, my gun. I give and bequeath to Sarah Pope, wife of Henry Pope, the grinding toll free all the corn she brings for her family's use to the mill during her natural life to have that liberty whenever the mill shall grind. And lastly I do leave all the remaining part of my estate to pay my debts and the use of the mill five years and I do constitute make and appoint my daughter, Hannah Farecloth, and my son, Benjamin Farecloth, and my son, Moses Farecloth, to be Executrix and Executors of this my last will and testament and my will and desire is that the use of the mill fi9ve years and remaining part of my estate after my just debts and dues are to be equally divided between my three Executors and this I own to be my last will and testament revoking and disannulling all other wills and testaments made by me as witness my hand and seal this 9th day of January one thousand seven hundred and twenty seven."

This will was signed sealed and delivered in the presence of John R. Revell, Joseph I. Cobb, and Robert Scott. The last will and testament of William Farecloth, deceased was presented in the court by Hannah Farecloth on the 27th day of May 1728 in the Isle of Wight County, VA.

THOMAS FAIRCLOTH

The rent rolls of the Land of James City County, VA show that a Thomas Faircloth owned 277 acres of land in 1704. Thomas was born circa 1670.

Notes:

Immigration Lists

Additional American Settlers Born in England who Came to America.

Name	Census	Location	Yr Immigrated	Born	Married	From
John	1870	NJ	c. 1835-40		1820	Olive

From England; married Olive;

| Olive | 1870 | NJ | c. 1835-40 | | 1825 | John |

From England; Fairclough; wife of John above;

| Richard | 1870 | NJ | | | 1835 | Hester |

From England; married Hester;

| Peter | 1860 | NJ | | | 1835 | Sarah |

From England; Fairclough; married Sarah;

| Sarah | 1860 | NJ | | | 1802 | Peter |

From England; wife of Peter above; Fairclough

| David | 1850 | NJ | after 1831 | | 1805 | Ann |

From England

| Ann | 1850 | NJ | after 1831 | | 1805 | David |

From England; wife of David above; Fairclough

| John | 1850 | NJ | | | 1829 | |

From England; Fairclough; married Olivia;

| Richard | 1850 | NJ | | | 1831 | Hannah |

From England; Fairclough; married Hannah;

| Toni | | | prior 1858 | c. 1839; | | |

From London area; b. 1839.

| Francis | | VA | summer 1750; from Cambridgeshire, Eng. | | | |
| Joseph | | PA | 10 Oct 1726 | | | London |

"indentured servant who came to PA with Cpt. Laborious Pearce"

| Ellen | | VA | c. 1664 | | | |

"James Ward proved right by testimony to 400 acres of land in Charles County, VA for charge of importancon of 8 persons including her." Last name spelled: ffaircloth. 3 June 1664. VA Colonial Abstracts.

| William | | VA | 1699 | | 1687 | Leyland |
| Anne | | VA | 1699 | | | Leyland |

Was 3_ years old; Listed with Ann, Chorly who was

37 years old. Aboard the ship Elizabeth. Married Roger Sharples in 1677.

William		VA	1665	listed on passenger lists to VA		
Jane		VA	1665; possible wife of William above.			
Margery		VA	1699		1685	Chorly

Last name: Fairclough, 14 yrs old

Name	Census	Location	Yr Immigrated	Born	Married	From
Ann		VA	1699		1685	Chorly

Was 37 years old. Aboard the ship Elizabeth.

Name	Census	Location	Yr Immigrated	Born	Married	From
Margaret		VA	1699		1685	

Aboard the Ship "Elizabeth"; six years to serve Gilbert Leivsay
Last name: Fairclough, 16 yrs old;

Name	Census	Location	Yr Immigrated	Born	Married	From
John		VA	1659-60		m. Margery	Berkley

Mariner who transported many others to America   London

Name	Census	Location	Yr Immigrated	Born	Married	From
Margery		VA	1659-60		m. John	Hertford

The Mariner's wife

Wm   Came to Isle of Wight, VA in 1710-1718; 275 acres.

Sarah R.   Immigrated; was supposed to go to Barbados, 1717. Felon, sentenced on Dec 1716; bonded passenger to America from London 1656-1775. from Newgate prison with 6,000 others; penal servitude in the plantations for seven years; probably left on 15 Dec 1716 on ship called Lewis; Capt Roger Laming or Jan 1717 on Queen Elizabeth, with Capt. Nehemiah Shelding;

Sarah   Immigrated, was supposed to go to Jamaica;

Johnathan   came to James City, VA in 1714.

Name	Census	Location	Yr Immigrated	Born	Married	From
Mary		West Point	1849			Ireland

Mary was age 15 when she came from Liverpool, out of Ireland, to West Point, 004, 6 March of 1849.

Michael   1868 to Philadelphia, PA

Notes:

FAIRCLOTH'S BORN CIRCA 1600-1700'S

At this point we have the following Williams in Virginia:

Name	Date arriving in America	Poss. Birth date	Poss.Death Date
William	C. 1662	C. 1640	
William Farlowe		C. 1648	
Wife: Jane			
William	C. 1665		
William	C. 1699	C. 1687	
Mother: Ann			
Sisters: Margaret and Margery			
William Farecloth:		C. 1728	

Children:

    Benjamin Farecloth
    Moses Farecloth
    Elizabeth Farecloth Merser
    Sarah Farecloth Revell
    William Farecloth
    Sam Farecloth
    Hannah Farecloth
        Granddaughter: Martha Farecloth, daughter of Sam Farecloth

William III who was born c. 1710?

William III died Glasgow/Green County, NC after 1797?

William II OR III ? Revolutionary War July 1777 roster of Sheppard's Battalion

William and his wife Susan Edwards came to NC from VA and MD, born
    c. 1700's
    son was William Turner Faircloth, b. 1829

And the following others in Virginia:

Thomas	B. 1670	Living in Va in 1704	
John		1664-1670 Mariner who transported many persons to America	

And these in Pennsylvania:

Joseph   to PA, in 1726

And these in New Jersey in the early 1800's:

Name	Census	Location	Yr Immigrated	Born	Married	From
John	1870	NJ	c. 1835-40	1820	Olive	
Olive	1870	NJ	c. 1835-40	1825	John	
Richard	1870	NJ		1835	Hester	
Peter	1860	NJ		1835	Sarah	
Sarah	1860	NJ		1802	Peter	
David	1850	NJ	after 1831	1805	Ann	
Ann	1850	NJ	after 1831	1805	David	
John	1850	NJ		1829		
Richard	1850	NJ		1831	Hannah	
Toni			prior 1858	c.1839		

And the following in GA:

B.   GA state militia in 1800 ....maybe 18 yrs old....poss. born c. 1782

Other military personnel with births prior to War of 1812
(when they served: making births probably in the last quarter of the 1700's)

Isham	served 1814-15
Joel	served 1814-15
Kinchen	served 1813
Kinchen	served 1813
Noah	served 1813-14
Raiford	served 1813-14
Raphel or Raiford	served 1814-15
Solomon	served 1813-1814

The Indian War – Whose service made Births likely pre 1800 through 1814)

Robert	served 1816-18	GA
Richard	served 1814	GA
Thomas	served 1819	GA
Ethelred	served 1819	GA
Wm	served 1828	GA
Caleb	served 1831	GA
John	served 1814-16	VA

Revolutionary War	Participants whose births are prob. In the 1700's Era:
Benjamin	was 83 yrs old in 1840…b. c. 1757
Ephraim	served 1780, born in VA
Frederick	pay vouchers from 1777
John	in Wilmington in 1783
John	pay vouchers in 178-
John	enlisted 1777
John Robert	served 1778 – died 1779
John Smith	died 1796 in service
Newsom	payroll service for 1782-85
Thomas	prior to 1800
William	service 1761
William	service 1778
William	service prior to 1796, 84 months
William	24 months service
William	Tn filed for acreage in 1796
William	acreage filed for 84 months service in 1797
William, Jr.	service 1777
Zachariah	service 1782

Dobbs Militia mid 1700's; Dobbs County, NC

Last name	First name	Dates	Rank	Wife	Father	Where Born	Where Died
Faircloth	John		Private				
Faircloth	Thomas		Private				
Faircloth	William		Private				

Roster of Columbus County, NC Confederate Veterans D-J

Faircloth, Joseph, Company B, Carr's Regiment
Faircloth, Luke, Company D, 20th Regiment

Notes:

Faircloth's of America - 1600's

Ann
Passenger lists to VA   1699   1685   Chorly
Jane
Passenger lists to VA in 1665
John   m. Margery
Passenger lists to VA   1659-60   m. Margery   Berkley
Mariner who transported many others to America   London
Margery
          m. John Faircloth
Passenger lists: VA   1659-60   m. John   Hertford
     The Mariner's wife
Margery
Passenger lists to VA   1699   1685   Chorly
Margaret
Passenger lists to VA   1699   1685
          Aboard the Ship "Elizabeth"; six years to serve Gilbert Leivsay
Mary
          b. 1834
The US National Archives and Records Administration lists Mary Faircloth, age 15 coming from Ireland (during the Famine Irish Passenger Record Data File, 1/12/1846 to 12/31/1851), embarking on the ship Steerage in Liverpool, England. Passenger arrived on 3/6/1849.
Thomas
          b. c. 1670
The rent rolls of the Land of James City County, VA show that a Thomas Faircloth owned 277 acres of land in 1704. Thomas was born circa 1670.
William
Passenger lists to VA 1665
William   b. c. 1640
          William came to America as a Headright with Colonel John Carter, Esquire, circa 1662. John Carter, Councellor of State, was granted 4000 acres being a neck of land on the north side of Rappahannock River in Virginia. The tract was bounded on the westward side by the Cassatta Woman Creek which runs north and east northeast towards the head of Wiccocomica River. This tract was originally granted to Captain Samuel Mathews on August 1, 1643 but was deserted by him. Upon petition of Col. Carter, the land was granted to him by order of the General Court bearing the date October 12, 1665 and further due for transportation of 80 persons, among whom was William Faircloth. This William was born in England, circa 1640.
William Farecloth   m. probably Jane
On March 17, 1674, an inventory of the estate of Ambrose Fielding of Wickocomoca Hall was made after this death, for the Northumberland County Court. Among the inventory is a list of servants including:

1 servt man	William Farecloth	3 years to serve
1 Do	Thos. Holmes	2 do
1 Servt. Boy	Jno. Sonpin	7 years
2 Do Maide	Jane Farecloth	3 do Do.
1 Do Maide	Jane Cooper	2 do

Wm Farlowe

        b. 1648   m. apparently Jane

A Court Record in Northumberland County, VA, on 9 May 1660, shows "Wm. Farlowe, adjudged 12 years of ageThe Jane listed in the Fielding estate is apparently his wife.

William FAIRCLOUGH

        b. c. 1687 in Chorly, Lancashire, England

        mother: Anne

                b. 1662

                c.   William, b. c. 1687

                          Margery, b. 1685

                          Margaret, b. 1683

      A WILLIAM Fairclough came to VA with his family in 1699.

William

Passenger Lists to VA;1699; 1687 from Leyland

William FARECLOTH: Wills & Administrations of Isle o Wight Co, VA, 1647-1800, Book II, p. 39. d. after 9 Jan 1727

                c.   Benjamin Farecloth

                        Moses Farecloth

                        Elizabeth Farecloth Merser

                        Sarah Farecloth Revell

                        William Farecloth

                        Sam Farecloth

                        Hannah Farecloth

                          Granddaughter: Martha Farecloth, daughter of Sam

        Farecloth

        father: William Farecloth

A WILL WAS FILED ON 27 May 1728 in the Isle of Wight County, VA

Note: Cemetery notes from those who were born in the 1890-1900 or later are not included in this listing. Names may be repeated and actually the same person who entered the military, left and returned or had a reference to deed transactions, however, each is listed separately.

A.   Civil War: Pvt, Co C, 5th Batt, enl 5 Nov 1864 in Lenoir Co, NC

A. E.   Civil War: Pvt, resided in Cumberland County; enl in Lenoir Co on 6 Nov 1854;   paroled 1 May 1865 in Greensboro;

A. J.   Civil War: Pvt, G Co, 74th Regt; enl 23 Jun 1864 in Co H, 74th Regt

Abraham   FLA Creek Seminole War: 1836, Read's Batt, FLA volunteers, enl for 4 months

Achsah   8 Apr 1811: NC Deed dated 8 April 1811 Achsah Faircloth sold 100 acres in Sampson County to John Johnston, Jr. said parcel being part of a patent granted to Samuel Faircloth on 1 January 1793. Although this deed transaction does not directly state that Achsah Faircloth was Samuel's daughter, it seems obvious to me that she obtained this land as her part upon his death or probably received it as a gift during Samuel's lifetime. (as per Robert J. Faircloth).

Alex   b. 1822 Civil War: Private, enlisted in Cumberland County at age 41, September 2, 1863, for the war. Present or accounted for through August, 1864. No further records. 1812-1814.

Alexander   Civil War: 3rd Regt, Wimberlips, GA Militia

Alexander B. Civil War: Pvt, B Co, 10th Batt; enl 23 Apr 1864; discharged;

Alex B.   Faircloth, Alex B.   1898   1960
          No stone marker-only small metal marker similar to funeral home markers. Faircloth Cemetery, Sampson County, NC

Allen   Civil War: 3rd Regt, Wimberlips, GA Militia;

Allen   FLA Creek Seminole War: Cpt Holloman's Com, McCan'ts Batt, Jefferson Co, Middle FLA; drafted militia

Allen D.   FLA Creek Seminole War; Norton's Co, FLA mounted militia, 3 months, 1840-41; FLA Creek Seminole War; Miner Co, 9th Regt, 1st Brig, FLA mounted militia FLA Creek Seminole War: Newsom's Company, Taylor's Batt, middle FLA mounted volunteers in 1836. FLA Creek Seminole War: Hall's, Co, Bailey's Batt, FLA mounted militia 1840 for three months

Ann   1860 VA Census

Arthur   1820 Bladen Census

Arthur b. betw. 1794-1802
              c. b. 1810-1820; female under 10 in 1820 living in household
       1820 Sampson Census

MALES						FEMALES INFO					District	Page	Family
10	16	18	26	45	45+	10	16	26	45	45+			
Faircloth	Arthur												
0	0	0	1	0	0	1	0	0	0	0	Hall's	300	

       1840 Sampson Census

B.   GA State Militia: Sgt Ogeechee Guard, Effingham County; ordered into   service 23 Jun – 30 June 1800 by Maj Thomas Polhill

B.   Pvt, US Army, d. 17 Feb 1862; Buried Section F, Site 5132, Hampton National Cemetery, VA

Barnabus   b. 1827

Civil War: Born 1827; Pvt, Co C, 2nd Art, Regt 36; Owenville farmer; enl 9 Feb 1863, age 36, in Clinton, NC; assigned detached service in construction of wharf at Ft. Phillip; hospitalized 25 Oct 1864 at Wilmington with febris typhoids; furloughed 29 Oct 1864 for 30 days.

Barnabus   b. 1839   d. 15 Apr 1864

Civil War: Born 1839; Pvt, Co H, 20th Regt; Sampson farm laborer; enl 10 Jun 1861 in Clinton at age 21; captured 1-3 July 1863 at Gettysburg, PA; confined Ft Delaware, Del and Point Lookout, MD; died 15 Apr 1864 of diarrhea; Infantry, Civil War. Buried Section 1, Site 1, Point Lookout confederate Cemetery, Point Lookout, St. Mary's County, MD

Barnabus   Civil War: Pvt, Co I, 20th Regt; enl 10 Jun 1861 in Sampson Co, NC; prisoner of war in Spotsylvania on 12 May 1864; 1840 Sampson Census (listed as Rarna)

Note: Some names may be a duplicate as there is no way to know if the   person was the same one in another unit, or transferring from one unit to another in the military records.

Benjamin   b. 1757   d. aft 1840

Rev. War applied for pension compensation for Rev. War Service on
1 Jan 1840 in Emanual Co., GA at age of 83

Benjamin   b.   bef. 1752 (figuring 20 yrs old with first child)
            d.   after 1790
            m.   prob. by 1782 due to # of children by 1790
            c.   b. c. 1775 -1790 male under 16 by 1790 Census
                  b. c. 1774-1790 male under 16 by 1790 Census
                  b. c. 1773 –1790 male under 16 by 1790 Census
                  b. bef 1774; male over 16 by 1790
                  b. bef 1774; male over 16 by 1790
                  b. female by 1790
                  b. female by 1790
                  b. female by 1790

1784-86 Sampson County State Census: 200 acres, 1 wp, 1 bp
1790 Fayette Census: 3-4-4-0-0
Attributed to two Benjamin's possible:?
(1751 Deed, Edgecombe County (unsure if same person)
 ? 1761 – 22 Dec: deed to Benj F for 100 acres, DB 1, p. 49
 ?1766 – 30 Sep: DB 00, p. 85; from Benj to John skinner, 200   acres, south side of Wrights Creek ?1793 -Jonathan listed in Glasgow County as having voted along with Benj, Fredrick and Kinchen.

Benjamin   b. bef. 1775   m. b. 1794-1810

1820 VA Census, South Hampton; 1790 Tax List , VA; 1794 Southampton Witness to a will in 1791. Attributed to two Benjamin's possible:?
(1751 Deed, Edgecombe County (unsure if same person)
 ? 1761 – 22 Dec: deed to Benj F for 100 acres, DB 1, p. 49; ?1766 – 30 Sep: DB 00, p. 85; from Benj to John skinner, 200 acres, south side of Wrights Creek

Benjamin   b. 1840

Civil War: Born 1840; Co. C, 38th Inf; enl in GA

Benjamin F.   b. 1809, 1799 NC
                    m. Frances Bedsole, b. 1803, m. 1820, died ALA c. 1870;
                    c.   Sarah, b. 1829
                              Susan , b. 1833
                              Polly, b. 1835
                              Solomon, b. 1837
                              Thomas, b. 1841
                              Nancy, b. 1849
                              Duncan, b. 1848
          1850 Bladen Census, 41, laborer, b. 1809; b. 1803, m. Frances, b. 1803,   children
          Owned land in Bladen County in 1842. 100 acres deed to Benjamin Bladen County, NC
Benjamin   1800 Wayne County Census: 0-1-0-0-1-0-0-0-1-0-0-0-0-0
Benjamin P.   b. 1840
          Civil War: Born 1840; Co F, 5th FLA Inf; enl in FLA
Benjamin   b. 1841
                    Civil War: Born 1841; Co D, 27th Bn, GA Inf; enl in GA
Benjamin   Civil War; 8th Regt, Magien's VA militia
Bettie   1860 VA Census
C. M.   Civil War: Col who enl in Cumberland County, NC
Caleb   m.   by 1790
                    c.   b. 1774-1790; male, under 16 in 1790 Census
                              b. 1774-1790; male, under 16 in 1790 Census
                              female
                              female
                              female
                              female
                    1790 Fayette Census/Cumberland: 0-0-2-2-1-0-1
Caleb   m.   by 1790
                    c.   b. 1774-1790; male, under 16 in 1790 Census
                              b. 1774-1790; male, under 16 in 1790 Census
          1790 Fayette Census (not the preceding one unless counted twice?) 0-1-2-1-   0-0-
Caleb GA State Militia: 1831; Dooley County, 31 May
          2nd Seminole War of 1835-1842: Graham's Company, Ross's Battalion, GA Militia;
          Dooley and Pulaski County, GA
Ceasseyat?   1881 Sampson Census
          Ceasseyat? 55 mother in law living with William Culbreath
Charlotte   b. 1848
          Sampson County Cemetery marker: Charlotte Died 1931 83 years old; Hand etched
          Stone-Butler Funeral Home marker still present. Charlotte looks to be the wife of
          Stanley.
Cinthia 1850 Ashe Co Census
          Lists Elizabeth first, age 35, but lists Jackson, age 25, farmer with $800   property
          value, then lists, Cinthia, 47, Henry, 49, Hesther, 13, Jackson 25,   John   8,   Mary   43,
          Mary 37, Mikel 6
          (unsure of whom is who?) – Cinthia was married to Henry as per an earlier Censes and
          their children at that time were John and Mikel
Cordial   Listed in 1850 Census as at home in Lawrenceville, ALA
Cyrus Mills   b. 1 Dec 1876
          From the political graveyards site on the internet., Sampson County, NC
D.   Civil War: Pvt; Co A, Regt 8; wounded; enl Cumberland County, NC

D.   Civil War: Pvt, I Co, 72nd Regt, enl 1 Jun 1864;

Daniel Civil War: Pvt, Co E, Regt 8; enl 5 Aug 1861 in Cumberland County, NC

Daniel   b. 1825
          Civil War: Born in Sampson County where he resided as a farmer prior to enlisting in Cumberland County at age 36, on 1 Aug 1861.

Daniel B.   Civil War: Pvt, B Co, 8th Batt, enl 5 Mar 1862 in Harnett County, NC

Daniel J.   b. 1828 in Sampson County, NC
          d. 14 Nov 1864, Elmira, NY or 29 Dec 1864 at Elmira, NY.
          Civil War: Born 1828; Pvt Co E, Regt 8, Inf; Sampson Farmer; enl 1 Aug 1861   in Cumberland County, NC at age 33; captured 8 Feb 1862 on Roanoke Island; escaped; captured 1 Jun 1864 at Cold Harbor, VA. Confined Point Lookout, MD until transferred to Elmira, NY; died 14 Nov 1864 of chronic diarrhea; buried in grave #1316, Woodlawn Cemetery, Elmira, NY. Born Sampson County. Another account shows him dying at Elmira on 29 Dec 1864 of chronic diarrhea.

Edward Faircluff: Will in 1753 of Edward Faircluff – Pasquotank County.

Edward Farecloth   Landowner in 1723, son – Benjamin

Edward Smithwick   Landowner in 1723; probably same as one listed above;

Elijah 1860 VA Census

Ellen Passenger lists to VA c. 1664; "James Ward proved right by testimony to 400   acres of land in Charles County, VA for charge of importacon of 8   persons including her."

Elizabeth   1820 Camden Census

Elizabeth   b. 1815
          1850 Ashe Co Census Lists Elizabeth first, age 35, but lists Jackson, age 25, farmer with $800 property value, then lists, Cinthia, 47, Henry, 49, Hesther, 13, Jackson 25, John 8, Mary 43, Mary 37, Mikel 6 (unsure of who is whom?)

Ephraim   b. 1759
          c.   Charlotte (listed in his will in 1802)
                  Cordy (listed in his will in 1802)
          Rev War: Enl at age 21 on 1 Sept 1780; listed on Southampton Co Muster Roll as born in VA; Chesterfield Co. Court House size roll of troops lists him   as 5' 11", brown hair, grey eyes, fair complexion; shoemaker; on 4 Nov 1780 he deserted on a March from Chesterfield Court House, VA while listed with Cpt. Scott's Company of the 1st and 2nd Battalion; 1798 Tax List VA; 1791 witness to Will Signature, VA; 1802 Will, 18 Oct 1802, his own, VA

Ethelrred   2nd Seminole War of 1835-1842: Graham's Co, Ross' Batt, GA Militia; Dooley and Pulaski County, GA

Ethelred   GA State Militia, 1819. Screven Co, Pvt, 1st Class, 2nd Brig, 1st Div

Evan   b. 1840   m.   b. 1790-1800
          c.   b. 1825-1830; male
                  b. 1820-1825; male
                  b. 1825-1830; female
                  b. 1825-1830; female
          Civil War: Born 1840; Pvt, Co C. Regt 54, Inf; Sampson turpentine laborer; enl 7 Apr 1863 at Camp Mangum, Wake county, NC; reported missing 7 Nov 1863 on Rappahannock in VA; received 11 Nov 1863 at Old Capitol Prison, Washington, DC; confined Point Lookout, MD; released 29 Jan 1864 to   join Union Forces. Males: 1 (under 5), 1 (5-10), 1 (30-40) Females: 2 (under 5), 1 (30-40)

Evan b. 1800-1810; 20-30 by 1830
          1830 Sampson Census
          Evan (Green?):   Males: 1 (15-20), 2 (20-30),

27

Females: 1 (under 5), 1 (5-10), 1 (20-30), 1 (30-40),
1 (40-50), 1 (50-60)
4 slaves

Unsure of who is related to whom with the varying ages in this household. Probably a multi family house.

b. 1810-1815; male 15-20 by 1830
b. 1800-1810; male 20-30 by 1830
b. 1825-1830; female under 5 in 1830
b. 1820-1825; female 5-10 in 1830
b. 1800-1810; female 20-30 in 1830
b. 1790-1800; female 30-40
b. 1780-1790; female 40-50
b. 1770-1780; female 50-60

1840 Sampson Census

<u>Evans, Jr.</u>   b. 1837   d. 24 Sep 1862
Civil War: Born 1837; Pvt, Co E, Regt 2, Inf; Sampson farmer; enl 15 Jul 1862 in Wake county, NC; died 24 Sept 1862 at Boonesboro, MD of disease;

<u>Evlin</u> b. 1836   d. died 17 Sep 1862 (missing in action and reported dead)
Civil War: Born 1836; Pvt, Co F, Regt 2, Inf; Sampson farmer; enl 15 Aug 1862 in Wake county, NC; missing in action 17 Sept 1862, Sharpsburg, MD; later reported to have died.

<u>Francis F.</u>   b. 1837   Civil War: Born Sampson County; lived Cumberland co; Pvt; enl age 24, 3 Sept 1861; took Oat on 27 Jun 1865; G Co, 33rd Regt;

<u>Frederick</u>   c.   female   female
Pay vouchers, Dobbs Co, NC Copies of those pay vouchers for Frederick and   John Faircloth on file, dated 178(1 or 4…unreadable…most likely 84).
Dobbs Voting Lists-1779, Mar; 1790 Dobbs Census
1-0-3-0-0- i.e. male, other male, female, other, b 1792, Aug, Glasglow   County,   NC; Petition to move location of Courthouse, stocks & prison to another location signed by Wm, John, Fredrick, Thomas, J Frederick,   Kinchen 1793 -Jonathan listed in Glasgow County as having voted along with Benj, Fredrick and Kinchen. 1792, Aug, Glasglow County, NC; Petition to move location of Courthouse, stocks & prison to another location signed by Wm, John, Fredrick, Thomas, J Frederick, Kinchen

<u>F. J.</u>   Voted in 1800 in Greene County. Is this Frederick John and John Frederick the same person? J. Frederick: 1792, Aug, Glasglow County, NC; Petition to move location of Courthouse, stocks & prison to another location signed by Wm, John, Fredrick, Thomas, J Frederick, Kinchen

<u>Francis</u>Passenger lists to VA; summer 1750; from: Cambridge
<u>F. G.</u>   Civil War: Pvt, Co K, 40th;
<u>Grey</u>   Civil War: Pvt, F Co, 6th Batt; enl 4 Sep 1863 in Cumberland County
<u>H.</u>   b. 1819   d. 29 Aug 1864, 45 yrs old, GA
Civil War, VA

<u>Hanson </u>Asberry   b. 1863
Sampson County Cemetery Marker:
Faircloth, H. Asbury   January 27, 1941
Age 78, 8 months, 10 days? This grave is marked only with the funeral home marker which is very deteriorated and hard to read.

<u>Harden</u> Civil War: Pvt, D Co, 31st Regt; enl 17 Sep 1861 in Johnston, Co, NC; discharged for disability;

<u>Hardin</u>   d. 30 Dec 1864

Civil War: Pvt, E Co, 8th Regt; enl 5 Aug 1861 in Sampson Co; died 30 Dec 1864

Hardwick (Hardy) b. abt 1754

        d. (abt. 1810 or moved to Sampson County by that time)

        m. by 1785 with number of children

        c.   m. b. 1775-1790; under 16 by 1790

                m b. 1775-1790; under 16 by 1790

                m b. 1775-1790; under 16 by 1790

                m b. 1775-1790; under 16 by 1790

                m b. 1775-1790; under 16 by 1790

                listed by name:

Reason, Isham, James, Thomas, Jacob, Benjamin, Elizabeth, Achsah, Saber, Hardwick, Jr., Nancy, Jonah, Arthur, Wilson, Jonathan

        Private Duplin Militia; Soldier drew 1 RW pay voucher and lived in Sampson in 1790 and had five young males in his household. Soldier was born about 1754 to William and Sarah Faircloth and is also listed in Sampson in 1785 tax list. Soldier married Sarah Suggs. Issue: 1-Reason, 2-Isham, 3-James, 4-Thomas, 5-Jacob, 6-Benjamin, 7-Elizabeth or Betty, 8-Achsah, 9-Sabar, 10-Hardwick (Hardy) Jr., 11-Nancy, 12-Jonah, 13-Arthur, 14-Wilson, and 15-Jonathan. Soldier's brothers were John and Zechariah Faircloth. Soldier died about 1810. Listed in the Duplin Revolutionary War Records...as per perhaps he enlisted in Duplin County but lived in Sampson.1784-86 Sampson County State Census: Hardy: 300 acres, 1 wp, 1 bp 1790 Fayette Census: 1-5-1-0-0

Hardy	Civil War: Co E, 24th Regt;		
Hardy	b. 1822	d. Penny, b. 1837	
	c.	Lucy A., b. 1871 nephew: Levi, b.1861-1880	
	Sampson Census		
Hardy	_8	farmer	married
Penny	43	keeping house	married
Lucy A	9	daughter	
Levi	19	nephew	single

Hardy	b. 1832	
	m. widowed or divorced by 1880 Census	
	c.	Elizabeth, b. 1846
		Sally, b. 1840

Granddaughter, M. Jane b. 1873 (Listed after Elizabeth on the census)

1880 Sampson Census

Hardy, Sr.	89	widowed or divorced
Elizabeth	34	daughter single
M. Jane	7	grand-daughter
Sallie	40	daughter single
Hardy	b. 1841 in Sampson County, NC	

Civil War: Pvt, Born in Sampson County where he resided as a farmer prior to enlisting in Cumberland County at age 20 on 5 Aug 1861. Captured at Roanoke Island on 8 Feb 1862 but escaped. Present or accounted for until captured at Fort Harrison, VA on 30 Sept 1864. Confined at Point Lookout, MD until paroled and transferred to Boulware's Wharf, James river, VA, where he was received 19 Mar 1865 for exchange.

Harphrey	b. 1847	d. after 1889

Civil War: Born 1847; Pvt, A Co, 2nd Jr., Reserves, Regt 41; Sampson farmer; enl Apr 1864 in Clinton; left Company 24 Oct 1864 due to illness; admitted to hospital #3 on Apr 1865 in Greensboro; in Clinton 26 Sept 1889 for veteran reunion;

Henry b. 1845
Civil War: Born 1845; Pvt, Co C, Regt 54, Inf; Sampson farmer; records   lost;

Henry Civil War: Pvt, B Co, 7th Batt; enl 12 Apr 1864;

Henry b. 1801
1850 Ashe Co Census
Lists Elizabeth first, age 35, but lists Jackson, age 25, farmer with $800 property value, then lists, Cinthia, 47, Henry, 49, Hesther, 13, Jackson 25, <u>John 8, Mary</u> 43, <u>Mary</u> 37, <u>Mikel</u> 6 (unsure of whom is who?)

Henry b. 1811
  m. Cinthia, b. 1813
  c. John, b. 1852
   Mikel, b. 1854
1860 Ashe County Census
Lists wife Cinthia, age 47, Henry, age 49, John 8, Mikel 6, Mary 43 yrs old
(Unsure of what relationship is with Mary?)

Henry Civil War: Pvt, E Co, 70 Regt; enl 11 Apr 1864;

Hester b. 1837
1850 Ashe Co Census
See Henry above

Isaac 1790 Camden County Census, with wife
1820 Camden Census
FLA Seminole/Indian War: 1836, Read's Batt, FLA volunteers, 4 months

Inchen 1820 Wayne Census

Isham b. 1775
  m. b. 1775-1794
  c. b. 1811-1820; male under 10 in 1820
   b. 1804-1810. male 10-16 yrs in 1820
   b. 1811-1820; female, under 10 in 1820
   b. 1805-1810; female 10-16 yrs in 1820

War of 1812.: Pvt., 3rd Regt of Moore's, NC; Cpt Caleb Stephen's Co of   Infantry;11 Oct 1814-10 Mar 1815.
1820 Sampson Census

MALES	FEMALES INFO	District	Page	Family
10 16 18 26 45 45+	10 16 26 45 45+			

Isham
 1 1 0 0 1 0 1 2 1 0 0   Hall's 302
1840 Sampson Census

J. b. 1806 d. 2 Jan 1865, 59 yrs old, GA
Civil War, VA

J. b. 1818 d. 10 may 1864, 46 yrs old, NC
Civil War, VA

J. 1840 Sampson Census

J. Cemetery Marker in Blade County:
 Bessie Viola , daughter of J. & Miranda FAIRCLOTH
 Born June 5 1880 Died Oct 15, 1883

J. A. Civil War in VA

Jackson   b. 1825
    1850 Ashe Co Census
    Lists Elizabeth first, age 35, but lists Jackson, age 25, farmer with $800 property value,
    then lists, Cinthia, 47, Henry, 49, Hesther, 13, Jackson 25, John 8, Mary 43, Mary 37,
    Mikel 6 (unsure of whom is who?)
Jacob War of 1812 Muster rolls, 3d Co, detached from Cumberland County Regmt 1812-14;
    Cumberland County Records.
Jacob (possible son of Jacob above) b. 1827
    1820 Cumberland Census
        1850 Sampson Census: JACOB FAIRCLOTH 23   MALE   TIMBER
James Civil War: 2nd Regt; Sampson County;
James   b. 1775-1794
        c.   male, b. 1810-1820   female, b. 1810-1820
    1790 Anson County Census, alone; 1800 Anson Census
James   b.   1775   m   b. 1775-1794
        c.   b. 1811-1820; male under 10 in 1820
            b. 1811-1820, female under 10 in 1820
    1820 Sampson Census:
    MALES   FEMALES INFO   District   Page Family
    10 16 18 26 45 45+ 10 16 26 45 45+
    Faircloth   James
    1 0 0 0 1 0 1 0 1 0 0   Hall's   302
James J.   Cemetery Markers in Bladen County, NC; Annie M. Culbreth
    wife of James J. Faircloth; born *** 22, 1844; died Sep * 1921
    James J born May 8, 1848   Died Dec 21 1922 -
James W.   Civil War: enlisted 16 May 1861 in Wayne County; a lawyer;
Jeremiah   Civil War: enlisted 15 Jun 1861 in Wayne County.
Jerusha   1840 Sampson Census
Joel   War of 1812: Cpt John Woodward's Co of Infantry, 25th Regt, Maj
    Loveless Gasque's Batt, SC Militia; Pvt; 7 Nov 1814-15, Dec 1814 for 28 days;Camp
    Cat Island; paid $7.00 for service (rate of pay was $8.00 for one month's service)
J. Frederick   1792, Aug, Glasglow County, NC; Petition to move location of
    Courthouse, stocks & prison to another location signed by Wm, John, Fredrick, Thomas,
    J Frederick, Kinchen; 1793 -Jonathan listed in Glasgow County as having voted, along
    with Benj, Fredrick and Kinchen. (Could be Jonathan Frederick??) 1792, Aug, Glasglow
    County, NC; Petition to move location of Courthouse, stocks & prison to another location
    signed by Wm, John, Fredrick, Thomas, J Frederick, Kinchen
John   b. abt. 1750
    c. 3 males and 3 females
    Private Duplin Militia   Soldier drew 6 RW pay vouchers and lived in
    Sampson in 1790 and had three young sons and three young females and
    wife in his household. Soldier was born about 1750 to William and Sarah
    Faircloth and is also listed in 1785 state tax list for Sampson. Brother of
    Hardwick and Zecharia. Parents were William and Sarah Faircloth and are
    also listed in Sampson in 1785 tax list. Sampson in 1790
John   b. abt. 1760 in Edgecombe Co.   d. about 1820 Sumter Co, SC
    m. Catherine Holton
John   1784-86 Sampson County State Census: 0 acres, 1 wp, 0 bp
Jn   d. 5 Apr 1770

31

Cpt. Sharpe Company; enl 26 Aug 1778; died 5 Apr 1770; Pvt, 10h Regt, Col. Abraham Sheppard's Company of Sharpe

John   1774 Will of John Faircluff– Pasquotank County

John   Pvt; enl 4 May 1777 Cpt Abraham Sheppard's Company of Col. Abraham Sheppard's Batt.; discharged 1782 or later; Listed on Sheppard's Battalion   Roster on 1 Jun 1777.

John   Rev. War: Pay vouchers, Dobbs Co, NC, 1783; Private; listed in   Wilmington, Oct. 1783; 1788 voted in Dobbs; 1779 Dobbs Voting Lists-1779, Mar 1792, Aug, Glasglow County, NC; Petition to move location of Courthouse, stocks & prison to another location signed by Wm, John, Fredrick, Thomas, J Frederick, Kinchen; 1793 -Jonathan listed in Glasgow County as having voted along with Benj, Fredrick and Kinchen.

John   Sgt. 6th Regt, transferred to 4th Regt and mustered into Sharpe's Company;

John   1783-94 Court Records, Dobbs County:

20 Nov 1788: Wm, John summoned to curt to Sheriff bond, plus six other people for trespass, assault and battery and damage; went to court 1789;

John   1792, Aug, Glasglow County, NC; Petition to move location of Courthouse, stocks & prison to another location signed by Wm, John, Fredrick, Thomas, J Frederick, Kinchen

John   b. bef 1798   1810 VA Census, 3 slaves

John   b. 1836   1850 VA Census

John   b. 1839   1850 VA Census

John   b. 1842   1850 Ashe Co Census

See listing for Cinthia

1784-86 Sampson County State Census: 250 acres-1 wp-0 bp

John J. 1860 VA Census

John Smithwick   Landowner in 1723

John M.   b. bef. 1775   1820 VA Census, South Hampton

John Robert   d. 5 Apr 1779

Sgt.; F co, 10 Regt, Col Abraham Sheppard's Company of Cpt Bradley; enl 20 May 1778; died 5 Apr 1779;

John Smith   d. 3 Sept 1796

Pvt; died in service while serving in the Continental line of the 3rd Regt of NC; filed in Raleigh on 3 Sept 1796.

Joseph   Passenger Lists: to PA 10 Oct 1726 from London'; "indentured servant who came to PA with Cpt. Laborious Pearce"

John   VA State Militia: Ensign, 2nd Batt, 65 Regt, 8th Brig, VA Militia; Sept 1814-16; Artillery Company commanded by Francis Ridley, 4th Div, state militia.

John   Civil War: Pvt, G Co, 55th Regt, enl 28 Feb 1863 in Johnston Co; killed 2-3 Jul 1863 in Gettysburg;

John   b. 1835   d. 10 Feb 1863

Civil War Born 1835; Pvt, A Co, 30th Regt, Inf; Sampson turpentine maker; enl 1 Sept 1861 in Clinton; died 10 Feb 1863 at camp in Fredericksburg, VA of pneumonia;

John   Civil War 1st Regt, Cumberland Co

John   Civil War 2nd Regt, Bruton's NC militia

John   Civil War 3rd Regt, Sampson Co, Moore's

John   Civil War 2nd Regt, Sampson

John   Civil War 65th Blow's, VA Paymaster

John   b. betw. 1794-1802   m.   b.betw. 1794-1802   c.

1820 Sampson Census

MALES						FEMALES INFO					District	Page	Family
10	16	18	26	45	45+	10	16	26	45	45+			

John

0 0 0 1 0 0 0 0 1 0 1   Hall's   302

Note: a female, over 46 years old lives in the household. John is listed as head of household. Could be his mother living with John and his wife, or could be his mother, living with son, John and daughter; but more likely to be his mother, birth date c. before 1775; 1840 Sampson Census

Jonathan   1793 -Jonathan listed in Glasgow County as having voted.

Johnathan   b. 1820, b. 1817 as per the 1880 Census   m. Carolina,

b. 1823   c.   Franklin, b. 1851
Solomon, b. 1854
Shepherd, b. 1855
Sarah, b. 1857
Love D. b1880
Jasper, b. 1862

1870 Sampson Census

Johnathan	50	farmer
Caroline	47	keeping house
Franklin	19	farm hand
Solomon	16	farm hand
Shepherd	15	farm hand
Sarah	13	keeping house
Love D	10	farm hand
Jasper	8	farm hand

1880 Sampson Census

Jonathan 63   farmer   married

John F.   Civil War H Co, 41st Regt; surrendered at Appomattox

?F. J. Faircloth Voted in 1800 in Greene County. Is this Frederick John and John Frederick the same person?

John L.   b. 1838   d. 15 Jan 1863

Civil War Born 1838; Pvt, A Co, 30th Regt, Inf; Sampson Co farmer; enl 1 Sept 1861 in Clinton; died 15 Jan 1863 in hospital in Richmond, VA of smallpoxand plueropneumonia;

John W.   b. 1841 in Brunswick County, NC   d. 17 Mar 1862

Civil War Pvt; born Brunswick Co; resided Cumberland; enl age 20 on 31 Aug1861; killed in New Bern on 14 mar 1862; G Co, 33 Regt; also listed as enl on 6 Sep 1861 in Cumberland County;

Jonas   b. 1817   d. 12-13 Dec 1862

Civil War Born 1817; Pvt, C Co, 30th Regt, Inf; Sampson farm laborer; enl 19 May 1962, Camp Mangum, as substitute for Thomas Cole; named on report of casualties in engagement in front of Fredericksburg, VA 12-13 Dec 1862...killed;

Joseph M.   Civil War 8th Regt, Magnien's VA, Pvt; also Sgt in 7th.

Joseph   Civil War: Company B, Carr's Regiment

Kinchen   War of 1812: 7th Co., 2 Regt of Bruton's of Green Co, NC; detached for 2nd, 12th and 3rd Brigade; served 6 months including 15 July 1813; discharged 7 Aug 1813 for a six day march home which was 90miles away.

1792, Aug, Glasglow County, NC; Petition to move location of Courthouse, stocks & prison to another location signed by Wm, John, Fredrick, Thomas, J Frederick, Kinchen

1792, Aug, Glasglow County, NC; Petition to move location of Courthouse, stocks & prison to another location signed by Wm, John, Fredrick, Thomas, J Frederick, Kinchen

1793 Glasgow County court records: Kinchen F appearing in Wayne Co, voting book lists misplaced, he was witness to the fact that they had disappeared on 29 Nov 1793; 1793 Kinchen listed as voting in the elections.

1800 Greene County, not allowed to vote as doesn't own land—note two <u>Kinchen</u>s listed, one can't vote and one voting….same person???

1816 Tax Lists from Greene County: Kinchen, 1 white pole, 1 black pole

<u>Kinchen</u>   War of 1812: Cpt Heymrick Hooker's Co, NC; served 24 days including 19 July – 7 Aug 1813.

<u>Kinchen</u>   Civil War: Co 7, 2nd Regt, detached from the Green Regt, Sampson Co; 2nd, 12th, and 3rd Brig;

<u>Kinchen</u>   Co 7, 2nd Regt, detached from the Green Regt, Sampson Co; 2nd, 12th, and 3rd Brig;

<u>L.</u>   Civil War: Pvt, C Co, 26th Regt; enl 4 Nov 1863 at Orange Co, VA

<u>L. T.</u>   m. Janie bef. 1910

        c.   Livvie J., b. 10 Jun 1916

               Janie E., b. 26 Jul 1923

               Levada, b. 7 Nov 1927

               Loren G., 1 Nov 1910

Samson County Cemetery

<u>Livvie</u> J. Son of L. T. And Janie Faircloth June 10, 1916   June 11, 1916

    35.   Janie E.

Daughter of L.T. and Janie Faircloth July 26, 1923 August 2, 1923

    36.   Levada

Daughter of L.T. and Janie Faircloth November 7, 1927   November 7, 1927

    37.   Loren G.

Son of L.T. and Janie Faircloth November 1, 1910 July 29, 1933

<u>Leonides</u>   b. 1836   d. 26 Mar 1862

    Civil War: Pvt, enl at age 25 in Wayne Co on 15 June 1861; died Richmond,   VA on 26 March 1862; D Co, 4th Regt; Pvt, enl at age 25 in Wayne Co on 15 June 1861; died Richmond, VA on 26 March 1862; D Co, 4th Regt;

<u>Levi</u>   b. 1836   d. 1-3 Jul 1863 at Gettysburg, PA

    Civil War: Born 1836; Pvt, F Co, 20th Regt, Inf; Sampson farmer; enl 9 May 1861 in Clinton; wounded in head 27 Jun 1862 at Fox's Gap, MC; confined Ft Delaware, Del; received 2 Oct 1862, Aiken's Landing, VA; captured 1-2   May 1863, Chancellorsville, VA; paroled 4 May 1863; killed 1-3 Jul 1863 at Gettysburg, PA;

<u>Luke</u>   b. 1814-1815   d. 16 Dec 1862   m. Lydia, b. 1828

             c.   Joseph F., b. 1847

                  Patsy, b. 1848

                  Mary A., b. 1851

                  Edward, b. 1853

                  Elisha, male, b. 1854

                  Alfred J., b. 1860

                  Nancy, b. 1858

       c. see Columbus County, NC Census list below: (note all born in NC)

<u>Luke</u> FAIRCLOTH   46   M   Farmer

    Horry Cty, SC/Co D,20th Regt

 <u>Lydia</u> Faircloth   32   F   NC

<u>Joseph</u> [F.] Faircloth   13   M

    NC/ Co B, 7th Jr Reserve

<u>Patsy</u> Faircloth   12   F   NC

Mary A. Faircloth	9	F	NC
Edward Faircloth	7	M	NC
Elisha Faircloth	6	M	NC
Alfred J. Faircloth	4	M	NC
Nancy Faircloth	2	F	NC

       Civil War: Pvt, born Horry Co, SC enl Columbus County, age 46 on 26 Apr 1861; died in hospital at Petersburg, VA on 16 Dec 1862; D Co, 20th Regt; 1860 Columbus County Census

M. 1810-1826?: W. J. and M. Faircloth: notes and accounts due; court action, due to Col. Thos. Edwards. (not sure who this is?) Dobbs County, NC

M. M. Civil War: Pvt; enl 20 Jul 1862 in Ashe Co, NC

Margaret b. 1785 in NC
       1820 Hertford Census
       1850 Census lists Margaret E. at 65 yrs old, b. NC living with Harrell Family #78

Mark b. 1821
       1860 Sampson Census

Mark 39 yrs old, m

Mary b. 1807
       1850 Ashe Co Census
       See listing for Cinthia

Mary b. 1813
       1850 Ashe Co Census
       See listing for Cinthia

Mary 1840 Sampson Census

Mary c. five females
       1790 Montgomery Co Census: 0-0-0-5-0-4; 4 females plus four slaves

Mary E. M. b. 23 Feb 1832   d. 26 Dec 1856
       Cemetery Records Greene County
       Father: William: b. 6 Jul 1800; , died age 82, 3 mo, 15 days
                      d. 21 Sep 1882
       m. Susan, b. 22 Feb 1800, d. 25 Oct 1854
       Wife Susan, b. 22 Feb 1800, d. 25 Oct 1854
       Next to them is Mary E. M., b. 23 Feb 1832, d. 26 Dec 1856
       Buried in Cox Cemetery, Wilson County, NC

Matthew b. bef 1765
           c.   male, b. 1800-1810
                     male, b. 1794-1800
                     female
       1778: Murder trial witness in Wayne County. 1798 VA Tax List
       1810 VA Census, 1 slave, original copy of census page on file
       1-1-0-1-0-0-0-0-1-0-0-0-1

Matthew b. 1838
       Civil War: Pvt; enl age 23 on 12 Jun 1861; musician from Wayne County; A Co, 27th Regt;

Mikel b. 1854
       1850 Ashe Co Census
       See listing for Cinthia

Moris 1840 Sampson Census —most likely MOSES—below:

Moses b.1790-1800 (30-40 in 1830); 1801 (59 in 1860 Census)

m.   Penelope b. 1790-1800 (30-40 in 1830) 1799 (61 in 1860)

c.   Owen b. 1825-1830; male under 5 in 1830 (prob Owen b. 1832)

Barney b. 1825-1830; male under 5 in 1830 (prob   Barney, b. 1823)

Phillip b. 1825-1830; male under 5 in 1830 (prob. Phillip, b. 1834)

b. 1820-1825; male 5-10 in 1830 (not listed in 1860 census)

b. 1820-1825; female 5-10 in 1830 (prob. Sylvannia)

Sarah, born 1838 (as per 1860 Census), b. 1840 in 1870 Census

Sylvannia, b. 1822 (listed on the 1870 Sampson Census)

Note: . birthday errors...note parents most likely illiterate and dates soon forgotten...Sylvannia, b. 1828 (should have been on the 1830 Census, so may assume that she is the only female listed and should have been listed as 0-5 in the 1930 Census.

1830 Census: Males: 3 (under 5), 1 (5-10)1 (30-40)

Females: 1 (5-10), 1 (30-40)   9 slaves

1830 Census: another source for the 1830 census does not list one of the males under 5...perhaps census taker missed him or he died by the time   this was written or taken for the second time; all other data fits; Males: 2 (under 5), 1 (5-10), 1 (30-40) Females: 1 (5-10), 1 (30-40)

1860 Census

Moses	59
Penelope	61
Sylvania	32
Owen	28
Barny	23
Phillip	26
Sarah	22

1870 Sampson Census

Moses	69	farmer
Penelope	73	keeping house
Sylvannia	48	keeping house (dau of Moses, sister of Moses, Jr.)
Sarah	30	keeping house (daugh of Moses, sister of Moses Jr.)
Hanson	7	farm hand
Charlotte	8	keeping house

Note Hanson and Charlotte are children of Moses McLaine, Jr....may have been visiting with Grandma Penelope and Grandpa Moses, or could be living there with them.

Moses McLaine,

This would be Moses McLaine, Jr.

b. 1825-26, 1825   d. 22 Mar 1863

m. Ann, b. 1839 (died or divorced by 1870 as not listed on the census in Sampson with Mack and Patia, the daughter)

c.	Scott	b. 1856 male
	Patience	b. 1857 female
	Thomas J	b. 1860
	Sabra	b. 1644

Living with Moses "Mack" in 1870 was: Patia Hall, b. 1845 and her child: c. Nancy Hall, b. 1868

Civil War: Co, 54th Regt, Inf; born 1825; Pvt; Sampson farmer; enl 4 Mar 1862 in

Fayetteville; discharged as being over 35 years of age on 26 May 1862; enl 16 Oct 1862 in Cumberland county and assigned to E co, 8th Regt; died 22 March 1863 of fever in Charleston, SC hospital; served as a cook;

Samson 1860:

    McIlvary (Moses McLaine), 34 yrs old,

    Ann, his lst wife, 21 years old, listed as illiterate; divorced or died by

        1870 as is not listed on the 1870 Sampson Census

    Scott, his son, 4 yrs old

    Patience, his daughter, 3 years old

    Thomas J., his son, 11 months old

    Sabra   16 yrs old, female

    Shown as owning $400 worth of real estate and $100 in personal property

    on the reverse side of the census. Listed as illiterate. Hanson and Charlotte, children of

    Moses Jr. are listed as living with Moses, Sr. on the 1870

Sampson Census.1870 Census

Mack	45	farmer , b. 1825
Patia	13	keeping house, b. 1857 (Patience, his daughter)

Another 1870 version:

Mack	45	farmer
Patia	13	keeping house
Hall, Patia	25	keeping house
Hall, Nancy	2	at home
Nancy	b. 1805, VA	

        c.   Sarah, b. 1837

                James, b. 1838

                Rebecca J., b. 1844

                Wm T., b. 1846

1850 VA Census

Newsom   Rev. War: Nov 27, 1782 payroll list; vouchers for 1783 – 1785.

Newsom   c. b. 1774, male under 16

                             female in 1790 census list

        1790 Northampton Co Census; 1798 Tax List VA; 1816 Greene County

        Tax Lists: 191 3/4 acres, $242; 1827 – 27 Feb: adjoining lands of Newsom

        Faircloth N side of Autrys Creek on rd leading from arborough to Snow

        Hill; Newsome's Will dated 3 July 1830, probated Feb 1831 mentions the

        children Susanna, Lucy, Virginia, Feriby, Rita, Ridley, Winnefred, Cherry, Anna and

        Matilda, all girls, and the boys, Bright, Newsome, Jr. and John.

Noah   War of 1812: Maj Cameron's Command, 5th Co of Cumberland County, NC; Corporal; served for six months including 24 Jul 1813; drafted militia stationed at Deepwater Point; present 26 Sept 1813; detached all married men including him on 19 Oct 1813; present July 1813 through 19 Jan 1814; expiration date of pay was 19 Oct 1813.

Noah	Civil War: 5th Co, NC Cumberland Co, Maj. Cameron's Command
Nathan	Civil War: Pvt, A Co, 71st Regt; enl Apr 1864 in Sampson County;
Owen	b. 1830 m. Molly, b. 1832

        1870 Sampson Census

Owen	40	farmer
Molly	38	keeping house

Paterick   b. 1845   d. 10 Sep 1863
    Civil War: Born 1845; Pvt, C and F Company' 54 Regt, Inf; Sampson laborer; enl 22 Aug 1862 Camp Campbell; died 20 Sept 1863 in camp hospital at Orange Court House, VA;

Peggy   b. 1795
    1860 Hertford Census; Age 65, seamstress #985, appears to be an old age home   with multiple residents

Penelope   1860 Sampson Census   Penelope   45 yrs old, f

Penny Janie   b. 1 Dec 1883
    Sampson Co Cemetery
    38.   Faircloth
    A. Penny Janie   December 1, 1883 May 18, 1949

Phillip   b. 1834   d. 1 Jan 1865
    Civil War: Born 1834; Pvt, enl Orange Co Court House, VA on 1 Nov 1863; deserted 12 Apr 1864; returned 24 Sep 1864; captured 27 Oct 1864 near   Petersburg, VA.; Confined at Point Lookout, MD where he died 1 Jan 1865   in prison; C. Co, 26th Regt;

Raiford   War of 1812: 4th Regt of Cumberland Co, NC; Maj Cameron's Command; detached from 4th and 14th Brigade; six months of service from 24 July   1813; Cpt Thomas Boykin's Company, Deepwater point on 26 Sept 1813; Cpt David L. Evan's Company of Artillery 30 Nov – 31 Dec 1813 at   Deepwater; deserted; Cpt Boykin's Company from July 1813-19Jan 1814, deserted. Cpt Evans Company 19 Jan 1814, deserted;

Raiford   Civil War: 4th Co, detached from the Sampson Co, 2nd Regt of Maj.
    Cameron's

Raiford   b.   betw. 1794-1802   m.   by 1820; b. betw. 1794-1802
    c.   b. 1811-1820; female under 10 in 1820
    1820 Sampson Census

MALES						FEMALES INFO					District	Page Family
10	16	18	26	45	45+	10	16	26	45	45+		

    Faircloth   Raiford
    0   1   0   1   0   0   1   0   1   0   0   Hall's   302
    1840 Sampson Census

Raphel or Raiford   War of 1812: Pvt, 3rd Regt of Moore's Sampson County, NC; six months service from 11 Oct 1814; Cpt Caleg Stephens Co of Infantry, 3rd Regt, NC   militia; stated at Greenfield, near Wilmington through 15 Feb 1815;

Raphael   Civil War: 2nd Regt, Sampson Co.

Reasom   b. 1778
    Civil War: Born 1778; Pvt, E Co, 8th Regt; enl Cumberland County

Reason b. 1831   d. 12 Nov 1864
    Civil War: Born 1831; Pvt, E Co, 8th Regt, Inf; Sampson County farmer; enl 5 Aug 1861 Cumberland County at age 30;; captured 9 (8?) Feb 1862 on Roanoke Island; paroled 21 Feb 1862 Elizabeth City and exchanged in Aug 1862. wounded 30 Jan 1863 Morris Island, Charleston Harbor, SC; furloughed until 2 Nov 1863; captured 1Jun 1864 Cold Harbor, VA; confined Point Lookout, MD and Elmira, NY; died 14 Nov 1864 of chronic diarrhea; buried in grave #804 at Woodlawn Cemetery, Elmira, NY;

Rebecca   1860 VA Census

Rebecca   b. 1820
    1860 Columbus county Census: 40 yrs old, living with Cox Family #0786

Reddin b. 1846
    Civil War: Enl in Cumberland County on 16 Oct 1862. Present and accounted for through Apr 1863. Cook. No further records.

Richard   Civil War: Cpt, E, Blacksheair Co., GA

Richard   1870 VA Census

Richard   GA State Militia: Cartman in Cpt Elijah Blackshear's Co, GA Militia; 2 Jun – 7 Jun 1814 "to cut road in Pulaski County".

Richard M.   d. 2-3 Jul 1863

Civil War: L Co, 5th FL; casualty at Gettysburg on 2-3 Jul 1863.

Robert   c.   b. 1775-1790; male under 16 as per 1790 Census

                    b. 1775-1790male under 16 as per 1790 Census

                    female

                    female

                    female

                    female

1790 Fayette Census: 0-1-2-5-0-0-

?1766 – 1 Sep: DB o, p. 70: Robert Faircloth from John Hall, N side Town Creek, 100 acres in Edgecombe County.

Robert ?Edgecombe County: 1766 – 1 Sep: DB o, p. 70: Robert Faircloth from John Hall, N side Town Creek, 100 acres

1784-86 Sampson County State Census 100 acres, 1 wp, 0 bp

Robert   2 Seminole War of 1816-1818: Dean's County, GA Militia

Sampson   b. 1823

Civil War: Born 1823; Pvt, C Co, 26th Regt; enl 1 Nov 1863 at Orange Co., Court House, VA; deserted 11 Apr 1864; returned 24 Sept 1864; deserted 14 Feb 1865; captured by the enemy in Sampson County on 16 mar 1865; Confined at Hart's Island, New York Harbor until released / paroled 19 June 1865 after taking the Oath of Allegiance.

Sampson   1840 Sampson Census

Sampson   b. 1828, born 1823 in 1880 Sampson Census, so probably the same Sampson as listed in the Civil War born 1823.

            m. Ann, b. 1835, or b. 1833 as per the 1870 Census, b. 1830 in the 1880 Census (getting younger each year)

         c.   Hinton   b. 1853-54

                Mary   b. 1856-57

                Barna   b. 1862

                William,   b. 1864 (listed in the 1880 Census)

1860 Sampson Census

Sampson   32 yrs old, male

    Ann   25 yrs old, fe

    Hinton   7 yrs old, m

    Mary   4 yrs old, fe

1870 Sampson Census

Samson 42   farmer

    Ann   37   Housekeeper

    Hinton   16   farm hand

    Mary   13   keeping house

    Barna   8   farm hand

1880 Sampson Census

Sampson 57   farmer   married

    Ann   50   wife   married

    William   16   son   single

    Sampson

b. 1838

Civil War: Pvt, E Co, 8th Regt; enl 20 Jul 1961 Sampson Co, at age of 23; Oath   on   19 May 1965.

Sampson   b. 1838   d. Pvt, born in Sampson County where he resided as a farmer prior to enlisting in Cumberland County at age 23, 20 Jul 1861, for the war. Captured at Roanoke Island on 8 Feb 1862, but escaped. Present or accounted for until captured at Cold Harbor, VA on 1 Jun 1864. Confined at Point Lookout, MD, until transferred to Elmira, NY on 29 May 1865 after taking the Oath of Alliance.

Samuelm   by 1787 with three children by 1790 census
            c.   1 male under 16 in 1790 Census
                    2 females by 1790 Census

Sampson County, NC – Nicholas Sessums to Samuel Faircloth deed of land in 1790

1784-86 Sampson County State Census, 200 acres, 1 wp

1790 Fayette Census: 1-1-3-0-0

Samuel   Civil War: Pvt, C Co, 5th Batt; enl 2 Sept 1863 in Cumberland Co.
            Civil War: Pvt, B Co, 10th Batt; enl 11 Apr 1864; discharged;

Sarah   Passenger Lists: to Barbados Dec. 1716 from London

Sarah   Listed in South Carolina Census in 1800

Smith   Civil War: Pvt, g Co, 55 Regt, enl 8 May 1862 Johnston Co.

Smith F.   b. 1820

Civil War: Born 1820; Pvt, F Co, Regt 54, Inf; Sampson farmer; 3nl 7 Apr 1962; blockers, as substitute for G. W. Williams; captured 7 Nov 1863 on the Rappahannock, VA; confined Pt. Lookout, MD; received 16 Mar 1864, City Point, VA for exchange; captured 19 Sept 1864 in Winchester, VA; confined Point Lookout, MD; exchanged 15 Mar 1865;

Smiddick   b. bef. 1775   m. b. bef 1775
            c.   b. 1811-1820; male under 10 in 1820
                    b. 1804-1810; male 10 – 16 yrs old in 1820
                    b. 1794-1802 ; male 18-26 in 1820
                    b. 1794-1802; male 18-26 in 1820
                    b. 1811-1820; female under 10 in 1820
                    b. 1811-1820; female under 10 in 1820
                    b. 1804-1810; female 10-16 yrs in 1820
                    b. 1804-1810; female 10-16 in 1820
                    b. 1775-1794; female 26-45 in 1820
                    b. 1775-1794female 26-45 in 1820

1820 Sampson Census

MALES						FEMALES INFO					District	Page	Family
10	16	18	26	45	45+	10	16	26	45	45+			
Faircloth		Smiddick											
1	1	0	2	0	1	2	2	2	0	1	Hall's	302	

Cannot be sure who is related to who in this census record as it could be that Grandma Smiddick and Grandma Smiddick were living with their children and their grandchildren in multi family home.

Smithwick   b.   1800-1810   m.b. 1790-1800; prob. Female listed as 30-40 yrs old
            c.   b. 1820-1825; male 5-10 in 1830
                    b. 1815-1820; male 10-15 in 1830
                    b. 1815-1820; female 10-15 in 1830
                    b. 1805-1820; female 10-15 in 1830

1830 Sampson Census: Males: 1 (5-10), 1 (10-15), 1 (20-30)
Females: 2 (10-15), 1 (30-40), 1 (40-50)
9 slaves
Probably also includes another female relative 40-50 years old. B. 1780-1790

<u>Solomon</u>   War of 1812: Maj Cameron's Command, Cpt thomas Boykin's Company; July 1813 – 19 Jan 1814; stationed at Deepwater Point from 30 Nov – 31 Dec 1813; CptEvans com from 31 Dec - 19 Jan 1814 at Camp Deepwater Point;

<u>Solomon</u>   b. 1811   d. after 1862
     m. Edney A., b. 1801 (49 yrs old in 1850 Census)
     c.   Matilda J., b. 1839
     Thomas H., b. 1842
     John L., b. 1843
     Henry C., b. 1849

Civil War: Born 1811; Pvt, F Co, 2nd Art, 36 Regt; Sampson farm laborer; enl 26 Feb 1862 at Ellisville; hospitalized 11 Jul 1862 with acute diarrhea; C Co, 2nd Regt, Art, 36th Regt; enl 3 Mar 1862 for 3 yrs at age of 51 in Bladen County; h. co, 3rd Regt, enl 15 Jul 1862 Bladen ; 1850 Bladen Census Farmer, m. Edney A (49, $500 value property

<u>Solomon</u>   Civil War: 3rd Regt, Cumberland co, Maj Cameron's Command

<u>Solomon</u>   b. 1775-1794 (26 – 45 in 1820)   m. b. 1775-1794 (26-45 in 1820)
     c.   b. 1811-1820; male under 10 in 1820
     b. 1811-1820; male under 10 in 1820
     b. 1804-1810; male 10-16 in 1820
     b. 1804-1810; male 10-16 in 1820
     b. 1794-1802; male 18-26 in 1820
     b. 1811-1820; female under 10 in 1820
     b. 1804-1810; female 10-16 in 1820

MALES						FEMALES				INFO	District	Page	Family
10	16	18	26	45	45+	10	16	26	45	45+			
										Faircloth	Solomon		
3	2	0	1	1	0	1	1	0	1	0	Hall's	302	

1820 Sampson Census; 1840 Sampson Census

<u>Solomon</u>   b. 1800-1810 (20-30 yrs old by 1830)   m. b. 1800-1810 (20-30 in 1830)
     c.   b. 1815-1820; male 10-15 yrs in 1830
     b. 1810-1815; male; 15-20 yrs old in 1830
     b. 1820-1825; female; 5-10 yrs in 1830
     b. 1805-1820 female; 10-15 in 1830
     b. 1810-1815 female; 15-20 in 1830

plus one female 40-50 yrs old in 1820, b. 1780-1790;may be the grandmother or the mother of all these children with Solomon being her son.
1830 Sampson Census
Males: 1(10-15), 1 (15-20, 1 (20-30)
Females: 1 (5-10), 1 (10-15), 1 (15-20), 1 (20-30), 1 (40-50)
1840 Sampson Census

Stanley/Stantley   b. 1850   d. 1935
        Sampson County Cemetery marker:
        Faircloth, Stanley   Died 1935   85 years
        This is a hand made stone –Butler Funeral Home marker still present.
        That is all that is readable on the Butler Funeral Home Marker.
        Buried beside Charlotte, Faircloth, b. 1848   Charlotte Died 1931   83 years old; Hand etched Stone-Butler Funeral Home marker still present.
        Charlotte is the wife of Stanley.
Stephen   War of 1812: Pvt; Cpt John Woodward's Company of Infantry, 25th Regt, Maj Loveless Gasque's Batt, SC militia 7 Nov 1814- 5 Dec 1814 for 28 days at Camp Cat Island;
Stephen   Civil War: Pvt, G Co, 55 Regt; enl 8 May 1862 Johnston Co.
Susan b. 1793
        1850 Greene County Census; 57 yrs old,
            237a   20   FAIRCLOTH Susan 57   North Carolina pg 0235a.txt
T.   Civil War: Pvt, E co, 36th Regt; captured at Ft. Fisher on 15 Jan 1865.
Thelbert A.   Civil War: Pvt, B co, 37th Regt; enl 15 Feb 1864 Ashe Co; served 17 Mar 1864 - 7 Mar 1865.
Theopheles   b. 1813   m. Rebecca, b. 1819
                        c.   Jautha, b.1841 or Gerusha A., b. 1839
                                Lucy J., b. 1851, b. 1850
                                David, b. 1853 (not on 1850 census)
                                Benjamin, b. 1855
                                Rebecca, b. 1857
                                Millard, b. 1861
                                Sarah S., b. 1845 (not on 1870 Census)
        1850 Bladen County Census
        Lists Rebecca, , c. Gerusha A., b. 1839, thomas G., b. 1843, Sarah S, b. 1845, Lucy J., b. 1850
1870 Sampson Census

Theophilus	57	farmer	
Rebecca	51 (?)	keeping house	
Jarutha	29	keeping house	b. 1841
Lucy J.	19	keeping house	b. 1851
David	17	works on farm	b. 1852
Benjamin	15	works on farm	b. 1855
Rebecca	13	keeping house	b. 1857
Milliard	9	at home	b. 1861

Tho   1840 Sampson Census
Thomas   War of 1812 Muster Roll, Hertford Militia
Thomas
        NC Pasquotank County muster roll of Robert Murden's Regt of S. County; probably of Surry County; filed a petition for a duplicate warrant and a grant to be issued to him for an entry of land; rejected initially by the committee; Senate members over ruled this decision on 2 Dec 1800.
        Note: Pasquotank County has a will on file. See Wills section for address to obtain will. Will dated 1772 and last name spelled Faircluff.
        Thomas Faircluff– 1772 Pasquotank County
Thomas   1704 James City, VA Land Rolls

Thomas   m. probably by 1785 due to five children by 1790 census
              c.   male born by 1790
                        male born by 1790
                        male born by 1790
                        male born by 1790
                        female born by 1790
       Dobbs County Militia, Rev War Period.
       Dobbs Voting Lists-1779; 1780 Dobbs Tax Lists
         8   56   Thomas   Faircloth $126
       1788 Dobbs voted; 1790 Dobbs Census plus one slave: 1-5-2-0-1 i.e. 1-0-3-0-0- i.e. male, other male, female, other, b
       ? Craven County Court Action for John on 19 Sep 1792, Glasgow County; testimony of John, Thomas and William.
Thomas   1834, Feb, and 1835 voter lists in Dobbs county
Thomas   b. c. 1670   m. married in 1790
              c.   female
                        female
                        female
                        female
       1790 Surry Census, no longer listed in Surry in 1810.
       1820 Surry DOES list a Thomas head of household, also listed separately in another Thomas listing on this data sheet.
Thomas   GA State Militia: Screven Co, Pvt, 1st class, 2nd Brig, 1st Div, 1814;
Thomas   Civil War: 2nd Regt, Hertford Co;
Thomas   b. 1838
       Civil War: Pvt, A Co, 18th Regt; enl 15 Jun 1861 New Hanover Co.; enl age 23 on 23 Jul 1861; Bladen farmer; retired an invalid on 31 Aug 1864;
Thomas   1820 Hertford Census
Thomas   1820 Surry Census
Thomas   Will of Rachel Best, 1859, Wayne County, lists niece Sally Faircloth, niece Araminter Faircloth and witnessed by Thomas Faircloth. Will on file.
Thomas G.   b. 1841   d. 15 Jan 1865
       Civil War: Pvt, K Co, 2nd Co, 40th Regt, 3rd Art.; enl Brunswick County at age of 21 on 7 Jul 1862; killed at Fort Fisher on 15 Jan 1865.
Thomas H.   b. 1820   d. 14 Mar 1865
       Civil War: Born 1820; Pvt, F Co, 2nd Art, 36th Regt; Sampson farm laborer; enl 20 Feb 1862 Terebinth; captured 15 Jan 1865 Fort Fisher; confined Elmira, NY; died 14 Mar 1865 of rheumatism; buried in grave #243_ Woodlawn Cemetery, Elmira; a second source says he enl in Cumberland co, C Co, 3rdt, Art, 35th Regt;
Vusom   1820 Greene Census
Wiley   Civil War: Gasques Batt, SC
William   Mentioned in a Will in Oct 1735, VA; 1790 Tax List of VA
William   1790 Tax List VA, (a second one)
William   Coronet, listed on 11 Mar 1761.
William   Dobbs County Militia, Rev. War Period.
William   Lt, 10th Regt, Col Abraham Sheppard's Co; enl 20 Jan 1778; discharged 1 Jun 1778; was charged with a major pay scandal involving payments made to himself from state militia funds; (Seems he created extra soldiers and cashed their paychecks...as he was the quartermaster...paymaster.)
William   1st Lt; took Oath to US

William   1792, Aug, Glasglow County, NC; Petition to move location of   Courthouse, stocks & prison to another location signed by Wm, John, Fredrick Thomas, J Frederick, Kinchen? Craven County Court Action for John on 19 Sep 1792, Glasgow County; testimony of John, Thomas and William.

William

The Army Accounts of the North Carolina Line

ABSTRACT of the ARMY ACCOUNTS OF THE NORTH CAROLINA LINE - settled by the commissioners at Halifax from the 1st September, 1784, to the 1st Feb, 1785 and at Warrenton in the year 1786, designating by whom the claims   were receipted for respectivelyFrom the State Records of North Carolina, Vol. XVII, pub. 1899.

(WARRENTON)

By whom Received

| 1265 | John Suggs | William Faircloth |
| 1697 | Joseph Samford | William Faircloth |

1936	Henry Stomer	William Faircloth
2849	Raymond Solomons	William Faircloth
1711	Lawrance Floyd	Wm. Faircloth
1937	Henry Fitner	William Faircloth
2855	Levi Forehand	William Faircloth
1468	Francis Fowler	William Faircloth
1408	Thomas Winstell	William Faircloth
1710	Josiah Wimberty	William Faircloth
2869	Mason Weatherington	William Faircloth

William   Pvt, received 640 acres of land on 13 Dec 1796 for 84 months of service;

William, III   Lt., received 731 acres for 24 months of service;

William   filed for acreage due in Tennessee on 5 Dec 1796.

William   Rev War: no rank given; filed for 640 acres of land for 84 months of service on 15 Dec 1797.

William, Jr.   b. bef. 1754 (as per most likely 15 or over when listed on Dobbs
    Tax lists in 1769.; d. aft. 1790; 1769 Dobbs Tax Lists
    Rev War: Pvt, Cpt Abraham Sheppard's Co, Col Abraham Sheppard's Batt; listed 1 July 1777; enl 22 Apr 1777.
    Dobbs Voting Lists-1779, Mar; 1780 Dobbs Tax Lists
    1780 Green County Tax lists
    8   6   William   Faircloth $2,240
    1784 Craven County Court Records: Wm, Jr. assault in Dobbs County.
    1790 Census; 1-0-3-0-1 i.e. male, other male, female, other, b
    ? 1793 Court in Craven County, Glasgow County: testimony of John, Thomas and William in John's court case.

William, Sr.   b. bef. 1751 (as per at least 18 when son was born?)
        c. male born by 1769, son William
    1769 Dobbs Tax List – WM, 2 males, 2 whites, son WM
    1780 Dobbs Tax Lists
    8   34   William Faircloth, Sr. $5,659 Property value
    1790 Dobbs Census -4-0-4-4-15 i.e. male, other male, female, other, b

? 1793 Court in Craven County, Glasgow County: testimony of John, <u>Thomas</u> and William in John's court case.

? Craven County Court Action for John on 19 Sep 1792, Glasgow County; testimony of John, Thomas and William.

<u>William</u>   1792, Aug, Glasglow County, NC; Petition to move location of Courthouse, stocks & prison to another location signed by Wm, John, Fredrick, Thomas, J Frederick, Kinchen

<u>William</u>   1784-86 Sampson County State Census: 100 acres, 1 wp

<u>William</u>   b. 6 Jul 1800   d. 21 Sep 1882
            m. Susan, b. 22 Feb 1800, d. 25 Oct 1854
      Wife Susan, b. 22 Feb 1800, d. 25 Oct 1854
      Next to them is Mary E. M., b. 23 Feb 1832, d. 26 Dec 1856
      ?Cemetery Records: Cox Cemetery in Wilson County, NC lists a Wm b. 6 Jul 1800 and d. 21 Sep 1882, wife Susan, b. 22 Feb 1800, d 25 Oct 1851, and buried beside them is Mary E. M., b. 25 Feb 1832 and died 26 Dec 1856.

<u>William</u>   b. 1835
      1850 VA Census

<u>William</u>   b. 1848
      Civil War: Born 1848; Pvt, F Co, 20th Regt, Inf; Sampson laborer; 20 Apr 1864; Clinton enl; wounded 19 May 1864 at Spotsylvania Court House, VA; discharged Apr 1865.

<u>William</u>
      1820 Surry Census

<u>William (possible Wm II)</u>
      1816 Green County Tax Lists:
<u>FAIRCLOTH, Wm</u>, 1 white pole
      do John, not given in ???, 1 white pole
do Moses, not given in ?????, 1 white pole
William

<u>Australian   Convict   Index,   1788-1868</u>   Record about William FAIRCLOTH

Name:	William FAIRCLOTH
Year:	1790
Trial Place:	Hertford
State:	NSW
Ship:	Surprise
Comments:	d1790
Born:	c1766

Source Information:
Reakes, J., comp. *Australian Convict Index, 1788-1868* [database on-line]. Provo, UT, USA: MyFamily.com, Inc., 2001. Original data: *1788-1868 Convict Records..* Records kept at the New South Wales State Records Office, P.O. Box R625, Royal Exchange, NSW 2000; at the Archives Office of Tasmania, 77 Murray St., Hobart, TAS 7000; and at the State Records Office of Western

<u>William H.</u>   b. 1843   d. 6 May 1864
      Civil War: Pvt, enl age `18 on 9 Aug 1861; born Forsythe Co; farmer; I Co, 33rd Regt; killed at Wilderness on 6 May 1864;

Civil War: 1861 Enl Wayne County militia, 15 Apr 1861

William Turner   b. 8 Sep 1829

                                m. Evelyn on 10 Jan 1867;, father: Council Wooten

Civil War: Born 1829; Pvt C Co, 2nd NC State Troops of Col C. C. Tew,   Northern   ,
VA; enl 16 May 1861 as 1st Lt; promoted to Captain 14 Mar 1862, then   Assistant
Quarter Master; surrendered at Appomattox Court House in Apr 1865; Cpt. Faircloth was
described as a faithful officer in a most responsible position. He later became Chief
Justice of the Supreme Court in North Carolina. Father was William and mother was
Susan Edwards (1850 was 57 years old, b. 1793), Edgecombe County area./Greene.

William Turner Faircloth, born Jan. 8, 1829 on Otter Creek in Edgecombe
County, NC. His father was William Faircloth, and his mother, Susan
Edwards, had five children, of whom he was the oldest. His ancestors were English
and they came to NC from the eastern shores of Maryland and Virginia. His father was
an agriculturist, and the subject of this sketch bore his hand to the ploy until he was 18
years old. Having attended the common schools and an academy, and having had other
preparatory instruction, in June, 1850, he entered Wake Forest college, where he
completed the college course in June, 1854, standing with the head of his class. His
means being limited, he taught school during vacation and thus earned the money to
pay the principal part of his college expenses. In July, 1854, he entered the law school
of Chief-Justice Pearson at Richmond Hill, NC and on Jan. 1, 1856, was licensed to
practice in all the state courts, and located at Snow Hill, Greene county, NC, and in a
few weeks was elected county solicitor by the county court. He was still then in debt
for necessary expenses at college and at the law school, which he soon discharged with
the first fruits of his practice. In May, 1856, he located in Goldsboro, NC and has
resided there ever since in the pursuit of his profession with slight interruptions.
Politically he was a Henry Clay Whig, and was opposed to the doctrine of secession,
but after his state seceded, he volunteered as a private in Company C, Second NC state
troops, commanded by Col. C. C. Tew and was on duty in the army of northern
Virginia until its surrender at Appomattox C. H. in Aril, 1865, when he retired with the
rank of captain of cavalry, and resumed his professional work. In August, 1865, he
was elected by the people of his county (Wayne) as a delegate to the provisional state
convention which convened Oct 2, 1865. In the fall of 1865, he represented his county
in the first legislature after the war, which convened Nov. 27, 1865. During his
legislature he was elected solicitor of the Third judicial district of NC, and held the
office until displaced in the reconstruction of the state in 1868.

On Jan 10, 1867, Mr. Faircloth married Evelyn, the oldest living daughter of the late
Council Wooten, of Mosely Hall (now La Grange), in Lenoir County, NC. He
followed his profession closely, but in 1875, he was again sent by his county as a
delegate to the state constitutional convention, which assembled in Raleigh, in
September

Cyclopedia of Eminent and representative men of the Carolinas of the Nineteenth Century, Vol.
2, S. C. reprinted 1973. The Reprint Company, pp. 145-146.

William Faircloth m. Susan Edwards

          Five Children:

                    William Turner Faircloth   b. 8 Jan 1829
                    c.   b. after 1829
                    c.   b. after 1829
                    c.   b. after 1829
                    c.   b. after 1829

WM   Apr 1784- Apr 1789 Deed Book from Lenoir County: p. 502, WM to   FREDERICK
1783-94 Court Records, Dobbs County:
20 Nov 1788: Wm, John summoned to curt to Sheriff bond, plus six other people for trespass, assault and battery and damage; went to court 1789;
15 Nov 1790 Wm on bond, appeared in court to answer Nathan Smith; also going were Abram Sheppard and James Clark.
1790 Court: WM
16 Nov 1790, Dobbs Court House, Wm and John against Graves Bright court action.
18 Mar 1791, Dobbs, Wm and John, assault Andrew Green and have to go to court.

WM   Civil War: 3rd Regt, Wimberlip, GA

Wm   Civil War: Pvt, Co, 3rd Regt; enl 21 Jun 1861 Cumberland County;
Wounded at Gettysburg.

Wm   Civil War: Pvt, A Co, 58th Regt; enl 2 Oct 1863 at Martin;

WM   GA State Militia: 1828. 16 May, Baker Co

Wm J   b. 10 Jun 1858   d. 16 Jul 1936
As per Cumberland County Cemetery
1810-1826?: W. J. and M. Faircloth: notes and accounts due; court action, due to Col. Thos. Edwards. (not sure who this is?) Dobbs County, NC; William Forecloth and son; William's negroes were Sam and Rachel, Dobbs Tax List 1769, 2 males over 16 yrs of age, and two slaves.

Zachariah   b. c. 1750's Edgecombe Co.
     m. Mary Armstrong, b. 1757 in Montgomery County.
     c. Martha Jane, b. abt 1785
Loyalist, Sgt, served 98 days from 25 Dec – 1 Apr 1782 and 34 days from 2 Apr – 5 May 1782. Brother of John and Hardwick. Parents were:

William and Sarah Faircloth. Born abt 1750 Edgecombe County; Married Mary
     Armstrong, b. 1757 in Montgomery Co. C. Martha Jane, b. Montgomery
     County abt 1785. Discussion of notes on Zachariah Faircloth (b. 1751 Edgecombe
     County, NC and d. 1820 in Sampson County, NC.) and his children.
Sampson County, NC Court Minutes:
23 Aug. 1820: Administration on the estate of Zachariah Faircloth, dec'd, granted James Faircloth and entered into bond in the sum of $100 with Mark Johnston and Matthew Johnston his security. [This James Faircloth would be James Faircloth, (Sr.)]
21 Nov. 1820: James Faircloth, Administrator, returned the amount of the account of the sales of the estate of Zachariah Faircloth, dec'd, which was filed.

Zachariah   b. 1829
Civil War: Born 1829; Pvt, I Co, 46th Regt, Inf; Sampson farmer; enl 15 Mar 1862 in Clinton; on detached service Mar-Apr 1863; wounded 5 May 1864 in Battle of Wilderness, VA and hospitalized at Richmond, VA; assigned 15 Aug 1864 to light duty in Winder hospital,in Richmond; paroled 20 Apr 1865.

EARLY TAX LISTS, Voting Records AND CENSUS RECORDS
Dobbs Militia mid 1700's

Faircloth	John
Faircloth	Thomas
Faircloth	William

1769 Tax List - Dobbs County, NC

FAIRCLOTH   William son William   2   2

This was spelled "Forecloth and son in another resource. Negroes Sam and Rachel with William Forecloth and son, both Wm and Son over 16 yrs of age. No females listed; just two males over 16 and 2 slaves.

1779 Voter List - Dobbs County, NC

It Was Not Easy To Vote in 1779
Kinston Daily Free Press
Friday - November 2, 1962, Page 10

In 1779 the outlook for the success of the American Revolution had grown very dim. This year and the next were to be the darkest hours for the patriots. Kinston, the home town of Governor Richard Caswell, had become the de facto capital of the new State. Here the State's Board of War usually met in secret sessions. Sometimes the Council of State met here. Sessions of the General Assembly, being more a matter of public knowledge, usually were convened at larger and more heavily guarded towns. While the name of the town was changed from Kingston to Kinston by law in 1784, already by 1779 the patriots were calling it Kinston in derision of the King of England from whose title the original name derived.

The vote in the general election in 1779 required the highest patriotic conviction. If the Revolutionary cause failed, each of these voters would be marked as among the rankest seditionists. For these were the men of Dobbs County who closest held to heart the pledge of the Declaration of Independence, the pledge of "our sacred honor." This list of Dobbs voters is complete but does not complete her roll of honor, for there were those who were away with the armies in the field and the women whose names do not appear on this list. Still, these are the fathers and brothers and staunch supporters of those who fought, and each of them deserves to be remembered.

Even to those whose resolute patriotism stilled all fear of the possibility of danger in defeat, to vote was no easy matter. The voting place was at the old Dobbs County Courthouse erected near Walnut Creek about midway between present LaGrange and Goldsboro. Dobbs County included practically all of the areas now comprised in Lenoir, Greene and Wayne Counties, and it was from these areas that the voters came on horseback to cast the vote of freemen in a __ State. Because of the distances, the polls were open for two days, March 10th and 11th.

STATE OF NORTH CAROLINA
At an election of one Senator and Two Members of the House of Commons to Represent the county of Dobbs held at the Court House the 10th and 11th of March, 1779, the following persons voted for Members of the House of Commons to wit:

> Faircloth, Frederick
> Faircloth, John
> Faircloth, William Junr

1788 Dobbs 2nd Vote - Dobbs County, NC State of North Carolina
(Seal)
His Excellency Samuel Johnston Esquire Governor, Captain General &
Commander in Chief of the said State
To the Sheriff of Dobbs County. Greeting
Whereas it hath been made appear to me that the Ballots taken by you at the last General Election for Delegates to the State Convention, were forcibly & violently seized and taken from you by some riotous and disorderly persons, so that you had it not in your power to ascertain who were the persons who had the greatest number of votes and therefore cannot make a Return of any Persons as duly elected to serve as delegates in the said Convention. And whereas a number of respectable Inhabitants of the said County have by Petition represented to me that the Inhabitants of the said County are desirous that I should appoint another Day for the purpose of electing Delegates to represent them in the said Convention. I do therefore recommend to such of the Inhabitants of Dobbs County aforesaid, as are entitled to vote for Representatives in the house of Commons to meet at the Court House of the said County on the fourteenth & fifteenth days of July next then and there to elect five Freeholders to represent them in the State Convention to be held at the Town of Hillsborough on the third Monday of July next, and I do hereby require you to give notice to the Inhabitants to meet accordingly and that you attend at the same time & place and conduct the said Election in the manner prescribed by the Resolve of the last General Assembly held at Tarborough.

> Given under my Hand & Seal at Arms at Denton this 28th day of June in the twelfth year of the Independence of America & in the year of our Lord 1788 - Saml Johnston
State of North Carolina Dobbs County

North Carolina – Dobbs County, NC
In obedience to the within recommendation of his Excellency the Governor
I Benjamin Caswell Sheriff of the County aforesaid did on Receipt of the same, to wit, on or about the second & third days of July instant, Notify the Inhabitants of the County aforesaid by posting up at the Court House and other public places in the said County Advertisements in the usual & accustomed manner requiring the Freeholders & Freemen in the said County to attend at the times and place within mentioned for the purpose within required and they did then & there choose and Elect Richard Caswell, James Glasgow, Winston Caswell, Benjamin Sheppard & Nathan Lassiter their Representatives duly Qualified to it & Vote in the Convention of the State to be held in the Town of Hillsborough on the third Monday in July instant, agreeable to a resolution of the General Assembly held at Tarbourough in December last, and I do here by mention the said Richard Caswell, James Glasgow, Winston Caswell, Benjamin Sheppard & Nathan Lassiter, the Representatives of the said County accordingly.

July 16th 1788
Benj Caswell Sheriff State of North Carolina
At an election held for the County of Dobbs on the 14th & 15th days of July 1788. At the Court House there offered for representatives to set & vote in Convention at Hillsborough in the third Monday of this last pursuant to and issued by the Governors.

3 Jno. Faircloth
80 Thos. Faircloth

Dobbs Voting Lists-1779
      Faircloth, Frederick
      Faircloth, John
      Faircloth, William Junr
      3 Jno. Faircloth
      80 Thos. Faircloth

DOBBS COUNTY, NC, 1780 TAXLIST
District # 8 DAVIS
Greene County - West of Great Contentnea Creek in northern Greene County and adjacent to Wayne County.

DIST/Payee # #	FIRST	LAST NAME	VALUE	COMMENT
8 34	William	Faircloth, Sr.	5,659	

District # 8 DAVIS
Greene County - West of Great Contentnea Creek in northern Greene

North Carolina – Dobbs County, NC
County and adjacent to Wayne County.

8	6	William	Faircloth	2,240

DOBBS COUNTY, NC, 1780 TAXLIST

8	56	Thomas	Faircloth	126

DOBBS COUNTY, NC, 1780 TAXLIST

William	Faircloth, Sr.	5,659
William	Faircloth	2,240

DOBBS COUNTY, NC, 1780 TAXLIST
Thomas   Faircloth

State Census for 1784-86

SURNAME	Name	Acres-Wp-Bp Acres
FAIRCLOTH	John	250-1-0
FAIRCLOTH	Robert	100-1-0
FAIRCLOTH	John	0-1-0
FAIRCLOTH	Benjamin	200-1-1
FAIRCLOTH	Hardy	300-1-0
FAIRCLOTH	William	100-1-0
FAIRCLOTH	Samuel	200-1-0

1790 CENSUS – FAYETTE DISTRICT, pt. 1

1st # is for free white males 16 years and upwards including heads of families
2nd # is for free white males under 16 years
3rd # is for free white females including heads of families
4th # is for all other free persons
5th # is for slaves

Faircloth, Samuel	1-1-3-0-0
Faircloth, Benjamin	3-4-4-0-0
Faircloth, Hardy	1-5-1-0-0
Faircloth, John	1-3-4-0-0
Faircloth, Samuel	1-1-4-0-0

1790 US Census – Dobbs County, NC

		M-0M-F-0-B
Faircloth	Frederick	1-0-3-0-0
Faircloth	Thomas	1-5-2-0-1
Faircloth	William Jr.	1-0-3-0-1
Faircloth	William Sr.	4-0-4-0-15

1790 Dobbs County

Faircloth	Frederick
Faircloth	Thomas
Faircloth	William Jr.
Faircloth	William Sr.

1790 NC Cumberland Cty, Fayette dis pg 38c

1st #   free white males 16 year upwards and head of families
2nd #   free white males under 16 years
3rd #   free white   females and head of families
4th #   all other free persons
5th #   slaves

Faircloth, Caleb	1-2-1-0-0
Faircloth, Robert	1-2-5-0-0
Faircloth, Caleb	1-2-1-0-0

Note references may include multiple names of the same individual. References just cite known sources.

1790 Census Wilmington District - Bladen County, NC _NONE listed

1st #   free white males 16 year upwards and head of
 families
2nd #   free white males under 16 years
3rd #   free white   females and head of families
4th #   all other free persons
5th #   slaves

1791 Southampton, VA Tax Roles (1791-1836)

Benj,	1791 and 1792
Ephraim	1791, 1793 through 1800 (each year)
Newsom	1794 through 1800 (each year)
Matthew	1798

<u>1796 Southampton, VA</u>
Sally   1796, 12 Oct.; married Simon Everett, Southampton, VA

Notes:

CENSUS RECORDS – 1800 TO 1900

Various sources of information are available to track Faircloth's throughout the US. A daunting task to collect all information about all Faircloth's is not yet complete, and unlikely to be by anyone. However, the resources in North Carolina have been explored for many years. Part of that information is included in this section. The information contained herein is presented alphabetically by NC County when county is known. THIS IS ONLY A PARTIAL LISTING WITH SELECTED INDIVIDUALS.

1800 North Carolina

m   under   10,   10-16,   16-26,   26-45,   45+,   females,   other   free,   slaves

Sampson Co.

Allen	10100-00100-00	b. 1774-1784
Benjamin	10001-00211-00	b. 1755-1774
Caleb	32010-10010-01	b.1774-1784
Hardy	30301-20010-00	bef. 1755
John	30101-11110-00	bef. 1755
John	00100-10100-00	b. 1784-1784
Samuel	21010-11110-00	b. 1755-1774
Smidie	10010-20101-00	b. 1755-1774
Solomon	10100-00100-00	b. c. 1774-1784

Greene Co.

Benjamin	00010-10010-00	b. 1755-1774
Frederick	50010-21010-01	b. 1755-1774
Johnathan	20110-00010-05	b. 1755-1774
Kenchin	00010-10010-01	b. 1755-1774
Mary	00000-00101-01	b. c. 1775
Newsom	11010-21010-00	b. 1755-1774

Cumberland Co

| Richard | 20010-10010-00 | b.1755-1774 |

Surry Co.

| Thomas | 02001-21010-00 | bef. 1755 |

Anson Co.

GREENE CO. 1816 TAX LIST

FAIRCLOTH, Newsom, 191 3/4 acres, $242

FAIRCLOTH, Kinchen, 1 white pole, 1 black pole

A list of Taxables & Taxable Property in Captain Henry Westbrook District for the year 1816

FAIRCLOTH, Wm, 1 white pole
do John, not given in ???, 1 white pole
do Moses, not given in ?????, 1 white pole

NORTH CAROLINA 1820 CENSUS
All Last Names of Faircloth

	First Name	County
1.	Margaret	Hertford
2.	Thomas	Hertford
3.	Arthur	Sampson
4.	Arthur	Bladen
5.	Elizabeth	Camden
6.	Isaac	Camden
7.	Jacob	Cumberland
8.	James	Sampson
9.	John	Samp
10	Inchen	Wayne
11.	Raiford	Samp
12.	Smiddick	Samp
13.	Solomon	Samp
14.	Thomas	Surry
15.	Vusom	Greene
16.	William	Surry

North Carolina – Sampson County   C. 1800 Census Extract
[head/FWM:10 16 26 45 45+/FWF:10 16 26 45 45+/clrd pers.(not ind.)/slaves]

1820 US CENSUS – Sampson County

MALES						FEMALES					INFO	District	Page	Family
10	16	18	26	45	45+	10	16	26	45	45+				

Faircloth   Arthur

| 0 | 0 | 0 | 1 | 0 | 0 | 1 | 0 | 0 | 0 | 0 | Hall's | 300 |

Faircloth   Isham

| 1 | 1 | 0 | 0 | 1 | 0 | 1 | 2 | 1 | 0 | 0 | Hall's | 302 |

Faircloth   James

| 1 | 0 | 0 | 0 | 1 | 0 | 1 | 0 | 1 | 0 | 0 | Hall's | 302 |

Faircloth   John

| 0 | 0 | 0 | 1 | 0 | 0 | 0 | 0 | 1 | 0 | 1 | Hall's | 302 |

Faircloth   Raiford

| 0 | 1 | 0 | 1 | 0 | 0 | 1 | 0 | 1 | 0 | 0 | Hall's | 302 |

Faircloth   Smiddick

| 1 | 1 | 0 | 2 | 0 | 1 | 2 | 2 | 2 | 0 | 1 | Hall's | 302 |

Faircloth   Solomon

| 3 | 2 | 0 | 1 | 1 | 0 | 1 | 1 | 0 | 1 | 0 | Hall's | 302 |

1830 Sampson County Census – All Faircloths

Males: 5 & under 10, M 10& under 15, M 15 & under 20, M 20 & under 30, M 30 & under 40, M 40 & under 50, M 50 & under 60

Females: same age groups

Evan (Green?):
- Males: 1 (15-20), 2 (20-30),
- Females: 1 (under 5), 1 (5-10), 1 (20-30), 1 (30-40), 1 (40-50), 1 (50-60)
- 4 slaves

Smithwick
- Males: 1 (5-10), 1 (10-15), 1 (20-30)
- Females: 2 (10-15), 1 (30-40), 1 (40-50)
- 9 slaves

Moses
- Males: 3 (under 5), 1 (5-10)1 (30-40)
- Females: 1 (5-10), 1 (30-40)
- 9 slaves

1830 Sampson County Census – All Faircloths

Name   Males: 5 & under 10, M 10& under 15, M 15 & under 20, M 20 & under 30, M 30 & under 40, M 40 & under 50, M 50 & under 60

Females: same age groups

Evan
- Males: 1 (under 5), 1 (5-10), 1 (30-40)
- Females: 2 (under 5), 1 (30-40)

Solomon
- Males: 1(10-15), 1 (15-20, 1 (20-30)
- Females: 1 (5-10), 1 (10-15), 1 (15-20), 1 (20-30), 1 (40-50)

Moses
- Males: 2 (under 5), 1 (5-10), 1 (30-40)
- Females: 1 (5-10), 1 (30-40)

1840 Sampson County Census – All Faircloths

Moses   Males: (1 (5-10)-(prob Barnabus), 2 (10-15)(probably Phillip & Owen), 2 (15-20) (prob Sampson & Moses, Jr.), 1 (20-30) (prob Jasper), 1 (30-40) (prob Moses Sr)

Females: 2 (under 5) (prob Sarah and Janie), 1 (15-20) (prob Sylvannia), 1 (30-40) (prob Penelope)

1840 Sampson County Census

Arthur Faircloth	Evans Faircloth	Isam	Faircloth
J Faircloth	Jerusha Faircloth	John	Faircloth
Mary Faircloth	Moris Faircloth	Raiford	Faircloth
Rarna Faircloth	Sampson Faircloth	Solomon	Faircloth
Solomon Faircloth	Tho Faircloth		

1850, Partial Census - FEDERAL CENSUS- LOCKERMAN FAMILY

GEORGE AUTRY	44	MALE	FARMER
FANNY	38	FEMALE	
_IHAM	2	MALE	
EDNEY	1	FEMALE	
JACOB FAIRCLOTH	23	MALE	TIMBER

237a 20   FAIRCLOTH Susan   57   North Carolina
pg 0235a.txt

1860 Sampson County Census
(assumed families are grouped together as they are listed consecutively on the census records.)
McIlvary (Moses McLaine), 34 yrs old,
       Ann, his lst wife, 21 years old, listed as illiterate
       Scott, his son, 4 yrs old
       Patience, his daughter, 3 years old
       Thomas J., his son, 11 months old
Shown as owning $400 worth of real estate and $100 in personal   property on the reverse side of the census. Listed as illiterate.

Sabra   16 yrs old, female

Sampson 32 yrs old, male
Ann   25 yrs old, fe
Hinton   7 yrs old, m
Mary   4 yrs old, fe

Mark   39 yrs old, m

Penelope 45 yrs old, f
Moses   59
Penelope 61
Sylvania   32
Owen   28
Barny   23
Phillip   26
Sarah   22

1870 Sampson County Census – June
Samson   42   farmer
Ann   37   Housekeeper
Hinton   16   farm hand
Mary   13   keeping house
Barna   8   farm hand

Moses   69   farmer
Penelope 73   keeping house
Sylvannia   48   keeping house
Sarah   30   keeping house
Hanson   7   farm hand
Charlotte 8   keeping house

Mack   45   farmer
Patia   13   keeping house

Owen   40   farmer

Molly	38	keeping house

Johnathan	50	farmer
Caroline	47	keeping house
Franklin	19	farm hand
Solomon	16	farm hand
Shepherd	15	farm hand
Sarah	13	keeping house
Love D	10	farm hand

Jasper	8	farm hand

Samson	42	farmer
Ann	37	keeping house
Hinton	16	farm hand
Mary	13	keeping house
Barna	8	farm hand

Moses	69	farmer
Penelope	73	keeping house
Sylvania	48	keeping house

Sarah	30	keeping house
Hanson	7	farm hand
Charlotte	8	keeping house

1870 Sampson County Census – June
(birth dates estimated from age given)

Mack	45	farmer
Patia	13	keeping house
Hall, Patia	25	keeping house
Hall, Nancy	2	at home

Owen	40	farmer
Molly	38	keeping house

Theophilus	57	farmer	
Rebecca	51 (?)	keeping house	
Jarutha	29	keeping house	b. 1841
Lucy J.	19	keeping house	b. 1851
David	17	works on farm	b. 1852
Benjamin	15	works on farm	b. 1855
Rebecca	13	keeping house	b. 1857
Milliard	9	at home	b. 1861

1880 Sampson County Census

Hardy	_8	farmer	married
Penny	43	keeping house	married
Lucy A	9	daughter	

Levi	19	nephew	single

Hardy, Sr.	89	widowed or divorced	
Elizabeth34		daughter single	

M. Jane	7	grand-daughter	
Sallie	40	daughter single	

Ceasseyat?	55	mother in law living with William Culbreath

Sampson 57	farmer	married

Ann	50	wife	married
William	16	son	single

Jonathan 63	farmer	married

Greene County, NC - County Index to NC Marriages Database
49. Woodard, Calvin   Faircloth, Sudie   1890

1900 Sampson County Census
Berry	b. Mar 1863	37 yrs old
Lizzie	b. Feb 1871	29
Stephen F	b. Oct 1888	11
George W	b. Apr 1892	8
Lalister L.	b. Oct 1894	6
Lula J	b. Dec 1897	2
Santford	b. Mar 1900	

Hisk	b. Feb 1870		
Elizabeth	b. 1846 ?	mother	54
Ruffin	b. Mar 1844?	brother	56 ?
Nancy	b. Oct 1887	sister	12
William	b. Feb 1844	husband	56
Isabella	b. Mar 1833	wife	66
Jasper A.	b. 1875 (?)	son	25 (?)

<u>1633:</u> William Faircloth, I came to America as a Headright with Colonel John Carter, Esquire, in circa 1664. John Carter, Councellor of State, was granted 4000 acres being a neck of land on the north side of Rappahannock River in Virginia. The tract was bounded on the westward side by the Cassatta Woman Creek which runs north and east northeast towards the head of Wiccocomico River, and etc. This tract was originally granted to Captain Samuel Mathews on 1 Aug 1643 but was deserted by him. Upon Petition of Colonel Carter, the land was granted to him by order of the General Court bearing the date 12 Oct 1665 and further due for the transportation of 80 persons among whom was William Faircloth. William Faircloth, I, was born in England in c. 1640. No record has been found of his wife's name or when he married but he settled in the area near the County of Isle of Wight, Virginia. He was apparently the father of several children, among who were William, II and Thomas. The Rent Rolls of the Land of James City County, VA, show that Thomas Faircloth owned 277 acres of land in 1704. Thomas was born in VA, c. 1670. William, I, died in VA, c. 1710 when he was about 70 years old. Ref: Cavaliers, and Pioneers, Abstracts of Virginia Land Patents and Grants, 1623-1666 by Marian Nugent (Virginia Land Office, Richmond, VA), Gen. Publishing Co, INC. 1963, p. 536. The Planters of Colonial VA, by Thomas S. Wertenbaker, Princeton Univ. Press, 1922, p. 212.

<u>1713:</u> William Faircloth, II born c. 1663 patented 275 acres of land in Isle of Wight County, VA on 13 Nov 1813 and lived in the Isle of Wight County, VA all of his life. Died there c. 1728 at 65 years of age.

<u>1759</u> – 200 Acres surveyed for William in Johnson County

<u>1761</u> – 22 Dec: deed to Benj F for 100 acres, DB 1, p. 49'

<u>1765</u> – Colony of NC, 1765-1775 Land Patents by Margaret Hofmann, p. 10. Simon turner 6 Apr 1765, 400 acres in Dobbs Co on Cow branch, joining Thomas Turner, Parkes's Corner, William Faircloath, and Thomas Williams; also referred to on 26 Oct 1767 and 27 Apr 1767.

<u>1766</u> – 1 Sep: DB o, p. 70: Robert Faircloth from John Hall, N side Town Creek,
             100 acres

<u>1766</u> – 30 Sep: DB 00, p. 85; from Benj to John skinner, 200 acres, south side
         of Wrights Creek

1775: William II, Moved to Edgecombe Co, NC about 1745 and patented a tract of land on the Tar River where he lived until 1755. In 1755 he sold his land and moved into Dobbs Co (later named Greene County) where he settled and was still living in 1790.

1777- 27 Feb: mentions Faircloths line

1778- NORHUNTY SWAMP, NORTH SIDE

6 Jan 1778 #39(1). SAMUEL TARVIN, WILLIAM FAIRCLOTH, BENJAMIN EXUM, SHERROD BARROWS [also mentions COW BRANCH and BUTTON BRANCH].

1779- 4 Feb. 1779 #595. 640 acres to WILLIAM FAIRCLOTH ADJ: CAPTAIN PRIDGEON, THOMAS ALDRIDGE, WILLIAM HAM, SIMON TURNER.

1782: John Robert, son of William III, came with his father into Dobbs County, NC but left home early in life and went down in Brunswick County, NC where he was living when he enlisted (1778) in the Wilmington District Militia during the American Revolution. He served in the Militia until about 1782 or later. While in the war, he found an area of desirable land in North Duplin County, NC (which later became Sampson County), situated on Little Coharie River, somewhere east of where Autryville now stands. John received a grant for 300 acres in 1782 and later acquired other lands. In 1784, about the time of the new county of Sampson being formed, John and his brothers Thomas, Samuel, Hardy and William set out up the Cape Fear River, thence the South River until they reached about where Autryville, NC now stands. Here they all went forth located John's land, except for Thomas, who continued on northwestward finally settling in Tennessee. Samuel, Hardy, and William IV, all entered claims for grants on Great Swamp, a few miles west of John's tract. These grants were made in 1784, and soon after John, Hardy, and Samuel settled on their lands. However, William IV decided to return to Dobbs County where he remained the balance of his life.

1786- 4 April 1786. 50 acres to RYSTON FLOYD on east side of north east prong of Bear Creek, head Spring Branch ADJ: MICAJAH PARKER, WILLIAM HAM, WILLIAM FAIRCLOTH.

1791: Samuel to Ben, 100 acres, Duplin Co Deed book; N side of s. River; wit: Benj; 3 May 1791

1791: 18 Oct; Joh, Sr. to Wm Hobbs Deed east side of Little Coherra

1792: 8 Oct: John wit to deed in Little Coherie

1794 to 1804 Sampson Co. Deeds:

Benj: seller and witness	
Benj, seller	
Benj, Sr – buyer	
Rezen – witness	Caleb, seller, buyer, witness
Hardy – seller	James – witness
John – witness	Richard – seller
Sampson – witness	Samuel – buyer and seller
Smedick – witness	Smidick – witness
Smidwick – witness	Solomon – buyer
Thos – witness	Thomas – seller, witness

1 Jan 1793: In the Sampson County, NC Deed dated 8 April 1811 Achsah Faircloth sold 100 acres in Sampson County to John Johnston, Jr. said parcel being part of a patent granted to Samuel Faircloth on 1 January 1793. Although this deed transaction does not directly state that Achsah Faircloth was Samuel's daughter, it seems obvious to me that she obtained this land as her part upon his death or probably received it as a gift during Samuel's lifetime.

1798- 1 Nov: mentions Faircloths line, Burket Swamp & Sorrowful Branch

1800: Land survey 28 July 1800, 150 acres, Allen, Robert in Cumberland County

<u>8 Apr 1811</u>: NC Deed dated 8 April 1811 Achsah Faircloth sold 100 acres in Sampson County to John Johnston, Jr. said parcel being part of a patent granted to Samuel Faircloth on 1 January 1793. Although this deed transaction does not directly state that Achsah Faircloth was Samuel's daughter, it seems obvious to me that she obtained this land as her part upon his death or probably received it as a gift during Samuel's lifetime.

<u>18 Nov 1826</u>: There was a Sampson County, NC deed (vol. 21, p. 257) dated 18 <u>Nov. 1826</u> whereby Arthur Faircloth sold 150 acres and Wilson Faircloth sold his 50 acres including the interest of their siblings to their brother Raiford Faircloth; the others (siblings) who had interests in these properties were named as follows: Achsah "Axsey" (Faircloth) Butler, Betsey (Faircloth) Ellis, Isaac Sessoms and his wife Nancy (Faircloth), and Sabrey Faircloth. I thought I had a copy of the original of this deed, but I can't put my hands on it right now; what are stated above were my notes on the abstract of this deed. In the Sampson County,

<u>1827</u> – 27 Feb: adjoining lands of Newsom Faircloth which N side of Autrys Creek on rd leading from Tarborough to Snow Hill.

<u>Nov 1746 – Apr 1750</u>, Johnston County Deed Book 1: Thomas Jarrell to WM Faircloth, p. 84

<u>1732</u>-Southampton , VA Deed books; 190 acres on the south side of the Nottoway River adj. the east side of Sweathouse Swamp below the mouth of the Wolf Pit Branch (part of a patent to WILLIAM POPE on 28 Sep 1732), S: BENJAMIN (B) FAIRCLOTH and ANN (A) FAIRCLOTH, W: BENJAMIN (signed) DENSON, JACOB (signed) VICK, and CHARLES (signed) BRIGGS

<u>1753-1760</u>- <u>Southampton, VA Deed Books</u>

Pages 263-264   BENJAMIN FAIRCLOTH   MICHAEL VICK

Pages 263-264: BENJAMIN FAIRCLOTH and wife ANN to MICHAEL VICK dated 8 Feb 1755

<u>1756-1757</u>, Johnston County Deed Book 4, p. 27, WM and wife to James Calcote.

<u>1756-1757</u> Lenoir County Deed Book 4, p. 27: WM and wife to James Calcote
   AND Span, John to WILLIAM, p. 318

<u>1759</u> – 30 Apr, John Simones deed, next to William property; Dobbs County

<u>1761</u> - Edge. Co Db 1, page 49, deed date 22 Dec 1761, recorded Dec Ct 1761, James Permenter, Edge. Co to (Benjamin Faircloth), Edge. Co for 4 pds proc money a tract of land containing 100 acres beginning on the south side of (   ) Creek (   ) a large branch in said creek then along said creek to a small branch (below the plantation) then up the said branch to the (back line) to a pine so along the back line (   ) to a pine then down the (   ) being part of a patent to James Permenter for 300 acres, signed James Permenter, wit John Permenter, Robt. Wright (proved). (Film hard to read). Abstracted 6-07-05, NCA film C.037.40002, CTC.

<u>1759</u> - WAYNE COUNTY DEEDS

8. This document in several parts - 30 April 1759 - JOHN SPANN to ROBERT IVE - all of Dobbs - 30 pds - 440 acres - NS Nuse SS Great Contentena,
Nauhunty Branch, Butten Branch adj JOHN SIMONSES, survey of ROBERT PARKSES
adj WILLIAM FAIRCLOTH - part of patent granted to ROBERT PARKS on
2 September 1745

<u>1766</u> - Edge. Co Db 00, page 85, deed date 30 Sep 1766, recorded Oct Ct 1766,
Benjamin Faircloth, Edge. Co to John Skinner, county aforesaid for 45 pds, 10 shillings, proc money, a tract 200 acres on the south side of Wrights Creek beginning at a live oak in the mouth of a large branch in the said creek then down the said creek to a small branch to a gum in the said creek then down the said creek to the lower line to the midst of the said line so along the said line south 110 poles to a red oak and then west 220 feet to a pine in a fork a branch so down the said

61

branch to the first station and is part of a patent granted to the said James Permenter dated 1745 for 300 acres, signed Benjamin Faircloth (X), wit Nichs. Sessums, Demsey Skinner (O). Abstracted 4-11-06, RD

copy, CTC.

1766 - Edge. Co Db O, page 71, deed date (1 Sep 1766), recorded Oct Ct 1766, Thomas White and Elinor White, Edge. Co to Robert Killebrew, said county for 60 pds proc money, a tract on the north side of Town Creek on both sides of a branch beginning at a red oak then east 140 poles to a pine then north 160 poles to the center of three pines then west 140 poles to the first station, containing 157 acres, it being granted by Earl Granville to Thomas White date 26 Apr 1753, signed Thomas White, Elinor White(mark), wit Thos Merritt, Harry Irwin. Additional entry: receipt from Thomas White stating that he had been paid in full, witnessed by Henry Irwin, Oct Ct 1776. Abstracted 11-03-05, NCA

film C.037.00013, CTC.

Apr 1773-May 1775, Lenoir County Deed Book 10, p. 159, Span, John to WM

1774 – land given to son Benjamin by Benjamin of South Hampton, VA on 12 Mar 1774. Also mentions Frances, heir of John (Could this be the father of Benjamin who had a son named Ephraim?)

1777 – Edgecombe County, Edge. Co Db 3, page 106, deed date 27 Feb 1777, recorded (Apr Ct 1777), Thomas Laurence, Edge. Co to James Garner, county

aforesaid for 40 pounds, a tract of land beginning at a spruce pine in Faircloths line then along a contracted line to Burket Swamp then up the various courses of the swamp to Teagle Taylors line a eastward course to the corner to two small hickories then down a branch called Sorrowful Branch to Faircloths line then

along Faircloths line to the beginning, containing 150 acres.

Abstracted 3-3-05, NCA film C.037.40005, CTC.

1778, 6 Jan, Norhunty Swamp, north side TO WM

4 Feb. 1779 #595. 640 acres to WILLIAM FAIRCLOTH ADJ: CAPTAIN PRIDGEON,THOMAS ALDRIDGE, WILLIAM HAM, SIMON TURNER.

1780 – William, deed in Dobbs Co, 26 Jan 1780, also lists Thos, Fred (possible sons?)

1783 – Land Benjamin, South Hampton, VA, father of Ephraim, gave land to his son on 9 Oct 1783.

Apr 1784- Apr 1789 Deed Book from Lenoir County: p. 502, WM to FREDERICK

1784 – Deed of Samuel, 30 Nov 1784 in Sampson County lists son, Benjamin

1784 - 1784-1789; Lenoir County Deeds JOHNSTON/DOBBS/LENOIR COUNTIES GRANTOR INDEX - BOOK 16 - Lenoir County

1793, 1794, 1795

Faircloth, William   Frederick Faircloth 502

1786 Deed in Dobbs, "next to Wm"

1786 - DOBBS DEEDS

4 April 1786. 50 acres to RYSTON FLOYD on east side of north east prong of Bear Creek, head Spring Branch ADJ: MICAJAH PARKER, WILLIAM HAM, WILLIAM FAIRCLOTH.

6 Jan 1778 #39(1). SAMUEL TARVIN, WILLIAM FAIRCLOTH, BENJAMIN EXUM, SHERROD BARROWS [also mentions COW BRANCH and BUTTON BRANCH].

1784: Samuel Faircloth's father was Benjamin Faircloth, Sr. b. ca 1738 (place Va. or NC); verified in the Deed dated 30 Nov. 1784 whereby Nicholas Sessoms sold 100 acres in Sampson County on the east side of Great Swamp to Samuel Faircloth son of Benjamin Faircloth (Ref: Sampson County, NC Deed vol. B, pp 59 & 60; vol.8, pp 47 & 48).

1789 - 1784-1789; Lenoir County Deeds JOHNSTON/DOBBS/LENOIR COUNTIES GRANTOR INDEX - Lenoir County

1793, 1794, 1795

Book 14, Apr 1789-apr 1792:

Faircloth, William   John Howell   230

1778 – Dobbs: 6 Jan 1778 #39(1). SAMUEL TARVIN, WILLIAM FAIRCLOTH, BENJAMIN EXUM, SHERROD BARROWS [also mentions COW BRANCH and BUTTON BRANCH].

1779 – Dobbs: 4 Feb. 1779 #595. 640 acres to WILLIAM FAIRCLOTH ADJ: CAPTAIN PRIDGEON,

THOMAS ALDRIDGE, WILLIAM HAM, SIMON TURNER.

NORHUNTY SWAMP, NORTH SIDE

Apr 1790-Apr 1792 Lenoir County Deed Book: p. 230, WM to John Howell

1790 - North Carolina – Sampson County

NICHOLAS SESSUMS TO SAMUEL FAIRCLOTH, 1790

State of North Carolina Sampson County

This indenture made this fifth (5th) day of August in the year of our

Lord one thousand seven hundred and ninety 1790. Between NICHOLAS SESSUMS of Sampson County and in the state of North Carolina of the one part and SAMUEL FAIRCLOTH of the same county and state aforesaid of the other part.

Witnesseth that the said NICHOLAS SESSUMS for and in consideration of the sum of ninety (90) pounds special money to him in hand already paid and satisfied hath given granted alliend bargain sold and confirmed by these present and also duly give grant bargan sell and alien enfeffer and confirm to the said SAMEUL FAIRCLOTH his heirs and assign forever. One certain tract or parcel of land containing two hundred acres (200) of land it lying an being in Sampson County on the north side of the Caw Branch beginning at apine and white oak the edge of the Caw Branch running north 210 poles to apaplis in the Cabben Branch thence west 152 poles to a stake thence south 192 poles to a stake thence to the beginning with all and singular the rights hereditaments and appertainced whatsoever to the said lands in any ___ thereunto belonging.

To have and to hold the said tract of land or parcel of land with all ___ and dependencys until the said SAMUEL FAIRCLOTH his heirs and assigns forever in as full clear perfect manner to all intents and purposes as the said NICHOLAS SESSUMS ever did might or could have held the same before the making here of cleared and freed from all widows dowers jointure or thirds and all manner of such incumbrances whatsoever and this deed the said NICHOLAS SESSUMS hereby finds and obliges himself his heirs executors and adminstrators and assigns forever to defend from me and my heirs to be good valued and suffiecient unto the said SAMUEL FAIRCLOTH his heirsand assigns against his heirs and assigns an against all manner such whatsoever or any of them claiming by him from or under or any of them.In Witness whenceth the said NICHOLAS SESSUMS have hereunto set his hand an affix his seal this day an year first above written.   Signed Sealed and Delivered in the presence of }   Signed NICHOLAS SESSUMS

SOLOMON SESSUMS (Seal   and ISAAC SESSUMS}

State of North Carolina Sampson County August session of court one

thousand seven hundred and ninety 1790 the within deed from NICHOLAS

SESSUMS to SAMUEL FAIRCLOTH was proved in open court and ordered to be registered.

1793-95 Deed Book 16, p. 159: Exum, Ben TO JOHN Faircloth, Lenoir County

Lenoir County Deeds JOHNSTON/DOBBS/LENOIR COUNTIES GRANTOR INDEX - BOOK 16 - Lenoir County

1793, 1794, 1795

Exum, Benjamin to John Faircloth book 16,   P. 159; Old Dobbs County

1794 – August, Caleb to Sampson , Cumberland Co

1794 – 4 Aug 1794, Robert, Cumberland County 100 acres

1798 –Smeddic, 27 Sept 1798 deed in Sampson County

1798 - Edge. Co Db 9, page 98, deed date 1 Nov 1798, recorded Nov Ct

1798, Solomon Walker, Edge. Co to Samuel Raynor, same county for 200 pounds, a tract of land containing 100 acres beginning at a spruce pine in (Faircloths) line then along a contract line to Burkets Swamp then up the various courses of said swamp to Teagle Taylors line then along Taylors line to Hodges line then along Hodges line an eastwardly course to the corner to two small hickories then down a branch called Sorrowfull Branch to Faircloths line then along Faircloths line to the first station; also one other tract beginning at a spruce pine a corner tree of Laurences line then at easterly course to a white oak and so on to a gum on Sorrowful Branch then running up said branch with Solomon Walkers line to a poplar a corner tree then running along said Walkers line to the first station, containing 25 acres, the first being a tract I of John Dawson and the other being the land I bought of James Laurence, signed Solomon Walker (X), wit Thomas Newsom, John Brown. Abstracted 8-06-04, NCA film C.037.40009, CTC.

1799 – Dobbs, 4 Feb., 640 acres to WM

1799 – 150 acres to Allen on 31 Jan 1799

1799 – 24 Jan 1799 Robert to Benjamin, Cumberland County

1804 - 29 Dec 1804, Richard to _____, Montgomery, GA

1811   There was a Sampson County, NC deed (vol. 21, p. 257) dated 18 Nov. 1826 whereby Arthur Faircloth sold 150 acres and Wilson Faircloth sold his 50 acres including the interest of their siblings to their brother Raiford Faircloth; the others (siblings) who had interests in these properties were named as follows: Achsah "Axsey" (Faircloth) Butler, Betsey (Faircloth) Ellis, Isaac Sessoms and his wife Nancy (Faircloth), and Sabrey Faircloth. Above were my notes on the abstract of this deed. In the Sampson County, NC Deed dated 8 April 1811:   Achsah Faircloth sold 100 acres in Sampson County to John Johnston, Jr. said parcel being part of a patent granted to Samuel Faircloth on 1 January 1793. Although this deed transaction does not directly state that Achsah Faircloth was Samuel's daughter, it seems obvious to me that she obtained this land as her part upon his death or probably received it as a gift during Samuel's lifetime. Notes from Robert June Faircloth.

1816 – John gives land to his son, James on 24 Apr 1816. Witness was Raiford of Sampson County.

1819 - Untitled document located at the NC State Archives; my title "Report To Settle The Property Line Boundaries Between Arthur Faircloth and Wilson Faircloth". Report states: We the committee considers that the main coras[sic] of Cabbin Branch to the fork thence the south prong to the upper line shall be the dividing line between Arthur Faircloth and Wilson Faircloth heirs of Samuel Faircloth, dec'd. Arthur Faircloth to hold the north side and Wilson the south side. Certified by us this 16th day of April 1819. signed: Solomon Sessoms, Charles Butler, and Robert Butler.

1826 - There was a Sampson County, NC deed (vol. 21, p. 257) dated 18 Nov. 1826 whereby Arthur Faircloth sold 150 acres and Wilson Faircloth sold his 50 acres including the interest of their siblings to their brother Raiford Faircloth; the others

 (siblings) who had interests in these properties were named as follows: Achsah "Axsey" (Faircloth) Butler, Betsey (Faircloth) Ellis, Isaac Sessoms and his wife Nancy (Faircloth), and Sabrey Faircloth. I thought I had a copy of the original of this deed, but I can't put my hands on it right now; what is stated above were my notes on the abstract of this deed. In the Sampson County, NC Deed dated 8 April 1811 Achsah Faircloth sold 100 acres in Sampson County to John Johnston, Jr. said parcel being part of a patent granted to Samuel Faircloth on 1 January 1793. Although this deed transaction does not directly state that Achsah Faircloth was Samuel's daughter, it seems obvious to me that she obtained this land as her part upon his death or probably received it as a gift during Samuel's lifetime.

1827 - Edge. County Db 19, page 219, date of deed 27 Feb, 1827, date recorded May Ct. 1828, James Blow, executor of William Gay, decd to Eli Gay for $426 a tract of land on the north side of Autreys Creek on the road leading from Tarborough to Snow Hill adjoining the lands of William Edwards, Joshua Killebrew and others beginning in said creek at the mouth of Deep Bottom branch at William Edwards corner then up the said Branch along said Edwards line to Newsom Faircloth line then with his lint nearly north a course to a corner in the back line of the land of William Wooten then west along the said old line to the corner of the land drawn for Nancy Taylor then along her line nearly south course to the corner of the land drawn for Elijah Owens in right of his wife Sally Owens then along said line bearing west from south to a lightwood stake in the old field near the road opposite the corner of (Norvel) fence then a north course with lot Owens line (?) a branch then down the various courses of said branch to the said Norvel former line near the road then with said line to Autreys creek then down said creek to the beginning containing 140 acres, which land was sold to said Eli Gay at public sale in accordance with the last will of said William Gay duly proved in the Court of Please and Quarter session of Pitt County, signed James Blow, wit. Allen Gay, Elizabeth Rogers. Proved in court by Allen Gay. FHC
film 0018895.
1838 – 8 Dec 1838 to Greenville, Cumb/Sampson
1841 – 5 Jun 1841, Jacob to Jane, dau of Jacob, 200 acres, Cumberland County
1871 - No. 2288, on 13 Apr 1871 to Allen, 150 acres (may be 1771???)
Edgecombe thru 1820, books 1-15 scanned; 33 books total

Additional Deeds which may be in the same area as Faircloth deeds:
Bladen County, NC - Abstracts of Bedsole Family Land Entries, #4
Page 146-911; Feb. 7, 1779. Thomas Bedsole (Sr.)enters 100 acres on NE side of Beaverdam Swamp; Includes where he now lives and runs up the Swamp...
Paqge 154-955, Mar. 10, 1779. Thomas Bedsole (Sr.) enters 100 acres beginning on the head of Short Spring Branch and runs up the Branch...
Page 204--1231, Nov. 2, 1779. Thomas Bedsole (Sr.) enters 100 acres on the E side of Beaverdam Swamp. Borders his own land.....
2278 (5083) Thomas Bedsole (Sr.) 100 acres, Warrant # 1169 issued May 1, 1795 by W.R. Singletary to Simon Pharis for 100 acres between Archibald McDaniel & Samuel Hales, joins both, along the road on both sides & entered Jan. 1, 1795. Warrant sold on Oct. 10, 1798 by Jesse Hair, heir of Simon Pharis Hair, to Thomas Bedsole. (signed by Jesse Hair, but no witness or date) John Pharis swears purchase money for within mentioned land was paid & Warrant obtained without fraud. (Signed by John Pharis. Witness: Will White. This 100 acres was surveyed Nov. 24, 1798 by A. Weatherbee. Chain Carriers were: Samuel Pharis and H. Thomas. Grant # 2183, issued Mar. 9, 1799.
616, Sept. 30, 1799. William Bedsole (William
Henry Bedsole, Jr. b. 1727 in Va. Father of Thomas Bedsole, Sr.) paid 0.75 pound sterling for 150 acres and enters land in Book # 1799, dated Nov. 16, 1795. Grant # 2686, issued Nov. 27, 1802. Signed: John Haywood. 2822-5615. William Bedsole enters 50 acres. Warrant # 1799 issued Nov. 14, 1798 by William Robeson to William Bedsole for 50 acres on S side of South R, between & joins Archibald McDaniels and said Bedsoles own line & entered Apr. 26, 1797.
Land is on N side of Weathersbees Mill Bay & surveyed Nov. 20 1799 by A. Weathersbee. (No chain carriers listed). Grant # 2687, issued Nov. 27, 1802.
(Note: Although the following 6 patents were in Virginia, they pertain to the father of the above William (Henry) Bedsole (Jr.): July 11, 1719. Va. Land Office.
Patent # 11, Page 20, book for 1719-1724: William Henry Bledsoe/Bedsole, Sr. (b. ca. 1698?), Land Patent for 274 acres ; St. Marys Parish, Russel County, Va.

May 30, 1726, Va. Land Office. Patent # 12, book for 1623-1774. William Henry Bledsoe/Bedsole, Sr. and (his brother) Abraham Bledsoe, 1,000 acres, Spotsylvania County, Va.
Sept. 28, 1728. Va. Land Office. Patent # 13, book for 1725-1730. Isaac Bledsoe/Bedsole. (Brother of William Henry, Sr.) 1,000 acres . Spotsylvania County, Va.
Mar. 12, 1739. Va. Land Office. Patent # 18, book for 1738-1739. William Henry Bledsoe/Bedsole, Sr. 700 acres, Spotsylvania County, Va.
Jun. 16, 1768. Va. Land Office. Northern Neck Grants. Grant # 0 in Book for 1767-1770. 48 acres.
William Henry Bledsoe/Bedsole, Sr. Culpepper County, Virginia.

Bladen County, NC - Abstracts of Bedsole Family Land Entries, #3
23 March, 1842- Daniel Bedsole (son of William Bedsole), Thomas Parker and wife Charity Bedsole (Daughter of William Bedsole) of Cumberland County, NC, Nusen Autry & wife Clarry Bedsole (Daughter of William Bedsole)also of Cumberland County, NC to Love McDaniel (Attorney, Bladen County, NC) all our right, interest, title & claim to lands of William Henry Bedsole, of Bladen County, NC, deceased, being undivided and containing 417 acres on the S side of South River. First tract adjoins lands of Thomas Bedsole (Sr.) granted to William Bedsole on 12
December 1816-another tract of 107 acres being part of a tract granted to Samuel Hales on 9 March, 1791 on the south side of South River, east of the Stage Road, adj. lands of Mathew Hales-3rd tract of 100 acres granted to Thomas Bedsole (Sr.) & by him conveyed to Benjamin Faircloth (son in-law of Thomas Sr., married daughter of Thomas, Francis Bedsole) & by him to William Henry Bedsole on W side of South River -5th tract of 10 acres -6th tract of 100 acres being part of tract granted to Samuel Hales on March 9, 1797 including that part not sold or give to John Bedsole (uncle of Thomas Bedsole, Sr.) & adjoining lands of Samuel Pharesalso our interest in 100 acres "Which we have not got the Grant nor Courses" to the 3/8th part of the above land. Wit: J.B. Simpson, John McDaniel. Feb.'s term 1843. David Lewis, Clerk Of The Court, Bladen County, NC.
10 Oct. 1820 Thomas Bedsole, Jr. to Daniel Melvin- $140 for 50 acres adj. lands of Francis Davis and including the plantation on which I now live and 10 acres on N side of Archibald McDaniels pond adj. lands patented by Archibald McDaniel, Sr. Wit: Robert Melvin and Elizabeth Melvin. Feb. term, 1825.

April 23, 1762- John Melton, Planter, Bladen County, NC party of the first part hereby sells and conveys unto Vincent Bedsole, (Uncle of Thomas Bedsole, Sr.) party of the second part, Bladen County, NC, a certain tract of 300 acres lying, being and situate in Bladen County, NC, for 4 pounds sterling, as follows:
To Wit: Beginning at two white oaks near a ridge and running along the line of Thomas Bedsole (Sr., Nephew of Vincent), N 156 poles, and 12 Links.
 Aug. 20, 1764- Vincent Bedsole (Uncle of Thomas Bedsole, Sr.), Bladen County, to James Bailey 4 pounds sterling for 190 acres, adj. lands of Thomas Bedsole, Sr. (This appears to be part of the 300 acres above, which Vincent bought in 1762).
From Book # 107, 1779; Captain Johnson's District: Deeds Of Bladen County, NC; John Bedsole enters 200 acres on Beaverdam.
From Book # 107, 1779; Captain Johnson's District; Deeds Of Bladen County, NC; Thomas Bedsole (Sr.) enters 100 acres on Beaverdam.

From Book # 119; Feb. 2, 1779; John Bedsole, Bladen County, NC, enters 100 acres about 600 yards below Watson's Branch by a place called the "Thick Bolk".

Jan.1, <u>1793-</u> William (Henry) Bedsole (brother of Vincent and John. Uncle of Thomas Sr.) of Bladen County, NC party of the first part sells conveys and transfers unto William Gray, planter, Bladen County, NC, part of the second part, a certain tract of land lying, being and situate in Bladen County, NC and containing 50 acres, for 15 Shillings. To Wit: Beginning at a white oak and running along the N side of the Beaverdam, 32 poles, 43 chains and 12 links.

Notes:

LAST WILL AND TESTAMENTS

Faircloth Wills Known to be in existence:

1727: William, son Benjamin

1727: Will of Sarah (widow of Edward, Albermarle county, son Thomas, son John
: probably FAIRCLUFF listed below

1751: Discussion of notes on Zachariah Faircloth (b. 1751 Edgecombe County, NC and d. 1820 in Sampson County, NC.) and his children.
Sampson County, NC Court Minutes:

1753   Edward Faircluff – Pasquotank County.

1760 – Garner, John WILL: Will naming grandson, William Faircloth, Edgecombe County, NC
- Miscellaneous Wills, Book A

Garner, John, will date 25 Sep 1760, proved Dec Ct 1760. In the Name of God Amen, I John Garner, Sr of (Coeneto) in Edgecombe County being old and weake in body but of sound mind and memory thanks be to God... Imprimis I give and bequeath to my daughter Sarah Wright my Negro boy (Nead) to her and the lawful heirs of her body; Item- I give and bequeath unto my daughter Jayn Garner to my Negro Lucy to her and the lawful heirs of her body; Item- I give and bequeath to my son, John Garner my boy (Isaac); Item- I give and bequeath unto my (   ) son Jonathan Garner my Negro boy Peter; Item- I give and bequeath unto my son Absalom Garner my Negro boy Sam; Item- I give and bequeath to my daughter (Judy Garner) my Negro fellow (Quamines) to her and her lawful heirs of her body; Item- I give and bequeath unto my youngest daughter Onner Garner my Negro wench named (Dot) to her and the lawful heirs of her body; Item- I give unto my two youngest daughters (Jodey) and (Onner) each of them a young Negro (apiece) if (there) is any at the time of the division of my estate and if there is no young Negroes then the same above mentioned (Judy & Anner) and if there be young Negroes (   ) gets them. I give and bequeath unto my son John Garner the above mentioned Nan to the only use and behoof him and his heirs my Negro (Quamine) if there be young ones for (   ) Jonathan Garner to the only use and behoof of him. Item- I give and bequeath in the same manner my Negro wench Dot to my son Absalom Garner to the only use and behoof him providing there be young Negroes for my above mentioned (Judy and Anner). Item- I give and bequeath unto my daughter Martha Garner (five shillings sterling in remembrance that she is my daughter. Item- I give and bequeath to my grandson William Faircloth 25 shillings sterling. Item- I give and bequeath to my son John Garner the manor and dwelling plantation with 170 acres of land for the only and behoof of him. Item- I give and bequeath to my son Jonathan Garner 100 acres of land where (William Wiggins) formerly lived to the only use and behoof of him. Item- I give and bequeath unto my son Absalom Garner 100 acres of land being between (his   ) above mentioned to the only use and befoof of (   ). Item- I give and bequeath unto my loving wife Martha Garner all my workings (   ) from the date thereof in during her widowhood and my personal estate to my loving wife Martha Garner during the time of her widowhood. Item- I give and bequeath all my working (   ) and rest of my estate at the time of my wife's death or marriage to be equally divided to all my children but the two above mentioned Mathew Garner and William Faircloth. Item- I ordain my wife Martha and my son John Garner hole and sole executors till the day of marriage or death and then my son hole and sole executor. Item- I give and bequeath to my daughter Sarah (   ) two cows and calfes and after this whole (dividend) to be deducted of her share of this my last will and testament revoking all wills or other testament ever by me made or ordained in witness whereof I have set my hand and seal this twenty fifth of September of 1760. John Garner (Mark). Test William Wright, Thos Clark (mark), Reed Bottom (mark). Edgecombe County - (   ). December Inferior Court 1760. The within will was in open Court exhibited by the exrs therein named and proved by the oath of Thomas one of the subscribing (   ) thereto who likewise swore that he saw the other two (   ) subscribe the same and at the same time the exeors was qualified according to law which is ordered to be qualified and the will to be recorded. Test James Hall (CC Cir). Will Book A, page 13. Abstracted 2-23-06, NCA film C.037.80001, CTC.

1772   Thomas Faircluff– Pasquotank County

1774   John Faircluff– Pasquotank County

1791 – Benjamin and Ephraim signed the will of James Porter, 6 Oct 1791 in Southampton County, VA

1794   Ben and Ephraim witnessed Will of James Porter

1802: Ephraim will, son Cordy "Cordial, South Hampton, VA, daughter Charlotte, 1 Sept 1802.

1802-1803: pp 87-88: the last will and testament of Ephraim Faircloth to us presented in court by Bailey Barnes, one of the executors – therein named (time allowed the other executor to qualify) proved by the oat of Henry Blunt and John Barrow, two of the witnesses, thereto and ordered to be recorded on the motion of the said executor who made oath according to law a certificate is granted him for obtaining a probate thereof in due form giving security where upon the said Bailey Barnes with Henry Bland and John Barnes his security, entered into and acknowledged their bond in the penalty of $500 for the said Bailey due and faithful administration of the estate of the said decedent and performance of his will.
P. 88 Ordered that Thomas Porter (of John), Thomas Porter (black), Buxton Barnes, and John Whitehead or any three of them being first sworn before a Justice of the Peace of this County, do appraise in current money the slaves, if any, and personal estate of Ephraim Faircloth, dec'd, and return the appraisement to the next court.

1807 Samuel will dated 6 Feb 1807

1808: Will of Drury Autry mentions his daughter, Sarah Charlotte Drury Faircloth; It also mentions that debts owed to Drury by Caleb Faircloth and Gary Faircloth. One of the executors of this will was Caleb Faircloth. Caleb and David Faircloth also signed this will. Sampson County Record of Wills, Vol A., 1882-1864, p. 54.

31 Aug. 1814 : *Will of John D. Johnston, (Sr.) dated 31 Aug. 1814 Sampson County, NC.* Names wife Elizabeth and son John Johnston executors. Subscribing witnesses: Solomon Sessoms, James Faircloth, (Sr.), and Robert Grice. *Sampson County, NC Court Minutes: 23 Nov. 1814.* Elizabeth Johnston exhibited in this Court this last will and testament of her deceased husband

[John Johnston, (Sr.)] which was admitted to probate by oaths of Solomon Sessoms and James Faircloth, (Sr.) two of the subscribing witnesses.

The Will of John Johnston, (Sr) named his sons and sons-in-law and two of his Faircloth grandchildren: {the parentheses ( ) and/or brackets [ ] are my additions}. John D. Johnston, (Jr.) [died Nov. 1829 and was married to Spicey (maiden name unknown)], Mark Johnston, Matthew Johnston, Elizabeth Johnston [married a Mr. Faircloth (still unidentified)], Hannah Johnston [married James Faircloth, (Sr.)], Mary Johnston [married a Mr. Hall], and Milly Johnston [married Isham Faircloth-their daughter Mary Faircloth was mentioned in Johnston's Will].

Note: James Faircloth, (Sr.) involvement in the Administration of Zachariah Faircloth leads me to believe that he was one of Zach's children; also, even though without more solid evidence, I would speculate that Isham Faircloth, and the yet unidentified Faircloth were Zach's sons.

17 Mar 1819: Will of John, Southampton , VA released a slave, named Potor, mullato boy, possible son named Peter??

1819: John will, 9 Mar 1819, names mother Sally Faircloth Everitte, Southampton, VA (note that Sally Everitte married Newsom Faircloth???) Would this mean John was the son of Newsom and just living with William and Sarah later in life?

23 Aug. 1820: Administration on the estate of Zachariah Faircloth, dec'd, granted James Faircloth and entered into bond in the sum of $100 with Mark Johnston and Matthew Johnston his security. [This James Faircloth would be James Faircloth, (Sr.)]

1820: 23 Aug. 1820: Administration on the estate of Zachariah Faircloth, dec'd, granted James Faircloth and entered into bond in the sum of $100 with Mark Johnston and Matthew Johnston his security. [This James Faircloth would be James Faircloth, (Sr.)]

21 Nov. 1820: James Faircloth, Administrator, returned the amount of the account of the sales of the estate of Zachariah Faircloth, dec'd, which was filed.
Note: I've looked high and low for the account of sales mentioned above of Zachariah's estate but haven't found it.

21 Nov. 1820: James Faircloth, Administrator, returned the amount of the account of the sales of the estate of Zachariah Faircloth, dec'd, which was filed.

1829: Will of Isaac, Cumberland County, sister: Elizabeth, brother: Edward, wife Rosann (Rose), sister: Sara, sister: Abegail (ab dau-Brittainia.

16 Nov. 1849: Henry Faircloth b. 1821-1823;d. 1848-1849. Three of his siblings James, Robinson, and Bluford Faircloth were purchasers at the time of his estate sale on 16 Nov. 1849.

1853: Will of Cordilo, d. 18 Sept 1853 at 67 years old in Tennessee. B. 31 Mar 1786 in South Hampton, VA; Tenn. 1809, married 1816. Alabama 1822, 1824 married ___Barksdale.

1830: Newsome's Will, dated 3 July 1830, probated Feb 1831, mentions the children Susanna, Lucy, Virginia, Feriby, Rita, Ridley, Winnefred, Cherry, Anna and Matilda, all girls, and the boys, Bright, Newsome, Jr. and John.

22 Nov 1830: A deed of sale from Newsom Faircloth to Joshua Everitt proved by William Jenkins. From county Court Minutes of Please and Quarter Sessions held at Tarboro, 1820-1826 and 1826-1833.

Also in those County Court Minutes was:
28 Feb 1831: the last will and testament of Newsom Faircloth dec'd was exhibited in open court for probate and was proven by the oath of Richard T. Eagle, one of the subscribing witnesses thereto and John R. Scarborough, the executor therein named (and the same time qualified thereof ordered that the same be certified, and the will recorded and that the executor sell the perishable property on a credit of six months. Sarah Faircloth, widow of Newsom Faircloth came into open court and entered her deposit to her husband's will.

23 May 1831: Inventory and account of sales for the estate of Newsome Faircloth dec'd returned by the executor.

22 Aug 1831: William Faircloth is appointed overseer of the road leading from dead tree branch to Davis Howell in lieu of William Wooten.

29 Aug 1832: Ordered that Phesanton S. Sugg, Joab P. Pitt, Turner Bynum, Amos Wooten, and John F. Hughes or a majority of them be appointed commissioners to and settle the accounts of John R. Scarborough, executor of Newsom Faircloth, dec'd and also to divide the estate between the heirs equally to the will of said dec'd and report, etc.

29 Aug 1832: William Faircloth is appointed guardian to Newsom and John Faircloth. He entered into bond of $500 with James Wooten and William Edwards as securities.

26 Nov 1832: Account current of the estate of Newsom Faircloth returned by the executor.

20 August 1864: Will of James Faircloth, (Jr.) County of Cumberland dated 20 August 1864. Value of estate about $100.
Abstracted: James bequeaths his plantation whereupon he lives to his mother Hannah Faircloth and all his money to his mother after his debts are paid. After his mother's death estate goes to his sister Mary Susan Faircloth. Names N. Wales as executor of his estate.

12 Oct 1878: Request for the Administration of James Faircloth, dec'd," dated 12 October 1878 Cumberland County, NC.
"Our beloved brother James Faircloth has lately died, and we want you Mr. Clerk to appoint Thomas Bullock administrator to tend to the estate of our brother. Witness to the signatures hereto annexed G.T. Bullock.
Signatures annexed: Raford Faircloth, Bluford Faircloth, Jane Howell, Mary Faircloth, Prisey Faircloth. *Note: these would be the deceased James's siblings.*
Note: [This James Faircloth would be James Faircloth, (Jr.)].

1823: Thomas, Hertford County

1829: Isaac, Camden County

1859: Will of Rachel Best in Wayne County, NC
Niece: Sally Faircloth, Niece Araminter Faircloth, Witness: Thomas Faircloth

1864: Wilson, Cumberland County

1877: James, Cumberland County

1878: "Request for the Administration of James Faircloth, dec'd," dated 12 October 1878 Cumberland County, NC.
"Our beloved brother James Faircloth has lately died, and we want you Mr. Clerk to appoint Thomas Bullock administrator to tend to the estate of our brother. Witness to the signatures hereto annexed G.T. Bullock.
Signatures annexed: Raford Faircloth, Bluford Faircloth, Jane Howell, Mary Faircloth, Prisey Faircloth.
Note: these would be the deceased James's siblings.
Note: [This James Faircloth would be James Faircloth, (Jr.)].

1882: William, Greene County

1884: Greenville, Cumberland County

1896: William R., Sampson

1898: Lucy, Sampson County

Notes:

Court Actions

1744 - Re: Edgecombe County, NC Court Records on the baseborn children Hardwick, John, and Zachariah Faircloth:

Two sources:
1). The Edgecombe County, NC Court Records from which the above Faircloth siblings or half-siblings were taken are scattered and some years are missing: the records begin in 1744 but May 1746-Aug. 1757 are missing and July 1776-Aug. 1778 are missing. Be that as it may, April 1746-Aug. 1772 are the ones where the Faircloth siblings are recorded, and there was no mention of their father; in both entries of 9 July 1765 and 11 July 1765, Zachariah Faircloth (aged 14 yrs.), a baseborn child, was bound to Noah Sugg, and John Faircloth (aged 5yrs.), and Hardy Faircloth (aged 11) also baseborn children, were bound to Benjamin Faircloth, who obviously were close relatives of the children's mother Sarah Faircloth. Also note that the published book written by Marvin K. Dorman, Jr. entitled Edgecombe County, North Carolina Abstracts of Court Minutes 1744-1746, 1757-1794 does not include the full details of the original text and leaves out the word baseborn.
2). See page 111 of "Orphanage In Colonial North Carolina: Edgecombe County As A Case Study" by Alan D. Watson recorded in The North Carolina Historical Review, pp. 105-119, vol. 52, no. 2, April 1975. "The Court further eased the transition to orphanage by apprenticing siblings to the same master where possible. This was particularly true in the case of illegitimate offspring--the Quinn Brothers, Faircloth brothers, Johnson sisters, and Revel sisters--and belied a sympathetic understanding on the part of the justices of the more difficult adjustments to be made by those children

1783-94 Court Records, Dobbs County:
20 Nov 1788: Wm, John summoned to curt to Sheriff bond, plus six other people for trespass, assault and battery and damage; went to court 1789;

1788- Dobbs County - Stephanus Sheppard, Graves Bright, Jesse Lassiter, James
Holmes, Wm. Faircloth, John Sheppard,& John Faircloth - Benjamin
Caswell Sheriff - bond - all to appear in court 20 Nov 1788-

1788- Dobbs County - Stephanus Shepherd, Graves Bright, Jesse Lassiter, James Holmes, &
Wm. Faircloth - court 20 Nov 1788 - issued 23 May 1788 -
answer James How Hutchins of a plea of trespass assault & Battery &
damage 1000 lbs. Benjamin Caswell sheriff

1788- Dobbs County - Stephanus Sheppard, Graves Bright, Jesse Lassiter, James Holmes, Wm.
Faircloth, John Sheppard,& John Faircloth - Benjamin
Caswell Sheriff - bond - all to appear in court 20 Nov 1788-

1788- Dobbs County - Stephanus Shepherd, Graves Bright, Jesse Lassiter, James Holmes, & Wm. Faircloth - court 20 Nov 1788 - issued 23 May 1788 - answer James How Hutchins of a plea of trespass assault & Battery & damage 1000 lbs. Benjamin Caswell sheriff

1788- Dobbs County - Stephanus Sheppard, Graves Bright, Jesse Lassiter, James Holmes, Wm. Faircloth, John Sheppard,& John Faircloth - Benjamin Caswell sheriff - bond - all to appear in court 20 Nov 1788-1789- Stephen Shepperd vs. Mills Barfield - 1789 – file; wit: Graves Bright, John Herritage, Nathl Walker, Benjamin Sheppard Thomas Branton,Wm. Sheppard, Martin Gardner Sheppard, James Glasgow, Susannah Sheppard, John Faircloth, John C. Ponsmly, Teresa Salter, Asa Barfield, Nancy Barfield, Priscilla Barfield, Nathaniel Walker, Louisa Barfield, Abraham Sheppard Jr., Wm. Bearfield, John Bearfield, Jonas Bearfield, Thomas sharp, Thomas Bearfield, Ann Barfield, widow, - Stephanus Sheppard charges Miles Barfield, Wm. Barfield, John Barfield, & Jonas Barfield all of Dobbs county and yeoman - with trespass assault battery - 13 Apr 1788 Ann Barfield, widow, granddaughter Nancy Barfield called her to her house as a party of men were there to son Mills house - her sons were Wm. and Mills - Wm. Sheppard, Martin Gardner Sheppard, Thomas Branton, James Martin clubbed and shot Wm. and Mills - 20 Feb 1788 her mark she in 81st year - Barfields attacked Stepahanus Sheppard a minor on 13 Apr 1788 earlier than when his relatives took revenge on Barfields –

1789-Stephen Shepperd vs. Mills Barfield - 1789 - file
 wit: Graves Bright, john Herritage, Nathl Walker, Benjamin Sheppard Thomas Branton, Wm. Sheppard, Martin Gardner Sheppard, James Glasgow, Susannah Sheppard, John Faircloth, John C. Ponsmly, Teresa Salter, Asa Barfield, Nancy Barfield, Priscilla Barfield, Nathaniel Walker, Louisa Barfield, Abraham Sheppard Jr., Wm. Bearfield, John Bearfield, Jonas Bearfield, Thomas Sharp, Thomas Bearfield, Ann Barfield, widow, - Stephanus Sheppard charges Miles Barfield, Wm. Barfield, John Barfield, & Jonas Barfield all of Dobbs county and yeoman - with trespass assault battery - 13 Apr 1788 Ann Barfield, widow, granddaughter Nancy Barfield called her to her house as a party of men were there to son Mills house - her sons were Wm. and Mills - Wm. Sheppard, Martin Gardner Sheppard, Thomas Branton, James Martin clubbed and shot Wm. and Mills - 20 Feb 1788 her mark she in 81st year - Barfields attacked Stepahanus Sheppard a minor on 13 Apr 1788 earlier than when his relatives took revenge on Barfields -

1789- Stephen Shepperd vs. Mills Barfield - 1789 – file; wit: Graves Bright, john Herritage, Nathl Walker, Benjamin Sheppard Thomas Branton, Wm. Sheppard, Martin Gardner Sheppard, James Glasgow, Susannah Sheppard, John Faircloth, John C. Ponsmly, Teresa Salter, Asa Barfield, Nancy Barfield, Priscilla Barfield, Nathaniel Walker, Louisa Barfield, Abraham Sheppard Jr., Wm. Bearfield, John Bearfield, Jonas Bearfield, Thomas sharp, Thomas Bearfield, Ann Barfield, widow, - Stephanus Sheppard charges Miles Barfield, Wm. Barfield, John Barfield, & Jonas Barfield all of Dobbs county and yeoman - with trespass assault battery - 13 Apr 1788 Ann Barfield, widow, granddaughter Nancy Barfield called her to her house as a party of men were there to son Mills house - her sons were Wm. and Mills - Wm. Sheppard, Martin Gardner Sheppard, Thomas Branton, James Martin clubbed and shot Wm. and Mills - 20 Feb 1788 her mark she in 81st year - Barfields attacked Stepahanus Sheppard a minor on 13 Apr 1788 earlier than when his relatives took revenge on Barfields –

1790- Dobbs County - Superior Court of Law -Sheriff of Dobbs County John Jones esquire - bring forth the body of William Faircloth certain capias against him. November Term 1790 - Silas Cook clerk New Bern District.

1790- Dobbs County - Superior Court of Law -Sheriff of Dobbs County John

Jones esquire - bring forth the body of William Faircloth certain
capias against him. November Term 1790 - Silas Cook clerk New Bern
District.

1790:   1788-1868   Australian   Convict   Index,   1788-1868   Record
about William FAIRCLOTH ; trial place: Hertford, State: NSW; Ship-Surprise, d1790, born c
1766;

Name:	William FAIRCLOTH
Year:	1790
Trial Place:	Hertford
State:	NSW
Ship:	Surprise
Comments:	d1790
Born:	c1766

Source Information:
Reakes, J., comp. *Australian Convict Index, 1788-1868* [database on-line]. Provo, UT, USA:
MyFamily.com, Inc., 2001. Original data: *1788-1868 Convict Records.*. Records kept at the New
South Wales State Records Office, P.O. Box R625, Royal Exchange, NSW 2000; at the Archives
Office of Tasmania, 77 Murray St., Hobart, TAS 7000; and at the State Records Office of
Western

15 Nov 1790: Wm on bond, appeared in court to answer Nathan Smith; also going were Abram
Sheppard and James Clark. Dobbs County.

1790 Court: WM

16 Nov 1790, Dobbs Court House, Wm and John against Graves Bright court action.

18 Mar 1791, Dobbs, Wm and John, assault Andrew Green and have to go to court.

1792, Aug, Glasglow County, NC; Petition to move location of Courthouse, stocks & prison to
another location signed by Wm, John, Fredrick, Thomas, J Frederick, Kinchen

1793 Glasgow County court records: Kinchen F appearing in Wayne Co, voting book lists
misplaced, he was witness to the fact that they had disappeared on 29 Nov 1793

1804: December: Ormond VS Kinchin Faircloth re a negro was property of William Faircloth
(deceased) Lenoir Co/Glasgow, from documents of Jan 1793-1802.

Southampton Co, VA Court Records:
1802-1803:
Milly Faircloth against Simon Evritt, p. 169 and p. 423.

1778-Dec 1804: North Carolina Reports, Vol . Original Case Ormand VS Faircloth:
New Bern District Minutes: 176801772 through 1778-1788:

#35 13 Nov 1769: Thos. Lockey VS Wgrcott Ormond – Replevin

#94 21 Nov 1769: Wy Ormond VS Hen Lockey, not guilty

#51 12 May 1770 Robt Newell vs. Hen. Ormond – Awarded

#39 11 Nov 1770 Tho Blackburn VS Myriott Ormond – Reversed

#94 12 Nov 1770 Roger Ormond VS Moses Pode? – Guilty recovered 108 pounds

#92 13 Nov 1770 – Admn Wyriett Ormond VS Colemen Roes – debt.

63 11 May 1771 Roger Ormond vs Wriotte Ormond, Adam Henry Ormond. Awarded 190 pounds.

65 12 May 1771 Wriott Ormond VS Stephen Denning: 1 shilling

#60 11 May 1772 Wyriett Ormond and Roger Ormond VS Admr Alexander Stewart 23 pounds and costs

#87 11 May 1772 Wyriette & Roger Ormond VS Jno Patton, 31 pounds

#88 11 May 1772 Wyriette Ormond & Roger Ormond VS Admr Alexander Stewart, 23 pounds and costs

#87 11 May 1772 Wriette & Roger Ormond VS Jno Patton, 31 pounds

88 11 May 1772 Wriette Admr, Henry Ormond, damages and costs

Dobbs County, NC - 1779 Voter List

It Was Not Easy To Vote in 1779
Kinston Daily Free Press
Friday - November 2, 1962, Page 10

In 1779 the outlook for the success of the American Revolution had grown very dim. This year and the next were to be the darkest hours for the patriots. Kinston, the home town of Governor Richard Caswell, had become the de facto capital of the new State. Here the State's Board of War usually met in secret sessions. Sometimes the Council of State met here. Sessions of the General Assembly, being more a matter of public knowledge, usually were convened at larger and more heavily guarded towns. While the name of the town was changed from Kingston to Kinston by law in 1784, already by 1779 the patriots were calling it Kinston in derision of the King of England from whose title the original name derived.

The vote in the general election in 1779 required the highest patriotic conviction. If the Revolutionary cause failed, each of these voters would be marked as among the rankest seditionists. For these were the men of Dobbs County who closest held to heart the pledge of the Declaration of Independence, the pledge of "our sacred honor." This list of Dobbs voters is complete but does not complete her roll of honor, for there were those who were away with the armies in the field and the women whose names do not appear on this list. Still, these are the fathers and brothers and staunch supporters of those who fought, and each of them deserves to be remembered.

Even to those whose resolute patriotism stilled all fear of the possibility of danger in defeat, to vote was no easy matter. The voting place was at the old Dobbs County Courthouse erected near Walnut Creek about midway between present LaGrange and Goldsboro. Dobbs County included practically all of the areas now comprised in Lenoir, Greene and Wayne Counties, and it was from these areas that the voters came on horseback to cast the vote of freemen in a __ State. Because of the distances, the polls were open for two days, March 10th and 11th.

1779- STATE OF NORTH CAROLINA

At an election of one Senator and Two Members of the House of Commons to Represent the county of Dobbs held at the Court House the 10th and 11th of March, 1779, the following persons voted for Members of the House of Commons to wit:

Bass, John
Faircloth, Frederick
Faircloth, John
Faircloth, William Junr

At the close of the Poll on opening the Scrolls, I found the candidates had the following number of votes respectively Viz: Thos Gray 493, Jesse Cobb 535, Etheldred Ruffin 333, John Sheppard 5, James Bradbury 3, Major
Croom 1, Abram Sheppard 1. I Further certified that on Examining the Scrolls for the Senate and House of Commons there were in the Senate Box two tickets for Gray and Ruffin and in the Commons Box were also two tickets for Exum which Scrolls or votes are not including in the foregoing numbers.
Benja Caswell, Sheriff - March 1779

1781

Dobbs County, NC - Dobbs and Lenoir County Court Records, 1768-1801
Nov 1781 - Menan Patrick, James Bright, Jonas Williams, Wm. Faircloth, Jeremiah Loftin, David Smith
An Account of Letters of Administration Granted for Dobbs County in the Year
1772
1st column - date of the letters
2nd column - To whom Granted
3rd column - on whose Estate
4th column - Names of the Securities
5th column - Value of the Bond
6th column - at what Court taken

Mary Hopton - CHAR. HOPTON - Wm Faircloth, Thos Edwards - 250 pds - January Court 1772

#16 Nov 1782 "The Sheriff of Dobbs County returned the following list of jurors".....William Faircloth

17 Nov 1782: Ordered that 13 jurors including William Faircloth be fined NISI for not attending as jurors this term. (nisi prius: a court that tried issues before a jury and single judge as opposed to courts sitting with a full quorum of justices present.

1784-

1784 Craven County records for Dobbs assault:

Capias STEPHANUS SHEPPARD,GRAVES BRIGHT,JESSE LASITER,WILLIAM FAIRCLOTH JR and JAMES HELMS to answer indictment for assault Dobbs Co

26 Nov 1788: State vs Fred Faircloth, Thos Faircloth and Roger Roberts. "The same jury as in last case find the deft. Guilty of assault of Benajah White in manner and form and c." Benajah White was the prosecutor

New Bern District Minutes, 1768-1772 and 1778-88:

1786 – 26 Nov 1786. (could be 1788) The state vs. Step. Shephard, Graves Bright, Jesse Lassiter, Wm Faircloth, Jr., James Holmes. Prosecuted by James Hutchens: Witnesses Jacob Jackson, Jos. Tillmen, Jesse Skean, Marm. Cox; Martin Caswell Junr. Also a witness for the state being called and failed to appear is defaulted according to act of assembly. Fined the defend plus guilty in manner and form & c. (493 written in pencil at bottom of page is evidently an attempt to number pages).

1786: 1 Dec, (could be 1788) Ordered that Frederick Faircloth, Tho, Roger Roberts, James Homes, Sherrard Barrow & Wm Andrews, John Muncy, Wm Sheperd, Martin G. Shepard, Jesse Lassiter, William Faircloth, Graves Bright, Benj Shepherd, Mills Barfield, Wm Barfield, be in custody of the Sheriff until fines and fees are paid.

DSCR: 206-301-2 Superior Court Minutes, New Bern District, 1787-1794:

1788- Dobbs County - Stephanus Sheppard, Graves Bright, Jesse Lassiter, James Holmes, Wm. Faircloth, John Sheppard,& John Faircloth - Benjamin Caswell sheriff - bond - all to appear in court 20 Nov 1788-

1788, 26 Nov: The state versus Frederick Faircloth, Thomas Faircloth, Roger Roberts. Prosecutor Benajah White. Guilty in manner and form as charged in the bill of indictment.

1788: 1 Dec: 29 persons fined and ordered Sheriff of Craven to keep them in custody until all fines were paid. Among them were:

Frederick – 20 pounds

Thomas – 20 pounds

William – 10 pounds

1788- State of North Carolina   Dobbs County

        In obedience to the within recommendation of his Excellency the Governor I Benjamin Caswell Sheriff of the County aforesaid did on Receipt of the same, to wit, on or about the second & third days of July instant, Notify the Inhabitants of the County aforesaid by posting up at the Court House and other public places in the said County Advertisements in the usual & accustomed manner requiring the Freeholders & Freemen in the said County to attend at the times and place within mentioned for the purpose within required and they did then & there choose and Elect Richard Caswell, James Glasgow, Winston Caswell, Benjamin Sheppard & Nathan Lassiter their Representatives duly Qualified to it & Vote in the Convention of the State to be held in the Town of Hillsborough on the third Monday in July instant, agreeable to a resolution of the General Assembly held at Tarbourough in December last, and I do here by mention the said Richard Caswell, James Glasgow, Winston Caswell, Benjamin Sheppard & Nathan Lassiter, the Representatives of the said County accordingly.

July 16th 1788   Benj Caswell Sheriff   State of North Carolina

1788- Kinchin Faircloth   Richard Hamm JP
Dobbs County, NC - 2nd 1788 Dobbs Vote
State of North Carolina
(Seal)

His Excellency Samuel Johnston Esquire Governor, Captain General &Commander in Chief of the said State To the Sheriff of Dobbs County. Greeting Whereas it hath been made appear to me that the Ballots taken by you at the last General Election for Delegates to the State Convention, were forcibly & violently seized and taken from you by some riotous and disorderly persons, so that you had it not in your power to ascertain who were the persons who had the greatest number of votes and therefore cannot make a Return of any Persons as duly elected to serve as delegates in the said Convention. And whereas a number of respectable Inhabitants of the said County have by Petition represented to me that the Inhabitants of the said County are desirous that I should appoint another Day for the purpose of electing Delegates to represent them in the said Convention.

I do therefore recommend to such of the Inhabitants of Dobbs County afore said, as are entitled to vote for Representatives in the house of Commons to meet at the Court House of the said County on the fourteenth & fifteenth days of July next then and there to elect five Freeholders to represent them in the State Convention to be held at the Town of Hillsborough on the third Monday of July next, and I do hereby require you to give notice to the Inhabitants to meet accordingly and that you attend at the same time & place and conduct the said Election in the manner prescribed by the Resolve of the last General Assembly held at Tarborough.

Given under my Hand & Seal at Arms at Denton this 28th day of June in the twelfth year of the Independence of America & in the year of our Lord 1788
- Saml Johnston

1788- At an election held for the County of Dobbs on the 14th & 15th days of July 1788. At the Court House there offered for representatives to set & vote in Convention at Hillsborough in the third Monday of this last pursuant to and issued by the Governors.
Candidates:

Richard Caswell	James Glasgow
Benjamin Sheppard	Winston Caswell
Nathan Lasitter	John Herritage
Bryan Whitfield	W. Sheppard
Jesse Lasitter	

No. Voters Names
 3 Jno. Faircloth   80 Thos. Faircloth

1789- 1 Dobbs - summons William Shepppard & Martin Gardner Sheppard to court 20 Nov1789 to answer Miles Barfield of a plea of trespass - damage 100 pounds. William Barfield called to testify for Miles - Jesse Hicks witness - John Farecloth and Benjamin Sheppard to testify for William Shepharrd - Asa Barfield to testify for Miles Barfield - William /Barfield, John Barfield, Jesse Hicks, Nancy Smith to testify for Miles Barfield - Nancy Barfield & William Torrons witnesses for Miles - James Glasgow and Doctor John Leigh witnesses for William Sheppard - William Lorrow wit Miles - Thomas Branton, Wm. Sheppard, Susannah Sheppard, Nathaniel Walker, Benj. Sheppard wit.for William Sheppard –

1790- Dobbs - Abram Sheppard (sg), William Farrcloth (sg) and James Clark (mark) bound to Benjamin Sheppard high Sheriff Dobbs - Abram to appear in court answer Nathan Smith- 15 Nov 1790 - witn J. JONES sign

1790-DOBBS   Folder: 1790   Date: 20 May 1790   Date   of: Summons County: Dobbs   Information: Summons for John MASTEN (?MARTEN), Willoughby WILLIAMS, and Thomas BRANTON to testify on behalf of William FARECLOTH

Folder: 1790   GREEN; Date: 20 May 1790   Date of: Warrant   County: Dobbs Information: Arrest warrant for William FAIRCLOTH on charge of assault on Andrew

Folder: 1790   Date: 20 Nov 1790   Date of: Warrant: County: Dobbs Information: Arrest warrant for William FAIRCLOTH on charge of assault on Andrew GREEN

Folder: 1790   Mar 1791   Date of: Bond   County: Dobbs   Information: Appearance bond for William FAIRCLOTH with John FAIRCLOTH and John GARLAND, bondsmen to appear and answer a charge of assault on Andrew GREEN

Folder: 1790   Date: 16 Nov 1790   Date of: Bond County: Dobbs   Information: Appearance bond for William FAIRCLOTH with John FAIRCLOTH and Graves BRIGHT to appear and answer and indictment against him.

Folder: 1790 (second folder)   Date: 20 May 1790   Date of: County: Edgecombe Information: Summons for Andrew GREER to appear and testify against Benj. SHEPARD, Wm. SHEPARD, & Wm. FAIRCLOTH

1790 – 22 Nov: William Ormond on jury from Dobbs County. Also 19 mar 1792.
Sept Term 1792 John Faircloth on a jury from Glasgow County. Also March 1793 and March 1794. March 1794 Wyriott Ormond on jury from Beaufort County.

DSCR 206-301-3: Minutes Superior Court, New Bern District, 1794-1801:

1793-Summon TOBIAS COBB for State vs Faircloth CRAVEN CO
1793   Folder: 1793   Information: Summons for John Charles PONSONBY and John FAIRCLOTH to forfeit bond for failure of PONSONBY to appear and answer charge against him.   Date: 19 Sept 1792   Date of: Summons County: Glasgow

Folder: 1793 Information: Verdict of coroner's jury on view of body of Reddick BARFIELD that he was killed at the hand of Micajah BARROW, who was violently attacked by Reddick BARFIELD and he was acting in his own defense. Based on testimony of Pearcy BARFIELD and sundry others. Jurors: Wm. SHEPPARD, John FAIRCLOTH, William MARTIN, John WILLIAMS, Moses Holmes, JESSE HOLMES, Thomas FAIRCLOTH, Mark HEATH, William ANDREWS, William FAIRCLOTH, Joshua GOODSON, Harrod BARROW.

Date:1 Sept 1788   Date of: Verdict   County: Dobbs

Folder: 1793   Information: [Note: Edge of this document is torn away-sbg]. Deposition of Pearce BARFIELD (female) taken near the house of Willie BARROW upon view of the body of Reddick BARFIELD then and there lying dead. Stated she was riding with Reddick BARFIELD and Micajah BARROW on the way to Stephen CADES when one of them mentioned a dispute between them which they had settled. After some time Micajah BARROW asked Reddick BARFIELD why he would be so unkind to his daughter, this deponent [Pearce BARFIELD] "that he would not give her a ring which he had taken from her and after some talk on the subject Reddick BARFIELD said he would give to her as soon [torn] he got to the house & took a drink of grog but still mentioned at times that it was his own ring, at length Micajah BARROW said to [Pearce BARFIELD] You don't care so much about the rind do you she said she did because her grandmother gave it to her on which Reddick BARFIELD told Micajah BARROW that he had a good mind to drive his, Micajahs teeth down his throat with his gun. Micajah asked him why he would attempt to do that [torn] as that they had made friends he Micajah would not strike him Reddick for five hundred pounds. The said Reddick BARFIELD immediately dismounted himself ...and made a blow with his gun and struck...Micajah BARROW on the head & knocked him off his horse. [Goes on to describe a fight with many blows exchanged]. "Reddick called out and said God Cajah I will kill you I will Damned if I don't and repeated his blow again." [Describes more fighting]. "Micajah BARROW got hold the barrell part of the gun ... [torn] he struck ...Reddick and as [torn] blows Reddick says Cajah I beg and no other words past between them and ...Reddick lay dead." Pearce
BARFIELD goes on to say that she had often heard Reddick say that he would kill Micajah "and that he would never be at rest until he had done it and that she was at the house of William BARFIELD sometime past and that ... Reddick [over in the neighborhood of the said Micajah BARROW] and he come to the house of ...William BARFIELD and William asked him if he was come Reddick said yes, ...William asked him ...if he had done what he went to do Reddick told him no. ...William very warmly exclaimed agt him and asked ...why he did not kill the damnd son of a bitch at once [torn] have done with it for that he was a fool and would go poking [torn] and not do it until it would be too [torn] for that he might have killed fifteen Micajah BARROWS before this and have [torn] the ring and never been troubled about it and been gone to sea and damn him for a fool do it the next time went before he returned again. Reddick BARFIELD nodded his head at William BARFIELD and said to him as this deponant understood, not talk so ferce, for that it should soon be done.

Date: 31 Aug/1 Sept [year torn]   Date of: Event/deposition   County: Dobbs

1794: 24 Sept: Henry Ormond on jury for case.

1795 – 19 Sep – John Faircloth on jury from Glasgow County.

1796- 19 Mar: Wherriot Ormond on jury for Beaufort, also Sept 1796.

1817- Greene County, NC - Court Records 1817
Inventory of the notes & accounts due to or in possession of Col. Thos.
Edwards decd: W. J. & M. Faircloth   John Faircloth

NC Archives: Craven County Superior Court Minutes # 18.311.1, July 1801 – 1820:
1804: Jan., case 16, p. 99: Detinue – General Issue: Thomas Ormond VS Kinchen Faircloth: Statute of Limitation. The same jury as No 15 except Henry Rouse in the room of Thomas Smith impaneled and charged, fined that the defendant named in the plaintiff's declaration. Rule

to show cause why a new trial should not be granted. Case to be made up and sent to the Court of Conference.

1804: Jan: p. 107: Rule to shew cause why a new trial should not be granted; case to be made up and sent to Court of Conference.

1804 - NC Supreme Court found at the NC Archives, Raleigh, NC   New Bern District – Jan Term 1804 – Greene Co   Regarding the ownership of a Negro – it was the property of William Faircloth, dec at his death and came into the hands of his administrator – Benjamin Sheppard obtained two judgments against the adm in the Court of Lenoir – then writs in Glasgow County – Negro allotted to the defSubsequent term in Jan 1793 the sheriff of Glasgow sold the Negro at a private sale to John Grimsley for the full worth – Grimsley had the Negro for about 4 years and devised him to his daughter the wife of the plf – the plf had him in his possession until May 1802 when the def took him – jury instructed that the sale was not valid because it was done at a private Sheriff's sale - plf moved for a new trial because of the instructions to the jury This day persininaly appeared before me one of the Justices of the Peace of Wayn County Kinchen Faircloth of Glasgow County and made oth on the hold Evengilist of Almighty God that at the last day of the Election held for the County of Glasgow for _____representatives in the next General Assembly that when the Election was closed and the Tickets Counted out that the Clerks took their Books and went out before they were call up to see who was Elected and then they was caled in by the inspectors to Bring Back their Books and when they were come in with their Books the Deponant saith that he then saw one of the Clerks Books __ and misplased to with John Williams book one of the Clerks who kept the pole for the Commons and further this deponant saith not November 29, 1793
Sworn to before me

1805: Jan, p. 148: Thomas Ormond VS Kinchen Faircloth; judgment of the court of conference for the defendant.

1807:, April, p. 203; Court becomes Craven Co Superior Court.

1807: Samuel, Sampson

1810-1826?: W. J. and M. Faircloth: notes and accounts due; court action, due to Col. Thos. Edwards. (not sure who this is?); Dobbs County, NC

BLADEN COUNTY, NC - CEMETERIES - Culbreth Family Cemetery
Culbreth Family Cemetery, Jerome, Bladen County, NC
Directions: On west side of Hwy 53 in Jerome. It has a chain link fence
around it.
Large newer looking stone in the middle of the cemetery has the following inscription:

CULBRETH
Archibald, son of Neil & Martha Autry Culbreth, B. CA. 1770 D. After 1844
WIFE Mary "Polly" Horne B. CA. 1772 D. after 1850

CHILDREN
Fleet B. CA. 1800 D. after 1850
  M. Annah WEST B. CA. 1814 D. after 1850
Martha B. Jan. 17, 1801 D. Mar. 11, 1882
  M. Samuel WEST B. CA. 1803 D. Jun. 29 1880
Mary B. CA. 1808 D. before 1850
  M. David JOHNSON
Druscilla B. CA. 1813 D. CA. 1894
  M. Rayford HALL B. CA. 1816 D. after 1850
Job B. Feb 2 1814 D. Sep 21 1885
  M. Zada PRICE B. Mar 6 1821 D. Jan 16 1902
John J. B. 1816 D. 1894
  M. 1st Sophia HALL B. 1807 D. 1887
    2nd Catherine (HALL) PARKER B. Feb 24 1835 D. Aug 22 1922
POSSIBLY A SON & DAUGHTER BORN BEFORE 1800

Annie CULBRETH; wife of Ed McDANIEL
Born about 1880   Died about 1927

Annie M. Culbreth wife of James J. Faircloth
born*** 22, 1844   died Sep * 1921------------------ (inscription illegible)

Carrie Lee daughter of McK & Rachel CULBRETH; Apr. 9, 1867, Sept. 28, 1868
------------------------suffer **** children****** ***** to me-------------------

Tho lost to **** **** memory dear

Bessie Viola daughter of J. & Miranda FAIRCLOTH
Born June 5 1880 Died Oct 15, 1883
------------------------****** ****** of love ******** ******* ****

James J FAIRCLOTHborn May 8, 1848   Died Dec 21 1922
----------------------(inscription illegible)

Mount   Sinai   Cemetery
Sidney, Columbus County, North Carolina Lat: 34° 11' 11"N, Lon: 78° 47' 54"W

Faircloth,	Dorma	Ward,	b.	7/28/1879,	d.	12/21/1949
Faircloth,	John	Morris,	b.	6/23/1878,	d.	12/13/1928
Faircloth,	Luther	R,	b.	4/30/1911,	d.	7/13/1965,	"Marine	WWII"

Faircloth, Venson L, b. 7/16/1909, d. 10/3/1965

Sampson County, NC - Faircloth Cemetery
This Faircloth Cemetery is located on Nirvana Road which is a dirt road. It is one of many other Faircloth Cemeteries in the area. From Highway 24 between Autryville and Roseboro going west you will come to Horseshoe Road, which turns to the right and is a loop road that joins back up with Highway 24. Turn onto Horseshoe Road. Nirvana is a dirt road that turns off to the left from Horseshoe Road. The cemetery is about a mile off Horseshoe Road. Although the road leading back is dirt is it a good quality dirt road.

Name	Birth	Death	Comments
Williams, Infant		March 23, 1961	

Infant son of John H. & Annie Williams

Family Section outlined in stone Double Marker

Culbreth, Sarah E.   March 15, 1899 Aged 47 years-His Wife
Culbreth, William M.   September 20, 1905 Aged 52 years

Edge, William Arch   1940   1991 Butler Funeral Home Marker Only

Horne, Neil Clem   May 10, 1905   October 2, 1975
Husband of Lucy Edge Faircloth-Son of D.G. Horne & M.A.
Faircloth-brother of Berry Horne

Horne, Lucy Edge   January 6, 1922 February 28, 1997
Wife of Neil Clem Horne-Daughter of Taylor McC "Bunk" Edge &
Mary Jannie Jennie Faircloth

Unknown   1904   19?? Butler Funeral Home Marker Only

Horne, Annie L.   January 3, 1956 Aged 40 years, 4 months, 27 days
possible daughter of Taylor McC "Bunk" Edge & Mary Jannie
Jennie Faircloth- unknown who she married if she is their daughter

Edge, Marion Tom   January 19, 1949   Aged 19 years, 7 months, and 4 days
Butler Funeral Home Marker Only

Unknown
Metal Funeral Home Marker-possibly another Edge burial

E. Bunk
-SHOULD BE- Taylor McC "Bunk" Edge-Stone is handmade and
etched. No dates on stone or anything else readable. Looks like there
may have been at one time. Bunk was the son of David S. Edge & Margaret
New of Bladen County, North Carolina

Culbreth
Infant Twins of W.M. & Sarah E. Culbreth-this plot is surrounded by stone

Tanner, Cleab   October 3, 1933   May 18, 1968

Lockwood, Patrick W.   1963   1996 Butler Funeral Home Marker Only;
Possible burial but no marker-ground has been disturbed

Unmarked Grave
Tanner, Luther C.   July 17, 1940   April 18, 1993

Tanner, J. Grady   February 15, 1958 Aged 67 years, 7 months, 11 days
Butler Funeral Home Marker Only

Unknown Moses F.   1867
Aged 82 years-handmade stone

Tanner, Alton   August 10, 1921   April 14, 1995
US Army World War II –Also Funeral Home Marker from Butler Funeral Home

Ray, Lessie M.   1912   1995 Butler Funeral Home Marker Only
My Notes-Lessie is Lessie May Sessoms Ray wife of Burton Lee Ray

Ray, Burton Lee   1906   1984 Butler Funeral Home Marker Only
My Notes- Husband of Lessie Mae Sessoms Ray- son of Clemant R. "Clem"

S. Gillespie Ray & Sarah Jeanette/Janet/Jennette Jackson

New, Murphy E.   June 27, 1900   March 24, 1959

New Alice M.   February 16, 1910   May 15, 1938

Hall, George Franklin   February 15, 1941   Aged 63 years, 6 months & 0 days
Butler Funeral Home Marker Only

Tanner, Eva Jane   June 22, 1924   1968
Tanner, William Henry   April 28, 1889   May 29, 1966

Tanner, Carrie P.   March 9, 1900   October 2, 1982

Parker, Francis—NO DATES-ASSUMED STILL LIVING

Parker, Jane—NO DATES-ASSUMED STILL LIVING

Parker, Blannie Ann   1893   1960

Parker, George W.   1910   1976

Sessoms, Hattie Lee   May 7, 1906   May 7, 1964
Wife of Roy New

New, Roy Albert   February 8, 1898   March 11, 1978

Hall, Troy Minson   September 30, 1911   August 3, 1977

Hall, Elizabeth C.   1937   2001 Butler Funeral Home Marker only
Assumed wife of Troy Minson Hall

Suspected Infant Grave-Unmarked

Hall, Walter Jr.   August 24, 1943?   Unreadable
Possible age 2 months and 23 days?? Cannot read years if any

Faircloth, Stanley W.   August 6, 1910   June 7, 1959

Faircloth, Mamie E.   December 25, 1892   June 7, 1947

Faircloth, Mary E.   February 28, 1942
Aged 30 yrs 5 months 29 days-funeral home marker only

Faircloth, Alex B.   1898   1960 No stone marker-only small metal marker similar to funeral home markers.

Faircloth, James R.   December 22, 1956
Aged 22 years, 6 months- Butler Funeral Home Marker only

Evans James Franklin   October 24, 1898   March 3, 1953
NC Private CO A 168 Infantry 42 Division WWI

Double Stone
Horne, Minnie Hall   May 25, 1911   November 7, 1987
Horne, William R.   June 12, 1914   Living 1-2004

Faircloth, Rufus   August 13, 1911   February 9, 1993
US Army WWII

Unmarked Grave (possibly infants)

Unmarked Grave (possibly infants)

Unmarked Grave (marble pillar, no etching)

Faircloth, Stanley   Died 1935   85 years
This is a hand made stone –Butler Funeral Home marker still present.
That is all that is readable on the Butler Funeral Home Marker

Faircloth, Charlotte   Died 1931   83 years old
Hand etched Stone-Butler Funeral Home marker still present.
Charlotte looks to be the wife of Stanley.

Faircloth, H. Asbury   January 27, 1941
Age 78, 8 months, 10 days? This grave is marked only with the funeral home marker which is very deteriorated and hard to read.

Faircloth, Christine Dale   February 6, 1965
Infant Daughter of Christine & Roy Faircloth

Faircloth, Roy Julius   September 2, 1954   September 1, 1977
Our Son (Assumed to be the son of Roy & Christine)

Double Stone
Faircloth, Roy Cosby   November 15, 1928   October 3, 1997
Faircloth, Christine E.   September 04, 1934   February 07, 1987
Married: June 22, 1952

SEPARATE SECTION-SAME CEMETERY-HALL SECTION
Hall, N.J.   1942   1976 Butler Funeral Home Marker
Also marked by a marble pillar, no data recorded on pillar

Hall, Frankie Lee   NO DATES
This is a hand made grave area surrounded by a cement border with hand
etchings of his name only. This appears to be an infant.

Funeral Home Marker Only-Unreadable

Hall, Earnie Lee   January 3, 1913   July 5, 1990

Hall, Joseph F.   1919   1982 Butler Funeral Home Marker

Also marked by a marble pillar, no data recorded on pillar

Faircloth, Sarah   1898   1975
Butler Funeral Home Marker
Also marked by a marble pillar, no data recorded on pillar

Walton, Robert   August 30, 1960   September 24, 1977

Walton Hall, Mary Lelia(SIC) October 31, 1938   May 23, 2003

Red Hill Church Cemetery, Coats, Harnett County, North Carolina

Faircloth, Jessie A.(Allen), b. 08-25-1873, d. 04-08-1945, DH: Lissie P.(Pollard); 2/11/2000
Faircloth, Lissie P.(Pollard), b. 04-15-1883, d. 05-23-1967, DH: Jessie A.(Allen); 2/11/2000
Faircloth, Major D, b. 04-22-1933, d. no date, Wed Oct 4, 1952", DH: Patricia N.; 4/12/1996
Faircloth, Patricia N, b. 04-18-1938, d. no date, Wed Oct 4, 1952", DH: Major D.; 4/12/1996
Faircloth, Willie, b. 02-20-1913, d. 10-23-1915,

Wilmington National Cemetery, Wilmington, New Hanover County, North Carolina

Faircloth, Tate Jr, b. 11/10/1923, d. 11/09/1993, SSGT USAF, Plot: 8 405-D, bur. 11/15/1993, *
Faircloth, Tate Sr, b. 07/28/1894, d. 08/30/1953, SGT CO A 32ND INF 16TH DIV, Plot: 5 1452,
bur. 09/01/1953, *

New Bern National Cemetery; New Bern, Craven County, North Carolina

Faircloth, Harry Leon, b. 04/20/1921, d. 11/24/1995, US Merchant Marine, PANTRYMAN, Res:
Pascagoula,   MS,   Plot: 14   0   6513,   bur.   04/28/1997
Fairclough, Nat, d. 06/08/1865, 14 US CT, Plot: 2751, *

SAMPSON COUNTY, NC - CEMETERIES - Spell Cemetery
Spell Cemetery, Sampson Co. NC; The Spell Family Cemetery is located on State Road 1002,
(also called Dunn Road) in the Spelltown Community. It is on the Dunn to Roseboro Road.   It
is approximately five mile west of Salemburg, N.C.

		Born	Died
11.	Liston Ray Son of W.M. and Emma Faircloth	January 15, 1938	August 10, 1939
12.	Harace Jolly Son of W.M. and Emma Faircloth	May 24, 1932	September 22, 1934
13.	Bronzie Claxton Son of W.M. and Emma Faircloth	July 10, 1940	February 9, 1943
14.	Alfestus Faircloth, Jr.	October 14, 1940	October 15, 1940
15.	A. Pauline Spell	(no dates as of 7-26-1998)	
	B. Alfestus Faircloth	October 1, 1916	November 5, 1989
16.	Junious Clifton Spell, Jr. Son of Clifton and Ruth Spell	April 22, 1940	April 22, 1940
32.	Rubert Elthon Son of A.A. and Lillie Tyndall	September 27,1924	December 12, 1925
33.	Tillman A. Son of A.A. and L.C. Tyndall	September 20, 1918	December 4, 1919
34.	Livvie J.		

Son of L. T. And Janie Faircloth June 10, 1916   June 11, 1916

35.   Janie E.
       Daughter of L.T. and Janie Faircloth July 26, 1923 August 2, 1923

36.   Levada
       Daughter of L.T. and Janie Faircloth November 7, 1927 November 7, 1927

37.   Loren G.
       Son of L.T. and Janie Faircloth November 1, 1910 July 29, 1933

38.   Faircloth
       A. Penny Janie   December 1, 1883   May 18, 1949
       B. Live Thomas   May 6, 1887 July 14, 1959

39.   Henry Lee Bullard   November 25, 1907 December 12, 1943

Sampson County, North Carolina - C. A. Williams Cemetery
              [Updated August, 2004]
This cemetery was documented April 2004. Directions: Take S.R. 1418,
that is one mile north of S.R. 1233 in Little Coharie Township,
Autryville, North Carolina. Turn left on Leroy Autry Road; go about
a mile or so. There is no marker pointing the way to the cemetery,
but any neighbor in the area will know of the location of the cemetery.
You will turn left off of Leroy Autry Road to get to the cemetery and
wind back in on a dirt road to the cemetery, which is surrounded by
farming fields and woods. Submitter is Sharon Dover Romanek, a
descendant of John Dewitt Williams and wife Minnie Mae Edge Williams.

NAME   BIRTH   DEATH   COMMENTS
Faircloth, David N.   July 12, 1946 Dec. 31, 1990
Husband of Linda Faye Williams

Double Stone Williams, J. Dewitt   March 18, 1894 Nov. 20, 1975
Husband of Minnie;US Army WWI

Williams, Donald Gene   Sept. 7, 1959 July 7, 1997
Son of Donald & Mildred McCombs Williams

Faircloth, Jeffrey Vernon   Aug. 1, 1982 Oct. 14, 1995   Son of Alda Faircloth

Double Marker   Faircloth, G. Vernon June 30, 1924 Sept. 11, 1984
Husband of Christelle

Faircloth, Christelle S.   April 7, 1927 Nov. 20, 1996
Wife of George Vernon;   Married April ,1947

Faircloth, Infant   b. & d. Dec. 5, 1952   Son of Vernon & Christelle

Double Marker   Faircloth, Marion   May 28, 1905   Dec. 30, 1980
Husband of Callie.   Son of George & Repsie Williams Hall

Faircloth, Callie Hall Sept. 24,1904 May 15, 1974
Wife of Marion. Dau of John & Margaret Willis Hall

Faircloth, Nova Kermit   Oct. 24, 1926 May 25, 1928 Son of Marion & Callie

Faircloth, Repsie Williams   Dec. 9, 1881   Aug. 7, 1952
Wife of George Faircloth   Dau of Charles & Susan Williams Williams

Hall Infant   b. & d.1961   Son of Mr. & Mrs.James R. Hall

Williams, Evander   Dec. 5, 1864   May 16, 1923
husband of Rosa Lane Williams, son Of Reddin William and Rosa Lane Williams.
Father of John DewittWilliams

Double Marker Williams, Susan Anner   May 19, 1857   Oct. 22, 1929
Wife of Charlie A.   Dau of William & Rebecca Autry Williams

Williams, Charlie A. Feb 1, 1860   Oct. 29, 1915
Husband of Susan.   Son of Reddin & Nancy Faircloth Williams

Williams, Suley Lee   Sept. 22,1885 Dec 4, 1920
Daughter of Charles & Susan Williams Williams

Williams, Harvey A.   June 12, 1922   Dec. 28, 1978
Husband of Margaret B.   Son of George & Vinnie Ezell Williams

Double Marker   Faircloth, Void   March 3, 1920   Aug 22, 1997
Husband of Emily

Faircloth, Emily W.   Nov. 22, 1919   May 21, 1992
Wife of Void.   Dau of George & Vinnie Ezell Williams
Married November 18,1944

Faircloth, Jimmie V.   Aug 28, 1947   Jan 21, 1948
Son of Void & Emily

Double Marker   Williams, Winifred Scott   May 27, 1929   June 30, 1978
Son of Jessie Carrie Horn Williams. Husband Of Lettie Williams CPL US ARMY Korea

Williams, Lettie Lou   Feb 1, 1933   Wife of Winifred
Living 2004   Married February 24,1951

Williams, Novah Lee   Jan. 29,1933   Feb. 14, 1933
Son of Paul & Jincie Faircloth Williams

Williams, Roy Clifton   April 29,1934 July 20, 1936
Son of Paul & Jincie Faircloth Williams

USA – Sampson County, NC , Michigan and Florida
Misc. Political Graveyards

- FAIRCLOTH: *See also* Iris Faircloth Blitch.
- Faircloth, Cyrus Mills (b. 1876) — also known as Cyrus M. Faircloth — of Clinton, Sampson County, N.C. Born near Salemburg, Sampson County, N.C., December 1, 1876. Republican. Lawyer; member of North Carolina state house of representatives from Sampson County, 1913. Methodist. Member, Freemasons. Burial location unknown.
- Faircloth, Duncan McLauchlin (b. 1928) — also known as Lauch Faircloth — of North Carolina. Born in North Carolina, January 14, 1928. Republican. Candidate for Governor of North Carolina, 1984; U.S. Senator from North Carolina, 1993-99; defeated, 1998. Presbyterian. Still living as of 2001.
- Faircloth, E. V. — of West Palm Beach, Palm Beach County, Fla. Mayor of West Palm Beach, Fla., 1954. Still living as of 1954.
- Faircloth, Ernest E. (b. 1892) — of Michigan. Born in 1892. Democrat. Member of Michigan state house of representatives from Cheboygan District, 1933-38; defeated, 1940; candidate for Michigan state senate 29th District, 1938. Burial location unknown.
- Faircloth, Lauch *See* Duncan McLauchlin Faircloth

Info from the Political Graveyard web site: http://politicalgraveyard.com/bio/faircloth-farleigh.html

Militia

Faircloth's
who served their country during the Revolutionary through Civil Wars

<u>FAIRCLOTH SOLDIERS - REVOLUTIONARY WAR</u>

Benjamin   applied for pension compensation for Rev. War Service on
               1 Jan 1840 in Emanual Co., GA at age of 83

Ephraim   Enl at age 21 on 1 Sept 1780; listed on Southampton Co
        Muster Roll as born in VA; Chesterfield Co. Court House   size
roll of troops lists him as 5' 11", brown hair, grey eyes,   fair   complexion;
shoemaker; on 4 Nov 1780 he deserted on   a march from Chesterfield
Court House, VA while listed with   Cpt Scott's Company of the 1st and 2nd
Battalion;

Frederick   Pay vouchers, Dobbs Co, NC
               Copies of those pay vouchers for Frederick and John
        Faircloth follows:

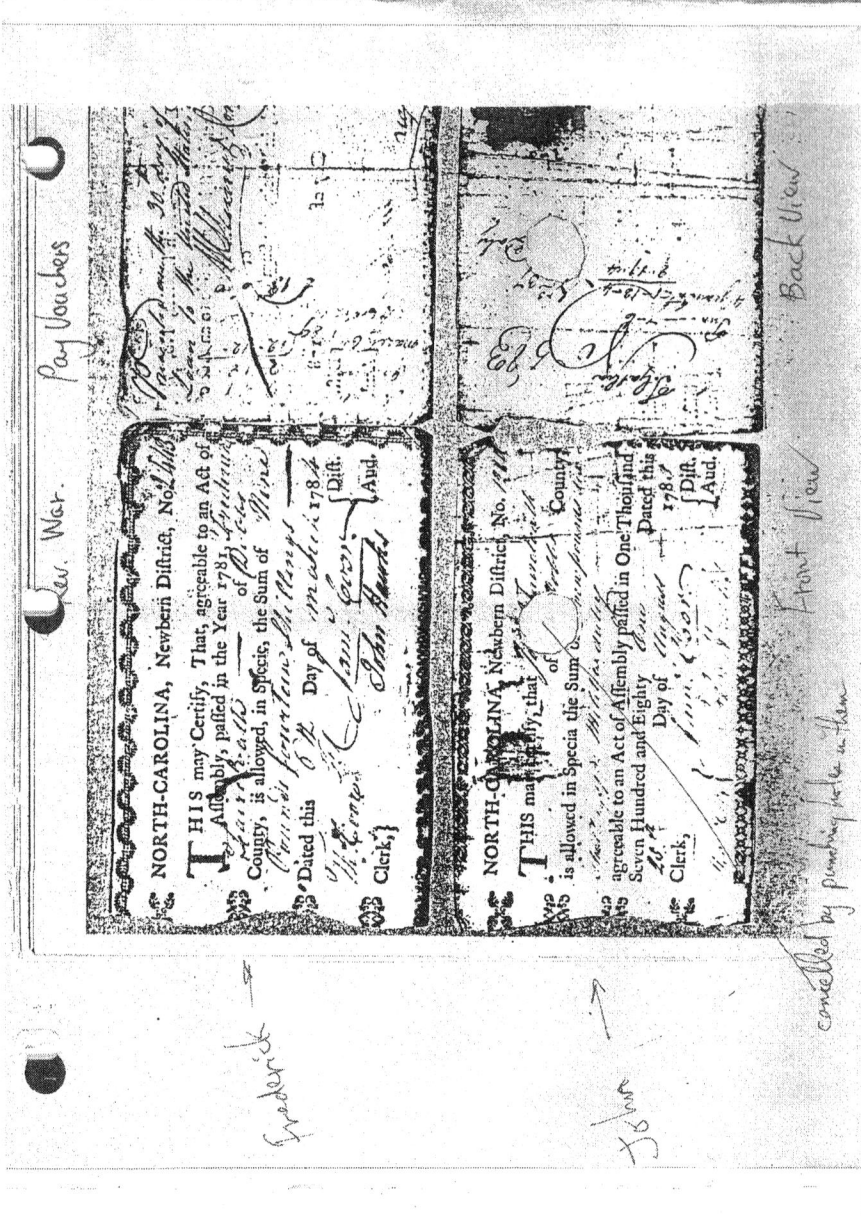

NORTH-CAROLINA, Newbern District, No.

THIS may Certify, That, agreeable to an Act of Assembly, passed in the Year 1783, _____ of _____ County, is allowed, in Specie, the Sum of _____

Dated this _____ Day of _____ 1784.

Clerk.

NORTH-CAROLINA, Newbern District, No.

THIS may certify, that _____ County

is allowed in Specie the Sum of _____ agreeable to an Act of Assembly passed in One Thousand Seven Hundred and Eighty One

Dated this _____ Day of August 178

Clerk.

John listed in Wilmington, Oct 1783, NC

FAIRCLOTH SOLDIERS - REVOLUTIONARY WAR

John   Pay vouchers, Dobbs Co, NC, 178_;

John   Cpt. Sharpe Company; enl 26 Aug 1778; died 5 Apr 1770; Pvt, 10h Regt, Col. Abraham Sheppard's Company of Sharpe; Wilmington District Militia; enl. 10 Nov 1778; discharged 1779 or later.

John   Sgt. 6th regt, transferred to 4th Regt and mustered into Sharpes Company;

John   Pvt; enl 4 May 1777 Cpt Abraham Sheppard's Company of Col. Abraham Sheppard's Batt.; discharged 1782 or later;

John Robert   Sgt.; F co, 10 Regt, Col Abraham Sheppard's Company of Cpt Bradley; enl 20 May 1778; died 5 Apr 1779;

John Smith   Pvt; died in service while serving in the Continental line of the 3rd Regt of NC; filed in Raleigh on 3 Sept 1796.

Newsom   Nov 27, 1782 payroll list; vouchers for 1783 – 1785.

Thomas   NC Pasquotank County muster roll of Robert Murden's Regt of S. County; probably of Surry County; filed a petition for a duplicate warrant and a grant to be issued to him for an entry of land; rejected initially by the committee; Senate members over ruled this decision on 2 Dec 1800.

William   Coronet, listed on 11 Mar 1761. List is as follows:

... Lieut.
Benjamin Craswell Ens.   Lieut — James Craswell Ensign
... Craswell Capt.
Francis Harper — Lieut.
Dennis McClendon Ens.

Wm. Whitefield — Capt. — Resigned
Henry Goodman — Lieut. Capt.
Moses Prescote — Ens. — Lieut. Constantine Whitfield Ensign

Wm. Williams — Capt. Dead } John Murphy Capt.
Jacob McClendon — Lieut. removed } John Charleton Lieut.
Isaac Hardee — Ens. Do. — Wm. Skinner Ensign

Wm. Speight Junr. Capt.
William Speight Junr. Lieut.
Frances Speight — Ens.

Simon Herring — Capt. Resigned Major Croom Capt.
Joshua Herring — Lieut. — Joshua Herring Lieut.
Major Croom — Ens.

James Oats — Capt.
Anthony Herring — Lieut.
Stephen Blackman Ens.

Lewis Pipkin — Capt. Dead
Wm. McHennie — Lieut. Capt. — Jos. Pipkin Ensign
Jethro Oats — Ens.

James Caleote — Capt. removed
John Grade — Lieut. Capt.
Wm. Harm — Ens. ...

John Sheerod — Capt.
Thomas Lane — Lieut. removed — Wm. ... Lieut.
John Peacock — Ens.

Stephen Grade Josh — Capt. Wm. Randal Capt.
William Coode — Lieut. Stephen ... Lieut.
William Barnsloth — Cornet. A... Deacon Ensign

37

Col. Abraham Sheppard's Battalion: 1 July 1777. Lists William, Jr. and John Faircloth. Dates of enlistment: Wm: 22 Apr 1777, John: 11 May 1777.

Roster of Captain Abraham Sheppards Company in Col. Abraham Sheppards Battalion. July 1th 1777.

Names of the Officers & privates	No. of privates	Dates of Commissions & Time of enlistment
Abraham Sheppard Capt.	...	19th April 1777
James Edmundson 1st Lieut.	...	Do
William Sheppard 2d Lieut.	...	Do
Solomon Cooper Ensign	...	Do
William Faircloth jun.	1.	22d April 1777
Benjamin Coleson	2.	Do
Edm Bass	3.	27th Do
Luke Bates	4.	Do
Thomas Price	5.	28th Do
James Jordan	6.	1st May Do
John Jordan	7.	1. Do
Thomas Tail	8.	Do
Thomas Potter	9.	Do
Benjamin Davis	10.	2d May
Peter Harrele	11.	Do
Jesse Nelson	12.	Do
Zador Phelps	13.	Do
James Phelps	14.	Do
Joshua Lynch	15.	Do
Edward Evans	16.	3d May
		Do
Waddele Cade	18.	Do
Jesse Taylor	19.	Do
William Martin	20.	4th May
Abraham Kray	21.	Do
John Faircloth	22.	Do

99

FAIRCLOTH SOLDIERS - REVOLUTIONARY WAR

William   Lt, 10th Regt, Col Abraham Sheppard's Co; enl 20 Jan 1778; discharged 1 Jun 1778; was charged with a major pay scandal involving payments made to himself from state militia funds; (Seems he created extra soldiers and cashed their paychecks...as he was the quartermaster...paymaster.)

William   1st Lt; took Oath to US

William   Pvt, received 640 acres of land on 13 Dec 1796 for 84 months of service;

William   Lt., received 731 acres for 24 months of service;

William   filed for acreage due in Tennessee on 5 Dec 1796.

William   no rank given; filed for 640 acres of land for 84 months of service on 15 Dec 1797.

William, Jr.   Pvt, Cpt Abraham Sheppard's Co, Col Abraham Sheppard's Batt; listed 1 July 1777; enl 22 Apr 1777.

Zachariah   Loyalist, Sgt, served 98 days from 25 Dec – 1 Apr 1782 and 34 days from   2 Apr – 5 May 1782.

Dobbs County, NC - Military - Dobbs Militia Mid 1700's

Last name	First name	Rank
Faircloth	John	Private
Faircloth	Thomas	Private
Faircloth	William	Private

Duplin County, NC - **Revolutionary War** Military Services, Surnames E-H

FAIRCLOTH, Hardwick (Hardy), Private Duplin Militia
Soldier drew 1 RW pay voucher and lived in Sampson in 1790 and had five young males in his household. Soldier was born about 1754 to William and Sarah Faircloth and is also listed in Sampson in 1785 tax list. Soldier married Sarah Suggs. Issue: 1-Reason, 2-Isham, 3-James, 4-Thomas, 5-Jacob, 6-Benjamin, 7-Elizabeth or Betty, 8-Achsah, 9-Sabar, 10-Hardwick (Hardy) Jr., 11-Nancy, 12-Jonah, 13-Arthur, 14-Wilson, and 15-Jonathan. Soldier's brothers were John and Zechariah Faircloth. Soldier died about 1810.

FAIRCLOTH, John, Private Duplin Militia
Soldier drew 6 RW pay vouchers and lived in Sampson in 1790 and had three young sons and three young females and wife in his household. Soldier was born about 1750 to William and Sarah Faircloth and is also listed in 1785 state tax list for Sampson.

Famous Battles
Boston Massacre
Battle of Moore's Creek
Valley Forge

Fellow patriots of this time period include:
Thomas Paine
Benjamin Franklin
John Adams
Thomas Jefferson
John Hancock
George Washington
Samuel Adams

Do any of these names sound familiar in the Faircloth family lines?

Notes:

FAIRCLOTH SOLDIERS - REVOLUTIONARY WAR

Col. Abraham Sheppard – The American Revolution – History of the Battle of King's Mountain. Commanding Officers included several Faircloth's.

One of Col. Cleveland's vigilant troops was "Bill Nichols, a noted and desperate leader, whose wife is said to have been a sister of Captain William Riddle. On one occasion, Nichols had a difficulty with a Whig neighbor named Letchey. He snatched his gun from him and with it shot him down in his tracks. Nichols was speedily executed. At another time, one Tate and eight others were taken by Cleveland and his men, and had them near old Richmond, on the Yadkin, in Surry. When Cleveland was about to execute the leader, Colonel William Sheppard protested against such summary justice. "Why", said Cleveland, "Tate confesses that he has frequently laid in wait to kill you." "Is that so?" inquired Sheppard, turning to the Tory captain. Tate frankly acknowledged that it was true—that he was an influential Whig, and the Loyalists were anxious to have him out of the way. Sheppard now acquiesced in the opinion that Tate was a dangerous man, and that they had best make an example of him. So his fate was fixed while his associates suffered only imprisonment as other captives of the war.

On another occasion, Col. Cleveland visited Col. Sheppard at Richmond, where he had two notorious Tory house thieves in prison. Cleveland insisted on swinging them to the nearest tree, lest they should effect their escape, and yet further endanger the community—at least one of them, whose crimes undered him particularly obnoxious to the people. One end of the rope was fastened to his neck, when he was mounted on a log, and the other end made fast to the limb of a tree overhead, and the log then rolled from under the culprit." The surviving Tories had their choice of joining the first or cutting off their own ears. The remainder chose to cut off their own ears. "Truly civil wars are both savage and sanguinary in their character."

Col. Sheppard was an early settler of Surry County. He commanded a troop of Calvary on Rutherford's Cherokee campaign. He participated largely in opposing the Tories of his region. He represented his country in the state Senate for six years (from 1777-1782) and removing to Orange County served again in the Senate in 1793, 1801, and 1803. He was many years a magistrate. He died 8 February 1822 at the age of 76. This would have made him born approximately 1846.

"Information taken from the History of the Battle of King's Mountain – Oct 7, 1780. NC Heritage Series, No. 5. Library of Congress No. 67-25801. Author: Lyman C. Draper, LL.D., Cincinnati, Peter g. Thomson Publishers, c. 1881. Page 446-7.

FAIRCLOTH SOLDIERS – War of 1812

War of 1812:

This list was abstracted from Muster Rolls of the Soldiers of the War of 1812 Detached from The Militia of North Carolina in 1812 and 1814 from the Adjutant General's office. These are names of soldiers who are identified as being in regiments from Cumberland County. Just because your ancestor is not listed here and lived in Cumberland County does not necessarily mean that he did not participate. Be sure to check the index at the rear of the book

Detached from the 4th and 14th Brigades
Second Company, detached from First Cumberland Regiment

Third Company, detached from Cumberland Regiment
Jacob Faircloth

Isham   Pvt., 3rd Regt of Moore's, NC; Cpt Caleb Stephen's Co of Infantry;
     11 Oct 1814-10 Mar 1815.

Joel   Cpt John Woodward's Co of Infantry, 25th Regt, Maj Loveless
     Gasque's Batt, SC Militia; Pvt; 7 Nov 1814-15, Dec 1814 for 28 days; Camp Cat Island;
     paid $7.00 for service (rate of pay was $8.00 for one month's service)

Kinchen   7th Co., 2 Regt of Bruton's of Green Co, NC; detached for 2nd, 12th
     and 3rd Brigade; served 6 months including 15 July 1813;
     discharged 7 Aug 1813 for a six day march home which was 90 miles away.

Kinchen   Cpt Heymrick Hooker's Co, NC; served 24 days including 19 July –
     7 Aug 1813.

Noah   Maj Cameron's Command, 5th Co of Cumberland county, NC;
     Corporal; served for six months including 24 Jul 1813; drafted militia stationed at Deepwater Point; present 26 Sept 1813; detached all married men including him on 19 Oct 1813; present July 1813 through 19 Jan 1814; expiration date of pay was 19 Oct 1813.

Raiford   4th Regt of Cumberland co, NC; Maj Cameron's Command;
     detached from 4th and 14th Brigade; six months of service from 24 July 1813;Cpt Thomas Boykin's Company, Deepwater point on 26 Sept 1813; Cpt David L. Evan's Company of Artillery 30 Nov – 31 Dec 1813 at Deepwater; deserted; Cpt Boykin's Company from July 1813-19Jan 1814, deserted. Cpt Evans Company 19 Jan 1814, deserted;

Raphel or Raiford   Pvt, 3rd Regt of Moore's Sampson County, NC; six months
     service from 11 Oct 1814; Cpt Caleg Stephens Co of Infantry, 3rd Regt, NC militia; stated at Greenfield, near Wilmington through 15 Feb 1815;

Solomon   Maj Cameron's Command, Cpt thomas Boykin's Company; July
     1813 – 19 Jan 1814; stationed at Deepwater Point from 30 Nov – 31 Dec 1813; Cpt Evans com from 31 Dec - 19 Jan 1814 at Camp Deepwater Point;

Stephen   Pvt; Cpt John Woodward's Company of Infantry, 25th Regt, Maj
     Loveless Gasque's Batt, SC militia 7 Nov 1814- 5 Dec 1814 for 28 days at Camp Cat Island;

FAIRCLOTH SOLDIERS – Indian Wars

2 Seminole War 1816-1818
> Robert Dean's County, GA Militia

2nd Seminole War of 1835-1842

Caleb — Graham's Company, Ross's Battalion, GA Militia; Dooley and Pulaski County, GA

Ethelrred — Graham's Co, Ross' Batt, GA Militia; Dooley and Pulaski County, GA

GA State Militia
1800	B.	Sgt Ogeechee Guard, Effingham County; ordered into service 23 Jun – 30 June 1800 by Maj Thomas Polhill;
1814	Richard	Cartman in Cpt Elijah Blackshear's Co, GA Militia; 2 Jun – 7 Jun 1814 "to cut road in Pulaski County".
1819	Thomas	Screven Co, Pvt, 1st class, 2nd Brig, 1st Div
1819	Ethelred	Screven Co, Pvt, 1st Class, 2nd Brig, 1st Div
1828	WM	16 May, Baker Co, LT.
1831	Caleb	Dooley County, 31 May

VA State Militia
> John — Ensign, 2nd Batt, 65 Regt, 8th Brig, VA Militia; Sept 1814-16; Artillery Company commanded by Francis Ridley, 4th Div, state militia.

Florida Creek Seminole War

Abraham — 1836, Read's Batt, FLA volunteers, enl for 4 months

Allen D. — Newsom's Company, Taylor's Batt, middle FLA mounted volunteers in 1836.

Allen D. — Hall's, Co, Bailey's Batt, FLA mounted militia 1840 for three months

Allen — Cpt Holloman's Com, McCan'ts Batt, Jefferson Co, Middle FLA; drafted militia

Allen D. — Norton's Co, FLA mounted militia, 3 months, 1840-41

Allen D. — Miner Co, 9th Regt, 1st Brig, FLA mounted militia

Isaac — 1836, Read's Batt, FLA volunteers, 4 months.

FAIRCLOTH SOLDIERS – CIVIL WAR

Many Faircloth males enlisted and served their country during the Civil War under General Robert E. Lee. These men earned $11.00 a month as privates and were paid every other month. They also received a small clothing allowance and if they chose to re-enlist, they received a bonus of $50.00.

The Faircloth confederate soldiers fought bravely in various famous battles and many not so well known. Among those known are the battles occurring at Ft. Fisher, Appomattox, Gettysburg, Roanoke Island, Rappahannock, VA, Sharpsburg, MC, New Bert, Fredericksburg, VA, Richmond, VA, Gaine's Mill, VA, Petersburg, VA, Morris Island, Charleston Harbor, SC, Winchester, VA, Spotsylvania, VA, and the Battle of Wilderness, VA.

His enemies called him Johnny Reb, Johnny, or just Reb. He was comfortable with any of those names, although he was officially a Confederate—a soldier of the confederate States of America. Typically, he was eighteen to twenty-nine years old, although his ranks included the middle-aged and even old men. He was also most likely a farmer, but not a planter. Most soldiers in gray were small farmers and only a slim minority owned slaves or large amounts of land. Sprinkled among his ranks were teachers, laborers, artisans, politicians, lawyers, clerks, mechanics, merchants, and members of most nineteenth-century American professions. However, an estimated two thirds of Johnny Reb's ranks were filled by men of the soil-traditional Southern farmers.

Nobody knows how many Southerners wore the gray. Some authorities say as many as 1.4 million Confederates were in the field at one time or another during the course of the war. Others believe Confederate troops numbered as few as 600,000. The best estimate probably lies somewhere in between...some 750,000 Southerners were in Confederate service during the War between States.

The men in gray had more to worry about than camp life, combat and their next meal. They fretted about wives and had children left behind, mulled over unfinished business back home, and pondered the chances of an end to what had quickly become a very deadly war. A sick child, uncollected bills, underfed hogs, camp gossip----such were the subjects of the soldiers during their service to the Confederate States. (Descriptions taken from The Illustrated Confederate Reader.)

Three quarters of a million Union and Confederate troops marched through Fredericksburg during the Civil War from 1862 through 1864. They fought over its lands in four major battles where over 17,000 soldiers died and over 80,000 were wounded. The intensity of heavy and continuous fighting in Fredericksburg covered a 17-mile radius. The four major battles included Fredericksburg, Chancellorsville, the Wilderness, and Spotsylvania Court House Battles.

Lee and Grant battled over Petersburg, Virginia, a vital rail center, 23 miles south of Richmond. When Petersburg fell, the Confederates hurried from Richmond after setting the city on fire. Within a week, Appomattox and surrender followed.

Many were taken prisoners and confined at point lookout, MD and Elmira, NY. The prisons must have been extremely unsanitary and the men not well fed or cared for as many of them died in prisons at these locations. Even so, our heritage includes all of those who served their states as prisoners of war, even until death. Many were buried at the Woodlawn Cemetery, Elmira, New York.

Poor diet, exposure, and unsanitary conditions made southern prisoners susceptible to disease, producing a high mortality rate in most prisons. As New York's Elmira Prison, almost one third of the 10,000 inmates died of illness. The Illustrated Confederate Reader, a collection of personal experiences and eyewitness accounts, selected by Rod Gragg and copyrighted in 1989 describes the conditions of the Yankee prisons as:

"There were nearly 10,000 prisoners at Elmira one time; sometimes less and sometimes more. During the winter those who came from the south felt the cold exceedingly and died from pneumonia. Our clothes were poor. The pants I had when arriving in Elmira were in such bad condition that for a time I wore nothing but my underwear. However, when the cold weather appeared, I was glad to welcome old pants again and after much patching, they were a great comfort. In late winter, out-of-date government coats were presented to us for overcoats: for some reason unknown to us the tails had been cut unevenly, one side being a foot long and the other extending only a few inches below the waist line. They helped us to keep warm, but should we have been out in the world in such costume, one might have mistaken us for scarecrows eloping from the neighboring cornfield. Oilcloth and two blankets was the covering in our bunks, with a big snow outside and the bitter wind raging around the plank building and whistling in at the cracks. "

"We didn't dream of comforts and many of us had very poor shoes. Mine were ready to be cast aside and I did not get a new pair until the last day of February. While in the house, I wrapped my feet in old rags which kept them warm, but in the late winter, we were compelled to stand in the snow every morning for roll call, consequently my feet and shins were badly frozen. In the spring they had the appearance of a boggler's legs, and it was many years after I returned home before they were entirely cured. Many besides myself had frozen feet."

"The man who looked after the fires made only two fires in 24 hours. Each ward had two stoves. The first fire was made at 8 o'clock in the morning, and the other at 8 pm. Near noon and midnight, we were comfortable, but during the twelve hours between fires when the temperature of the stoves lowered, we often suffered with the cold. A dead line nailed to the floor three feet in circumference surrounded the stoves. Of course we could not cross the dead lines and often a petty officer who entered on a cold evening would find some of the ragged shivering men standing too near the fast-cooling stove, would become enraged and would run cursing, striking right and left through the crowd, little caring who received the blows or what he did."

"Much sickness prevailed among the prisoners. In the latter part of the winter, many came from near Mobile Bay and brought with the smallpox. There were more than forty cases in our ward, and many died. When seven years of age I was vaccinated, and although surrounded by it, I escaped."

"There were also many cases of pneumonia and measles, and thousands of us were afflicted with the stubborn diarrhea. The poor fellows died rapidly, despondent, homesick, hungry and wretched. I have stood day after day watching the wagons carrying the dead outside to be buried, and each day for several weeks sixteen dead men were taken through the gate. While the prison was occupied by us, which was about one year, it was estimated that 3,000 men died. The physicians were very good, but it was impossible to save all."

"Our dead were buried outside with a detail of 16-17 prisoners. The name, company, and regiment of the dead were written on a piece of paper, put in a tightly corked bottle and buried with the corpse. All were buried in that way. Their caskets were made in the pen by prisoners detailed for that purpose."

"After warm weather came we had many visitors, often ladies. Some of them spoke pleasantly and were well behaved, while others were impudent and insulting. I remember on day colonel Moore's son came in our pen with a few young girls. Colonel Moore was commander of the post, his son was a foppish young fellow, and one of the girls overdressed and attracted him. While passing through our ward, with her dainty fingers she tipped up her rustling silken skirts and passed along with an affected air and a disdainful look on her countenance, saying, "Oh, the nasty, dirty, ignorant, beastly Rebels. How filthy they are." On she continued with a peculiar air, while some of the girls gave us kindly words and looks, and were embarrassed by her rudeness. But she was punished for being so unlady-like. One of our number, Bish Fletcher, a daredevil, took the opportunity as the girl passed by him to present her with some body lice, "Gray Backs," we called them." (Account documented by Pvt. John r. King of the 25th Virginia Infantry who survived Elmira.)

The following account describes prison discipline by the Confederate I. W. K. Handy at Ft Delaware in 1864:

"July 3, 1864 – a lamentable affair occurred at the rear about dusk this evening. Many persons are now suffering with diarrhea, and crowds are frequenting that neighborhood. The orders are to go by one path and return by the other. Two lines of men, going and coming, are in continual movement. I was returning from the frequented spot and, in much weakness, making my way back when suddenly I heard the sentinel challenge from the top of the water-house. I had no idea he was speaking to me, until some friends called my attention to the order. I suppose my pace was too slow for him. I passed on; and as frequent inquiries were made in regard to my health, I was obliged to say to friends "We have no time to talk; the sentinel is evidently restless or alarmed, and we are in danger."

I had scarcely reached my quarters before a musket fired and it was immediately reported that colonel e. P. Jones had been shot. The murder of Colonel Jones is the meanest and most inexcusable affair that has occurred in the officers' quarters; or that has come under my observation since my imprisonment at Fort Delaware. I did not see him fall; but I have heard from Captain J. b. Cole, who was an eye-witness to the whole scene, that although he was standing within ten steps of the man that killed him, he heard no challenge and no order to move on. The first intimation he had of the sentinel's displeasure was the discharge of the musket, and the simultaneous exclamation of the colonel: "Oh, God! Oh, God! My God, what did you shoot me for? Why didn't you tell me to go on? I never heard you say anything to me!" With a few such exclamations, he sank upon the ground; and then fell, or rather rolled, down the embankment." Colonel Jones lingered a few hours, and died in great agony." Many others were wounded or killed in militia action across the east coast from New York to Florida.

Ft. Fisher, NC, kept Federal blockade ships at a distance from the Cape Fear River, saving Wilmington from attack and insuring relatively safe passage to Confederate naval travel. Wilmington was the last major port open to the confederacy, and the destination of steamers called blockade runners which smuggled provisions into the southern states and supplied General Lee's Army of Northern Virginia.

The Union Army and Navy planned several attacks on Fort Fisher and the port of Wilmington but made no attempt until December 24, 1864. After two days of fighting, with little headway, Union commanders concluded that the Fort was too strong to assault, and they withdrew their forces. However, they returned for a second attempt on January 12, 1865. The Fort was bombarded on both land and sea face by Federal ships and assaulted on land face by more than 3,300 Union infantry troops. On January 15, after six hours of fierce combat, the Fort was captured by the Union. (information on Fort Fisher taken from a pamphlet distributed at the camp and NC Division of Archives.)

On April 7th, a charge was made for the relief of Mahone, who was hard pressed. The enemy was driven back and a number of prisoners captured. General Lee again expressed his appreciation of the conduct of the North Carolinians. The general seemed to have the gift of prophecy, and gave the North Carolinians on the field the meed of praise which was to be long withheld in the history of their country.

The 8th was spent marching towards Appomattox, which was passed during the night. Sunday, the 9th of April, found the regiment in front of the town, where it engaged the enemy, and were driving him when withdrawn and ordered to join the other division of Gordon's Corps.

The highest claim to distinction that any man in this country can make is that he enlisted for the defense of his state at the first call to arms, and fought with the armies in the field to the last day at Appomattox. (NC Regiments, Vol. 1, pp. 157, 159, 175.)

The last scene of the greatest drama of modern times, the surrender, the cry of mortification, the curse of defiance, the tears of sorrow for our friends slain in battle, and above all, the noble word of the great-hearted leader: "Human fortitude should be above human calamity!"

Sometimes one may note that a soldier deserted and returned to duty only to desert the troops a second or third time. One should not hold this as extremely disgraceful as they often deserted in the spring so as to return home to plant the crops. After the growing season, when the harvest was done, and the assurance made to provide for their families, they would return to service. They certainly must have loved their families.

Remembering these brave men and the many Faircloth's that were members of the Confederates, this work is dedicated. Your heirs remember you and your service to our great country.

FAIRCLOTH SOLDIERS – CIVIL WAR

A. E.   Pvt, resided in Cumberland County; enl in Lenoir Co on 6 Nov 1854; paroled 1 May 1865 in Greensboro;

A.   Pvt, Co C, 5th Batt, enl 5 Nov 1864 in Lenoir Co, NC

A. J.   Pvt, G Co, 74th Regt; enl 23 Jun 1864 in Co H, 74th Regt

Alex   Private, enlisted in Cumberland County at age 41, September 2, 1863, for the war. Present or accounted for through August, 1864. No further records.

Alexander   3rd Regt, Wimberlips, GA Militia

Alexander B.   Pvt, B Co, 10th Batt; enl 23 Apr 1864; discharged;

Anderson   Ramseur-Cox Brigade, p. 463 of NC Regiments, Vol IV.

Allen   3rd Regt, Wimberlips, GA Militia;

Barnabus   Born 1827; Pvt, Co C, 2nd Art, Regt 36; Owenville farmer; enl 9 Feb 1863, age 36, in Clinton, NC; assigned detached service in construction of wharf at Ft. Phillip; hospitalized 25 Oct 1864 at Wilmington with febris typhoids; furloughed 29 Oct 1864 for 30 days.

Barnabus   Born 1839; Pvt, Co H, 20th Regt; Sampson farm laborer; enl 10 Jun 1861 in Clinton at age 21; captured 1-3 July 1863 at Gettysburg, PA; confined Ft Delaware, Del and Point Lookout, MD; died 15 Apr 1864 of diarrhea;

Barnabus   Pvt, Co I, 20th Regt; enl 10 Jun 1861 in Sampson Co, NC; prisoner of war in Spotsylvania on 12 May 1864;

Benjamin   Born 1840; Co. C, 38th Inf; enl in GA

Benjamin P.   Born 1840; Co F, 5th FLA Inf; enl in FLA

Benjamin   Born 1841; Co D, 27th Bn, GA Inf; enl in GA

Benjamin   8th Regt, Magien's VA militia

C. M.   Col who enl in Cumberland County, NC

D.   Pvt; Co A, Regt 8; wounded; enl Cumberland County, NC

D.   Pvt, I Co, 72nd Regt, enl 1 Jun 1864;

Daniel   Pvt, Co E, Regt 8; enl 5 Aug 1861 in Cumberland County, NC

Daniel   Born in Sampson County where he resided as a farmer prior to enlisting in Cumberland County at age 36, on 1 Aug 1861. Captured at Roanoke Island on 8 Feb 1862 and paroled at Elizabeth City on 21 Feb 1862. Exchanged in Aug, 1862; Present or accounted for until admitted to hospital at Wilmington on 24 May 1863 with a gunshot wound. Roll of Honor states that he "shot off two desertion" through Dec 1863. Deserted to the enemy at New Bern on or about 1 Feb 1864. Confined at Fort Monroe, VA until released on 20 Mar 1864 after taking the Oath of Allegiance.

Daniel B.   Pvt, B Co, 8th Batt, enl 5 Mar 1862 in Harnett County, NC

Daniel J.   Born 1828; Pvt Co E, Regt 8, Inf; Sampson Farmer; enl 1 Aug 1861 in Cumberland County, NC at age 33; captured 8 Feb 1862 on Roanoke Island; escaped; captured 1 Jun 1864 at Cold Harbor, VA. Confined Point Lookout, MD until transferred to Elmira, NY; died 14 Nov 1864 of chronic diarrhea; buried in grave #1316, Woodlawn Cemetery, Elmira, NY. Born Sampson County. Another account shows him dying at Elmira on 29 Dec 1864 of chronic diarrhea.

Evan   Born 1840; Pvt, Co C. Regt 54, Inf; Sampson turpentine laborer; enl 7 Apr 1863 at Camp Mangum, Wake county, NC; reported missing 7 Nov 1863 on Rappahannock in VA; received 11 Nov 1863 at Old Capitol Prison, Washington, DC; confined Point Lookout, MD; released 29 Jan 1864 to join Union Forces.

Evans, Jr.   Born 1837; Pvt, Co E, Regt 2, Inf; Sampson farmer; enl 15 Jul 1862 in Wake county, NC; died 24 Sept 1862 at Boonesboro, MD of disease;

Evlin   Born 1836; Pvt, Co F, Regt 2, Inf; Sampson farmer; enl 15 Aug 1862 in Wake
          county, NC; missing in action 17 Sept 1862, Sharpsburg, MD; later reported to have died.
Francis F.   Born Sampson County; lived Cumberland co; Pvt; enl age 24, 3 Sept 1861; took
          Oath on 27 Jun 1865; G Co, 33rd Regt;
F. G.   Pvt, Co K, 40th;
Grey   Pvt, F Co, 6th Batt; enl 4 Sep 1863 in Cumberland County
Harden   Pvt, D Co, 31st Regt; enl 17 Sep 1861 in Johnston, Co, NC; discharged   for
          disability;
Hardin   Pvt, E Co, 8th Regt; enl 5 Aug 1861 in Sampson Co; died 30 Dec 1864
Hardy   Co E, 24th Regt;
Hardy   Pvt, Born in Sampson County where he resided as a farmer prior to
          enlisting in Cumberland County at age 20 on 5 Aug 1861.
          Captured at Roanoke Island on 8 Feb 1862 but escaped. Present or accounted for until
          captured at Fort Harrison, VA on 30 Sept 1864. Confined at Point Lookout, MD until
          paroled and transferred to Boulware's Wharf, James river, VA, where he was received 19
          Mar 1865 for exchange.
Harphrey   Born 1847; Pvt, A Co, 2nd Jr., Reserves, Regt 41; Sampson farmer;
          enl Apr 1864 in Clinton; left Company 24 Oct 1864 due to illness;
          admitted to hospital #3 on Apr 1865 in Greensboro; in Clinton 26 Sept 1889 for veteran
          reunion;
Henry   Born 1845; Pvt, Co C, Regt 54, Inf; Sampson farmer; records lost;
Henry   Pvt, B Co, 7th Batt; enl 12 Apr 1864;
Henry   Pvt, E Co, 70 Regt; enl 11 Apr 1864;
James   2nd Regt; Sampson County;
John   Pvt, G Co, 55th Regt, enl 28 Feb 1863 in Johnston Co; killed 2-3 Jul 1863 in
          Gettysburg;
John   Born 1835; Pvt, A Co, 30th Regt, Inf; Sampson turpentine maker; enl 1 Sept 1861
          in Clinton; died 10 Feb 1863 at camp in Fredericksburg, VA of pneumonia;
John   1st Regt, Cumberland Co
John   2nd Regt, Bruton's NC militia
John   3rd Regt, Sampson Co, Moore's
John   2nd Regt, Sampson

John   65th Blow's, VA Paymaster
John F.   H Co, 41st Regt; surrendered at Appomattox
John L.   Born 1838; Pvt, A Co, 30th Regt, Inf; Sampson Co farmer; enl 1
          Sept 1861 in Clinton; died 15 Jan 1863 in hospital in Richmond, VA of smallpox and
          plueropneumonia;
John W.   Pvt; born Brunswick Co; resided Cumberland; enl age 20 on 31 Aug 1861; killed
          in New Bern on 14 Mar 1862; G Co, 33 Regt; also listed as enl on 6 Sep 1861 in
          Cumberland County;
Jonas   Born 1817; Pvt, C Co, 30th Regt, Inf; Sampson farm laborer; enl 19
          May 1962, Camp Mangum, as substitute for Thomas Cole; named on report of casualties
          in engagement in front of Fredericksburg, VA 12-13 Dec 1862…killed;
Joseph M.   8th Regt, Magnien's VA, Pvt; also Sgt in 7th.
Kinchen   Co 7, 2nd Regt, detached from the Green Regt, Sampson Co; 2nd, 12th, and 3rd
          Brig;
Leonides   Pvt, enl at age 25 in Wayne Co on 15 June 1861; died Richmond,   VA   on   26
          March 1862; D Co, 4th Regt;

Levi   Born 1836; Pvt, F Co, 20th Regt, Inf; Sampson farmer; enl 9 May 1861 in Clinton; wounded in head 27 Jun 1862 at Fox's Gap, MC; confined Ft Delaware, Del; received 2 Oct 1862, Aiken's Landing, VA; captured 1-2 May 1863, Chancellorsville, VA; paroled 4 May 1863; killed 1-3 Jul 1863 at Gettysburg, PA;

Luke   Pvt, born Horry Co, SC enl Columbus County, age 46 on 26 Apr 1861; died in hospital at Petersburg, VA on 16 Dec 1862; D Co, 20th Regt;

L.   Pvt, C Co, 26th Regt; enl 4 Nov 1863 at Orange Co, VA

M. M.   Pvt; enl 20 Jul 1862 in Ashe Co, NC

Matthew   Pvt; enl age 23 on 12 Jun 1861; musician from Wayne County; A Co, 27th Regt;

Moses McLaine   Co, 54th Regt, Inf; born 1825; Pvt; Sampson farmer; enl 4 Mar 1862 in Fayetteville; discharged as being over 35 years of age on 26 May 1862; enl 16 Oct 1862 in Cumberland county and assigned to E Co, 8th Regt; died 22 March 1863 of fever in Charleston, SC hospital; served as a cook;

Noah   5th Co, NC Cumberland Co, Maj. Cameron's Command

Nathan   Pvt, A Co, 71st Regt; enl Apr 1864 in Sampson County;

Paterick   Born 1845; Pvt, C and F Company' 54 Regt, Inf; Sampson laborer; enl 22 Aug 1862 Camp Campbell; died 20 Sept 1863 in camp hospital at Orange Court House, VA;

Phillip   Born 1834; Pvt, enl Orange Co Court House, VA on 1 Nov 1863; deserted 12 Apr 1864; returned 24 Sep 1864; captured 27 Oct 1864 near Petersburg, VA.; Confined at Point Lookout, MD where he died 1 Jan 1865 in prison; C. Co, 26th Regt;

Raiford   4th Co, detached from the Sampson Co, 2nd Regt of Maj. Cameron's

Raphael   2nd Regt, Sampson Co.

Reasom   Born 1778; Pvt, E Co, 8th Regt; enl Cumberland County

Reason Born 1831; Pvt, E Co, 8th Regt, Inf; Sampson County farmer; enl 5 Aug 1861 Cumberland County at age 30;; captured 9 (8?) Feb 1862 on Roanoke Island; paroled 21 Feb 1862 Elizabeth City and exchanged in Aug 1862. ; wounded 30 Jan 1863 Morris Island, Charleston Harbor, SC; furloughed until 2 Nov 1863; captured 1 Jun 1864 Cold Harbor, VA; confined Point Lookout, MD and Elmira, NY; died 14 Nov 1864 of chronic diarrhea; buried in grave #804 at Woodlawn Cemetery, Elmira, NY;

Reddin Enl in Cumberland County on 16 Oct 1862. Present and accounted for through Apr 1863. Cook. No further records.

Richard   Cpt, E, Blacksheair Co., GA

Richard M. L Co, 5th FL; casualty at Gettysburg on 2-3 Jul 1863.

Sampson   Born 1823; Pvt, C Co, 26th Regt; enl 1 Nov 1863 at Orange co., Court House, VA; deserted 11 Apr 1864; returned 24 Sept 1864; deserted 14 Feb 1865; captured by the enemy in Sampson County on   16   Mar   1865; Confined at Hart's Island, New York Harbor until released/ paroled 19 June 1865 after taking the Oath of Allegiance.

Sampson   Pvt, E Co, 8th Regt; enl 20 Jul 1961 Sampson Co, at age of 23; Oath on 19 May 1865.

Sampson   Pvt, born in Sampson County where he resided as a farmer prior to enlistingin Cumberland County at age 23, 20 Jul 1861, for the war. Captured at Roanoke Island on 8 Feb 1862, but escaped. Present or accounted for until captured at Cold Harbor, VA on 1 Jun 1864. Confined at Point Lookout, MD, until transferred to Elmira, NY on 29 May 1865 after taking the Oath of Alliance.

Smith F.   Born 1820; Pvt, F Co, Regt 54, Inf; Sampson farmer; 3nl 7 Apr 1962; blockers, as substitute for G. W. Williams; captured 7 Nov 1863 on the Rappahannock, VA; confined Pt. Lookout, MD; received 16 Mar 1864, City Point, VA for exchange; captured 19 Sept 1864 in Winchester, VA; confined Point Lookout, MD; exchanged 15 Mar 1865;

Solomon   Born 1811; Pvt, F Co, 2nd Art, 36 Regt; Sampson farm laborer; enl 26 Feb 1862 at Ellisville; hospitalized 11 Jul 1862 with acute diarrhea; C Co, 2nd Regt, Art, 36th Regt; enl 3 Mar 1862 for 3 yrs at age of 51 in Bladen County; h. co, 3rd Regt, enl 15 Jul 1862 Bladen Co.

Solomon   3rd Regt, Cumberland co, Maj Cameron's Command

Samuel   Pvt, C Co, 5th Batt; enl 2 Sept 1863 in Cumberland Co.

Samuel   Pvt, B Co, 10th Batt; enl 11 Apr 1864; discharged;

Smith   Pvt, g Co, 55 Regt, enl 8 May 1862 Johnston Co.

Stephen   Pvt, G Co, 55 Regt; enl 8 May 1862 Johnston Co.

T.   Pvt, E co, 36th Regt; captured at Ft. Fisher on 15 Jan 1865.

Thelbert A.   Pvt, B co, 37th Regt; enl 15 Feb 1864 Ashe Co; served 17 Mar 1864 - 7 Mar 1865.

Thomas   2nd Regt, Hertford Co;

Thomas   Pvt, A Co, 18th Regt; enl 15 Jun 1861 New Hanover Co.; enl age 23 on 23 Jul 1861; Bladen farmer; retired an invalid on 31 Aug 1864;

Thomas G.   Pvt, K Co, 2nd Co, 40th Regt, 3rd Art.; enl Brunswick County at age of 21 on 7 Jul 1862; killed at Fort Fisher on 15 Jan 1865.

Thomas H.   Born 1820; Pvt, F Co, 2nd Art, 36th Regt; Sampson farm laborer; enl 20 Feb 1862 Terebinth; captured 15 Jan 1865 Fort Fisher; confined Elmira, NY; died 14 Mar 1865 of rheumatism; buried in grave #243_ Woodlawn Cemetery, Elmira; a second source says he enl in Cumberland co, C Co, 3rdt, Art, 35th Regt;

Wiley   Gasques Batt, SC

William   Born 1848; Pvt, F Co, 20th Regt, Inf; Sampson laborer; 20 Apr 1864; Clinton enl; wounded 19 May 1864 at Spotsylvania Court House,   VA; discharged Apr 1865.

WM   3rd Regt, Wimberlip, GA

Wm   Pvt, Co, 3rd Regt; enl 21 Jun 1861 Cumberland County; wounded at Gettysburg.

Wm   Pvt, A Co, 58th Regt; enl 2 Oct 1863 at Martin;

William H.   Pvt, enl age 18 on 9 Aug 1861; born Forsythe Co; farmer; I Co, 33rd Regt; killed at Wilderness on 6 May 1864;

William Turner   Born 1829; Pvt C Co, 2nd NC State Troops of Col C. C. Tew, Northern , VA; enl 16 May 1861 as 1st Lt; promoted to Captain 14 Mar 1862, then Assistant Quarter Master; surrendered at Appomattox Court House in Apr 1865; Cpt. Faircloth was described as a faithful officer in a most responsible position. He later became Chief Justice of the Supreme Court in North Carolina. W. T. Faircloth, Captain and A.Q.M., Dec 1861, NC Regiments, Vol IV, p. 463;, Cox's Brigade. William Turner is the bottom right photo.

SECOND REGIMENT.

1. William R. Cox, Colonel.
2. Charles C. Tew, Colonel.
3. John P. Cobb, Colonel.
4. George L. Kirby, Surgeon.
5. D. W. Hurtt, Major.
6. W. M. Norman, Captain, Co. A.
7. W. T. Faircloth, Captain and Assistant Q. M.

Hon. William Turner Faircloth

(born January 8, 1829)

Engr by C.H. Campbell, N.Y.

Yours truly
W. T. Faircloth

BRANT & FULLER, PUB

FAIRCLOTH SOLDIERS – CIVIL WAR

Zachariah   Born 1829; Pvt, I Co, 46th Regt, Inf; Sampson farmer; enl 15 Mar   1862   in Clinton; on detached service Mar-Apr 1863; wounded 5 May 1864 in Battle of Wilderness, VA and hospitalized at Richmond,VA; assigned 15 Aug 1864 to light duty in Winder hospital, in Richmond; paroled 20 Apr 1865.

Wilmington, NC Confederate General Hospital #4

www.onhgs.org, p. 94 – locations are where their home was.
#1708 & #1709: A. 32d, GA, Oela_tas, 5 Jan 1863 – 7 Jan 1863, Col. G = 4, H=30, Green Bond, GA, Col. K=2
#1710 D., 8th NCT, Co E., Vul Sclop, 24 May 1863 to 27 May 1863; Blocksville for 30 days.
#1711 D. C. 32nd GA, Gonorrhea; 31 Dec 1862 to 7 Jan 1863, Green Pond, GA
#1712 I., 30 the NCT, lcterus, 29 May 1862, Clinton, NC
#1713 R. 8th NCT, Co E, Feb, Typhy; 24 May 1863 to 30 May; Blocksville;
#1714 S. 36th NC, 2nd Co; Cpt Blocker, diarrhea, acuta, 11 Jul 1862; Cedar Creek.
#1715 S – 8th NC Co E#, Feb Typh 27 May 1863 to 30 May 1863; Blocksville.

==

PART TWO: GENEALOGY RECORDS

The Descendents of William Faircloth, I

Descendants of William Faircloth I

Generation No. 1

1. WILLIAM[1] FAIRCLOTH I was born Abt. 1640 in England, and died Abt. 1710 in VA. William Faircloth, I, came to America as a Headright with Colonel John Carter, Esquire, in circa 1664. John Carter, Councellor of State, was granted 4000 acres being a neck of land on the north side of Rappahanock River in Virginia. The tract ws bounded on the westward side by the Cassatta Woman Creek which runs north and east northeast towards the head of Wiccocomico River, and etc. This tract was originally granted to Captain Samuel Mathews on 1 Aug 1643 but was deserted by him. Upon Petition of Colonel Carter, the land was granted to him by order of the General Court bearing the date 12 Oct 1665 and further due for the transportation of 80 persons among whom was William Faircloth. William Faircloth, I, was born in England in c. 1640. No record has been found of his wife's name or when he married but he settled in the area near the County of Isle of Wight, Virginia. He was apparently the father of several children, among whom were William, II and Thomas. The Rent Rolls of the Land of James City County, VA, show that Thomas Faircloth owned 277 acres of land in 1704. Thomas was born in VA, c. 1670. William, I, died in VA, c. 1710 when he was about 70 years old. Date born 2: Bet. 1640 – 1650

```
/William Faircloth b: BET 1640 AND 1650
 /William Faircloth b: 1670 d: 1728
/William Faircloth b: ABT 1690 d: AFT 1782
/William Faircloth b: ABT 1720 d: 1765
 |    \Mary ?
Hardwick Faircloth b: 1754 d: 1810
 \Sarah ? b: ABT 1730
```

Children of WILLIAM FAIRCLOTH I are:
2.   i.   WILLIAM[2] FAIRCLOTH II, b. Abt. 1663, Southeast VA; d. Abt. 1728,
3.   ii.   THOMAS FAIRCLOTH, b. Abt. 1670.

Generation No. 2

2. WILLIAM[2] FAIRCLOTH II *(WILLIAM[1])* was born Abt. 1663 in Southeast VA, and died Abt. 1728 in Died in Isle of Wight County, VA at age 65.
Wm II patented 175 acres of land in Isle of Wight County, VA on 13 Nov 1713 and settled there with his wife who name has not been determined at this time. Ref: English Duplicates of Lost VA Records by Louis des Cognets, Jr. A list of patents granted for land in this colony by the Honorable Alexander Spotswood, His Majesty's Lieutenant Governor and commander-in chief of this dominion. Ref: VA Wills and Administrations, 1632-1800 by Clayton Torrence Gen. Pub. Co,1965. 1816 Green County Tax Lists: FAIRCLOTH, Wm, 1 white pole; do John, not given in ???, 1 white pole; do Moses, not given in ?????, 1 white pole

Children of WILLIAM FAIRCLOTH II are:
    i.   ELIZABETH[3] FAIRCLOTH, b. Bef. 1728.
    ii.   SARANAH FAIRCLOTH.

4.   iii. WILLIAM FAIRCLOTH III, b. Abt. 1710, Isle of Wight Co, VA; d. Abt. 1791, Died at 81 years old.
     iv. SAMUEL FAIRCLOTH, b. Bef. 1728.
     v.   BENJAMIN FAIRCLOTH, b. Bef. 1728.
     vi. SARAH FAIRCLOTH, b. Bef. 1728; m. JOHN REVELL, 1731, Isle of Wight, VA; D. B. 4, p. 129.
     vii. HANNAH FAIRCLOTH, b. Bef. 1728.
    viii. MOSES FAIRCLOTH, b. Bef. 1728.

3. THOMAS[2] FAIRCLOTH (*WILLIAM[1]*) was born Abt. 1670 in VA. He married UNKNOWN 1790. The rent rolls of the Land of James City County, VA show that a Thomas Faircloth owned 277 acres of land in 1704. 1790 Surry Census, no longer listed in Surry in 1810. 1820 Surry DOES list a Thomas head of household, also listed separately in another Thomas listing on this data sheet.

Children of THOMAS FAIRCLOTH and UNKNOWN are:
     i.   UNKNOWN[3] FAIRCLOTH, b. Bef. 1790.
     ii. UNKNOWN FAIRCLOTH, b. Bef. 1790.
     iii. UNKNOWN FAIRCLOTH, b. Bef. 1790.
     iv. UNKNOWN FAIRCLOTH, b. Bef. 1790.

Generation No. 3

4. WILLIAM[3] FAIRCLOTH III (*WILLIAM[2], WILLIAM[1]*) was born Abt. 1710 in Isle of Wight Co, VA, and died Abt. 1791 in Died at 81 years old. He married (1) MARY ANN JOHNSON. Date born 2: Abt. 1690. Date born 3: Abt. 1700; Died 2: Aft. 1782, Edgecombe Co., NC. Moved to Edgecombe Co, NC about 1745 and patented a tract of land on the Tar River where he lived until 1755. In 1755 he sold his land and moved into Dobbs Co (later named Greene County) where he settled and was still living in 1790. Note in the Will of Robert Vick, Isle of Wight County, VA, Oct 25th 1735, land adjoining William Faircloth is mentioned.
     Hardwick and John Robert are possibly William III's children. They are also listed under William IV and Sara's children. Speculation is that they were actually the children of William III, but went to live with William IV and his wife Sara about 1765 as being under 14 yrs old. Notes that John Robert and Hardwick were William III's children come from my early notes when just beginning my genealogical research. Lt., received 731 acres for 24 months of service

Children of WILLIAM FAIRCLOTH and MARY JOHNSON are:
5.   i.   WILLIAM[4] FAIRCLOTH IV, b. Bet. 1740 - 1749; d. 1765.
6.   ii. SAMUEL FAIRCLOTH, b. Bet. 1750 - 1759.
          Fought in the Dobbs Co. Militia. 1784 – Deed of Samuel, 30 Nov 1784 in Sampson County lists son, Benjamin DEED. Unsure if this is the same Samuel. Listing Benjamin as his son, based upon this deed.
     iii. THOMAS FAIRCLOTH, b. Bet. 1750 - 1759. Fought in Dobbs Co. Militia, Newbern District
     iv. BENJAMIN FAIRCLOTH, b. 1757; d. Aft. 1840, Died in Thomas Cty. Georgia. Rev. War applied for pension compensation for Rev. War Service on 1 Jan 1840 in Emanual Co., GA at age of 83

118

5. WILLIAM⁴ FAIRCLOTH IV *(WILLIAM³, WILLIAM², WILLIAM¹)* was born Bet. 1740 - 1749, and died 1765. He married SARAH. She was born Abt. 1730, and died Abt. 1727. Date born 2: Abt. 1720

Children of WILLIAM FAIRCLOTH and SARAH are:

1). The Edgecombe County, NC Court Records from which the above Faircloth siblings or half-siblings were taken are scattered and some years are missing: the records begin in 1744 but May 1746-Aug. 1757 are missing and July 1776-Aug. 1778 are missing. Be that as it may, April 1746-Aug. 1772 are the ones where the Faircloth siblings are recorded, and there was no mention of their father; in both entries of 9 July 1765 and 11 July 1765, Zacheriah Faircloth (aged 14 yrs.), a baseborn child, was bound to Noah Sugg, and John Faircloth (aged 5yrs.), and Hardy Faircloth (aged 11) also baseborn children, were bound to Benjamin Faircloth, who obviously were close relatives of the children's mother Sarah Faircloth. Also note that the published book written by Marvin K. Dorman, Jr. entitled Edgecombe County, North Carolina Abstracts of Court Minutes 1744-1746, 1757-1794 does not include the full details of the original text and leaves out the word baseborn.

2). See page 111 of "Orphanage In Colonial North Carolina: Edgecombe County As A Case Study" by Alan D. Watson recorded in The North Carolina Historical Review, pp. 105-119, vol. 52, no. 2, April 1975. "The Court further eased the transition to orphanage by apprenticing siblings to the same master where possible. This was particularly true in the case of illegitimate offspring--the Quinn Brothers, Faircloth brothers, Johnson sisters, and Revel sisters--and belied a sympathetic understanding on the part of the justices of the more difficult adjustments to be made by those children.

   i. HARDWICK⁵ FAIRCLOTH, b. 1754, Edgecombe Co., NC or Sampson County, NC; d. Abt. 1810, Sampson County, NC. m. SARAH SUGGS. Name 2: Hardwick "Hardy" Faircloth;

   ii. JOHN ROBERT FAIRCLOTH, b. 1760, Edgecombe, North Carolina, near Autryville?; d. 1819, Sumpter, SC; other accounts say he died at 69 years old and is laid to rest in the family Cemetery in Ala between 1831-1840.; m. (1) CATHERINE HOLTON; b. Abt. 1750; m. (2) UNKNOWN UNKNOWN, Abt. 1780.
Date born 2: 1750, Edgecombe, North Carolina

   iii. ZECHARIAH FAIRCLOTH, b. 1751, Edgecombe Co., NC; d. 1810, Washington, Louisiana; m. MARY ARMSTRONG; b. 1757, Montgomery County, NC.

6. SAMUEL⁴ FAIRCLOTH *(WILLIAM³, WILLIAM², WILLIAM¹)* was born Bet. 1750 - 1759.
   Child of SAMUEL FAIRCLOTH is:
   i.   BENJAMIN⁵ FAIRCLOTH.

Descendants of Hardwick Faircloth

Generation No. 1

1.   HARDWICK⁵ FAIRCLOTH   *(WILLIAM⁴, WILLIAM³, WILLIAM², WILLIAM¹)* was born 1754 in Edgecombe Co., NC or Sampson County, NC, and died Abt. 1810 in Sampson County, NC?. He married SARAH SUGGS by 1785.
Name 2: Hardwick "Hardy" Faircloth
     On 11 Jul 1765, Hardy, age 11 and John, 5 yrs old, sons of Sarah are bound to Benjamin of Edgecombe County, NC.
Father of Hardwick may be Samuel Faircloth, baseborn child of Sara. See description of the situation in William's notes previously.   He was assigned to live with William and Sarah while he was under 14 years old in the Orphans Court. This may also have been because of his father and mother's death?
     1784 Duplin/Sampson Tax lists show Hardy with 300 acres of land.
Private Duplin Militia; Soldier drew 1 RW pay voucher and lived in Sampson in 1790 and had five young males in his household. Soldier was born about 1754 to William and Sarah Faircloth and is also listed in Sampson in 1785 tax list.
     1785 Tax Rolls; FAIRCLOTH, Hardwick (Hardy), Private Duplin Militia   Soldier drew 1 RW pay voucher and lived in Sampson in 1790 and had five young males in his household. Soldier was born about 1754 to William and Sarah Faircloth and is also listed in Sampson in 1785 tax list. Soldier married Sarah Suggs. Issue: 1-Reason, 2-Isham, 3-James, 4-Thomas, 5-Jacob, 6-Benjamin, 7-Elizabeth or Betty, 8-Achsah, 9-Sabar, 10-Hardwick (Hardy) Jr., 11-Nancy, 12-Jonah, 13-Arthur, 14-Wilson, and 15-Jonathan. Soldier's brothers were John and Zechariah Faircloth. Soldier died about 1810.

     1 Jan 1793: In the Sampson County, NC Deed dated 8 April 1811 Achsah Faircloth sold 100 acres in Sampson County to John Johnston, Jr. said parcel being part of a patent granted to Samuel Faircloth on 1 January 1793. Although this deed transaction does not directly state that Achsah Faircloth was Samuel's daughter, it seems obvious to me that she obtained this land as her part upon his death or probably received it as a gift during Samuel's lifetime.
     8 Apr 1811: NC Deed dated 8 April 1811 Achsah Faircloth sold 100 acres in Sampson County to John Johnston, Jr. said parcel being part of a patent granted to Samuel Faircloth on 1 January 1793. Although this deed transaction does not directly state that Achsah Faircloth was Samuel's daughter, it seems obvious to me that she obtained this land as her part upon his death or probably received it as a gift during Samuel's lifetime.
Hardwick (Hardy)
          m. by 1785
          c.   m. b. 1775-1790; under 16 by 1790
                  m b. 1775-1790; under 16 by 1790
                  m b. 1775-1790; under 16 by 1790
                  m b. 1775-1790; under 16 by 1790
                  m b. 1775-1790; under 16 by 1790

Children of HARDWICK FAIRCLOTH and SARAH SUGGS are:

i. REASON[6] FAIRCLOTH, b. 1778
Civil War: Born 1778; Pvt, E Co, 8th Regt; enl Cumberland County
2. ii. ISHAM FAIRCLOTH, b. 1775; possibly Zachariah's son.

Children of ISHAM FAIRCLOTH and MILLY JOHNSTON are:
i. MARY[7] FAIRCLOTH.
ii. UNKNOWN FAIRCLOTH, b. Bet. 1811 - 1820.
iii. UNKNOWN FAIRCLOTH, b. Bet. 1804 - 1810.
iv. UNKNOWN FAIRCLOTH, b. Bet. 1811 - 1820, Either of these females may be Mary.
v. UNKNOWN FAIRCLOTH, b. Bet. 1805 - 1810, Either of these females may be Mary.

3. iii. JAMES FAIRCLOTH, b. 1775; possibly Zachariah's child. Discussion of notes on Zacheriah Faircloth (b. 1751 Edgecombe County, NC and d. 1820 in Sampson County, NC.) and his children.
iv. THOMAS FAIRCLOTH, b. Bet. 1770 – 1780;
v. JACOB FAIRCLOTH, b. Bet. 1770 - 1780.
War of 1812 Muster rolls, 3d Co, detached from Cumberland County Regiment 1812-14; Cumberland County Records. 1820 Cumberland Census: possibly son of Jacob, son of Hardwick? 1850 Sampson Census: JACOB FAIRCLOTH   23   MALE   TIMBER
vi. BENJAMIN FAIRCLOTH, b. Bet. 1770 – 1780;
vii. ELIZABETH "BETTY" FAIRCLOTH, b. Bet. 1770 – 1780; possibly child of Samuel;; m. UNKNOWN ELLIS.
viii. ACHSAH FAIRCLOTH, b. Bet. 1770 - 1780, possible child of Samuel;.
There was a Sampson County, NC deed (vol. 21, p. 257) dated 18 Nov. 1826 whereby Arthur Faircloth sold 150 acres and Wilson Faircloth sold his 50 acres including the interest of their siblings to their brother Raiford Faircloth; the others (siblings) who had interests in these properties were named as follows: Achsah "Axsey" (Faircloth) Butler, Betsey (Faircloth) Ellis, Isaac Sessoms and his wife Nancy (Faircloth), and Sabrey; what is stated above were my notes on the abstract of this deed.
In the Sampson County, NC Deed dated 8 April 1811 Achsah Faircloth sold 100 acres in Sampson County to John Johnston, Jr. said parcel being part of a patent granted to Samuel Faircloth on 1 January 1793. Although this deed transaction does not directly state that Achsah Faircloth was Samuel's daughter, it seems obvious to me that she obtained this land as her part upon his death or probably received it as a gift during Samuel's lifetime?
ix. SABAR FAIRCLOTH, b. Bet. 1770 - 1780, possible child of Samuel;
x. HARDWICK "HARDY" FAIRCLOTH, JR., b. Bet. 1770 - 1780, child;.
Listed in 1830 Sampson Census, Hardy.
xi. NANCY FAIRCLOTH, b. Bet. 1770 - 1780, possible child of Samuel;; m. ISAAC SESSOMS.
There was a Sampson County, NC deed (vol. 21, p. 257) dated 18 Nov. 1826 whereby Arthur Faircloth sold 150 acres and Wilson Faircloth sold his 50 acres including the interest of their siblings to their brother Raiford Faircloth; the others (siblings) who had interests in these properties were named as follows: Achsah "Axsey" (Faircloth) Butler, Betsey (Faircloth) Ellis, Isaac Sessoms and his wife Nancy (Faircloth), and Sabrey Faircloth. I thought I had a copy of the original of this

deed, but I can't put my hands on it right now; what is stated above were my notes on the abstract of this deed. In the Sampson County, NC Deed dated 8 April 1811 Achsah Faircloth sold 100 acres in Sampson County to John Johnston, Jr. said parcel being part of a patent granted to Samuel Faircloth on 1 January 1793. Although this deed transaction does not directly state that Achsah Faircloth was Samuel's daughter, it seems obvious to me that she obtained this land as her part upon his death or probably received it as a gift during Samuel's lifetime.

More about ISAAC SESSOMS: Name 2: Isaac Sessoms, Jr.

    xii.   JONAH FAIRCLOTH, b. Bet. 1770 - 1780, child.

    xiii.   WILSON FAIRCLOTH, b. Bet. 1770 - 1780, possible child of Samuel;; d. Abt. 1864.

            1864: Wilson, Cumberland County Known WILL.

    xiv.   JONATHAN FAIRCLOTH, b. Bet. 1770 - 1780, child.

4.   xv.   ARTHUR FAIRCLOTH, b. 1775, Sampson Co., NC; possible child of Samuel; d. Aft.1840, Bladen Co., NC.

Generation No. 2

2. ISHAM[6] FAIRCLOTH *(HARDWICK[5], WILLIAM[4], WILLIAM[3], WILLIAM[2], WILLIAM[1])* was born 1775, possibly Zachariah's son. He married MILLY JOHNSTON Bet. 1775 - 1794, daughter of JOHN JOHNSTON.

Will of John D. Johnston, (Sr.) dated 31 Aug. 1814 Sampson County, NC. Names wife Elizabeth, and son John Johnston, executors. Subscribing witnesses: Solomon Sessoms, James Faircloth, (Sr.), and Robert Grice. Sampson County, NC Court Minutes: 23 Nov. 1814. Elizabeth Johnston exhibited in this Court this last will and testament of her deceased husband [John Johnston, (Sr.)] which was admitted to probate by oaths of Solomon Sessoms and James Faircloth, (Sr.) two of the subscribing witnesses. The Will of John Johnston, (Sr) named his sons and sons-in-law and two of his Faircloth grandchildren: {the parentheses ( ) and/or brackets [ ] are my additions}. John D. Johnston, (Jr.) [died Nov. 1829 and was married to Spicey (maiden name unknown)], Mark Johnston, Matthew Johnston, Elizabeth Johnston [married a Mr. Faircloth (still unidentified)], Hannah Johnston [married James Faircloth, (Sr.)], Mary Johnston [married a Mr. Hall], and Milly Johnston [married Isham Faircloth-their daughter Mary Faircloth was mentioned in Johnston's Will].

Isham:

    m.   b. 1775-1794

    c.   b. 1811-1820; male under 10 in 1820

           b. 1804-1810. male 10-16 yrs in 1820

           b. 1811-1820; female, under 10 in 1820

           b. 1805-1810; female 10-16 yrs in 1820

War of 1812.: Pvt., 3rd Regt of Moore's, NC; Cpt Caleb Stephen's Co of Infantry; 11 Oct 1814-10 Mar 1815.

1820 Sampson Census

MALES						FEMALES				INFO	District	Page	Family
10	16	18	26	45	45+	10	16	26	45	45+			

Faircloth	Isham											
1	1	0	0	1	0	1	2	1	0	0	Hall's	302

1840 Sampson Census
Listed in Sampson County in 1860.

Children of ISHAM FAIRCLOTH and MILLY JOHNSTON are:
    i. MARY[7] FAIRCLOTH.
    ii. UNKNOWN FAIRCLOTH, b. Bet. 1811 - 1820.
    iii. UNKNOWN FAIRCLOTH, b. Bet. 1804 - 1810.
    iv. UNKNOWN FAIRCLOTH, b. Bet. 1811 - 1820, Either of these females may be Mary.
    v. UNKNOWN FAIRCLOTH, b. Bet. 1805 - 1810, Either of these females may be Mary.

Unverified information on Isham's descendents: (LIVING INDICATES IN 2004)

1 Isham FAIRCLOTH b: 1775
  2 Jonathan FAIRCLOTH b: 1820
   + Sarah Caroline (Mrs Jonathan) (FAIRCLOTH) b: 1828
    3 William L FAIRCLOTH b: 1851
     + Catharine (Mrs William) (FAIRCLOTH) b: 1856
      4 M---ie Lee? FAIRCLOTH b: 1878
      4 Stella A FAIRCLOTH b: 1879
    3 Franklin FAIRCLOTH b: 1852
    4 Solomon Jonathan FAIRCLOTH b: 1853 d: Aft 30 Apr 1930
     + Roena Dallis SPELL b: 1870 d: Aft 30 Apr 1930
      4 Charles Shepard FAIRCLOTH b: 8 Nov 1889 d: Abt 1961
       + Katie Jewell "Big Sis" OATES b: 11 Jan 1889 d: 11 Apr 1977
        5 Jewel "Baby Jewel" FAIRCLOTH b: Abt 1917 d: Abt 1919
        5 Charles Shepard FAIRCLOTH b: 10 Feb 1919 d: 29 Aug 1996
         + (Mrs. C S, Jr) (FAIRCLOTH)
         + Alberta (Mrs CS Jr) (FAIRCLOTH)
          6 Living FAIRCLOTH
           + Living (FAIRCLOTH)
          6 Living FAIRCLOTH
        5 Sylvia Jane FAIRCLOTH b: 25 May 1923 d: Living
         + Charles EDDINGS b: c 1920 d: Living
          6 Ronald Charles EDDINGS b: Abt 1954 d: Living
        5 Samuel Judson "Sam" FAIRCLOTH b: 25 May 1923 d: Living
        5 Jean FAIRCLOTH b: 25 Feb 1926 d: Living
         + Edward J HODGES b: 29 Aug 1927 d: 5 Jun 1980
          6 Cynthia Jewel "Cindy" HODGES b: Abt 1956 d: Abt 1982
        5 Jack FAIRCLOTH b: 25 Feb 1926 d: Living
         + Living (FAIRCLOTH)
          6 Living FAIRCLOTH
         + Birdye Hope BORLAND b: 11 Sep 1925 d: 24 Nov 1999
          6 Cheryl "Chery" FAIRCLOTH b: 23 Nov 1948 d: Living
           + Gary William BUSBY b: 5 Oct 1947 d: Living
           + Gregory Lawrence "Greg" LABBE b: 3 May 1948 d: Living
          6 Jane Ellen FAIRCLOTH b: 5 Dec 1950 d: Living
           + Tony A PAYSON b: 20 Jun 1952 d: Living
          6 Charles Shepard FAIRCLOTH b: 18 Dec 1951 d: Living
          6 Ann Oates FAIRCLOTH b: 30 Dec 1955 d: Living
           + Living BENTON

+ Living RAVARY
      6 Julie Kate FAIRCLOTH b: 9 May 1957 d: Living
      + Dennis Paul MUSSETT b: 26 May 1948 d: Living
      6 John Murray FAIRCLOTH b: 19 Sep 1959 d: Living
      + Living BOWEN
      6 Lynette FAIRCLOTH b: 12 Nov 1961 d: Living
      + Living SCHWAB
      + Living
      + Living MARTELL
      6 Jacqueline Hope "Jacque" FAIRCLOTH b: 12 May 1964 d: Living
      + Living SECCO
      + Living
      6 William Lamar FAIRCLOTH b: 19 Feb 1966 d: Living
      + Tina Rochelle NELSON d: Living
    4 Bessie Leroy FAIRCLOTH d: Bef 1926
    + Walter Teachy NORRIS b: Abt 1880
     5 Walter Teachy NORRIS b: 27 Jul 1913 d: 31 May 1986
    4 Ira Vaughn FAIRCLOTH b: 1892
    4 Edgar Byron FAIRCLOTH b: 27 Nov 1895 d: 23 Aug 1961
    + Ida Lorena AUTRY b: 19 Sep 1902 d: 11 Feb 1986
     5 Ossie Virginia FAIRCLOTH
     + (h McLAMB o Ossie V Faircloth)
     5 Harold Gibson FAIRCLOTH b: 25 Feb 1926 d: 9 Sep 1982
     + Living SPELL
      6 Living FAIRCLOTH
      6 Living FAIRCLOTH
     5 Wayne McNeil FAIRCLOTH b: 7 Nov 1927 d: 20 Sep 1982
      6 Living FAIRCLOTH
     5 Living FAIRCLOTH
     5 Living FAIRCLOTH
     + Lester Waylon AUTRY
      6 Living AUTRY
      + Living BELLANDE
     5 Sylvia Joan FAIRCLOTH b: 13 Mar 1935 d: 18 Jun 1997
     + Living MOLETTIERE
   3 Shepard FAIRCLOTH b: 1855
   3 Sarah M FAIRCLOTH b: 1857
   3 Love D FAIRCLOTH b: 1861
   3 Jasper FAIRCLOTH b: 1863

3. JAMES[6] FAIRCLOTH (*HARDWICK*[5], *WILLIAM*[4], *WILLIAM*[3], *WILLIAM*[2], *WILLIAM*[1]) was born 1775. Possibly Zachariah's child.

    Discussion of notes on Zacheriah Faircloth (b. 1751 Edgecombe County, NC and d. 1820 in Sampson County, NC.) and his children. Sampson County, NC Court Minutes: 23 Aug. 1820: Administration on the estate of Zacheriah Faircloth, dec'd, granted James Faircloth and entered into bond in the sum of $100 with Mark Johnston and Matthew Johnston his security. [This James Faircloth would be James Faircloth, (Sr.)] 21 Nov. 1820: James Faircloth, Administrator, returned the amount of the account of the sales of the estate of Zacheriah Faircloth, dec'd, which was filed.

Will of John D. Johnston, (Sr.) dated 31 Aug. 1814 Sampson County, NC. Names wife Elizabeth, and son John Johnston, executors. Subscribing witnesses: Solomon Sessoms, James Faircloth, (Sr.), and Robert Grice.

Sampson County, NC Court Minutes: 23 Nov. 1814. Elizabeth Johnston exhibited in this Court this last will and testament of her deceased husband [John Johnston, (Sr.)] which was admitted to probate by oaths of Solomon Sessoms and James Faircloth, (Sr.) two of the subscribing witnesses.

The Will of John Johnston, (Sr) named his sons and sons-in-law and two of his Faircloth grandchildren: {the parentheses ( ) and/or brackets [ ] are my additions}.

John D. Johnston, (Jr.) [died Nov. 1829 and was married to Spicey (maiden name unknown)], Mark Johnston, Matthew Johnston, Elizabeth Johnston [married a Mr. Faircloth (still unidentified)], Hannah Johnston [married James Faircloth, (Sr.)], Mary Johnston [married a Mr. Hall], and Milly Johnston [married Isham Faircloth-their daughter Mary Faircloth was mentioned in Johnston's Will].

Possible James
 b. 1775-1794
 c.   male, b. 1810-1820
         female, b. 1810-1820
                  1790 Anson County Census, alone
                  1800 Anson Census

 James
 b.   1775
 m   b. 1775-1794
 c.   b. 1811-1820; male under 10 in 1820
      b. 1811-1820, female under 10 in 1820
1820 Sampson Census:
MALES   FEMALES INFO   District   Page Family
10 16 18 26 45 45+   10 16 26 45 45+

Faircloth   James
1   0 0 0 1 0   1 0 1 0 0   Hall's   302

Children of JAMES FAIRCLOTH are:
         i. UNKNOWN[7] FAIRCLOTH, b. Bet. 1810 - 1820.
        ii. UNKNOWN FAIRCLOTH, b. Bet. 1810 - 1820.

4. ARTHUR[6] FAIRCLOTH *(HARDWICK[5], WILLIAM[4], WILLIAM[3], WILLIAM[2], WILLIAM[1])* was born 1775 in Sampson Co., NC; possible child of Samuel;, and died Aft. 1840 in Bladen Co., NC. He married (1) MARY ANN MCDANIEL "DICEY ANN", daughter of ARCHIBALD MCDANIEL and MARY. She was born Bet. 1880 - 1890. He married (3) MARY ANN MCDANIEL Abt. 1818.

Children of ARTHUR FAIRCLOTH and MARY ANN" are:
5.   i. BENJAMIN[7] FAIRCLOTH, b. Abt. 1809, Bladen Co., NC; d. Aft. 1880.
6.   ii. SOLOMON FAIRCLOTH, b. 1811; d. Bladen County, NC.
7.   iii. THEOPHELES "AFFIE" FAIRCLOTH, b. 1812.
       iv. UNKNOWN FAIRCLOTH, b. Bef. 1810.
        v. UNKNOWN FAIRCLOTH, b. Aft. 1810.
       vi. UNKNOWN FAIRCLOTH, b. Aft. 1810.

125

5. BENJAMIN⁷ FAIRCLOTH *(ARTHUR⁶, HARDWICK⁵, WILLIAM⁴, WILLIAM³, WILLIAM², WILLIAM¹)* was born Abt. 1809 in Bladen Co., NC, and died Aft. 1880. He married (1) FRANCES BEDSOLE Abt. 1827, daughter of THOMAS BEDSOLE and REBECCA JONES. She was born Abt. 1802 in Bladen Co., NC, and died Abt. 1861. He married (2) HARRIET B. NEW Abt. 1862.

Children of BENJAMIN FAIRCLOTH and FRANCES BEDSOLE are:
8.　i.　DUNCAN⁸ FAIRCLOTH, b. 17 May 1846, Beaver Dam Twp., Bladen Co., NC; d. 13 Sep 1928, Hoke Co., NC.
　　ii.　SARAH FAIRCLOTH, b. Abt. 1828.
　　iii.　SUSAN FAIRCLOTH, b. Abt. 1830.
　　iv.　SOLOMON FAIRCLOTH, b. Abt. 1836.
　　　　Namesake: Named after Uncle Solomon Faircloth.
　　v.　THOMAS FAIRCLOTH b. Ab. 1838.
　　　　Namesake: Named after Uncle Thomas Bedsole
9.　vi.　NANCY FAIRCLOTH, b. Abt. 1843.
　　vii.　CHARLOTTE E. FAIRCLOTH, b. Abt. 1850.
　　viii.　POLLY FAIRCLOTH, b. Abt. 1835.
　　ix.　JOHN JAMES HENRY FAIRCLOTH.
　　x.　GEORGE B. FAIRCLOTH.
　　xi.　CORA FAIRCLOTH.
　　xii.　EDNA L FAIRCLOTH.
　　xiii.　MARIE M. FAIRCLOTH.

6. SOLOMON⁷ FAIRCLOTH *(ARTHUR⁶, HARDWICK⁵, WILLIAM⁴, WILLIAM³, WILLIAM², WILLIAM¹)* was born 1811, and died in Bladen County, NC. He married EDNA "EDNEY" ANN FORT Abt. 1838 in Bladen County, NC, daughter of JOHN FORT and JULIA UNKNOWN. She was born Bet. 1801 - 1802, and died 14 Jul 1873 in Bladen County, NC. Between 26 Feb and 11 Jul he was with Co. F, 2nd Artillery of the 36th Regmt as a Private with the NC Troops. Military service: 1862, Enlisted in Confederate army at age 51.

Children of SOLOMON FAIRCLOTH and EDNA FORT are:
　i.　MATILDA J.⁸ FAIRCLOTH, b. 02 Nov 1839, Bladen County, NC; d. 11 Oct 1894; m. STEVEN N. MELVIN, 07 Oct 1874, Home of Solomon and Edney Faircloth; b. 1843; d. 09 Oct 1907.
　ii.　THOMAS H. FAIRCLOTH, b. 03 Jun 1840, Bladen County, NC; d. 14 Mar 1865, Elmira, NY; buried 14 Mar grave #2430.
　　Notes for THOMAS H. FAIRCLOTH:
　　20 Feb 1862 - 15 Jan 1865 he was a Private, Co F, 2nd Artillery, 36th Regmt. enlisted in Confederate Army on 20 Jan 1862.at age 21 at Terebinth. On 15 Jan 1865 was captured at Fort Fisher at the Fall of Ft. Fisher, NC.
　iii.　JOHN L. FAIRCLOTH, b. 27 Nov 1842, Bladen County, NC; d. 15 Jan 1863, Succombed to smallpox and pleurapneumonia in the Hospital in Richmond, VA.
　iv.　HENRY C. FAIRCLOTH, b. 03 Apr 1844, Bladen County, NC; d. 10 Dec, ; He was in the 1870 Census but not in the 1880..

7. THEOPHELES "AFFIE"^{7} FAIRCLOTH (*ARTHUR^6, HARDWICK^5, WILLIAM^4, WILLIAM^3, WILLIAM^2, WILLIAM^1*) was born 1812. He married REBECCA CASHWELL, daughter of THOMAS CASHWELL.
Census: 1870, T. shown as living in Little Coharie Twp. Sampson Co., age 57.

Children of THEOPHELES FAIRCLOTH and REBECCA CASHWELL are:
      i. GERUSHA A.^{8} FAIRCLOTH, b. 1839.
          More About GERUSHA A. FAIRCLOTH:
          1870 Census: Jerutha was 29 years old at this time.
      ii. THOMAS G. FAIRCLOTH, b. 1841; d. 07 Jul 1862, Ft. Fisher, Brunswick County, NC, during the Civil War.
      iii. LUCY JANE FAIRCLOTH, b. Mar 1850.
          More About LUCY JANE FAIRCLOTH:
          1870 Census: Lucy J. was 19 years old on this Census
      iv. DAVID C. FAIRCLOTH, b. 1852.
          More About DAVID C. FAIRCLOTH:
          1870 Census: D. was 17 years old on this Census
      v. MILLARD FAIRCLOTH, b. Bet. 1861 - 1862.
10.   vi. BENJAMIN F. FAIRCLOTH, b. 1854, Roseboro at Rt. 2, Sampson County, NC; d. Buried at the home of Ralph Faircloth (531-3859).
      vii. SARAH S. FAIRCLOTH, b. 1845.
11.   viii. REBECCA C. FAIRCLOTH, b. 1857.

Generation No. 4

8. DUNCAN^8 FAIRCLOTH (*BENJAMIN^7, ARTHUR^6, HARDWICK^5, WILLIAM^4, WILLIAM^3, WILLIAM^2, WILLIAM^1*) was born 17 May 1846 in Beaver Dam Twp., Bladen Co., NC, and died 13 Sep 1928 in Hoke Co., NC. He married NANCY HALL Abt. 1866, daughter of JAMES HALL and JEANETTE (HAIR?). She was born 01 Mar 1839 in Bladen Co., NC, and died 11 Aug 1901 in Hoke Co., NC.
Burial: 1928, Ephesus Bapt. Ch. Cemetery, Hoke Co., NC. Military service: 01 Jun 1864, Enlisted in Confederate army at age 18. Served in C Co. 7th NC Reserve and 1 Co. 72nd Rgt. NC St. Troops. Applied for Conf. Vet. Pension from State of NC, June 14, 1909. Namesake: Named after Uncle Duncan Bedsole
    Nancy Hall was buried in 1901, Ephesus Bapt. Ch. Cemetery, Hoke Co., NC
Residence: The 1860 census indicates Nancy lived on an adjacent farm.

Children of DUNCAN FAIRCLOTH and NANCY HALL are:
      i. WILLIAM MARSHAL^9 FAIRCLOTH, b. 21 Jul 1869, NC; d. 16 Nov 1926, Moore Co., NC; m. MARY NEIL JACKSON, Abt. 1898; b. 19 May 1882, Robeson Co., NC; d. 08 Sep 1934, Moore Co., NC.
          William: Burial: 1926, Beulah Hill Ch. Cemetery, Moore Co., NC
          Mary: Burial: 1936, Beulah Hill Ch. Cemetery, Moore Co., NC
      ii. JAMES MAURICE FAIRCLOTH, b. 23 Aug 1867; d. 08 May 1931; m. (1) LESSIE JANE KOONCE; b. 16 Sep 1868; d. 13 Dec 1897; m. (2) BESSIE OPHELIA ADCOX, Abt. 1898; b. 12 Jun 1879; d. 09 Nov 1951. Burial: 1931, Ephesus Bapt. Ch. Cemetery, Hoke Co., NC
          Lessie: Burial: 1897, Ephesus Bapt. Ch. Cemetery, Hoke Co., NC
          Bessie: Burial: 1951, Ephesus Bapt. Ch. Cemetery, Hoke Co., NC

iii. STEPHEN SHERMAN FAIRCLOTH, b. 19 Mar 1872, (Grave marker shows 3-19-1870.); d. 12 Dec 1941; m. SARAH (UNK); b. May 1876.
Stephen: Burial: 1941, Ephesus Bapt. Ch. Cemetery, Hoke Co., NC
Census: 1880 - Shows Sherman as "Stephen S." and his age as 8. 1900 - shows birth date as Mar. 1872.
iv. KITTY L. FAIRCLOTH, b. Abt. 1866.
v. JEANETTE FAIRCLOTH, b. Abt. 1874.
vi. ELIZABETH FAIRCLOTH, b. Abt. 1877.
vii. GEORGE L. FAIRCLOTH, b. Abt. 1880.
viii. JOE FAIRCLOTH, b. Feb 1883; m. DELLA; b. Abt. 1890.
ix. ARCHIE FAIRCLOTH, b. Jan 1889; m. PHOEBE; b. Abt. 1887.

9. NANCY[8] FAIRCLOTH *(BENJAMIN[7], ARTHUR[6], HARDWICK[5], WILLIAM[4], WILLIAM[3], WILLIAM[2], WILLIAM[1])* was born Abt. 1843. She married REDDIN WILLIAMS.

Child of NANCY FAIRCLOTH and REDDIN WILLIAMS is:
i. LUCY R.[9] WILLIAMS, b. 17 Apr 1867; d. 19 Jul 1902; m. GEORGE W. FAIRCLOTH; b. 10 Sep 1867; d. 14 Jul 1907.

10. BENJAMIN F.[8] FAIRCLOTH *(THEOPHELES "AFFIE"[7], ARTHUR[6], HARDWICK[5], WILLIAM[4], WILLIAM[3], WILLIAM[2], WILLIAM[1])* was born 1854 in Roseboro at Rt. 2, Sampson County, NC, and died in Buried at the home of Ralph Faircloth (531-3859). He married ADLINE CATHERINE AUTRY, daughter of YOUNG AUTRY and NANCY. She was born 1865 in Cumberland County, NC, and died 23 Apr 1936 in Buried in the Faircloth Cemetery in Roseboro, NC; died from strangulation hernias.

Children of BENJAMIN FAIRCLOTH and ADLINE AUTRY are:
i. LAWRENCE C.[9] FAIRCLOTH, b. 13 Mar 1886, Sampson Co., NC; d. 20
Oct 1952, Fayetteville, NC;
Lawrence C. and Lula J. Faircloth descendents are listed in the section on the descendents of Edward Faircloth, under Lula Faircloth.
ii. ALLEN CLAY FAIRCLOTH, b. Bet. 28 Jul 1887 - 1888; d. 05 Jul 1944, m. (1) MISSOURI "ZUDE"; b. Abt. 1890; m. (2) MISSOURI "ZUDE" HALL, 02 Oct 1908
iii. ELLEN FAIRCLOTH, b. 1891; m. ALFRED OR ASHFORD "TATE" HALL, 03 Jan 1909, Sampson Co., NC
iv. JERE TATE FAIRCLOTH, b. 1894; d. Aug 1953, New Hanover County, NC; m. MURLENE WATKINS.
v. NITA FAIRCLOTH, b. Bet. 1898 - 1899, Sampson Co., NC; d. 18 Apr 1936,

11. REBECCA C.[8] FAIRCLOTH *(THEOPHELES "AFFIE"[7], ARTHUR[6], HARDWICK[5], WILLIAM[4], WILLIAM[3], WILLIAM[2], WILLIAM[1])* was born 1857. She married JOHN STALLINGS. He was born 1853 in Austria.

Children of REBECCA FAIRCLOTH and JOHN STALLINGS are:
i. GEORGE[9] STALLINGS, b. 1874, NC.
ii. SUSANNA STALLINGS, b. 1877.

Descendants of John Robert Faircloth

Generation No. 1

1. JOHN ROBERT[5] FAIRCLOTH *(WILLIAM[4], WILLIAM[3], WILLIAM[2], WILLIAM[1])* was born 1760 in Edgecombe, North Carolina, near Autryville?, and died 1819 in Sumpter, SC; other accounts say he died at 69 years old and is laid to rest in the family Cemetery in Ala between 1831-1840.. He married (1) CATHERINE HOLTON. She was born Abt. 1750. He married (2) UNKNOWN UNKNOWN Abt. 1780.

See the notes under William for complete discussion on possible father of John Robert....possibly baseborn child of Sara who went to live with William and Sara. Father of John may be Samuel Faircloth, baseborn child of Sara. Assigned to live with William and Sarah while he was under 14 years old in the Orphans Court. Hardwick and John Robert are possibly William III's children. They are also listed under William IV and Sara's children. Speculation is that they were actually the children of William III, but went to live with William IV and his wife Sara about 1765 as being under 14 yrs old. Notes that John Robert and Hardwick were William III's children come from my early notes when just beginning my genealogical research on 11 Jul 1765, Hardy, age 11 and John, 5 yrs old, sons of Sarah are bound to Benjamin of Edgecome County, NC

John Robert came with his father into Dobbs County, NC but left home early in life and went down in Brunswick County, NC where he was living when he enlisted (1778) in the Wilmington District Militia during the American Revolution. He served in the Militia until about 1782 or later. While in the war, he found an area of desirable land in North Duplin County, NC (which later became Sampson County), situated on Little Coharie River, somewhere east of where Autryville now stands. John received a grant for 300 acres in 1782 and later acquired other lands. In 1784, about the time of the new county of Sampson being formed, John and his brothers Thomas, Samuel, Hardy and William set out up the Cape Fear River, thence the South River until they reached about where Autryville, NC now stands. here they all went forth located John's land, except for Thomas, who continued on northwestward finally settling in Tennessee. Samuel, Hardy, and William IV, all entered claims for grants on Great Swamp, a few miles west of John's tract. These grants were made in 1784, and soon after John, Hardy, and Samuel settled on their lands. However, William IV decided to return to Dobbs County where he remained the balance of his life.

17 Mar 1819: Will of John, South Hampton , VA released a slave, named Potor, mullato boy, possible son named Peter?? Did this John Go back to his home state of VA in his older years or is this another John?

1819: John will, 9 Mar 1819, names mother Sally Faircloth Everitte, Southampton, VA..or is the death date a coincidence and there was another John in VA who died at the same time? 1819: John will, 9 Mar 1819, names mother Sally Faircloth Everitte, Southampton, VA (note that Sally Everitte married Newsom Faircloth???) Would this mean John was the son of Newsom and just living with William and Sarah later in life? or adopted/cared for by William and Sarah? John b. abt. 1750

      c.   three males and three females

Parents were William and Sarah Faircloth and is also listed in Sampson in 1785 tax list. Sampson in 1790

b. abt. 1760 in Edgecombe Co.
d. about 1820 Sumter Co, SC

Family Data: John Faircloth, Sr., b 1760 in Edgecombe County, NC; d. c 1822 Sumpter, SC
John was one of three known baseborn children born to Sarah Faircloth, a single, unmarried
woman, living in Edgecombe County, NC in the 1750's-1760's. John's other known siblings or
perhaps half-siblings were Zacheriah (b. 1751 Edgecombe Co., and Hardwick "Hardy", born
1754 when Sampson County was formed from part of Duplin County. The Sampson County
Deed Records show that Zacheriah Faircloth witnessed a deed on 2 Jul 1771 between Jacocb
Surginor and Benjamin Faircloth; likewise, Hardy witnessed a deed on Jan 1777 between
Zacheriah and Solomon Sessoms; Hardy also bought land from the State of NC on 10 Nov 1784.
Hardy didn't live long enough to become a significant part of the Sampson and Cumberland
County Records. He died between 1810and 1820, and apparently had six sons and two
daughters according to census records who were all born before 1800.

John and his family left the Sampson-Cumberland area between 1817and 1818 and moved to
Sumter County, SC. The only evidence found of their presence in Sumter County were the
following records;   1820 Federal Census and Witness to a deed between Noah Faircloth and
John Faircloth with w. H. Capers witnessed a deed of sale between David Peebles and Jane Mc
Cants dated 7 Dec 1818, AND 3. Court Litigation: The Sumter County Court of Please and
Quarter Sessions record litigation between the merchants Welsh and Dwyer and John Faircloth.
John had given these merchants a promissory note for payment of $104.88 due a few days
following the note date of 5 May 1819; apparently John couldn't pay, and Welsh and Dwyer filed
on him to collect their money. No further information has been found as to whether he was
jailed or the matter resolved.

Rayford and Noah Faircloth had moved again into Henry County in southeast Alabama by
1824, the same year that John Faircloth, Jrs' daughter, Mary, married David Harper.

FAIRCLOTH, John, Private Duplin Militia
Soldier drew 6 RW pay vouchers and lived in Sampson in 1790 and had three young sons and
three young females and wife in his household. Soldier was born about 1750 to William and
Sarah Faircloth and is also listed in 1785 state tax list for Sampson. Fought in the Wilmington
District Militia; Was a Sergeant in the 10th Regiment, Colonel Abraham Shepard, Co of Bradley;
enlistment and commission on 20 May 1778; Withdrew soon after. He was a Private in the 10th
Regiment, Col Abraham Shepard Co of Sharp; enlistment and commission on 10 Nov 1778;
served through Aug 1779.

The Power of Attorney Paper from John Faircloth, Jr. to his attorney, Joseph Gardner
indicated that John had returned to Cumberland County, NC by 11 Nov 1819, the date of this
paper signed by John's "mark" at Fayetteville, Cumberland County, NC. This document reads
"Know all men by these presents that I , John Faircloth, of Sumter district in the State of south
Carolina do hereby constitute and appoint Joseph Gardner of the county of Cumberland and State
of North Carolina, my lawful attorney for me in the name to receive all and every part of my
portion in the division of the estate of Nathaniel Holton which has reverted to me by the death of
his widow Jane Holton and give his receipts and dischargers for me in my name as well as i were
present--Given under my hand and seal at Fayetteville this 11day of November, 1819".

Children of JOHN FAIRCLOTH and CATHERINE HOLTON are:
2.
        i.   JOHN ROBERT[6] FAIRCLOTH II, b. Bet. 1778 - 1781, Sampson-Cumberland
            County area of NC; d. Abt. 1838, Henry County, ALA.

130

3. ii. NOAH FAIRCLOTH, b. 1788, Sampson Co., NC; d. Bet. 1851 - 1860, Jackson County, FLA.
    iii. JAMES FAIRCLOTH, b. 1792, Sampson Co., NC; m. NANCY ROYAL. There is a known WILL 1877: James, Cumberland County but unsure if this is the correct James for this will.
    iv. UNKNOWN FAIRCLOTH.
    v. UNKNOWN FAIRCLOTH.
    vi. UNKNOWN FAIRCLOTH.
    vii. EVAN FAIRCLOTH.
4. viii. RAIFORD FAIRCLOTH, b. 1795, Sampson Co., NC; d. Bet. 1860 - 1870, Alabama. War of 1812: 4th Regt of Cumberland Co, NC; Maj Cameron's Command; detached from 4th and 14th Brigade; six months of service from 24 July 1813 ; Cpt Thomas Boykin's Company, Deepwater point on 26 Sept 1813; Cpt David L. Evan's Company of Artillery 30 Nov – 31 Dec 1813 at Deepwater; deserted; Cpt Boykin's Company from July 1813-19Jan 1814, deserted. Cpt Evans Company 19 Jan 1814, deserted; Rayford remained in southeast Alabama and was living in Barbour County by 1830;

    Children of RAIFORD FAIRCLOTH and RUTH ANN are:
    i.   RAIFORD FAIRCLOTH[7] JR, b. 1825.
    ii. JANE M. RAIFORD, b. 1815.
    iii. MARY M. RAIFORD, b. 1822.

War of 1812: Pvt, 3rd Regt of Moore's Sampson County, NC; six months service from 11 Oct 1814; Cpt Caleg Stephens Co of Infantry, 3rd Regt, NC militia; stated at Greenfield, near Wilmington through 15 Feb 1815;
Child of JOHN FAIRCLOTH and UNKNOWN is:
    ix. JOHN ROBERT[6] FAIRCLOTH, JR., b. 1781.

Generation No. 2

2. JOHN ROBERT[6] FAIRCLOTH II (*JOHN ROBERT[5], WILLIAM[4], WILLIAM[3], WILLIAM[2], WILLIAM[1]*) was born Bet. 1778 - 1781 in Sampson-Cumberland County area of NC, and died Abt. 1838 in Henry County, ALA. He married CATHERINE HAIR 14 Mar 1805 in Cumberland County, NC.
 Served in the War of 1812 beginning in 29 Jul 1813 for five months and 20 days. He served in the 3rd Regiment of Cumberland County Militia, Capt Redding Shipp's Company of Drafted Militia (stationed at Beaufort, NC, under Maj. Cameron's Command. for his term of service he was paid a total of $45.16 ($8.00 per month) plus four days allowance to travel back home.

Children of JOHN FAIRCLOTH and CATHERINE HAIR are:
    i.   MARY[7] FAIRCLOTH, b. Abt. 1804; m. DAVID HARPER, 02 Sep 1824, Henry Co., ALA.
    ii. JOHN ALLEN FAIRCLOTH, b. 10 Apr 1815; d. 04 Oct 1899, LA; m. PRANDY COTTLE.
         Civil War Vet.; once for the Blue and once for the Gray!!
    iii. MARGARET FAIRCLOTH, b. Abt. 1812; m. JAMES MORGAN, 25 Aug 1825, Henry Co., ALA.
    iv. JACOB FAIRCLOTH.

v. PATIENCE FAIRCLOTH, b. Abt. 1802; m. DAVID B. STANLEY, 27 Feb 1825, Henry Co., ALA.

5.   vi. THOMAS DIDYMUS FAIRCLOTH, b. 1808, Cumberland County, NC; d. 1880, Polk Co., Texas.

3. NOAH[6] FAIRCLOTH *(JOHN ROBERT[5], WILLIAM[4], WILLIAM[3], WILLIAM[2], WILLIAM[1])* was born 1788 in Sampson Co., NC, and died Bet. 1851 - 1860 in Jackson County, FLA. He married JANE. She was born Bet. 1794 - 1796 in North Carolina, and died Bet. 187 - 1880 in Grant Parish, LA. War of 1812: Maj Cameron's Command, 5th Co of Cumberland County, NC; Corporal; served for six months including 24 Jul 1813; drafted militia stationed at Deepwater Point; present 26 Sept 1813; detached all married men including him on 19 Oct 1813; present July 1813 through 19 Jan 1814; expiration date of pay was 19 Oct 1813. Noah born 1788 or his possible son, Noah, if there was one: Civil War: 5th Co, NC Cumberland Co, Maj. Cameron's Command. Noah moved south from Henry County in to Jackson County, FLA about 1844-45. Noah's descendants made their final move c 1858 to Winn Parish , then Grant Parish, Louisiana.

Child of NOAH FAIRCLOTH and JANE is:
    i. JAMES[7] FAIRCLOTH, b. 1829.

4. RAIFORD[6] FAIRCLOTH *(JOHN ROBERT[5], WILLIAM[4], WILLIAM[3], WILLIAM[2], WILLIAM[1])* was born 1795 in Sampson Co., NC, and died Bet. 1860 - 1870 in Alabama. He married RUTH ANN. She was born Abt. 1795.

Children of RAIFORD FAIRCLOTH and RUTH ANN are:
    i. RAIFORD. FAIRCLOTH[7] JR, b. 1825.
    ii. JANE M. RAIFORD, b. 1815.
    iii. MARY M. RAIFORD, b. 1822.

Generation No. 3

5. THOMAS DIDYMUS[7] FAIRCLOTH *(JOHN ROBERT[6], JOHN ROBERT[5], WILLIAM[4], WILLIAM[3], WILLIAM[2], WILLIAM[1])* was born 1808 in Cumberland County, NC, and died 1880 in Polk Co., Texas. He married ELIZABETH REGISTER 26 Jan 1836. She was born 1820 in Georgia, and died Bet. 1860 - 1870 in Polk Co., Texas. He left Cumberland in 1899 for Texas from Alabama. He left Ala in 1899 for Texas. He moved to TX in late 1854 and purchased his first 320 acres of land on 6 Jan 1855. He had ten known children.

Children of THOMAS FAIRCLOTH and ELIZABETH REGISTER are:
6.   i. WILLIAM HENRY HARRISON[8] FAIRCLOTH, b. 10 May 1841, Henry County, Alabama; d. 25 Jan 1923, Erath Co., TX; Buried at Autman Cemetery, Erath Co., TX.
    ii. CHARITY JANE FAIRCLOTH, b. 14 Apr 1837, Henry County, ALA; d. Aug 1868, Polk Co., Texas; m. WILLIAM F. VARNER, 17 Jan 1861, Polk County, TX.
    iii. WINNAFREID EUFRACY FAIRCLOTH, b. 25 Jan 1840, Henry County, ALA; d. Aft. 1860.
    iv. JOHN FAIRCLOTH, b. 04 Oct 1842, Henry County, ALA; d. Died young..
    v. MARY ELIZABETH FAIRCLOTH, b. 28 Mar 1844, Henry County, ALA; d. Bet. 1880 - 1885, Stephens Co., TX; m. MEREDITY "MERDIA OR MERRITY" LOPER, 20 Jan 1867, Polk County, TX.

vi. LOUISA C. FAIRCLOTH, b. 21 Jan 1847, Henry County, ALA; d. 19 Dec 1919, Eastland Co., TX; m. C. P. PULLEN, 16 Aug 1876, Polk County, TX.

7. vii. JAMES KNOX POLK FAIRCLOTH, b. 23 Oct 1849, Henry County, ALA; d. 23 Mar 1921, Polk Co., Texas.

viii. INDIANA CAROLINE FAIRCLOTH, b. 23 Dec 1852, Henry County, ALA; d. 04 Jul 1923, Polk Co., Texas; m. WILLIAM JOHN KEEN, 27 Jul 1871, Henry Co., ALA.

ix. PRANDY COTTLE FAIRCLOTH, b. 23 Jan 1856, Polk Co., Texas; d. 06 Apr 1896, Eastland Co., TX; m. THOMAS JEFFERSON HILTON, 09 Jan 1879, Polk County, TX.

x. ARRELIA LAFATEE FAIRCLOTH, b. 16 Nov 1858, Polk Co., Texas; d. 20 Mar 1893, Robertson Co., TX; m. (1) RICHARD HENRY TEMPLETON, 21 Dec 1876, Polk County, TX; m. (2) GEORGE S. CASTELOW, 25 Sep 1892, Robertson Co., TX.

Generation No. 4

6. WILLIAM HENRY HARRISON[8] FAIRCLOTH (*THOMAS DIDYMUS[7], JOHN ROBERT[6], JOHN ROBERT[5], WILLIAM[4], WILLIAM[3], WILLIAM[2], WILLIAM[1]*) was born 10 May 1841 in Henry County, Alabama, and died 25 Jan 1923 in Erath Co., TX; Buried at Autman Cemetery, Erath Co., TX. He married MARY S. MCCROREY 25 Feb 1866 in Polk County, TX.

Child of WILLIAM FAIRCLOTH and MARY MCCROREY is:
    i. CHARLIE EDGAR[9] FAIRCLOTH, b. 1876, Polk Co., Texas.
       Child of Charlie: June Edgar Faircloth, b. 1906 in Polk County, TX
       Child of June Edgar: Robert June Faircloth, b. 1942 in Mc Lom Co., TX
       Child of Robert June: Matt L. Faircloth, b. 1972 in Harris Co., TX

7. JAMES KNOX POLK[8] FAIRCLOTH (*THOMAS DIDYMUS[7], JOHN ROBERT[6], JOHN ROBERT[5], WILLIAM[4], WILLIAM[3], WILLIAM[2], WILLIAM[1]*) was born 23 Oct 1849 in Henry County, ALA, and died 23 Mar 1921 in Polk Co., Texas. He married CLARA AMANDA DOBBINS 11 Dec 1878 in Polk County, TX, daughter of EDWARD DOBBINS and UNKNOWN SNELLING. She was born 23 Sep 1862 in Point Blank, San Jacinto Co., TX, and died 16 Jan 1937 in Polk Co., Texas.

Soon after their marriage, James contracted a severe case of pneumonia which collapsed one of his lungs. His doctor recommended that he move to a drier climate for his health. In 1879, James' brother-in-law, Meredith "Merrity" Loper, James and Clara lived with the Lopers until his health improved enough for him to work. He and Clara hired on as cooks at the railhead in Breckenridge, TX. As soon as they had enough money, they bought a farm in the Wayland Community, Stephens County, TX. They continued to do well and prospered with their farm until very dry seasons hit the area in 1881 and 1882. During these two years they barely got by and received as others in the community, aid from the US Government. laying farming aside as his main occupation, James began freighting between Ranger, Eastland County, TX and Breckenridge in Stephens County, TX. He continued this for many years but finally decided to return to Onalaska in Aug 1911 to visit his nephew Alexander "Eck" S. Faircloth. While there he was convinced by his relatives to move back there; so, they loaded all their belongings on two rented railroad boxcars and several covered wagons and started the seventeen day journey to Onalaska. The family arrived with great fanfare on 26 Dec 1911 at the home of his niece Asaleete Prozell Faircloth Tanner, Mrs. James Henry Tanner, Sr.

133

Children of JAMES FAIRCLOTH and CLARA DOBBINS are:
  i. JAMES THOMAS[9] FAIRCLOTH, b. 21 Mar 1882, Wayland Community, Stephens Co., TX; d. 12 Feb 1884, Died from measles; buried Wayland, TX.
  ii. WINNEFRED NAOMI FAIRCLOTH, b. 05 Dec 1884, Wayland Community, Stephens Co., TX; d. 22 Jul 1930, Died from tuberculosis of the stomach; Polke Co., TX. Never married; taught school in Stephens County, TX
  iii. JIMMIE SEYMOUR FAIRCLOTH, b. 07 Jun 1889, Wayland Community, Stephens Co., TX; d. 15 May 1964, Polk Co., Texas; m. WALTER MOLEN KEEN; b. 18 Dec 1886; d. 09 Sep 1942, Polk Co., Texas.
  Child: Stillborn, 29 Dec 1914.
  iv. GEORGIA COTTLE FAIRCLOTH, b. 17 Mar 1892, Wayland Community, Stephens Co., TX; d. 28 Aug 1963, Polk Co., Texas; m. WILLIAM ROBERT MILLER, 30 Aug 1916, Polk County, TX; b. 25 Aug 1890, Vidor, TX; d. 05 Sep 1965, Polk Co., Texas.

Children of GEORGIA FAIRCLOTH and WILLIAM MILLER are:
  i. GEORGIA MAURINE MILLER[10] MILLER, b. 30 Jun 1918; m. CLOVIS HASKELL, 12 Oct 1940.
  ii. ROBET MYRTH MILLER, b. 01 Oct 1922; m. EVELYN HELEN TIKAL.
  iii. JAMES MAURICE MILLER MILLER, b. 12 Jul 1925; m. (1) SUE MAYES; m. (2) VERNA UNKNOWN; m. (3) NELDA JEAN LOFTIN.
  iv. MARVIN ROYCE MILLER, b. 16 Oct 1932; m. VIOLET KENNEDY.
2.   v. JAMES EDWARD LEE MILLER, b. 29 Dec; d. 05 May 1964.

2. JAMES EDWARD LEE[10] MILLER (*GEORGIA COTTLE[9] FAIRCLOTH, JAMES KNOX POLK[8], THOMAS DIDYMUS[7], JOHN ROBERT[6], JOHN ROBERT[5], WILLIAM[4], WILLIAM[3], WILLIAM[2], WILLIAM[1]*) was born 29 Dec, and died 05 May 1964. He married THELMA MAE GILBERT 03 Mar 1923. She was born 12 Jul 1905, and died 12 May 1981.

Children of JAMES MILLER and THELMA GILBERT are:
  i. EDWARD MURL[11] MILLER, b. 29 Sep 1922, Liberty Co., TX; d. Bet. Feb 1986 - 1987.
  ii. EDWARD LEE "BILLY" MILLER, b. 13 Jun 1929, Polk Co., Texas; d. 17 Jun 1929.
  iii. JERALD LEE MILLER, b. 09 Mar 1926, Polk Co., Texas; d. 08 Dec 1989, Hardin, TX.
  iv. JAMES FREELAND MILLER, b. 19 Apr 1928, Polk Co., Texas; d. 05 Jun 1972, Liberty Co., TX.
  v. CECIL HORACE MILLER, b. 11 Aug 1920, Polk Co., Texas.
  vi. FNNIS WAYNE MILLER, b. 11 Sep 1932, Polk Co., Texas.

Descendants of Zechariah Faircloth

Generation No. 1

1. ZECHARIAH[5] FAIRCLOTH *(WILLIAM[4], WILLIAM[3], WILLIAM[2], WILLIAM[1])* was born 1751 in Edgecombe Co., NC, and died 1810 in Washington, Louisiana. He married MARY ARMSTRONG. She was born 1757 in Montgomery County, NC.

Notes for ZECHARIAH FAIRCLOTH:

1). The Edgecombe County, NC Court Records from which the above Faircloth siblings or half-siblings were taken are scatttered and some years are missing: the records begin in 1744 but May 1746-Aug. 1757 are missing and July 1776-Aug. 1778 are missing. Be that as it may, April 1746-Aug. 1772 are the ones where the Faircloth siblings are recorded, and there was no mention of their father; in both entries of 9 July 1765 and 11 July 1765, Zacheriah Faircloth (aged 14 yrs.), a baseborn child, was bound to Noah Sugg, and John Faircloth (aged 5yrs.), and Hardy Faircloth (aged 11) also baseborn children, were bound to Benjamin Faircloth, who obviously were close relatives of the children's mother Sarah Faircloth. Also note that the published book written by Marvin K. Dorman, Jr. entitled Edgecombe County, North Carolina Abstracts of Court Minutes 1744-1746, 1757-1794 does not include the full details of the original text and leaves out the word baseborn. 2). See page 111 of "Orphanage In Colonial North Carolina: Edgecombe County As A Case Study" by Alan D. Watson recorded in The North Carolina Historical Review, pp. 105-119, vol. 52, no. 2, April 1975. "The Court further eased the transition to orphanage by apprenticing siblings to the same master where possible. This was particularly true in the case of illegitimate offspring--the Quinn Brothers, Faircloth brothers, Johnson sisters, and Revel sisters--and belied a sympathetic understanding on the part of the justices of the more difficult adjustments to be made by those children.

Children of ZECHARIAH FAIRCLOTH and MARY ARMSTRONG are:

2. i.   JAMES[6] FAIRCLOTH, SR., b. 1783, Sampson Co., NC; d. Abt. 1850, Cumberland County, NC.
    ii. RAFORD FAIRCLOTH.
    iii. BLUFORD FAIRCLOTH.
    iv. MARY SUSAN FAIRCLOTH.
    v.   PRISEY FAIRCLOTH.
    vi. MARTHA JANE FAIRCLOTH, b. Abt. 1785, Montgomery County, NC.

Generation No. 2

2. JAMES[6] FAIRCLOTH, SR. *(ZECHARIAH[5], WILLIAM[4], WILLIAM[3], WILLIAM[2], WILLIAM[1])* was born 1783 in Sampson Co., NC, and died Abt. 1850 in Cumberland County, NC. He married HANNAH JOHNSTON. She was born Abt. 1793, and died Aft. 1880 in Cumberland County, NC

Children of JAMES FAIRCLOTH and HANNAH JOHNSTON are:

i. JAMES[7] FAIRCLOTH, JR., b. 1825; d. Oct 1876, Other dates: 1864 will of James, Jr. with mother Hanah;. 12 Oct 1878: Request for the Administration of James Faircloth, dec'd," dated 12 October 1878 Cumberland County, NC. "Our beloved brother James Faircloth has lately died, and we want you Mr. Clerk to appoint Thomas Bullock administrator to tend to the estate of our brother. Witness to the signatures hereto annexed G.T. Bullock. 20 August 1864: Will of James Faircloth, (Jr.) County of Cumberland dated 20 August 1864. Value of estate about $100. Abstracted: James bequeaths his plantation whereupon he lives to his mother Hannah Faircloth and all his money to his mother after his debts are paid. After his mother's death estate goes to his sister Mary Susan Faircloth. Names N. Wales as executor of his estate.

Signatures annexed: Raford Faircloth, Bluford Faircloth, Jane Howell, Mary Faircloth, Prisey Faircloth. Note: these would be the deceased James's sibliings. Note: [This James Faircloth would be James Faircloth, (Jr.)].

Henry Faircloth b. 1821-1823;d. 1848-1849. Three of his siblings James, Robinson, and Bluford Faircloth were purchasers at the time of his estate sale on 16 Nov. 1849.

ii. SUSANNAH FAIRCLOTH, b. Bet. 1810 - 1812, Could be the same as Mary Polly or Susanna was Mary Susanna. Unknown if ever married.

iii. JANE FAIRCLOTH, b. Abt. 1814; d. Living in 1876; m. THOMAS HOWELL.

iv. RAIFORD FAIRCLOTH, b. Bet. 1815 - 1816; m. NANCY ANN RILEY, 28 Jun 1853. Nancy was the daughter of Absolom Riley.

v. SAMUEL FRANCIS FAIRCLOTH, b. 20 Nov 1820; d. 13 Nov 1901; m. (1) ELIZA CARVER; m. (2) HOLLY ANN BYRD.

vi. HENRY FAIRCLOTH, b. Bet. 1821 - 1823; d. Bet. 1848 - 1849.
Three of his siblings James, Robinson, and Bluford Faircloth were purchasers at the time   of his estate sale on 16 Nov. 1849.

vii. JOHN ROBINSON FAIRCLOTH, b. 1831; m. SUSAN FAIRCLOTH, 08 Mar 1850.) Henry Faircloth b. 1821-1823;d. 1848-1849. Three of his siblings James, Robinson, and Bluford Faircloth were purchasers at the time of his estate sale on 16 Nov. 1849.

viii. BLUFORD FAIRCLOTH, b. 1826; m. MARY ELIZABETH AUTERY, 20 May 1865; b. Abt. 1826.) Henry Faircloth b. 1821-1823;d. 1848-1849. Three of his siblings James, Robinson, and Bluford Faircloth were purchasers at the time of his estate sale on 16 Nov. 1849.

ix. PRISCILLA ANN FAIRCLOTH, b. 1827; d. Bet. 1903 - 1906, Cumberland County, NC; m. (1) REASON FAIRCLOTH, 12 Apr 1846; b. Bet. 1830 - 1831; d. 14 Nov 1864, Civil War; m. (2) WILEY HORNE, 25 Dec 1872; b. 1817; d. Bet. 1883 - 1888.
Reason was in theCivil War: Born 1831; Pvt, E Co, 8th Regt, Inf; Sampson County farmer; enl 5 Aug 1861 Cumberland County at age 30;; captured 9 (8?) Feb 1862 on Roanoke Island; paroled 21 Feb 1862 Elizabeth City and exchanged in Aug 1862. Wounded 30 Jan 1863 Morris Island, Charleston Harbor, SC; furloughed until 2 Nov 1863; captured 1Jun 1864 Cold Harbor, VA; confined Point Lookout, MD and Elmira, NY; died 14 Nov 1864 of chronic diarrhea; buried in grave #804 at Woodlawn Cemetery, Elmira, NY;

x. MARY POLLY FAIRCLOTH, b. Bet. 1834 - 1835; d. Living in 1880; never married.

xi. MARY SUSAN FAIRCLOTH, b. Could be the same as Mary Polly or Susanna was Mary Susanna..

Generation No. 1

1. ARTHUR⁶ FAIRCLOTH *(HARDWICK⁵, WILLIAM⁴, WILLIAM³, WILLIAM², WILLIAM¹)* was born 1775 in Sampson Co., NC; possible child of Samuel;, and died Aft. 1840 in Bladen Co., NC. He married (1) MARY ANN MCDANIEL "DICEY ANN", daughter of ARCHIBALD MCDANIEL and MARY. About 1818. She was born Bet. 1880 - 1890.

Robert Earl Woodham, a Faircloth Family historian wrote:

Arthur Faircloth's house in Bladen County is the oldest known Faircloth home still standing. He and many others of the family are buried in the Faircloth family cemetery nearby. (WMF: I have not been able to confirm this nor locate a Faircloth house or cemetery in Bladen).

Arthur was also reported to be born 2: Abt. 1770

Commentary: The fact that Arthur named his first two sons after Sampson, Edgecombe and Isle of Wight (VA) County Faircloth patriarchs suggests a connection to these families not known for sure at this time. Residence: Bet. 1810 - 1820, Moved from Sampson to Bladen Co.

There was a Sampson County, NC deed (vol. 21, p. 257) dated 18 Nov. 1826 whereby Arthur Faircloth sold 150 acres and Wilson Faircloth sold his 50 acres including the interest of their siblings to their brother Raiford Faircloth; the others (siblings) who had interests in these properties were named as follows: Achsah "Axsey" (Faircloth) Butler, Betsey (Faircloth) Ellis, Isaac Sessoms and his wife Nancy (Faircloth), and Sabrey Faircloth.

1820 Bladen County Census Records list Arthur with 2 male children under the age of ten and one female under the age of ten. He was between 26 and 45 and his wife was between 16 and 26 years of age. 1820 Bladen County Census: lists Arthur with 2 males less than 10 years old, one female under 10, one female 16-26, and 1 male 26-45 years of age.

1830 Census lists: 1 male 5-10 years of age, 1 male 10-15 years of age, 1 female less than 5 years of age, 1 female 15-20 years of age, and 1 female 30-40 years of age.

1840 Census lists: 1 male 20-30, 1 male 60-70 years of age. It lists 1 female 10-15 years of age, 1 female 15-20 years of age and 1 female 50-60 years of age.

1840 Census also lists Theopheles with 1 male 20-30 years old, 1 female less than 5 years old and 1 female 20-30 years of age.

Another 1840 Census lists Solomon as 30-40 years old, 1 female 20-30 and one female less than 5 years old.

Arthur is no longer listed in the 1850 Bladen County Census Records. He moved from Bladen to Sampson sometime between 1840 and 1850. Solomon and Theopheles are not listed on the Sampson County 1850 Census even though they each had established themselves as heads of households, married and began having children. Solomon and Theopheles remained in Bladen County during the 1860's. By 1870, Theopheles had moved to Sampson County with his wife and children. Solomon and his family continue to be listed on the Bladen County Census in 1870.

Deed Books in Bladen County, NC, P. 327, deed Book 11, Lists Arthur Faircloth, dated 17 July 1823.

1799-186_: a wooden stake marks the grave of Arthur; located next to the graves of two wives, Kitsey and Catherine in the Faircloth Cemetery.

Children of ARTHUR FAIRCLOTH and MARY ANN" are:

2.　　i.　BENJAMIN[7] FAIRCLOTH, b. Abt. 1809, Bladen Co., NC; d. Aft. 1880.
3.　　ii.　SOLOMON FAIRCLOTH, b. 1811; d. Bladen County, NC.
4.　　iii.　THEOPHELES "AFFIE" FAIRCLOTH, b. 1812.
　　　iv.　UNKNOWN FAIRCLOTH, b. Bef. 1810.
　　　v.　UNKNOWN FAIRCLOTH, b. Aft. 1810.
　　　vi.　UNKNOWN FAIRCLOTH, b. Aft. 1810.

Generation No. 2

2. BENJAMIN[7] FAIRCLOTH (*ARTHUR[6], HARDWICK[5], WILLIAM[4], WILLIAM[3], WILLIAM[2], WILLIAM[1]*) was born Abt. 1809 in Bladen Co., NC, and died Aft. 1880. He married (1) FRANCES BEDSOLE Abt. 1827, daughter of THOMAS BEDSOLE and REBECCA JONES. She was born Abt. 1802 in Bladen Co., NC, and died Abt. 1861. He married (2) HARRIET B. NEW Abt. 1862.

Property: 1840, Bladen Co. deed book 8, pg. 423, Benjamin and Frances sold for $10 all right and title to a 10-acre tract including the home place of Thomas Bedsole, Sr.

Benjamin F.

b. 1803, 1799 NC

1850 Bladen Census, 41, laborer, b. 1809;

m. Frances Bedsole in 1820; She was born 1803 and died in Alabama about 1870.

Owned land in Bladen County in 1842: 100 acres deed to Benjamin

Bladen County, NC - Abstracts of Bedsole Family Land Entries, #3

23 March, 1842- Daniel Bedsole (son of William Bedsole), Thomas Parker and wife Charity Bedsole (Daughter of William Bedsole) of Cumberland County, NC, Nusen Autry & wife Clarry Bedsole (Daughter of William Bedsole)also of Cumberland County, NC to Love McDaniel (Attorney, Bladen County, NC) all our right, interest, title & claim to lands of William Henry Bedsole, of Bladen County, NC, deceased, being undivided and containing 417 acres on the S side of of South River. First tract adjoins lands of Thomas Bedsole (Sr.) granted to William Bedsole on 12 December 1816-another tract of 107 acres being part of a tract granted to Samuel Hales on 9 March, 1791 on the south side of South River, east of the Stage Road, adj. lands of Mathew Hales-3rd tract of 100 acres granted to Thomas Bedsole (Sr.) & by him conveyed to Benjamin Faircloth (son in-law of Thomas Sr., married daughter of Thomas, Francis Bedsole) & by him to William Henry Bedsole on W side of South River -5th tract of 10 acres -6th tract of 100 acres being part of tract granted to Samuel Hales on March 9, 1797 including that part not sold or give to John Bedsole (uncle of Thomas Bedsole, Sr.) & adjoining lands of Samuel Pharesalso our interest in 100 acres "Which we have not got the Grant nor Courses" to the 3/8th part of the above land. Wit: J.B. Simpson, John McDaniel. Feb.'s term 1843. David Lewis, Clerk Of The Court, Bladen County, NC.

Bladen County, NC - Bedsole Family Ancestors/Descendants

BEDSOLE FAMILY ANCESTORS/DESCENDANTS

Country of Origin for the surname Bedsole is Prussia which became Germany. Prior to Prussia, there are no records, so Germany in the country of origin, for
practical matters. In the German language, Bedsole is spelled BETZOLD, but
pronounced as Bedsole.

1. The first Bedsole ancestor into this country was William Henry Bledsoe, (Sr.),
from Germany as Wilhelm Heinrich Betzold. He was most likely born 1690-1710. His name was written by an English Scribe upon boarding the ship as; William Henry Bledsoe, since these names were close in English spellings to his German names. Also, except for Scribes, none of the Bedsole ancestors could read, write or

spell until about 1800. It appears William arrived here with brothers Abraham and Isaac. William married and had sons William Jr., Elisha, Vincent and John Bedsole, all born between 1726 and 1735. I have been unable to find his wifes name, or any more of his children, if any. William Henry Bedsole, Jr. was born in Virginia in 1727, in St. Marys Parish, Virginia, but moved to Beaverdam, NC (Bladen County), in 1747, together with his 3 brothers. He married Rhoda West, b. 1730,(a daughter of James West), in 1748 in NC. A son, Thomas Bedsole, (Sr) was born in 1750 at Beaverdam. They also had a son John Bedsole, b. 1753. Thomas Sr. married Rebecca Jones, b. 1753, in 1770, in Beaverdam, NC.

The Bedsole ancestor/Descendant list contains many thousands of name, dates and places and are contained in the Bedsole History Book, 1690-1990, along with all the old land records, etc,. The book is available from JD Bedsole, 100-B Beamon Avenue, Opp, Alabama 36467, for the $25 cost of copying, binding and mailing it. To get one, E-mail jbeds@oppcatv.com. However, due to the extreme length of that list, the following are only a summary for display here:

2. Thomas Bedsole, Sr. b. 1750, Beaverdam, NC
   + Rebecca Jones, b. 1753, Beaverdam, NC
      3. Rhoda Bedsole, b. 1770, Beaverdam, NC
         + John Parker, Jr., b. 1753
      3. Sarah Bedsole, b. 1779, Beaverdam, NC
         + Benjamin Muccei
      3. William Henry Bedsole, b.1773-1825
         + Sarah Smythe, b. 1775, NC
      3. Thomas Bedsole, Jr. b. 1785, NC
         + Charlotte English, b. 1788, NC
      3. Robert Bedsole, b. 1780, NC
         + Rebecca Starling, b. 1782, NC
      3. Travis Bedsole, b. 1782, NC
         + Nancy Simmons, n. 1784, NC
      3. Owen Bedsole, b. 1787, NC
         + Wife Unknown
      3. Duncan Bedsole, b. 1797, NC
         + Catherine Hair, b. 1798, NC
      3. Francis Bedsole, b. 1802, NC
        + Benjamin Faircloth, b. 1799, NC
      3. Elizabeth Bedsole, b. 1775, NC
         + Steven Ryals/Rials, b. 1773, NC

Children of BENJAMIN FAIRCLOTH and FRANCES BEDSOLE are:
5.   i.   DUNCAN[8] FAIRCLOTH, b. 17 May 1846, Beaver Dam Twp., Bladen Co., NC; d. 13 Sep 1928, Hoke Co., NC.
     ii. SARAH FAIRCLOTH, b. Abt. 1828.
     iii. SUSAN FAIRCLOTH, b. Abt. 1830.
     iv. SOLOMON FAIRCLOTH, b. Abt. 1836.
          Namesake: Named after Uncle Solomon Faircloth.
     v.   THOMAS FAIRCLOTH, b. Abt. 1838.
          Namesake: Named after Uncle Thomas Bedsole
6.   vi. NANCY FAIRCLOTH, b. Abt. 1843.
     vii. CHARLOTTE E. FAIRCLOTH, b. Abt. 1850.

viii. POLLY FAIRCLOTH, b. Abt. 1835.
  ix. JOHN JAMES HENRY FAIRCLOTH.
   x. GEORGE B. FAIRCLOTH.
  xi. CORA FAIRCLOTH.
 xii. EDNA L FAIRCLOTH.
xiii. MARIE M. FAIRCLOTH.

3. SOLOMON[7] FAIRCLOTH *(ARTHUR[6], HARDWICK[5], WILLIAM[4], WILLIAM[3], WILLIAM[2], WILLIAM[1])* was born 1811, and died in Bladen County, NC. He married EDNA "EDNEY" ANN FORT Abt. 1838 in Bladen County, NC, daughter of JOHN FORT and JULIA UNKNOWN. She was born Bet. 1801 - 1802, and died 14 Jul 1873 in Bladen County, NC. Solomon was a Pvt., Company F, 2nd Artillery, 36th Regiment in the Civil War. He was born in 1811 in Sampson County according to Army Records and was a farmer/laborer when he enlisted on 26 February 1862 in Ellisville. He was hospitalized on 11 July 1862 of acute diarrhea. Military service: 1862, Enlisted in Confederate army at age 51. Listed in the Bladen County Records of 1850, 1860, 1870 and listed as born 1812 and 1813. Civil War: 3rd Regt, Cumberland co, Maj. Cameron's Command.

Children of SOLOMON FAIRCLOTH and EDNA FORT are:
   i. MATILDA J.[8] FAIRCLOTH, b. 02 Nov 1839, Bladen County, NC; d. 11 Oct 1894; m. STEVEN N.
       MELVIN, 07 Oct 1874, Home of Solomon and Edney Faircloth; b. 1843; d. 09 Oct 1907.
       No children.
  ii. THOMAS H. FAIRCLOTH, b. 03 Jun 1840, Bladen County, NC; d. 14 Mar 1865, Elmira, NY; buried 14 Mar grave #2430.
       20 Feb 1862 - 15 Jan 1865 he was a Private, Co F, 2nd Artillery, 36th Regmt. Enlisted in Confederate Army on 20 Jan 1862.at age 21 at Terebinth. On 15 Jan 1865 was captured at Fort Fisher at the Fall of Ft. Fisher, NC.
 iii. JOHN L. FAIRCLOTH, b. 27 Nov 1842, Bladen County, NC; d. 15 Jan 1863, Succumbed to smallpox and pleurapneumonia in the Hospital in Richmond, VA. According to the Melvin Faircloth Bible, he served in the militia between 1 Sep and 15 Oct, 1861 served with the NC Troops.
  iv. HENRY C. FAIRCLOTH, b. 03 Apr 1844, Bladen County, NC; d. 10 Dec, ; He was in the 1870 Census but not in the 1880. Private, Co C, 54th Regiment, NC Troops.

4. THEOPHELES "AFFIE"[7] FAIRCLOTH *(ARTHUR[6], HARDWICK[5], WILLIAM[4], WILLIAM[3], WILLIAM[2], WILLIAM[1])* was born 1812. He married REBECCA CASHWELL, daughter of THOMAS CASHWELL (born 1819).

Children of THEOPHELES FAIRCLOTH and REBECCA CASHWELL are:
   i. GERUSHA A.[8] FAIRCLOTH, b. 1839.
  ii. THOMAS G. FAIRCLOTH, b. 1841; d. 07 Jul 1862, Ft. Fisher, Brunswick County, NC, during the Civil War
 iii. LUCY JANE FAIRCLOTH, b. Mar 1850.
  iv. DAVID C. FAIRCLOTH, b. 1852.
       1870 Census: D. was 17 years old on this Census
   v. MILLARD FAIRCLOTH, b. Bet. 1861 - 1862.
7.   vi. BENJAMIN F. FAIRCLOTH, b. 1854, Roseboro at Rt. 2, Sampson County, NC; d. Buried at the home of Ralph Faircloth (531-3859).

vii. SARAH S. FAIRCLOTH, b. 1845.
8.   viii. REBECCA C. FAIRCLOTH, b. 1857. was born 1857. She married
    JOHN   STALLINGS.

Generation No. 3

5. DUNCAN[8] FAIRCLOTH (*BENJAMIN[7], ARTHUR[6], HARDWICK[5], WILLIAM[4], WILLIAM[3], WILLIAM[2], WILLIAM[1]*) was born 17 May 1846 in Beaver Dam Twp., Bladen Co., NC, and died 13 Sep 1928 in Hoke Co., NC. He married NANCY HALL Abt. 1866, daughter of JAMES HALL and JEANETTE (HAIR?).

Children of DUNCAN FAIRCLOTH and NANCY HALL are:
9.   i. WILLIAM MARSHAL[9] FAIRCLOTH, b. 21 Jul 1869, NC; d. 16 Nov 1926, Moore
       Co., NC.
10.   ii. JAMES MAURICE FAIRCLOTH, b. 23 Aug 1867; d. 08 May 1931.
11.   iii. STEPHEN SHERMAN FAIRCLOTH, b. 19 Mar 1872, (Grave marker shows 3-19-
       1870.); d. 12 Dec 1941.
      iv. KITTY L. FAIRCLOTH, b. Abt. 1866.
      v. JEANETTE FAIRCLOTH, b. Abt. 1874.
      vi. ELIZABETH FAIRCLOTH, b. Abt. 1877.
      vii. GEORGE L. FAIRCLOTH, b. Abt. 1880.
      viii. JOE FAIRCLOTH, b. Feb 1883; m. DELLA; b. Abt. 1890.

12. ix. ARCHIE FAIRCLOTH, b. Jan 1889. ARCHIE[9] FAIRCLOTH (*DUNCAN[8], BENJAMIN[7], ARTHUR[6], HARDWICK[5], WILLIAM[4], WILLIAM[3], WILLIAM[2], WILLIAM[1]*) was born Jan 1889. He married PHOEBE. She was born Abt. 1887.

Child of ARCHIE FAIRCLOTH and PHOEBE is:
      i. EVA M.[10] FAIRCLOTH, b. 15 Sep 1909; d. 15 Jul 1968.
         Burial: 1968, Ephesus Bapt. Ch. Cemetery, Hoke Co., NC

6. NANCY[8] FAIRCLOTH (*BENJAMIN[7], ARTHUR[6], HARDWICK[5], WILLIAM[4], WILLIAM[3], WILLIAM[2], WILLIAM[1]*) was born Abt. 1843. She married REDDIN WILLIAMS.

Child of NANCY FAIRCLOTH and REDDIN WILLIAMS is:
13.   i. LUCY R.[9] WILLIAMS, b. 17 Apr 1867; d. 19 Jul 1902.
      LUCY R.[2] WILLIAMS (*REDDIN[1]*) was born 17 Apr 1867, and died 19 Jul   1902.
    She married GEORGE W. FAIRCLOTH, son of NEVER MARRIED and SYLVANNIA
    FAIRCLOTH. He was born 10 Sep 1867, and died 14 Jul 1907.
      The family of Sylvannia and George W. Faircloth are listed in the descendents of
    EDWARD FARECLOTH, of this manuscript.

Children of LUCY WILLIAMS and GEORGE FAIRCLOTH are:
      i. BEULAH[3] FAIRCLOTH, b. Abt. 1902; m. THOMAS MASON SESSOMS; b. Abt.
         1894.
      ii. MARION FAIRCLOTH.

7. BENJAMIN F.[8] FAIRCLOTH (*THEOPHELES "AFFIE"[7], ARTHUR[6], HARDWICK[5], WILLIAM[4], WILLIAM[3], WILLIAM[2], WILLIAM[1]*) was born 1854 in Roseboro at Rt. 2, Sampson

County, NC, and died in Buried at the home of Ralph Faircloth (531-3859). He married ADLINE CATHERINE AUTRY, daughter of YOUNG AUTRY and NANCY.

Children of BENJAMIN FAIRCLOTH and ADLINE AUTRY are:
14.   i.   LAWRENCE C.[9] FAIRCLOTH, b. 13 Mar 1886, Sampson Co., NC; d. 20 Oct 1952, Fayetteville, NC; Complete descendents of Lawrence C. and Lula J. Faircloth are found in The descendents of EDWARD FARECLOTH of this manuscript under Lula J. Faircloth.
15.   ii.   ALLEN CLAY FAIRCLOTH, b. Bet. 28 Jul 1887 - 1888; d. 05 Jul 19
      iii. ELLEN FAIRCLOTH, b. 1891; m. ALFRED OR ASHFORD "TATE" HALL, 03 Jan 1909, Sampson Co., NC
16.   iv. JERE TATE FAIRCLOTH, b. 1894; d. Aug 1953, New Hanover County, NC.
      v.   NITA FAIRCLOTH, b. Bet. 1898 - 1899, Sampson Co., NC; d. 18 Apr 1936

8. REBECCA C.[8] FAIRCLOTH (*THEOPHELES "AFFIE"[7], ARTHUR[6], HARDWICK[5], WILLIAM[4], WILLIAM[3], WILLIAM[2], WILLIAM[1]*) was born 1857. She married JOHN STALLINGS. He was born 1853 in Austria.

Children of REBECCA FAIRCLOTH and JOHN STALLINGS are:
      i.   GEORGE[9] STALLINGS, b. 1874, NC.
      ii. SUSANNA STALLINGS, b. 1877.

Generation No. 4

9. WILLIAM MARSHAL[9] FAIRCLOTH (*DUNCAN[8], BENJAMIN[7], ARTHUR[6], HARDWICK[5], WILLIAM[4], WILLIAM[3], WILLIAM[2], WILLIAM[1]*) was born 21 Jul 1869 in NC, and died 16 Nov 1926 in Moore Co., NC. He married MARY NEIL JACKSON Abt. 1898, daughter of RANDAL JACKSON and FANNIE S..

Children of WILLIAM FAIRCLOTH and MARY JACKSON are:
      i.   MILLARD[10] FAIRCLOTH, b. 17 Oct 1902, NC; d. 16 Sep 1983, Fayetteville, NC; m. (1) CAROLINE ECKHART; d. 1934; m. (2) HELEN FRANCES FRYE, 1937, Bennettsville, SC; b. 11 Nov 1919, NC; d. 31 Jul 2001, Fayetteville, NC.
      ii. ERNEST D. FAIRCLOTH, b. 16 Jan 1899.
      iii. ELBERT L. FAIRCLOTH, b. 02 May 1900.
      iv. WORTH A. FAIRCLOTH, b. 20 Sep 1905.
      v.   LACY G. FAIRCLOTH, b. 02 May 1908.
      vi. LYDIA FAIRCLOTH, b. 16 Nov 1910.
      vii. PETE FAIRCLOTH, b. 18 Mar 1913.
    viii. JAMES RUSSELL FAIRCLOTH, b. 1915.
      ix. GRADY FAIRCLOTH, b. Abt. 1919.
      x.   GEORGIA FAIRCLOTH, b. Aft. 1920.

10. JAMES MAURICE[9] FAIRCLOTH (*DUNCAN[8], BENJAMIN[7], ARTHUR[6], HARDWICK[5], WILLIAM[4], WILLIAM[3], WILLIAM[2], WILLIAM[1]*) was born 23 Aug 1867, and died 08 May 1931. He married (1) LESSIE JANE KOONCE. She was born 16 Sep 1868, and died 13 Dec 1897. He married (2) BESSIE OPHELIA ADCOX Abt. 1898, daughter of HAMPTON ADCOX. She was born 12 Jun 1879, and died 09 Nov 1951. James: Burial: 1931, Ephesus Bapt. Ch. Cemetery, Hoke Co., NC. More About LESSIE JANE KOONCE: Burial: 1897, Ephesus Bapt. Ch. Cemetery, Hoke Co., NC.

Child of JAMES FAIRCLOTH and LESSIE KOONCE is:
    i. WILLA[10] FAIRCLOTH, b. Dec 1897.

Children of JAMES FAIRCLOTH and BESSIE ADCOX are:
    ii. MELLA[10] FAIRCLOTH, b. Oct 1898.
    iii. PEARLY (NORA?) FAIRCLOTH, b. 24 Apr 1900.
    iv. JAMES FAIRCLOTH, b. 1904.
    v. ANNA FAIRCLOTH, b. 1906.
    vi. ALMA FAIRCLOTH, b. 1908.
    vii. MYRTLE FAIRCLOTH, b. 1910.
    viii. LILLIAN FAIRCLOTH, b. 1913.
    ix. CLYDE FAIRCLOTH, b. 1914.
    x. STANLEY ALTON FAIRCLOTH, b. 15 Feb 1916.
    xi. BLANCHE FAIRCLOTH, b. 1918.
    xii. THELMA FAIRCLOTH, b. 26 Feb 1921.

11. STEPHEN SHERMAN[9] FAIRCLOTH (*DUNCAN[8], BENJAMIN[7], ARTHUR[6], HARDWICK[5], WILLIAM[4], WILLIAM[3], WILLIAM[2], WILLIAM[1]*) was born 19 Mar 1872 in (Grave marker shows 3-19-1870.), and died 12 Dec 1941. He married SARAH (UNK). She was born May 1876. More About STEPHEN SHERMAN FAIRCLOTH: Burial: 1941, Ephesus Bapt. Ch. Cemetery, Hoke Co., NC; Census: 1880 - Shows Sherman as "Stephen S." and his age as 8. 1900 - shows birth date as Mar. 1872.

Children of STEPHEN FAIRCLOTH and SARAH (UNK) are:
    i. LESSIE[10] FAIRCLOTH, b. Jan 1895.
    ii. IDA M. FAIRCLOTH, b. Feb 1897.
    iii. GEORGE GIBSON FAIRCLOTH, b. Mar 1900; d. 23 Oct 1980, Raeford, NC; m. NELLIE HAIR; b. 29 Dec 1901, Robeson Co., NC.
        More About GEORGE GIBSON FAIRCLOTH:
        Burial: 1980, Raeford Cemetery, Raeford, NC
        Military service: WW I Veteran
        Occupation: Raeford City Policeman
        More About NELLIE HAIR:
        Burial: Raeford Cemetery, Raeford, NC
    iv. LULA (?) FAIRCLOTH, b. Aft. 1900.
    v. ROBERT R. FAIRCLOTH, b. 27 Aug 1908.

12. ARCHIE[9] FAIRCLOTH (*DUNCAN[8], BENJAMIN[7], ARTHUR[6], HARDWICK[5], WILLIAM[4], WILLIAM[3], WILLIAM[2], WILLIAM[1]*) was born Jan 1889. He married PHOEBE. She was born Abt. 1887.

Child of ARCHIE FAIRCLOTH and PHOEBE is:
    i. EVA M.[10] FAIRCLOTH, b. 15 Sep 1909; d. 15 Jul 1968.
        More About EVA M. FAIRCLOTH: Burial: 1968, Ephesus Bapt. Ch. Cemetery, Hoke Co., NC

13. LUCY R.[9] WILLIAMS (*NANCY[8] FAIRCLOTH, BENJAMIN[7], ARTHUR[6], HARDWICK[5], WILLIAM[4], WILLIAM[3], WILLIAM[2], WILLIAM[1]*) was born 17 Apr 1867, and died 19 Jul 1902. She married GEORGE W. FAIRCLOTH, son of NEVER MARRIED and SYLVANNIA FAIRCLOTH. He was born 10 Sep 1867, and died 14 Jul 1907.

Children of LUCY WILLIAMS and GEORGE FAIRCLOTH are:
  i.   BEULAH[10] FAIRCLOTH, b. Abt. 1902; m. THOMAS MASON SESSOMS; b. Abt. 1894.
  ii. MARION FAIRCLOTH.

14. LAWRENCE C.[9] FAIRCLOTH *(BENJAMIN F.[8], THEOPHELES "AFFIE"[7], ARTHUR[6], HARDWICK[5], WILLIAM[4], WILLIAM[3], WILLIAM[2], WILLIAM[1])* was born 13 Mar 1886 in Sampson Co., NC, and died 20 Oct 1952 in Fayetteville, NC; buried in Cross Creek Cemetery, Fayetteville, NC. He married LULA JANE FAIRCLOTH 10 Jan 1915 in Sampson County, NC, daughter of HANSON FAIRCLOTH and ELIZABETH HALL.
For the complete descendents of Lawrence C. and Lula J. Faircloth, see the Lula J. Faircloth entries under the descendents of Edward Faircloth.

Children of LAWRENCE FAIRCLOTH and LULA FAIRCLOTH are:

  i.   LILLIAN ELIZABETH[10] FAIRCLOTH, b. 15 Dec 1915, Sampson Co., NC; Little Coherie Township.; d. Fayetteville, NC;
  ii.   LEROY FAIRCLOTH, b. 05 May 1918, Hayne, NC; m. (1) ADDIE MAE CHEEK; m. (2) ALICE TAYLOR.
  iii. HERMAN REMUS FAIRCLOTH, b. 04 Feb 1927, Fayetteville, NC; m. ERIKA ELSE KREISLER, 07 May 1950, Germany; b. 05 Aug 1929, Stollenwasser, Germany (Jannusk, Poland).
  iv.   JOYCE MARIE FAIRCLOTH, b. 16 Oct 1929; m. (1) DONALD TAYLOR; m. (2) CHARLIE FLOYD FISHER; b. 04 Nov 1926; d. 28 Apr 1956.
  v.   HELEN FAIRCLOTH, b. 16 Sep 1924; m. WINFRED PAUL SAUNDERS, 06 Mar 1947, Raeford, NC; b. 08 Dec 1921; d. 06 Jul 1999.
  vi.   LOTTIE JUANITA FAIRCLOTH, b. 30 Oct 1932; m. ARWOOD HAMMOND, 25 Nov; b. Abt. 1930;
  vii. JUDY ADLINE FAIRCLOTH, b. 27 Mar 1938, B St., Fayetteville, NC; d. 2005; m. RAEFORD SMITH.
  viii. CARL HOUSTON FAIRCLOTH, b. 29 Oct 1920, Sampson Co., NC; d. 28 Dec 1971, m. (1) LILLIAN BERNICE BROWN; m. (2) LENA MAE BEARD, 27 Jan 1948, Dillon, SC.

15. ALLEN CLAY[9] FAIRCLOTH *(BENJAMIN F.[8], THEOPHELES "AFFIE"[7], ARTHUR[6], HARDWICK[5], WILLIAM[4], WILLIAM[3], WILLIAM[2], WILLIAM[1])* was born Bet. 28 Jul 1887 - 1888, and died 05 Jul. He married (1) MISSOURI "ZUDE".

Child of ALLEN FAIRCLOTH and MISSOURI "ZUDE" is:
  i.   VENNIE[10] FAIRCLOTH, b. 08 Jun 1923; d. 13 Mar 1975, Roseboro Cemetery, NC; m. HOUSTON TROY FAIRCLOTH, 20 Jan 1946, Dillon, SC; b. 23 May 1926, Sampson Co., NC; d. Roseboro Cemetery, NC.

Children of ALLEN FAIRCLOTH and MISSOURI HALL are:
  ii.   MARIE MARY[10] FAIRCLOTH, d. Died young..
  iii. ROBERT CLAY FAIRCLOTH, b. 22 Jul 1915; d. 13 Mar 1952; m. ETHEL DAVIS; b. 1916, Cumberland County, NC.
  iv.   CARLIE FAIRCLOTH, b. 14 Feb 1909; d. 07 Aug 1972; m. AMY CLYDE CULBRETH, 21 Feb 1942, Dillon, SC.

     v. GLADIS FAIRCLOTH, b. 29 Jul 1918; m. ROMMIE LEWIS.
    vi. AGNES FAIRCLOTH, b. 23 Sep 1921; m. (1) ALVIN PARKER; m. (2) JAMES SESSOMS.
   vii. ALLINE FAIRCLOTH, b. 12 Dec 1927; m. IVEY LAL FAIRCLOTH; b. 17 Mar 1927.
  viii. PAUL ERNEST FAIRCLOTH, b. 08 Feb 1913; m. EARNIE KATE SESSOMS, 1936; d. 08 Sep 1978, Buried in Roseboro, NC Cemetery..
    ix. VENIE FAIRCLOTH, b. 08 Jun 1923; d. 13 Mar 1965, Buried in Roseboro Cemetery.; m. HOUSTON TROY FAIRCLOTH, 20 Jun 1946, Dillon, SC; b. 23 May 1926, Sampson Co., NC; d. Roseboro Cemetery, NC.
     x. JOHN FAIRCLOTH, b. 08 Sep 1915.

16.   JERE TATE[9] FAIRCLOTH (*BENJAMIN F.*[8], *THEOPHELES "AFFIE"*[7], *ARTHUR*[6], *HARDWICK*[5], *WILLIAM*[4], *WILLIAM*[3], *WILLIAM*[2], *WILLIAM*[1]) was born 1894, and died Aug 1953 in New Hanover County, NC. He married MURLENE WATKINS.

Children of JERE FAIRCLOTH and MURLENE WATKINS are:
     i. BEN THOMAS[10] FAIRCLOTH, b. 18 Jan 1922, New Hanover Co., NC; d. 03 Apr 1922.
    ii. JERE TATE FAIRCLOTH, b. Nov 1923, New Hanover Co., NC; d. 1967.
   iii. CLYDE EARNEST FAIRCLOTH, b. Dec 1924, New Hanover Co., NC.

Descendants of George Gibson Faircloth

Generation No. 1

1. GEORGE GIBSON[10] FAIRCLOTH (*STEPHEN SHERMAN*[9], *DUNCAN*[8], *BENJAMIN*[7], *ARTHUR*[6], *HARDWICK*[5], *WILLIAM*[4], *WILLIAM*[3], *WILLIAM*[2], *WILLIAM*[1]) was born Mar 1900, and died 23 Oct 1980 in Raeford, NC. He married NELLIE HAIR. She was born 29 Dec 1901 in Robeson Co., NC.
More About GEORGE GIBSON FAIRCLOTH: Burial: 1980, Raeford Cemetery, Raeford, NC.
Military service: WW I Veteran. Occupation: Raeford City Policeman

More About NELLIE HAIR: Burial: Raeford Cemetery, Raeford, NC

Children of GEORGE FAIRCLOTH and NELLIE HAIR are:
     i. GEORGE ALFORD[11] FAIRCLOTH, b. 1928.
    ii. SAMUEL DUNCAN FAIRCLOTH, b. 1923.
2.   iii. FLORENCE FAIRCLOTH, b. 23 Feb 1925, Abbotsburg, NC.

Generation No. 2

2. FLORENCE[11] FAIRCLOTH (*GEORGE GIBSON*[10], *STEPHEN SHERMAN*[9], *DUNCAN*[8], *BENJAMIN*[7], *ARTHUR*[6], *HARDWICK*[5], *WILLIAM*[4], *WILLIAM*[3], *WILLIAM*[2], *WILLIAM*[1]) was

born 23 Feb 1925 in Abbotsburg, NC. She married THOMAS MACKO 16 Nov 1946 in Catskill, New York. He was born 11 Dec 1924 in Yonkers, NY.

Children of FLORENCE FAIRCLOTH and THOMAS MACKO are:
3.　　i.　PATRICIA ANNE[12] MACKO, b. 25 Jan 1952.
　　　ii.　THOMAS MICHAEL MACKO, b. 1947.

Generation No. 3

3.　PATRICIA ANNE[12] MACKO *(FLORENCE[11] FAIRCLOTH, GEORGE GIBSON[10], STEPHEN SHERMAN[9], DUNCAN[8], BENJAMIN[7], ARTHUR[6], HARDWICK[5], WILLIAM[4], WILLIAM[3], WILLIAM[2], WILLIAM[1])* was born 25 Jan 1952. She married MICHELE ERNEST PRINCE 30 Mar 1974. He was born Nov 1949.

Children of PATRICIA MACKO and MICHELE PRINCE are:
　　　i.　MICHELLE MACKO[13] PRINCE, b. 03 Feb 1979.
　　　ii.　BEVIN ANNE PRINCE, b. 23 Sep 1982.

Descendants of Millard Faircloth

Generation No. 1

1.　MILLARD[10] FAIRCLOTH *(WILLIAM MARSHAL[9], DUNCAN[8], BENJAMIN[7], ARTHUR[6], HARDWICK[5], WILLIAM[4], WILLIAM[3], WILLIAM[2], WILLIAM[1])* was born 17 Oct 1902 in NC, and died 16 Sep 1983 in Fayetteville, NC. He married (1) CAROLINE ECKHART. She died 1934. He married (2) HELEN FRANCES FRYE 1937 in Bennettsville, SC, daughter of WILLIAM FRYE and MARY BUNNELL. She was born 11 Nov 1919 in NC, and died 31 Jul 2001 in Fayetteville, NC.
　　Millard: Burial: 1983, Beulah Hill Ch. Cemetery, Moore Co., NC
　　Helen: Burial: 2001, Beulah Hill Ch. Cemetery, Moore Co., NC

Child of MILLARD FAIRCLOTH and CAROLINE ECKHART is:
　　　i.　DOROTHY ANNE[11] FAIRCLOTH, b. Jan 1933.

Children of MILLARD FAIRCLOTH and HELEN FRYE are:
2.　　ii.　WILLIAM MARSHALL[11] FAIRCLOTH, b. 05 Jan 1949, NC.
　　　iii.　MILLARD LEROY FAIRCLOTH, b. 19 Jun 1939.
3.　　iv.　MYRNA LOY FAIRCLOTH, b. 28 Feb 1942.

Generation No. 2

2.　WILLIAM MARSHALL[11] FAIRCLOTH *(MILLARD[10], WILLIAM MARSHAL[9], DUNCAN[8], BENJAMIN[7], ARTHUR[6], HARDWICK[5], WILLIAM[4], WILLIAM[3], WILLIAM[2], WILLIAM[1])* was born 05 Jan 1949 in NC.

Children of WILLIAM MARSHALL FAIRCLOTH are:

i. PHILIP LEA[12] FAIRCLOTH, b. 11 Dec 1972, Fayetteville, NC.
ii. WILLIAM EDWARD FAIRCLOTH, b. 30 Nov 1977, Fayetteville, NC.

3. MYRNA LOY[11] FAIRCLOTH (*MILLARD[10], WILLIAM MARSHAL[9], DUNCAN[8], BENJAMIN[7], ARTHUR[6], HARDWICK[5], WILLIAM[4], WILLIAM[3], WILLIAM[2], WILLIAM[1]*) was born 28 Feb 1942. She married (1) BILLY MERLE AVERITTE 16 Sep 1967 in Spring Lake, NC. He died Jan 1994 in Winston Salem, NC. She married (2) GARY L. GRAHAM 15 Apr 1996 in Winston Salem, NC.
Billy: Burial: Jan 1994

Child of MYRNA FAIRCLOTH and BILLY AVERITTE is:
i. WILLIAM BRADFORD[12] AVERITTE, b. 31 Jan 1972.

Descendants of *Myrna Loy Faircloth*

Generation No. 1

1. MYRNA LOY[11] FAIRCLOTH (*MILLARD[10], WILLIAM MARSHAL[9], DUNCAN[8], BENJAMIN[7], ARTHUR[6], HARDWICK[5], WILLIAM[4], WILLIAM[3], WILLIAM[2], WILLIAM[1]*) was born 28 Feb 1942. She married (1) BILLY MERLE AVERITTE 16 Sep 1967 in Spring Lake, NC. He died Jan 1994 in Winston Salem, NC. She married (2) GARY L. GRAHAM 15 Apr 1996 in Winston Salem, NC.
More About BILLY MERLE AVERITTE: Burial: Jan 1994

Child of MYRNA FAIRCLOTH and BILLY AVERITTE is:
i. WILLIAM BRADFORD[12] AVERITTE, b. 31 Jan 1972.

Descendants of *William Pilot Frye*

Generation No. 1

1. WILLIAM PILOT[1] FRYE was born 24 Nov 1869 in Moore Co., NC, and died 04 Apr 1950 in Moore Co., NC. He married ANNIE JANE JACKSON. She was born 17 Jan 1876 in Moore Co., NC, and died 13 Jun 1934 in Moore Co., NC.
More About WILLIAM PILOT FRYE:
Burial: 1950, Beulah Hill Ch. Cemetery, Moore Co., NC
More About ANNIE JANE JACKSON:
Burial: 1934, Beulah Hill Ch. Cemetery, Moore Co., NC

Child of WILLIAM FRYE and ANNIE JACKSON is:
2. i. WILLIAM LEE[2] FRYE, b. 14 Jun 1897, NC; d. 21 Oct 1977, Moore Co. NC.

Generation No. 2

2. WILLIAM LEE[2] FRYE *(WILLIAM PILOT[1])* was born 14 Jun 1897 in NC, and died 21 Oct 1977 in Moore Co. NC. He married MARY ETHEL BUNNELL 13 Jan 1917 in Moore Co., NC, daughter of DANIEL BUNNELL and MILLIE CADDELL. She was born 22 Jan 1896 in NC, and died 17 Oct 1965 in Pinehurst, NC.
William: burial: 1977, Beulah Hill Ch. Cemetery, Moore Co., NC
Mary: Burial: 1965, Beulah Hill Ch. Cemetery, Moore Co., NC

Child of WILLIAM FRYE and MARY BUNNELL is:
3.　　i.　HELEN FRANCES[3] FRYE, b. 11 Nov 1919, NC; d. 31 Jul 2001, Fayetteville, NC.

Generation No. 3

3. HELEN FRANCES[3] FRYE *(WILLIAM LEE[2], WILLIAM PILOT[1])* was born 11 Nov 1919 in NC, and died 31 Jul 2001 in Fayetteville, NC. She married MILLARD FAIRCLOTH 1937 in Bennettsville, SC, son of WILLIAM FAIRCLOTH and MARY JACKSON. He was born 17 Oct 1902 in NC, and died 16 Sep 1983 in Fayetteville, NC.
Helen: Burial: 2001, Beulah Hill Ch. Cemetery, Moore Co., NC
Millard: Burial: 1983, Beulah Hill Ch. Cemetery, Moore Co., NC

Children of HELEN FRYE and MILLARD FAIRCLOTH are:
4.　　i.　WILLIAM MARSHALL[4] FAIRCLOTH, b. 05 Jan 1949, NC.
　　　ii.　MILLARD LEROY FAIRCLOTH, b. 19 Jun 1939.
5.　　iii.　MYRNA LOY FAIRCLOTH, b. 28 Feb 1942.

Generation No. 4

4. WILLIAM MARSHALL[4] FAIRCLOTH *(HELEN FRANCES[3] FRYE, WILLIAM LEE[2], WILLIAM PILOT[1])* was born 05 Jan 1949 in NC.

Children of WILLIAM MARSHALL FAIRCLOTH are:
　　　i.　PHILIP LEA[5] FAIRCLOTH, b. 11 Dec 1972, Fayetteville, NC.
　　　ii.　WILLIAM EDWARD FAIRCLOTH, b. 30 Nov 1977, Fayetteville, NC.

5. MYRNA LOY[4] FAIRCLOTH *(HELEN FRANCES[3] FRYE, WILLIAM LEE[2], WILLIAM PILOT[1])* was born 28 Feb 1942. She married (1) BILLY MERLE AVERITTE 16 Sep 1967 in Spring Lake, NC. He died Jan 1994 in Winston Salem, NC. She married (2) GARY L. GRAHAM 15 Apr 1996 in Winston Salem, NC.
More About BILLY MERLE AVERITTE: Burial: Jan 1994

Child of MYRNA FAIRCLOTH and BILLY AVERITTE is:
　　　i.　WILLIAM BRADFORD[5] AVERITTE, b. 31 Jan 1972.

Descendants of Daniel R. Bunnell

Generation No. 1

1. DANIEL R.[3] BUNNELL *(THOMAS[2], ASA[1])* was born 02 Apr 1850, and died 03 Jun 1922 in Moore Co., NC. He married MILLIE ANN CADDELL, daughter of JOHN CADDELL and HANNAH MCKINNON. She was born 15 Aug 1856 in Moore Co., NC, and died 12 May 1945 in Moore Co., NC.

Child of DANIEL BUNNELL and MILLIE CADDELL is:
2.   i.   MARY ETHEL[4] BUNNELL, b. 22 Jan 1896, NC; d. 17 Oct 1965, Pinehurst, NC.

Generation No. 2

2. MARY ETHEL[4] BUNNELL *(DANIEL R.[3], THOMAS[2], ASA[1])* was born 22 Jan 1896 in NC, and died 17 Oct 1965 in Pinehurst, NC. She married WILLIAM LEE FRYE 13 Jan 1917 in Moore Co., NC, son of WILLIAM FRYE and ANNIE JACKSON. He was born 14 Jun 1897 in NC, and died 21 Oct 1977 in Moore Co. NC.
Ethel: Burial: 1965, Beulah Hill Ch. Cemetery, Moore Co., NC
William: Burial: 1977, Beulah Hill Ch. Cemetery, Moore Co., NC

Child of MARY BUNNELL and WILLIAM FRYE is:
3.   i.   HELEN FRANCES[5] FRYE, b. 11 Nov 1919, NC; d. 31 Jul 2001, Fayetteville, NC.

Generation No. 3

3. HELEN FRANCES[5] FRYE *(MARY ETHEL[4] BUNNELL, DANIEL R.[3], THOMAS[2], ASA[1])* was born 11 Nov 1919 in NC, and died 31 Jul 2001 in Fayetteville, NC. She married MILLARD FAIRCLOTH 1937 in Bennettsville, SC, son of WILLIAM FAIRCLOTH and MARY JACKSON. He was born 17 Oct 1902 in NC, and died 16 Sep 1983 in Fayetteville, NC.
Helen: Burial: 2001, Beulah Hill Ch. Cemetery, Moore Co., NC
Millard: Burial: 1983, Beulah Hill Ch. Cemetery, Moore Co., NC

Children of HELEN FRYE and MILLARD FAIRCLOTH are:
4.   i.   WILLIAM MARSHALL[6] FAIRCLOTH, b. 05 Jan 1949, NC.
      ii. MILLARD LEROY FAIRCLOTH, b. 19 Jun 1939.
5.   iii. MYRNA LOY FAIRCLOTH, b. 28 Feb 1942.

Generation No. 4

4. WILLIAM MARSHALL[6] FAIRCLOTH *(HELEN FRANCES[5] FRYE, MARY ETHEL[4] BUNNELL, DANIEL R.[3], THOMAS[2], ASA[1])* was born 05 Jan 1949 in NC.

Children of WILLIAM MARSHALL FAIRCLOTH are:
      i.   PHILIP LEA[7] FAIRCLOTH, b. 11 Dec 1972, Fayetteville, NC.
      ii. WILLIAM EDWARD FAIRCLOTH, b. 30 Nov 1977, Fayetteville, NC.

5. MYRNA LOY[6] FAIRCLOTH *(HELEN FRANCES[5] FRYE, MARY ETHEL[4] BUNNELL, DANIEL R.[3], THOMAS[2], ASA[1])* was born 28 Feb 1942. She married (1) BILLY MERLE AVERITTE 16 Sep 1967 in Spring Lake, NC. He died Jan 1994 in Winston Salem, NC. She married (2) GARY L. GRAHAM 15 Apr 1996 in Winston Salem, NC.
Billy: Burial: Jan 1994

Child of MYRNA FAIRCLOTH and BILLY AVERITTE is:
      i. WILLIAM BRADFORD[7] AVERITTE, b. 31 Jan 1972.

Descendants of Asa Bunnell

Generation No. 1

1. ASA[1] BUNNELL
Child of ASA BUNNELL is:
2.   i. THOMAS[2] BUNNELL.

Generation No. 2

2. THOMAS[2] BUNNELL *(ASA[1])*
Child of THOMAS BUNNELL is:
3.   i. DANIEL R.[3] BUNNELL, b. 02 Apr 1850; d. 03 Jun 1922, Moore Co., NC.

Generation No. 3

3. DANIEL R.[3] BUNNELL *(THOMAS[2], ASA[1])* was born 02 Apr 1850, and died 03 Jun 1922 in Moore Co., NC. He married MILLIE ANN CADDELL, daughter of JOHN CADDELL and HANNAH MCKINNON. She was born 15 Aug 1856 in Moore Co., NC, and died 12 May 1945 in Moore Co., NC.
Daniel: Burial: 1922, Beulah Hill Ch. Cemetery, Moore Co., NC
Millie: Burial: 1945, Beulah Hill Ch. Cemetery, Moore Co., NC

Child of DANIEL BUNNELL and MILLIE CADDELL is:
4.   i. MARY ETHEL[4] BUNNELL, b. 22 Jan 1896, NC; d. 17 Oct 1965, Pinehurst, NC.

Generation No. 4

4. MARY ETHEL[4] BUNNELL *(DANIEL R.[3], THOMAS[2], ASA[1])* was born 22 Jan 1896 in NC, and died 17 Oct 1965 in Pinehurst, NC. She married WILLIAM LEE FRYE 13 Jan 1917 in Moore Co., NC, son of WILLIAM FRYE and ANNIE JACKSON. He was born 14 Jun 1897 in NC, and died 21 Oct 1977 in Moore Co. NC.
Mary: Burial: 1965, Beulah Hill Ch. Cemetery, Moore Co., NC
William: Burial: 1977, Beulah Hill Ch. Cemetery, Moore Co., NC

Child of MARY BUNNELL and WILLIAM FRYE is:

i. HELEN FRANCES[5] FRYE, b. 11 Nov 1919, NC; d. 31 Jul 2001, Fayetteville, NC; m. MILLARD FAIRCLOTH, 1937, Bennettsville, SC; b. 17 Oct 1902, NC; d. 16 Sep 1983, Fayetteville, NC.
More About HELEN FRANCES FRYE:
Burial: 2001, Beulah Hill Ch. Cemetery, Moore Co., NC
More About MILLARD FAIRCLOTH:
Burial: 1983, Beulah Hill Ch. Cemetery, Moore Co., NC

Descendants of John McKinnon

Generation No. 1

1. JOHN[1] MCKINNON was born Abt. 1775 in Isle of Skye, Scotland.

Child of JOHN MCKINNON is:
2.   i. HANNAH[2] MCKINNON, b. 25 Jan 1829; d. 28 Jan 1918, Moore Co., NC.

Generation No. 2

2. HANNAH[2] MCKINNON *(JOHN[1])* was born 25 Jan 1829, and died 28 Jan 1918 in Moore Co., NC. She married JOHN CADDELL. He was born Abt. 1828, and died Bef. 1880 in Moore Co., NC.

Child of HANNAH MCKINNON and JOHN CADDELL is:
3.   i. MILLIE ANN[3] CADDELL, b. 15 Aug 1856, Moore Co., NC; d. 12 May 1945, Moore Co., NC.

Generation No. 3

3. MILLIE ANN[3] CADDELL *(HANNAH[2] MCKINNON, JOHN[1])* was born 15 Aug 1856 in Moore Co., NC, and died 12 May 1945 in Moore Co., NC. She married DANIEL R. BUNNELL, son of THOMAS BUNNELL. He was born 02 Apr 1850, and died 03 Jun 1922 in Moore Co., NC.
Millie: Burial: 1945, Beulah Hill Ch. Cemetery, Moore Co., NC
: Daniel: Burial: 1922, Beulah Hill Ch. Cemetery, Moore Co., NC

Child of MILLIE CADDELL and DANIEL BUNNELL is:
4.   i. MARY ETHEL[4] BUNNELL, b. 22 Jan 1896, NC; d. 17 Oct 1965, Pinehurst, NC.

Generation No. 4

4. MARY ETHEL[4] BUNNELL *(MILLIE ANN[3] CADDELL, HANNAH[2] MCKINNON, JOHN[1])* was born 22 Jan 1896 in NC, and died 17 Oct 1965 in Pinehurst, NC. She married WILLIAM LEE FRYE 13 Jan 1917 in Moore Co., NC, son of WILLIAM FRYE and ANNIE JACKSON. He was born 14 Jun 1897 in NC, and died 21 Oct 1977 in Moore Co. NC.

Mary: Burial: 1965, Beulah Hill Ch. Cemetery, Moore Co., NC
William: Burial: 1977, Beulah Hill Ch. Cemetery, Moore Co., NC

Child of MARY BUNNELL and WILLIAM FRYE is:
     i. HELEN FRANCES[5] FRYE, b. 11 Nov 1919, NC; d. 31 Jul 2001, Fayetteville, NC; m. MILLARD FAIRCLOTH, 1937, Bennettsville, SC; b. 17 Oct 1902, NC; d. 16 Sep 1983, Fayetteville, NC.
       Helen: Burial: 2001, Beulah Hill Ch. Cemetery, Moore Co., NC
       Millard: Burial: 1983, Beulah Hill Ch. Cemetery, Moore Co., NC

Descendants of Duncan Faircloth

Generation No. 1

1. DUNCAN[8] FAIRCLOTH (*BENJAMIN[7], ARTHUR[6], HARDWICK[5], WILLIAM[4], WILLIAM[3], WILLIAM[2], WILLIAM[1]*) was born 17 May 1846 in Beaver Dam Twp., Bladen Co., NC, and died 13 Sep 1928 in Hoke Co., NC. He married NANCY HALL Abt. 1866, daughter of JAMES HALL and JEANETTE (HAIR?). She was born 01 Mar 1839 in Bladen Co., NC, and died 11 Aug 1901 in Hoke Co., NC.
More About DUNCAN FAIRCLOTH: Burial: 1928, Ephesus Bapt. Ch. Cemetery, Hoke Co., NC. Military service: 01 Jun 1864, Enlisted in Confederate army at age 18. Served in C Co. 7th NC Reserve and 1 Co. 72nd Rgt. NC St. Troops. Applied for Conf. Vet. Pension from St. of NC, June 14, 1909. Namesake: Named after uncle Duncan Bedsole. Nancy: Burial: 1901, Ephesus Bapt. Ch. Cemetery, Hoke Co., NC
Residence: The 1860 census indicates Nancy lived on an adjacent farm.

Children of DUNCAN FAIRCLOTH and NANCY HALL are:
2.   i. WILLIAM MARSHAL[9] FAIRCLOTH, b. 21 Jul 1869, NC; d. 16 Nov 1926, Moore Co., NC.
3.   ii. JAMES MAURICE FAIRCLOTH, b. 23 Aug 1867; d. 08 May 1931.
4.   iii. STEPHEN SHERMAN FAIRCLOTH, b. 19 Mar 1872, (Grave marker shows 3-19-1870.); d. 12 Dec 1941.
     iv. KITTY L. FAIRCLOTH, b. Abt. 1866.
     v. JEANETTE FAIRCLOTH, b. Abt. 1874.
     vi. ELIZABETH FAIRCLOTH, b. Abt. 1877.
     vii. GEORGE L. FAIRCLOTH, b. Abt. 1880.
     viii. JOE FAIRCLOTH, b. Feb 1883; m. DELLA; b. Abt. 1890.
5.   ix. ARCHIE FAIRCLOTH, b. Jan 1889.

Generation No. 2

2. WILLIAM MARSHAL[9] FAIRCLOTH (*DUNCAN[8], BENJAMIN[7], ARTHUR[6], HARDWICK[5], WILLIAM[4], WILLIAM[3], WILLIAM[2], WILLIAM[1]*) was born 21 Jul 1869 in NC, and died 16 Nov 1926 in Moore Co., NC. He married MARY NEIL JACKSON Abt. 1898, daughter of RANDAL JACKSON and FANNIE S.. She was born 19 May 1882 in Robeson Co., NC, and died 08 Sep 1934 in Moore Co., NC.

William: Burial: 1926, Beulah Hill Ch. Cemetery, Moore Co., NC
Mary: Burial: 1936, Beulah Hill Ch. Cemetery, Moore Co., NC

William and Mary Faircloth

Children of WILLIAM FAIRCLOTH and MARY JACKSON are:
6.   i.   MILLARD[10] FAIRCLOTH, b. 17 Oct 1902, NC; d. 16 Sep 1983, Fayetteville, NC.
      ii.   ERNEST D. FAIRCLOTH, b. 16 Jan 1899.
    iii.   ELBERT L. FAIRCLOTH, b. 02 May 1900.
    iv.   WORTH A. FAIRCLOTH, b. 20 Sep 1905.
     v.   LACY G. FAIRCLOTH, b. 02 May 1908.
    vi.   LYDIA FAIRCLOTH, b. 16 Nov 1910.
   vii.   PETE FAIRCLOTH, b. 18 Mar 1913.
  viii.   JAMES RUSSELL FAIRCLOTH, b. 1915.
    ix.   GRADY FAIRCLOTH, b. Abt. 1919.
     x.   GEORGIA FAIRCLOTH, b. Aft. 1920.

3.   JAMES MAURICE[9] FAIRCLOTH *(DUNCAN[8], BENJAMIN[7], ARTHUR[6], HARDWICK[5], WILLIAM[4], WILLIAM[3], WILLIAM[2], WILLIAM[1])* was born 23 Aug 1867, and died 08 May 1931. He married (1) LESSIE JANE KOONCE. She was born 16 Sep 1868, and died 13 Dec 1897. He married (2) BESSIE OPHELIA ADCOX Abt. 1898, daughter of HAMPTON ADCOX. She was born 12 Jun 1879, and died 09 Nov 1951.
James: Burial: 1931, Ephesus Bapt. Ch. Cemetery, Hoke Co., NC
Lessie: Burial: 1897, Ephesus Bapt. Ch. Cemetery, Hoke Co., NC
Bessie: Burial: 1951, Ephesus Bapt. Ch. Cemetery, Hoke Co., NC

Child of JAMES FAIRCLOTH and LESSIE KOONCE is:
     i.   WILLA[10] FAIRCLOTH, b. Dec 1897.
Children of JAMES FAIRCLOTH and BESSIE ADCOX are:
     ii.   MELLA[10] FAIRCLOTH, b. Oct 1898.
    iii.   PEARLY (NORA?) FAIRCLOTH, b. 24 Apr 1900.
    iv.   JAMES FAIRCLOTH, b. 1904.
     v.   ANNA FAIRCLOTH, b. 1906.
    vi.   ALMA FAIRCLOTH, b. 1908.
   vii.   MYRTLE FAIRCLOTH, b. 1910.

    viii. LILLIAN FAIRCLOTH, b. 1913.
     ix. CLYDE FAIRCLOTH, b. 1914.
      x. STANLEY ALTON FAIRCLOTH, b. 15 Feb 1916.
     xi. BLANCHE FAIRCLOTH, b. 1918.
    xii. THELMA FAIRCLOTH, b. 26 Feb 1921.

4. STEPHEN SHERMAN[9] FAIRCLOTH (*DUNCAN*[8], *BENJAMIN*[7], *ARTHUR*[6], *HARDWICK*[5], *WILLIAM*[4], *WILLIAM*[3], *WILLIAM*[2], *WILLIAM*[1]) was born 19 Mar 1872 in (Grave marker shows 3-19-1870.), and died 12 Dec 1941. He married SARAH (UNK). She was born May 1876. Stephen: Burial: 1941, Ephesus Bapt. Ch. Cemetery, Hoke Co., NC Census: 1880 - Shows Sherman as "Stephen S." and his age as 8. 1900 - shows birth date as Mar. 1872.

Children of STEPHEN FAIRCLOTH and SARAH (UNK) are:
      i. LESSIE[10] FAIRCLOTH, b. Jan 1895.
     ii. IDA M. FAIRCLOTH, b. Feb 1897.
7.   iii. GEORGE GIBSON FAIRCLOTH, b. Mar 1900; d. 23 Oct 1980, Raeford, NC.
     iv. LULA (?) FAIRCLOTH, b. Aft. 1900.
      v. ROBERT R. FAIRCLOTH, b. 27 Aug 1908.

5. ARCHIE[9] FAIRCLOTH (*DUNCAN*[8], *BENJAMIN*[7], *ARTHUR*[6], *HARDWICK*[5], *WILLIAM*[4], *WILLIAM*[3], *WILLIAM*[2], *WILLIAM*[1]) was born Jan 1889. He married PHOEBE. She was born Abt. 1887.
Child of ARCHIE FAIRCLOTH and PHOEBE is:
      i. EVA M.[10] FAIRCLOTH, b. 15 Sep 1909; d. 15 Jul 1968.
          More About EVA M. FAIRCLOTH: Burial: 1968, Ephesus Bapt. Ch. Cemetery, Hoke Co., NC

Generation No. 3

6. MILLARD[10] FAIRCLOTH (*WILLIAM MARSHAL*[9], *DUNCAN*[8], *BENJAMIN*[7], *ARTHUR*[6], *HARDWICK*[5], *WILLIAM*[4], *WILLIAM*[3], *WILLIAM*[2], *WILLIAM*[1]) was born 17 Oct 1902 in NC, and died 16 Sep 1983 in Fayetteville, NC. He married (1) CAROLINE ECKHART. She died 1934. He married (2) HELEN FRANCES FRYE 1937 in Bennettsville, SC, daughter of WILLIAM FRYE and MARY BUNNELL. She was born 11 Nov 1919 in NC, and died 31 Jul 2001 in Fayetteville, NC. Millard: Burial: 1983, Beulah Hill Ch. Cemetery, Moore Co., NC Helen: Burial: 2001, Beulah Hill Ch. Cemetery, Moore Co., NC

Child of MILLARD FAIRCLOTH and CAROLINE ECKHART is:
      i. DOROTHY ANNE[11] FAIRCLOTH, b. Jan 1933.

Children of MILLARD FAIRCLOTH and HELEN FRYE are:
8.   ii. WILLIAM MARSHALL[11] FAIRCLOTH, b. 05 Jan 1949, NC.
     iii. MILLARD LEROY FAIRCLOTH, b. 19 Jun 1939.
9.   iv. MYRNA LOY FAIRCLOTH, b. 28 Feb 1942.

7. GEORGE GIBSON[10] FAIRCLOTH (*STEPHEN SHERMAN*[9], *DUNCAN*[8], *BENJAMIN*[7], *ARTHUR*[6], *HARDWICK*[5], *WILLIAM*[4], *WILLIAM*[3], *WILLIAM*[2], *WILLIAM*[1]) was born Mar 1900, and died 23 Oct 1980 in Raeford, NC. He married NELLIE HAIR. She was born 29 Dec 1901 in Robeson Co., NC. George: Burial: 1980, Raeford Cemetery, Raeford, NC. Military service:

WW I Veteran. Occupation: Raeford City Policeman; Nellie: Burial: Raeford Cemetery, Raeford, NC

Children of GEORGE FAIRCLOTH and NELLIE HAIR are:
    i.   GEORGE ALFORD[11] FAIRCLOTH, b. 1928.
    ii. SAMUEL DUNCAN FAIRCLOTH, b. 1923.
10. iii. FLORENCE FAIRCLOTH, b. 23 Feb 1925, Abbotsburg, NC.

Generation No. 4

8. WILLIAM MARSHALL[11] FAIRCLOTH *(MILLARD[10], WILLIAM MARSHAL[9], DUNCAN[8], BENJAMIN[7], ARTHUR[6], HARDWICK[5], WILLIAM[4], WILLIAM[3], WILLIAM[2], WILLIAM[1])* was born 05 Jan 1949 in NC.

Children of WILLIAM MARSHALL FAIRCLOTH are:
    i.   PHILIP LEA[12] FAIRCLOTH, b. 11 Dec 1972, Fayetteville, NC.
    ii. WILLIAM EDWARD FAIRCLOTH, b. 30 Nov 1977, Fayetteville, NC.

9. MYRNA LOY[11] FAIRCLOTH *(MILLARD[10], WILLIAM MARSHAL[9], DUNCAN[8], BENJAMIN[7], ARTHUR[6], HARDWICK[5], WILLIAM[4], WILLIAM[3], WILLIAM[2], WILLIAM[1])* was born 28 Feb 1942. She married (1) BILLY MERLE AVERITTE 16 Sep 1967 in Spring Lake, NC. He died Jan 1994 in Winston Salem, NC. She married (2) GARY L. GRAHAM 15 Apr 1996 in Winston Salem, NC. Billey: Burial: Jan 1994

Child of MYRNA FAIRCLOTH and BILLY AVERITTE is:
    i.   WILLIAM BRADFORD[12] AVERITTE, b. 31 Jan 1972.

10. FLORENCE[11] FAIRCLOTH *(GEORGE GIBSON[10], STEPHEN SHERMAN[9], DUNCAN[8], BENJAMIN[7], ARTHUR[6], HARDWICK[5], WILLIAM[4], WILLIAM[3], WILLIAM[2], WILLIAM[1])* was born 23 Feb 1925 in Abbotsburg, NC. She married THOMAS MACKO 16 Nov 1946 in Catskill, New York. He was born 11 Dec 1924 in Yonkers, NY.

Children of FLORENCE FAIRCLOTH and THOMAS MACKO are:
    i.   PATRICIA ANNE[12] MACKO, b. 25 Jan 1952; m. MICHELE ERNEST PRINCE, 30 Mar 1974; b. Nov 1949.
    ii. THOMAS MICHAEL MACKO, b. 1947.

Descendants of Allen Clay Faircloth

Generation No. 1

1. ALLEN CLAY[9] FAIRCLOTH *(BENJAMIN F.[8], THEOPHELES "AFFIE"[7], ARTHUR[6], HARDWICK[5], WILLIAM[4], WILLIAM[3], WILLIAM[2], WILLIAM[1])* was born Bet. 28 Jul 1887 - 1888, and died 05 Jul 1944 in Buried in Hollywood Cemetary in Roseboro. He married (1) MISSOURI "ZUDE". She was born Abt. 1890. He married (2) MISSOURI "ZUDE" HALL 02 Oct 1908 in Married at the home of Uriah Sessoms, Justice of the Peace. Allen Clay Faircloth was a farmer. He died of a brain abscess from a gunshot wound to the eye.

Children of ALLEN FAIRCLOTH and MISSOURI "ZUDE' Hall" are:

    i.   VENNIE[10] FAIRCLOTH, b. 08 Jun 1923; d. 13 Mar 1975, Roseboro Cemetery, NC; m. HOUSTON TROY FAIRCLOTH, 20 Jan 1946, Dillon, SC; b. 23 May 1926, Sampson Co., NC; d. Roseboro Cemetery, NC.

    ii.   MARIE MARY[10] FAIRCLOTH, d. Died young..

2.   iii.   ROBERT CLAY FAIRCLOTH, b. 22 Jul 1915; d. 13 Mar 1952.

3.   iv.   CARLIE FAIRCLOTH, b. 14 Feb 1909; d. 07 Aug 1972.

4.   v.   GLADIS FAIRCLOTH, b. 29 Jul 1918.

5.   vi.   AGNES FAIRCLOTH, b. 23 Sep 1921.

6.   vii.   ALLINE FAIRCLOTH, b. 12 Dec 1927.

7.   viii.   PAUL ERNEST FAIRCLOTH, b. 08 Feb 1913.

8.   ix.   VENIE FAIRCLOTH, b. 08 Jun 1923; d. 13 Mar 1965, Buried in Roseboro Cemetery..

    x.   JOHN FAIRCLOTH, b. 08 Sep 1915.

Generation No. 2

2. ROBERT CLAY[10] FAIRCLOTH *(ALLEN CLAY[9], BENJAMIN F.[8], THEOPHELES "AFFIE"[7], ARTHUR[6], HARDWICK[5], WILLIAM[4], WILLIAM[3], WILLIAM[2], WILLIAM[1])* was born 22 Jul 1915, and died 13 Mar 1952. He married ETHEL DAVIS. She was born 1916 in Cumberland County, NC.

Children of ROBERT FAIRCLOTH and ETHEL DAVIS are:

    i.   MARY LOIS[11] FAIRCLOTH, b. 19 Oct 1942.

    ii.   PAULINE FAIRCLOTH, b. 20 Oct 1943.

    iii.   ANNETTE FAIRCLOTH, b. 1952.

    iv.   DAVID NEAL FAIRCLOTH, b. 12 Jul 1946.

    v.   PERCY CLAY FAIRCLOTH, b. 18 Jul 1948.

3. CARLIE[10] FAIRCLOTH *(ALLEN CLAY[9], BENJAMIN F.[8], THEOPHELES "AFFIE"[7], ARTHUR[6], HARDWICK[5], WILLIAM[4], WILLIAM[3], WILLIAM[2], WILLIAM[1])* was born 14 Feb 1909, and died 07 Aug 1972. He married AMY CLYDE CULBRETH 21 Feb 1942 in Dillon, SC, daughter of LILLIE CULBRETH and JANIE SUTTON.

Children of CARLIE FAIRCLOTH and AMY CULBRETH are:
  i.   MALCOLM JENKINS[11] FAIRCLOTH.
9.   ii. ALLEN CLAY FAIRCLOTH, b. 09 Feb 1943.
  iii. CATHERINE JANIE FAIRCLOTH, b. 25 Feb 1945; d. 09 Mar 1950, Died from 2nd and 3rd degree burns when her clothes caught fire from a furnace; Buried in the Hollywood Cemetery in Roseboro, NC.
10. iv. MARTIN LANGISTER FAIRCLOTH.
11. v.   WILLIAM LAWRENCE FAIRCLOTH, b. 19 May 1950.

4.   GLADIS[10] FAIRCLOTH *(ALLEN CLAY[9], BENJAMIN F.[8], THEOPHELES "AFFIE"[7], ARTHUR[6], HARDWICK[5], WILLIAM[4], WILLIAM[3], WILLIAM[2], WILLIAM[1])* was born 29 Jul 1918. She married ROMMIE LEWIS.

Children of GLADIS FAIRCLOTH and ROMMIE LEWIS are:
  i.   BOBBY[11] LEWIS.
  ii. MARTIN LEWIS.
  iii. CHARLES LEWIS.
  iv. DONNIE LEWIS.

5.   AGNES[10] FAIRCLOTH *(ALLEN CLAY[9], BENJAMIN F.[8], THEOPHELES "AFFIE"[7], ARTHUR[6], HARDWICK[5], WILLIAM[4], WILLIAM[3], WILLIAM[2], WILLIAM[1])* was born 23 Sep 1921. She married (1) ALVIN PARKER. She married (2) JAMES SESSOMS.

Children of AGNES FAIRCLOTH and ALVIN PARKER are:
  i.   FLOYD[11] PARKER, m. JERDINE FAIRCLOTH.
  ii. UNKNOWN PARKER, m. TOM ISLEY.

6.   ALLINE[10] FAIRCLOTH *(ALLEN CLAY[9], BENJAMIN F.[8], THEOPHELES "AFFIE"[7], ARTHUR[6], HARDWICK[5], WILLIAM[4], WILLIAM[3], WILLIAM[2], WILLIAM[1])* was born 12 Dec 1927. She married IVEY LAL FAIRCLOTH. He was born 17 Mar 1927.

Children of ALLINE FAIRCLOTH and IVEY FAIRCLOTH are:
  i.   KAY[11] FAIRCLOTH, m. BOBBY MCLAMB.
  ii. JAMES FAIRCLOTH, m. BETTY UNKNOWN.

7. PAUL ERNEST[10] FAIRCLOTH *(ALLEN CLAY[9], BENJAMIN F.[8], THEOPHELES "AFFIE"[7], ARTHUR[6], HARDWICK[5], WILLIAM[4], WILLIAM[3], WILLIAM[2], WILLIAM[1])* was born 08 Feb 1913. He married EARNIE KATE SESSOMS 1936, daughter of HOLLY SESSOMS and MARRY PARKER. She died 08 Sep 1978 in Buried in Roseboro, NC Cemetery..

Children of PAUL FAIRCLOTH and EARNIE SESSOMS are:
  i.   VIVIAN MISSOURI[11] FAIRCLOTH, b. 28 Jun 1952; m. G. H. RAY.
  ii. MARY DORIS FAIRCLOTH, b. 29 Jan 1945.
12. iii. EARL JUNIOR FAIRCLOTH, b. 11 Jan 1939.
  iv. HERMAN JAMES FAIRCLOTH, b. 24 Oct 1942; m. HELEN JEAN MATTHEWS, 02 Sep 1961.
  v.   PAUL RUDY FAIRCLOTH, b. 31 Jan 1948; m. JOYCE ELAINE LUCAS.
  vi. BILLY DEAN FAIRCLOTH, b. 15 Nov 1957; m. MARTHA KAY HALL, 21 Dec 1974.

8. VENIE[10] FAIRCLOTH *(ALLEN CLAY[9], BENJAMIN F.[8], THEOPHELES "AFFIE"[7], ARTHUR[6], HARDWICK[5], WILLIAM[4], WILLIAM[3], WILLIAM[2], WILLIAM[1])* was born 08 Jun 1923, and died 13 Mar 1965 in Buried in Roseboro Cemetery.. She married HOUSTON TROY FAIRCLOTH 20 Jun 1946 in Dillon, SC, son of TROY FAIRCLOTH and PENNY FAIRCLOTH. He was born 23 May 1926 in Sampson Co., NC, and died in Roseboro Cemetery, NC.

Children of VENIE FAIRCLOTH and HOUSTON FAIRCLOTH are:
  i. FAYE[11] FAIRCLOTH, b. 05 Feb 1949.
  ii. DOROTHY FAIRCLOTH, b. 18 Sep 1947.
  iii. RUBEN ESTES FAIRCLOTH, b. 1951, Sampson Co., NC.
  iv. RICHARD " RICKY" HOUSTON FAIRCLOTH, b. 10 Oct 1955.
  v. LAWRENCE RAY FAIRCLOTH, b. 1952; d. Bef. 1984.
  vi. CATHY DIANE FAIRCLOTH, b. 10 Jan 1957.

Generation No. 3

9. ALLEN CLAY[11] FAIRCLOTH *(CARLIE[10], ALLEN CLAY[9], BENJAMIN F.[8], THEOPHELES "AFFIE"[7], ARTHUR[6], HARDWICK[5], WILLIAM[4], WILLIAM[3], WILLIAM[2], WILLIAM[1])* was born 09 Feb 1943. He married VADA LEE TURNER 01 Apr 1964.

Children of ALLEN FAIRCLOTH and VADA TURNER are:
  i. UNKNOWN[12] FAIRCLOTH.
  ii. KENNETH ALLEN FAIRCLOTH, b. 06 Mar 1967.

10. MARTIN LANGISTER[11] FAIRCLOTH *(CARLIE[10], ALLEN CLAY[9], BENJAMIN F.[8], THEOPHELES "AFFIE"[7], ARTHUR[6], HARDWICK[5], WILLIAM[4], WILLIAM[3], WILLIAM[2], WILLIAM[1])* He married JANETTE F. WILLIAMS.

Child of MARTIN FAIRCLOTH and JANETTE WILLIAMS is:
  i. TRAVIS MARTIN[12] FAIRCLOTH, b. 19 May 1950.

11. WILLIAM LAWRENCE[11] FAIRCLOTH *(CARLIE[10], ALLEN CLAY[9], BENJAMIN F.[8], THEOPHELES "AFFIE"[7], ARTHUR[6], HARDWICK[5], WILLIAM[4], WILLIAM[3], WILLIAM[2], WILLIAM[1])* was born 19 May 1950. He married ELMA DARLENE THOMPSON.

Children of WILLIAM FAIRCLOTH and ELMA THOMPSON are:
  i. ELMA MICHELLE[12] FAIRCLOTH, b. 30 Nov 1972.
  ii. UNKNOWN FAIRCLOTH.

12. EARL JUNIOR[11] FAIRCLOTH *(PAUL ERNEST[10], ALLEN CLAY[9], BENJAMIN F.[8], THEOPHELES "AFFIE"[7], ARTHUR[6], HARDWICK[5], WILLIAM[4], WILLIAM[3], WILLIAM[2], WILLIAM[1])* was born 11 Jan 1939. He married DORTHEA HALL 05 Oct 1957.

Children of EARL FAIRCLOTH and DORTHEA HALL are:
13. i. ROSA FAYE[12] FAIRCLOTH, b. 09 Jul 1958.
     ii. FRANKIE RAY FAIRCLOTH, b. 20 Mar 1961; m. LORI JANE HALL, 07 Nov 1981.
     iii. LONNIE PAUL FAIRCLOTH, b. 20 Aug 1965.

Generation No. 4

13.   ROSA FAYE[12] FAIRCLOTH *(EARL JUNIOR[11], PAUL ERNEST[10], ALLEN CLAY[9], BENJAMIN F.[8], THEOPHELES "AFFIE"[7], ARTHUR[6], HARDWICK[5], WILLIAM[4], WILLIAM[3], WILLIAM[2], WILLIAM[1])* was born 09 Jul 1958. She married LLOYD FAIRCLOTH, JR..

Child of ROSA FAIRCLOTH and LLOYD FAIRCLOTH is:
    i.   BRANDY ROSE[13] FAIRCLOTH, b. 28 Mar 1978.

Descendants of Benjamin F. Faircloth

Generation No. 1

1. BENJAMIN F.[8] FAIRCLOTH *(THEOPHELES "AFFIE"[7], ARTHUR[6], HARDWICK[5], WILLIAM[4], WILLIAM[3], WILLIAM[2], WILLIAM[1])* was born 1854 in Roseboro at Rt. 2, Sampson County, NC, and died in Buried at the home of Ralph Faircloth (531-3859). He married ADLINE CATHERINE AUTRY, daughter of YOUNG AUTRY and NANCY. She was born 1865 in Cumberland County, NC, and died 23 Apr 1936 in Buried in the Faircloth Cemetery in Roseboro, NC; died from strangulation hernias. According to Helen Faircloth (daughter of Lawrence and Lula), when Ben died, the family dressed him out and put him in a wooden box (related to author in Oct 1984).

According to Roy Faircloth (son of Lawrence and Lula), Ben picked his teeth with a quill from a goose and always carried a goose quill for a toothpick. when Roy was small, Lawrence told him that he (Lawrence) remembers his father (Ben), telling him about the time when Ben went to court to claim his part of the settlement of the estate of Ben's father. As the judge asked all to stand who had a claim on this estate, an Indian stood at the back of the courthouse to claim his share. Does this bring up the possibility of Indian blood in the Faircloth lineage?

According to Devotion Faircloth (interview in 1982 at the age of 92 years old), Ben and Adline lived on Baggets Bridge. He described Ben and Adline as "good ole people". He also states that Adline raised honeybees and made the best tray of flitters (flour bread) he had ever had. Adline died at home, close to highway 24, outside of Autryville, which is heading east at the intersection of the road which leads to Hayne.

Adline owned some land in Hayne (Sampson County). The exact location is unknown at this time.

According to Roy Faircloth, Adline was "a real pistol on alcohol. She used to pour out every bottle of alcohol she could find. She would go looking for the hiding places of the men and pour it out everytime." Roy also states that "Adline died of a gall bladder operation when he (Roy) was about 6-7 years of age". Since Roy was born in 1918, the death date of Adline can be placed between 1924-25.

Roy also stated that shortly after Adline's death, Adline's daughter, Nita died. (about a year later).

Adlines' birth date is unknown but is presumed to be before 1870. According to Helen, Daughter of Lawrence and Lula), she recalls when Adline died and estimates the she (Helen) was about 10-12 years of age, 1910 Census lists him as Benjamin R.
Medical Information: Adline died from strangulated hernias.

Children of BENJAMIN FAIRCLOTH and ADLINE AUTRY are:
2.   i.   LAWRENCE C.[9] FAIRCLOTH, b. 13 Mar 1886, Sampson Co., NC; d. 20 Oct 1952, Fayetteville, NC;
3.   ii.   ALLEN CLAY FAIRCLOTH, b. Bet. 28 Jul 1887 - 1888; d. 05 Jul 1944,
      iii.   ELLEN FAIRCLOTH, b. 1891; m. ALFRED OR ASHFORD "TATE" HALL, 03 Jan 1909, Sampson Co., NC Married by D. H. Vinsom, Justice of the Peace in Beaverdam Township.; b. 1887.
4.   iv.   JERE TATE FAIRCLOTH, b. 1894; d. Aug 1953, New Hanover County, NC.

v. NITA FAIRCLOTH, b. Bet. 1898 - 1899, Sampson Co., NC; d. 18 Apr 1936, Buried in Mozie Cemetary, Sampson County, NC; m. JOHN J. HALL; b. 26 Jan 1887; d. 23 Jul 1916.

Generation No. 2

2. LAWRENCE C.[9] FAIRCLOTH (*BENJAMIN F.[8], THEOPHELES "AFFIE"[7], ARTHUR[6], HARDWICK[5], WILLIAM[4], WILLIAM[3], WILLIAM[2], WILLIAM[1]*) was born 13 Mar 1886 in Sampson Co., NC, and died 20 Oct 1952. He married LULA JANE FAIRCLOTH 10 Jan 1915 in Sampson County, NC, daughter of HANSON FAIRCLOTH and ELIZABETH HALL

Children of LAWRENCE FAIRCLOTH and LULA FAIRCLOTH are:
5.   i.   LILLIAN ELIZABETH[10] FAIRCLOTH, b. 15 Dec 1915, Sampson Co., NC; Little Coherie Township.; d. Fayetteville, NC; 6.
      ii.   LEROY FAIRCLOTH, b. 05 May 1918, Hayne, NC.
7.   iii.   HERMAN REMUS FAIRCLOTH, b. 04 Feb 1927, Fayetteville, NC.
8.   iv.   JOYCE MARIE FAIRCLOTH, b. 16 Oct 1929.
9.   v.   HELEN FAIRCLOTH, b. 16 Sep 1924.
10.   vi.   LOTTIE JUANITA FAIRCLOTH, b. 30 Oct 1932.
11.   vii.   JUDY ADLINE FAIRCLOTH, b. 27 Mar 1938, B St., Fayetteville, NC; d. 2005.
12. viii.   CARL HOUSTON FAIRCLOTH, b. 29 Oct 1920, Sampson Co., NC; d. 28 Dec 1971

All descendents of Lawrence C. and Lula J. Faircloth are listed under Lula Jane Faircloth, of the Edward Farecloth Descendents.

3. ALLEN CLAY[9] FAIRCLOTH (*BENJAMIN F.[8], THEOPHELES "AFFIE"[7], ARTHUR[6], HARDWICK[5], WILLIAM[4], WILLIAM[3], WILLIAM[2], WILLIAM[1]*) was born Bet. 28 Jul 1887 - 1888, and died 05 Jul 1944 in Buried in Hollywood Cemetery in Roseboro. He married (1) MISSOURI "ZUDE". She was born Abt. 1890. He married (2) MISSOURI "ZUDE" HALL 02 Oct 1908 in Married at the home of Uriah Sessoms, Justice of the Peace. Medical Information: Allen died of a brain abscess from a gunshot wound to the eye.

Child of ALLEN FAIRCLOTH and MISSOURI "ZUDE" is:
      i.   VENNIE[10] FAIRCLOTH, b. 08 Jun 1923; d. 13 Mar 1975, Roseboro Cemetery, NC; m. HOUSTON TROY FAIRCLOTH, 20 Jan 1946, Dillon, SC; b. 23 May 1926, Sampson Co., NC; d. Roseboro Cemetery, NC.

Children of ALLEN FAIRCLOTH and MISSOURI HALL are:
      ii.   MARIE MARY[10] FAIRCLOTH, d. Died young..
13.   iii.   ROBERT CLAY FAIRCLOTH, b. 22 Jul 1915; d. 13 Mar 1952.
14.   iv.   CARLIE FAIRCLOTH, b. 14 Feb 1909; d. 07 Aug 1972.
15.   v.   GLADIS FAIRCLOTH, b. 29 Jul 1918.
16.   vi.   AGNES FAIRCLOTH, b. 23 Sep 1921.
17.   vii.   ALLINE FAIRCLOTH, b. 12 Dec 1927.
18. viii.   PAUL ERNEST FAIRCLOTH, b. 08 Feb 1913.
19.   ix.   VENIE FAIRCLOTH, b. 08 Jun 1923; d. 13 Mar 1965, Buried in Roseboro Cemetery..
      x.   JOHN FAIRCLOTH, b. 08 Sep 1915.

4.   JERE TATE[9] FAIRCLOTH *(BENJAMIN F.[8], THEOPHELES "AFFIE"[7], ARTHUR[6], HARDWICK[5], WILLIAM[4], WILLIAM[3], WILLIAM[2], WILLIAM[1])* was born 1894, and died Aug 1953 in New Hanover County, NC. He married MURLENE WATKINS.

Children of JERE FAIRCLOTH and MURLENE WATKINS are:
   i.   BEN THOMAS[10] FAIRCLOTH, b. 18 Jan 1922, New Hanover Co., NC; d. 03 Apr 1922.
   ii. JERE TATE FAIRCLOTH, b. Nov 1923, New Hanover Co., NC; d. 1967.
   iii. CLYDE EARNEST FAIRCLOTH, b. Dec 1924, New Hanover Co., NC.

.Continuation of Descendents of Allen Clay Faircloth:

13.   ROBERT CLAY[10] FAIRCLOTH *(ALLEN CLAY[9], BENJAMIN F.[8], THEOPHELES "AFFIE"[7], ARTHUR[6], HARDWICK[5], WILLIAM[4], WILLIAM[3], WILLIAM[2], WILLIAM[1])* was born 22 Jul 1915, and died 13 Mar 1952. He married ETHEL DAVIS. She was born 1916 in Cumberland County, NC.

Children of ROBERT FAIRCLOTH and ETHEL DAVIS are:
   i.   MARY LOIS[11] FAIRCLOTH, b. 19 Oct 1942.
   ii. PAULINE FAIRCLOTH, b. 20 Oct 1943.
   iii. ANNETTE FAIRCLOTH, b. 1952.
   iv. DAVID NEAL FAIRCLOTH, b. 12 Jul 1946.
   v.   PERCY CLAY FAIRCLOTH, b. 18 Jul 1948.

14.   CARLIE[10] FAIRCLOTH *(ALLEN CLAY[9], BENJAMIN F.[8], THEOPHELES "AFFIE"[7], ARTHUR[6], HARDWICK[5], WILLIAM[4], WILLIAM[3], WILLIAM[2], WILLIAM[1])* was born 14 Feb 1909, and died 07 Aug 1972. He married AMY CLYDE CULBRETH 21 Feb 1942 in Dillon, SC, daughter of LILLIE CULBRETH and JANIE SUTTON.

Children of CARLIE FAIRCLOTH and AMY CULBRETH are:
   i.   MALCOLM JENKINS[11] FAIRCLOTH.
39.   ii. ALLEN CLAY FAIRCLOTH, b. 09 Feb 1943.
   iii. CATHERINE JANIE FAIRCLOTH, b. 25 Feb 1945; d. 09 Mar 1950, Died from 2nd and 3rd degree burns when her clothes caught fire from a furnace; Buried in the Hollywood Cemetery in Roseboro, NC.
40.   iv. MARTIN LANGISTER FAIRCLOTH.
41.   v.   WILLIAM LAWRENCE FAIRCLOTH, b. 19 May 1950.

15.   GLADIS[10] FAIRCLOTH *(ALLEN CLAY[9], BENJAMIN F.[8], THEOPHELES "AFFIE"[7], ARTHUR[6], HARDWICK[5], WILLIAM[4], WILLIAM[3], WILLIAM[2], WILLIAM[1])* was born 29 Jul 1918. She married ROMMIE LEWIS.

Children of GLADIS FAIRCLOTH and ROMMIE LEWIS are:
   i.   BOBBY[11] LEWIS.
   ii. MARTIN LEWIS.
   iii. CHARLES LEWIS.
   iv. DONNIE LEWIS.

16. AGNES[10] FAIRCLOTH *(ALLEN CLAY[9], BENJAMIN F.[8], THEOPHELES "AFFIE"[7], ARTHUR[6], HARDWICK[5], WILLIAM[4], WILLIAM[3], WILLIAM[2], WILLIAM[1])* was born 23 Sep 1921. She married (1) ALVIN PARKER. She married (2) JAMES SESSOMS.

Children of AGNES FAIRCLOTH and ALVIN PARKER are:
    i. FLOYD[11] PARKER, m. JERDINE FAIRCLOTH.
    ii. UNKNOWN PARKER, m. TOM ISLEY.

17. ALLINE[10] FAIRCLOTH *(ALLEN CLAY[9], BENJAMIN F.[8], THEOPHELES "AFFIE"[7], ARTHUR[6], HARDWICK[5], WILLIAM[4], WILLIAM[3], WILLIAM[2], WILLIAM[1])* was born 12 Dec 1927. She married IVEY LAL FAIRCLOTH. He was born 17 Mar 1927.

Children of ALLINE FAIRCLOTH and IVEY FAIRCLOTH are:
    i. KAY[11] FAIRCLOTH, m. BOBBY MCLAMB.
    ii. JAMES FAIRCLOTH, m. BETTY UNKNOWN.

18. PAUL ERNEST[10] FAIRCLOTH *(ALLEN CLAY[9], BENJAMIN F.[8], THEOPHELES "AFFIE"[7], ARTHUR[6], HARDWICK[5], WILLIAM[4], WILLIAM[3], WILLIAM[2], WILLIAM[1])* was born 08 Feb 1913. He married EARNIE KATE SESSOMS 1936, daughter of HOLLY SESSOMS and MARRY PARKER. She died 08 Sep 1978 in Buried in Roseboro, NC Cemetery..

Children of PAUL FAIRCLOTH and EARNIE SESSOMS are:
    i. VIVIAN MISSOURI[11] FAIRCLOTH, b. 28 Jun 1952; m. G. H. RAY.
    ii. MARY DORIS FAIRCLOTH, b. 29 Jan 1945.
42.   iii. EARL JUNIOR FAIRCLOTH, b. 11 Jan 1939.
    iv. HERMAN JAMES FAIRCLOTH, b. 24 Oct 1942; m. HELEN JEAN MATTHEWS, 02 Sep 1961.
    v. PAUL RUDY FAIRCLOTH, b. 31 Jan 1948; m. JOYCE ELAINE LUCAS.
    vi. BILLY DEAN FAIRCLOTH, b. 15 Nov 1957; m. MARTHA KAY HALL, 21 Dec 1974.

19. VENIE[10] FAIRCLOTH *(ALLEN CLAY[9], BENJAMIN F.[8], THEOPHELES "AFFIE"[7], ARTHUR[6], HARDWICK[5], WILLIAM[4], WILLIAM[3], WILLIAM[2], WILLIAM[1])* was born 08 Jun 1923, and died 13 Mar 1965 in Buried in Roseboro Cemetery.. She married HOUSTON TROY FAIRCLOTH 20 Jun 1946 in Dillon, SC, son of TROY FAIRCLOTH and PENNY FAIRCLOTH. He was born 23 May 1926 in Sampson Co., NC, and died in Roseboro Cemetery, NC.

Children of VENIE FAIRCLOTH and HOUSTON FAIRCLOTH are:
    i. FAYE[11] FAIRCLOTH, b. 05 Feb 1949.
    ii. DOROTHY FAIRCLOTH, b. 18 Sep 1947.
    iii. RUBEN ESTES FAIRCLOTH, b. 1951, Sampson Co., NC.
    iv. RICHARD " RICKY" HOUSTON FAIRCLOTH, b. 10 Oct 1955.
    v. LAWRENCE RAY FAIRCLOTH, b. 1952; d. Bef. 1984.
    vi. CATHY DIANE FAIRCLOTH, b. 10 Jan 1957.

39. ALLEN CLAY[11] FAIRCLOTH *(CARLIE[10], ALLEN CLAY[9], BENJAMIN F.[8], THEOPHELES "AFFIE"[7], ARTHUR[6], HARDWICK[5], WILLIAM[4], WILLIAM[3], WILLIAM[2], WILLIAM[1])* was born 09 Feb 1943. He married VADA LEE TURNER 01 Apr 1964.

Children of ALLEN FAIRCLOTH and VADA TURNER are:
  i. UNKNOWN[12] FAIRCLOTH.
  ii. KENNETH ALLEN FAIRCLOTH, b. 06 Mar 1967.

40. MARTIN LANGISTER[11] FAIRCLOTH *(CARLIE[10], ALLEN CLAY[9], BENJAMIN F.[8], THEOPHELES "AFFIE"[7], ARTHUR[6], HARDWICK[5], WILLIAM[4], WILLIAM[3], WILLIAM[2], WILLIAM[1])* He married JANETTE F. WILLIAMS.

Child of MARTIN FAIRCLOTH and JANETTE WILLIAMS is:
  i. TRAVIS MARTIN[12] FAIRCLOTH, b. 19 May 1950.

41. WILLIAM LAWRENCE[11] FAIRCLOTH *(CARLIE[10], ALLEN CLAY[9], BENJAMIN F.[8], THEOPHELES "AFFIE"[7], ARTHUR[6], HARDWICK[5], WILLIAM[4], WILLIAM[3], WILLIAM[2], WILLIAM[1])* was born 19 May 1950. He married ELMA DARLENE THOMPSON.

Children of WILLIAM FAIRCLOTH and ELMA THOMPSON are:
  i. ELMA MICHELLE[12] FAIRCLOTH, b. 30 Nov 1972.
  ii. UNKNOWN FAIRCLOTH.

42. EARL JUNIOR[11] FAIRCLOTH *(PAUL ERNEST[10], ALLEN CLAY[9], BENJAMIN F.[8], THEOPHELES "AFFIE"[7], ARTHUR[6], HARDWICK[5], WILLIAM[4], WILLIAM[3], WILLIAM[2], WILLIAM[1])* was born 11 Jan 1939. He married DORTHEA HALL 05 Oct 1957.

Children of EARL FAIRCLOTH and DORTHEA HALL are:
  i.   ROSA FAYE[12] FAIRCLOTH, b. 09 Jul 1958; m. LLOYD FAIRCLOTH, JR..
  ii. FRANKIE RAY FAIRCLOTH, b. 20 Mar 1961; m. LORI JANE HALL, 07 Nov 1981.
  iii. LONNIE PAUL FAIRCLOTH, b. 20 Aug 1965.
Notes:

END OF DESCENDENTS OF WILLIAM FAIRCLOTH

Part Three – Genealogy Records
The Descendents of Edward Farecloth

The Descendents of Edward Farecloth

Edward – Benjamin Franklin – Solomon – Moses McLaine, Sr – Hanson Asberry – Herman R. – Joyce Christine – Jennifer Heather Brooke Judah – Isaih Dale Fisher.

The line of Edward Farecloth begins in the early 1700's and extends through the lines of Benjamin Franklin Faircloth, Sr. down to my grandson, Isaih Dale Fisher. The line of Moses McLaine Faircloth, Sr., is fairly well accepted throughout the Faircloth historians. It is my belief, based upon information contained therein, that the lines above Moses lead through Solomon Faircloth, to Benjamin Franklin Faircloth to his father, Edward. Therefore, this work begins with the elder, Edward Farecloth.

Descendants of Edward Farecloth

Generation No. 1

1. EDWARD[1] FARECLOTH was born Bet. 1700 - 1710. He married SARAH UNKNOWN. She was born Bet. 1700 - 1710, and died Aft. 1774.

Children of EDWARD FARECLOTH and SARAH UNKNOWN are:
2.   i.   BENJAMIN FRANKLIN[2] FAIRCLOTH, SR., b. 1735.
     ii.   THOMAS FAIRCLOTH, b. Bef. 1727.
    iii.   JOHN FAIRCLOTH, b. Bef. 1727.

Generation No. 2

2. BENJAMIN FRANKLIN[2] FAIRCLOTH, SR. *(EDWARD[1] FARECLOTH)* was born 1735. He married LETITIA "LEDDY" GARNER. She was born 1735.

Children of BENJAMIN FAIRCLOTH and LETITIA GARNER are:
3.   i.   SOLOMON[3] FAIRCLOTH, b. Abt. 1765.
4.   ii.   SAMUEL FAIRCLOTH, b. Bet. 1760 - 1780, Sampson Co., NC; d. Bet. 1807 - 1808.
    iii.   BENJAMIN FRANKLIN FAIRCLOTH, JR., b. Abt. 1780; m. LETITIA "LEDDY" GARNER.
        Will
        Will naming grandson, William Faircloth, Edgecombe County, NC - Miscellaneous Wills, Book A
        Garner, John, will date 25 Sep 1760, proved Dec Ct 1760. In the Name

of God Amen, I John Garner, Sr of (Coeneto) in Edgecombe County being old and weake in body but of sound mind and memory thanks be to God... Imprimis I give and bequeath to my daughter Sarah Wright my Negro boy (Nead) to her and the lawful heirs of her body; Item- I give and bequeath unto my daughter Jayn Garner to my Negro Lucy to her and the lawful heirs of her body; Item- I give and bequeath to my son, John Garner my boy (Isaac); Item- I give and bequeath unto my (   ) son Jonathan Garner my Negro boy Peter; Item- I give and bequeath unto my son Absalom Garner my Negro boy Sam; Item- I give and bequeath to my daughter (Judy Garner) my Negro fellow (Quamines) to her and her lawful heirs of her body; Item- I give and bequeath unto my youngest daughter Onner Garner my Negro wench named (Dot) to her and the lawful heirs of her body; Item- I give unto my two youngest daughters (Jodey) and (Onner) each of them a young Negro (apiece) if (there) is any at the time of the division of my estate and if there is no young Negroes then the same above mentioned (Judy & Anner) and if there be young Negroes ( ) gets them. I give and bequeath unto my son John Garner the above mentioned Nan to the only use and behoof him and his heirs my Negro (Quamine) if there be young ones for

(   ) Jonathan Garner to the only use and behoof of him. Item- I give and bequeath in the same manner my Negro wench Dot to my son Absalom Garner to the only use and behoof him providing there be young Negroes for my above mentioned (Judy and Anner). Item- I give and bequeath unto my daughter Martha Garner (five shillings sterling in remembrance that she is my daughter. Item- I give and bequeath to my grandson William Faircloth 25 shillings sterling. Item- I give and bequeath to my son John Garner the manor and dwelling plantation with 170 acres of land for the only and behoof of him. Item- I give and bequeath to my son Jonathan Garner 100 acres of land where (William Wiggins) formerly lived to the only use and behoof of him. Item- I give and bequeath unto my son Absalom Garner 100 acres of land being between (his   ) above mentioned to the only use and befoof of ( ). Item- I give and bequeath unto my loving wife Martha Garner all my workings (   ) from the date thereof in during her widowhood and my personal estate to my loving wife Martha Garner during the time of her widowhood. Item- I give and bequeath all my working (   ) and rest of my estate at the time of my wife's death or marriage to be equally divided to all my children but the two above mentioned Mathew Garner and William Faircloth. Item- I ordain my wife Martha and my son John Garner hole and sole executors till the day of marriage or death and then my son hole and sole executor. Item- I give and bequeath to my daughter Sarah (   ) two cows and calfes and after this whole (dividend) to be deducted of her share of this my last will and testament revoking all wills or other testament ever by me made or ordained in witness whereof I have set my hand and seal this twenty fifth of September of 1760. John Garner (Mark). Test William Wright, Thos Clark (mark), Reed Bottom (mark). Edgecombe County - (   ). December Inferior Court 1760. The within will was in open Court exhibited by the exrs therein named and proved by the oath of Thomas one of the subscribing (   ) thereto who likewise swore that he saw the other two (   ) subscribe the same and at the same time the exeors was qualified according to law which is ordered to be qualified and the will to be recorded. Test James Hall (CC Cir). Will Book A, page 13. Abstracted 2-23-06, NCA film C.037.80001, CTC.

    iv.   WILLIAM FAIRCLOTH, b. 1751; m. ELIZABETH SESSOMS; b. 1750.
    v.   CALEB FAIRCLOTH, b. Abt. 1780.
    vi.   RICHARD M. FAIRCLOTH, b. Abt. 1780.
    vii.   SMITHWICK FAIRCLOTH, b. Abt. 1780.
    viii.   THOMAS FAIRCLOTH b. Abt. 1780.
5.   ix.   ROBERT FAIRCLOTH, b. 1752.

Generation No. 3

3. SOLOMON[3] FAIRCLOTH *(BENJAMIN FRANKLIN[2], EDWARD[1] FARECLOTH)* was born Abt. 1765.

Children of SOLOMON FAIRCLOTH are:
6.   i.   MOSES MCLAINE[4] FAIRCLOTH, SR., b. Bet. 1795 - 1801; d. Bet. 1860 - 1870, 82 yrs old when died about 1860-70.Charleston, SC.
    ii.   UNKNOWN FAIRCLOTH.
    iii.   UNKNOWN FAIRCLOTH.
    iv.   UNKNOWN FAIRCLOTH.
    v.   UNKNOWN FAIRCLOTH.
    vi.   UNKNOWN FAIRCLOTH.
    vii.   UNKNOWN FAIRCLOTH.
    viii.   UNKNOWN FAIRCLOTH.

4. SAMUEL[3] FAIRCLOTH *(BENJAMIN FRANKLIN[2], EDWARD[1] FARECLOTH)* was born Bet. 1760 - 1780 in Sampson Co., NC, and died Bet. 1807 - 1808. He married ELIZABETH. She was born Abt. 1763, and died Abt. 1818 in Sampson Co., NC.

Robert June Faircloth believes that the following children were children of Samuel: Elizabeth, Achsah, Sabra, Nancy (who married Isaac Sessoms), Jonah, Arthur, b. 1760, Wilson, who later moved to Georgia, Raiford, Serenah and Betsy. Most of these are listed as children of Hardwick Faircloth and Sarah Suggs Faircloth on my documents at this time (2006). Further investigation is warranted as I have them listed as Hardwick's children, as per the militia information which he lists as all his children.

Children of SAMUEL FAIRCLOTH and ELIZABETH are:
    i.   NANCY[4] FAIRCLOTH, m. ISAAC SESSOMS.
       More About ISAAC SESSOMS:
       Name 2: Isaac Sessums, Jr.
    ii.   CALEB FAIRCLOTH.
    iii.   ELIZABETH FAIRCLOTH.
    iv.   JONAH FAIRCLOTH.

5. ROBERT[3] FAIRCLOTH *(BENJAMIN FRANKLIN[2], EDWARD[1] FARECLOTH)* was born 1752. He married ELIZABETH LANE. She was born 1754.

Child of ROBERT FAIRCLOTH and ELIZABETH LANE is:
    i.   ALLAN[4] FAIRCLOTH, b. 1770; d. Apr 1852.

6. MOSES MCLAINE[4] FAIRCLOTH, SR. *(SOLOMON[3], BENJAMIN FRANKLIN[2], EDWARD[1] FARECLOTH)* was born Bet. 1795 - 1801, and died Bet. 1860 - 1870 in 82 yrs old when died about 1860-70.Charleston, SC. He married (1) ELIZABETH "LIZZIE" HALL. 1870.

Child of MOSES FAIRCLOTH and ELIZABETH HALL is:
  i. ELIZABETH "LIZZIE"[5] HALL, b. Abt. 1862; d. Bet. 1901 - 1911; m. HANSON ASBERRY "BEAR" FAIRCLOTH, Bet. 1887 - 1888; b. 11 May 1862, Sampson Co., NC; d. 27 Jan 1941, Sampson Co., NC; buried in the Moses Cemetery in Sampson County, NC.

Children of MOSES FAIRCLOTH and PENELOPE are:
  ii. MOSES MCLAINE (MCLEWANEY)[5] FAIRCLOTH, JR., b. Abt. 1825; d. 22 Mar 1863. m. (1) ANNIE NANCY HALL; b. Abt. 1839; d. Bet. 1863 - 1868; m. (2) PATIENCE " PATIA" HALL; b. 1845.

  iii. SYLVANNIA C. FAIRCLOTH, b. 1826; d. Aft. 1880; m. NEVER MARRIED. Her birthdate fluctuates depending upon which census you are consulting. Living with widowed mother in 1880.

  iv. SAMPSON FAIRCLOTH, b. 23 Jan 1823; d. Aug 1906; m. (1) ANN HALL; b. Apr 1828; d. 1907; m. (2) NANNIE HOLLAND; b. May be the same individual as Ann Hall, b. 1828. Sampson's birthdate established by 1840, 1960 and 1870 Census Records.

  Resided in Sampson County, NC and enlisted in the Orange County Court House, VA on 1 Nov 1863 for the Civil War. He was present and accounted for until he deserted about 11 April 1864. He returned to duty on 24 Sept 1864. He deserted again on 14 February 1865. He was captured by the enemy in Sampson County on 16 March 1865 and confined at Hart's Island, New York Harbor on 10 April 1865. He was released from Hart's Island on 19 June 1865 after taking the Oath of allegiance. He was a member of C Company, 26th Regiment, NC State Troops. he applied and was granted a soldiers pension on 27 July 1903 at 80 years of age. At age 79, his widow, Annie, applied for a pension in Sampson County. She stated "My husband served all through the war." Sampson died in Sampson County in 1906.

  v. OWEN FAIRCLOTH, b. 1837; d. Aft. 1905; m. MOLLIE, 30 Nov 1865, Sampson County, NC; married by J. c. Autry;; b. 1832.
  Notes for OWEN FAIRCLOTH:
  Birth date is listed as 10 and under 15 in the 1840 Census putting his birth between 1830 and 1835. He is listed as 23 on the 1860 Census putting his birth at 1837. Owen was married by J. C. Autry, Justice of Peace in Sampson County, NC

  vi. PHILLIP FAIRCLOTH, b. 1834; d. 01 Jan 1865, Civil War, of chronic dysentery; m. JANE. Phillip is listed as of 5 and under 10 in the 1840 Census putting his birth at 1834. Phillip enlisted at the orange Court House, VA on November 1863 for the war. He was present or accounted for until he deserted on or about April 12, 1864. He returned to duty on September 24, 1864. He was present or accounted for until captured near Petersburg, VA on October 27, 1864 and confined at Point Lookout, Maryland where he died on Jan 1, 1865 of chronic dysentery.
  Died 2: 01 Jan 1865, in Civil War of Chronic dysentery

vii. BARNABUS FAIRCLOTH, b. 1837; d. 15 Apr 1864, Civil War; Died in MD at a POW Camp. Barnabus is listed as 5 and under 10 in the 1840 census putting his birth at 1837.Barnabus was a Private in Company H. Regt., 20th Infantry. He was born in 1839 according to military records and enlisted on 10 June 1861 in Clinton, NC. He was captured 1-3 July 1863 at Gettysburg, PA and confined to Fort Delaware, Del and Point Lookout, MD where he died 15 April 1864 of diarrhea. He enlisted at age 21. He was transferred to point Lookout on October 15-18, 1863. He died in a hospital.

viii. SARAH FAIRCLOTH, b. Abt. 1837.
Sarah is listed as 22 years old in 1860 and 30 years old in 1870 putting her birth year between 1838-40.

ix. JANIE FAIRCLOTH, b. Abt. 1842.:
Janie's age is listed as under 5 in 1850 and this puts her birth between 1845 and 1850.

x. JASPER JONATHAN FAIRCLOTH, b. Mar 1820, NC; d. Aft. 1900, Jasper and Sarah, his wife, buried at Autryville Baptist Church Cemetery;; m. (1) SARAH CAROLINE SESSOMS; b. Bet. 1823 - 1828; m. (2) SARAH CAROLINA SESSOMS.:
Possibly born March 1816.

xi. OWEN FAIRCLOTH, b. May 1830; d. Aft. 1905; m. MOLLIE FAIRCLOTH, 30 Nov 1865; b. 1832.

xii. BARNABUS FAIRCLOTH, b. 1839; d. 15 Apr 1864, Died in Civil War.

Descendants of Benjamin Franklin Faircloth, Sr.

Generation No. 1

1. BENJAMIN FRANKLIN[2] FAIRCLOTH, SR. *(EDWARD[1] FARECLOTH)* was born 1735. He married LETITIA "LEDDY" GARNER. She was born 1735. See under Last Wills and Testaments, John Gardner's will of 1760. LETITIA "LEDDY" GARNER was the daughter of JOHN GARNER and MARTHA.

Children of BENJAMIN FAIRCLOTH and LETITIA GARNER are:
2.   i. SOLOMON[3] FAIRCLOTH, b. Abt. 1765.
3.   ii. SAMUEL FAIRCLOTH, b. Bet. 1760 - 1780, Sampson Co., NC; d. Bet. 1807 - 1808.
     iii. BENJAMIN FRANKLIN FAIRCLOTH, JR., b. Abt. 1780;
     iv. WILLIAM FAIRCLOTH, b. 1751; m. ELIZABETH SESSOMS; b. 1750.
     v. CALEB FAIRCLOTH, b. Abt. 1780.
     vi. RICHARD M. FAIRCLOTH, b. Abt. 1780.
     vii. SMITHWICK FAIRCLOTH, b. Abt. 1780.
     viii. THOMAS FAIRCLOTH, b. Abt. 1780.
4.   ix. ROBERT FAIRCLOTH, b. 1752.

Descendants of Solomon Faircloth

Generation No. 1

1. SOLOMON[3] FAIRCLOTH *(BENJAMIN FRANKLIN[2], EDWARD[1] FARECLOTH)* was born Abt. 1765.

Children of SOLOMON FAIRCLOTH are:
2. i. MOSES MCLAINE[4] FAIRCLOTH, SR., b. Bet. 1795 - 1801; d. Bet. 1860 - 1870, 82 yrs old when died about 1860-70.Charleston, SC.
    ii. UNKNOWN FAIRCLOTH.
    iii. UNKNOWN FAIRCLOTH.
    iv. UNKNOWN FAIRCLOTH.
    v. UNKNOWN FAIRCLOTH.
    vi. UNKNOWN FAIRCLOTH.
    vii. UNKNOWN FAIRCLOTH.
    viii. UNKNOWN FAIRCLOTH.

Generation No. 2

2. MOSES MCLAINE[4] FAIRCLOTH, SR. *(SOLOMON[3], BENJAMIN FRANKLIN[2], EDWARD[1] FARECLOTH)* was born Bet. 1795 - 1801, and died Bet. 1860 - 1870 in 82 yrs old when died about 1860-70. He married (1) ELIZABETH "LIZZIE" HALL. She was born Feb 1871 in Sampson Co., NC, and died Bet. 1900 - 1907 in Sampson Co., NC. He married (2) PENELOPE. She was born Abt. 1799.

Child of MOSES FAIRCLOTH and ELIZABETH HALL is:
3. i. ELIZABETH "LIZZIE"[5] HALL, b. Abt. 1862; d. Bet. 1901 - 1911.

Children of MOSES FAIRCLOTH and PENELOPE are:
4. ii. MOSES MCLAINE (MCLEWANEY)[5] FAIRCLOTH, JR., b. Abt. 1825; d. 22 Mar 1863, Died in SC of a fever in a local hospital..
5. iii. SYLVANNIA C. FAIRCLOTH, b. 1826; d. Aft. 1880.
6. iv. SAMPSON FAIRCLOTH, b. 23 Jan 1823; d. Aug 1906.
7. v. OWEN FAIRCLOTH, b. 1837; d. Aft. 1905.
8. vi. PHILLIP FAIRCLOTH, b. 1834; d. 01 Jan 1865, Civil War, of chronic dysentery.
    vii. BARNABUS FAIRCLOTH, b. 1837; d. 15 Apr 1864, Civil War; Died in MD at a POW Camp..Barnabus is listed as 5 and under 10 in the 1840 census putting his birth at 1837. Barnabus was a Private in Company H. Regt., 20th Infantry. He was born in 1839 according to military records and enlisted on 10 June 1861 in Clinton, NC. He was captured 1-3 July 1863 at Gettysburg, PA and confined to Fort Delaware, Del and Point Lookout, MD where he died 15 April 1864 of diarrhea. He enlisted at age 21. He was transferred to point Lookout on October 15-18, 1863. He died in a hospital.

viii. SARAH FAIRCLOTH, b. Abt. 1837.
Sarah is listed as 22 years old in 1860 and 30 years old in 1870 putting her birth year between 1838-40.

ix. JANIE FAIRCLOTH, b. Abt. 1842.
Janie's age is listed as under 5 in 1850 and this puts her birth between 1845 and 1850.

9. x. JASPER JONATHAN FAIRCLOTH, b. Mar 1820, NC; d. Aft. 1900, Jasper and Sarah, his wife, buried at Autryville Baptist Church Cemetery;.

xi. OWEN FAIRCLOTH, b. May 1830; d. Aft. 1905; m. MOLLIE FAIRCLOTH, 30 Nov 1865; b. 1832.

xii. BARNABUS FAIRCLOTH, b. 1839; d. 15 Apr 1864, Died in Civil War.

Generation No. 3

3. ELIZABETH "LIZZIE"[5] HALL *(MOSES MCLAINE[4] FAIRCLOTH, SR., SOLOMON[3], BENJAMIN FRANKLIN[2], EDWARD[1] FARECLOTH)* was born Abt. 1862, and died Bet. 1901 - 1911. He married HANSON ASBERRY "BEAR" FAIRCLOTH Bet. 1887 - 1888, son of MOSES FAIRCLOTH and ANNIE HALL. He was born 11 May 1862 in Sampson Co., NC, and died 27 Jan 1941 in Sampson Co., NC;

Children of ELIZABETH HALL and HANSON FAIRCLOTH are:
10. i. LULA JANE[6] FAIRCLOTH, b. 16 Aug 1897, Sampson Co., NC; d. 23 Aug 1959, Cumberland County, NC;
11. ii. STEPHEN PHILLIP FAIRCLOTH, b. 17 Oct 1888; d. 17 Jan 1958.
12. iii. LAMAR LALLISTER FAIRCLOTH, b. 30 Oct 1893; d. 07 Nov 1943, Sampson Co., NC;
iv. UNKNOWN FAIRCLOTH, b. Bef. 1900.
Listed as a result of the 1900 Census records.
13. v. SANTFORD ALLEN FAIRCLOTH, b. 13 Mar 1900, Sampson Co., NC; d. 18 Mar 1971, Sampson Co., NC;
14. vi. TROY FAIRCLOTH, b. 13 Aug 1901, Cumberland County, NC; d. 03 Sep 1966,
15. vii. GEORGE WASHINGTON FAIRCLOTH, b. 02 Apr 1892; d. 23 Jan 1971, VA Hospital.

4. MOSES MCLAINE (MCLEWANEY)[5] FAIRCLOTH, JR. *(MOSES MCLAINE[4], SOLOMON[3], BENJAMIN FRANKLIN[2], EDWARD[1] FARECLOTH)* was born Abt. 1825, and died 22 Mar 1863 in Died in SC of a fever in a local hospital.. He married (1) ANNIE NANCY HALL.

Children of MOSES FAIRCLOTH and ANNIE HALL are:
16. i. HANSON ASBERRY "BEAR"[6] FAIRCLOTH, b. 11 May 1862, Sampson Co., NC; d. 27 Jan 1941, Sampson Co., NC;
17. ii. CHARLOTTE FAIRCLOTH, b. Mar 1861; d. 1931, Sampson Co., N
iii. SCOTT FAIRCLOTH, b. Abt. 1849.
iv. PATIENCE "PATRICIA"FAIRCLOTH, b. 1857.
v. THOMAS J. FAIRCLOTH, b. Jun 1859.
18. vi. PHILLIP FAIRCLOTH, b. Aug 1869; d. 27 Feb 1967

Children of MOSES FAIRCLOTH and PATIENCE HALL are:

vii. NANCY[6] HALL.

viii. IDA E. FAIRCLOTH, b. Feb 1875, Sampson Co., NC; d. 09 Mar 1959, Sampson Co., NC; m. GRADY TANNER.

ix. IRENE RENA FAIRCLOTH, b. 16 Jul 1879, Mother is Patience "Patia" Hall; m. M. O. MATTHEWS, 16 Dec 1903; b. 1876; d. 16 Dec 1903, Sampson Co., NC.

x. NANCY HALL FAIRCLOTH, b. adopted by Moses Jr..

5.   SYLVANNIA C.[5] FAIRCLOTH (*MOSES MCLAINE[4], SOLOMON[3], BENJAMIN FRANKLIN[2], EDWARD[1] FARECLOTH*) was born 1826, and died Aft. 1880 NEVER MARRIED.

Children of SYLVANNIA FAIRCLOTH and NEVER MARRIED are:
19.   i. GEORGE W.[6] FAIRCLOTH, b. 10 Sep 1867; d. 14 Jul 1907.
20.   ii. WRIGHT L. FAIRCLOTH, b. 28 Apr 1857; d. 05 Jul 1918.

6.   SAMPSON[5] FAIRCLOTH (*MOSES MCLAINE[4], SOLOMON[3], BENJAMIN FRANKLIN[2], EDWARD[1] FARECLOTH*) was born 23 Jan 1823, and died Aug 1906. He married (1) ANN HALL.

Children of SAMPSON FAIRCLOTH and ANN HALL are:
       i. BARNEY[6] FAIRCLOTH, b. 1849; d. Bef. 1860.
21.   ii. HINTON KELLY CARR FAIRCLOTH, b. 13 Aug 1853, Sampson Co., NC; d. 11 Nov 1927, Died of lobas pneumonia; Buried 14 Nov 1927 in the Joel Horne Cemetery, Sampson County..
       iii. MARY FAIRCLOTH, b. Abt. 1856; m. JAMES HALL.
22.   iv. WILLIAM BARNA FAIRCLOTH, b. 02 Oct 1862; d. 01 Sep 1923, Buried Horne Cemetery on 2 sep 1923; died from gallstones, TB & tumor in liver.
23.   v. BLACKMON FAIRCLOTH, b. 15 Oct 1848; d. 10 Mar 1924, Buried in Rich Faircloth Cemetery; Buried 11 Mar 1924.

7.   OWEN[5] FAIRCLOTH (*MOSES MCLAINE[4], SOLOMON[3], BENJAMIN FRANKLIN[2], EDWARD[1] FARECLOTH*) was born 1837, and died Aft. 1905. He married MOLLIE 30 Nov 1865 in Sampson County, NC; married by J. c. Autry;. She was born 1832.

Child of OWEN FAIRCLOTH and MOLLIE is:
       i. ABBIE[6] FAIRCLOTH, b. Sep 1881; m. D. MCK. HOWELL, 03 Sep 1905, Cumberland County, NC.

8.   PHILLIP[5] FAIRCLOTH (*MOSES MCLAINE[4], SOLOMON[3], BENJAMIN FRANKLIN[2], EDWARD[1] FARECLOTH*) was born 1834, and died 01 Jan 1865 in Civil War, of chronic dysentery. He married JANE.

Child of PHILLIP FAIRCLOTH and JANE is:
24.   i. STANTLEY[6] FAIRCLOTH, b. Dec 1859, Sampson Co., NC; d. 1935, Buried in the Moses Cemetery, Sampson County, NC.

9.   JASPER JONATHAN[5] FAIRCLOTH (*MOSES MCLAINE[4], SOLOMON[3], BENJAMIN FRANKLIN[2], EDWARD[1] FARECLOTH*) was born Mar 1820 in NC, and died Aft. 1900 in Jasper and Sarah, his wife, buried at Autryville Baptist Church Cemetery;. He married (1) SARAH CAROLINE SESSOMS. She was born Bet. 1823 - 1828. JASPER possibly born March 1816.

174

Children of JASPER FAIRCLOTH and SARAH SESSOMS are:

    i.   JASPER JONATHAN^6 FAIRCLOTH II, b. Feb 1861, Grave says he was born 1858.; d. 30 Dec 1950, Died of arteriosclosis & Pneumonia at 92 yrs of age.

    ii.   SARAH M. FAIRCLOTH, b. 10 Mar 1859, NC; d. 16 Dec 1927, Buried Autryville Baptist Church Cemetery; died of heart disease; tombstone says born 12 Jan 1858..

    iii.   WILLIAM FRANKLIN FAIRCLOTH, b. 1851.

25.   iv.   SOLOMON (JONATHAN JAMES) FAIRCLOTH, b. 28 Oct 1853, Samson Co., NC; d. 08 Apr 1931, Sampson Co., NC; of pneumonia;.

    v.   SHEPARD FAIRCLOTH, b. 1855.

    vi.   LOVE D. FAIRCLOTH, b. Abt. 1860, Possibly born between 1860-62.; d. 30 Dec 1950.

Generation No. 4

10.   LULA JANE^6 FAIRCLOTH *(ELIZABETH "LIZZIE"^{5} HALL, MOSES MCLAINE^4 FAIRCLOTH, SR., SOLOMON^3, BENJAMIN FRANKLIN^2, EDWARD^1 FARECLOTH)* was born 16 Aug 1897 in Sampson Co., NC, and died 23 Aug 1959 in Cumberland County, NC;. She married (1) SMITH. She married (2) LAWRENCE C. FAIRCLOTH 10 Jan 1915 in Sampson County, NC, son of BENJAMIN FAIRCLOTH and ADLINE AUTRY.

Children of LULA FAIRCLOTH and LAWRENCE FAIRCLOTH are:

    i.   LILLIAN ELIZABETH^7 FAIRCLOTH, b. 15 Dec 1915. D. Fayetteville, NC

    ii.   LEROY FAIRCLOTH, b. 05 May 1918, Hayne, NC;

    iii.   HERMAN REMUS FAIRCLOTH, b. 04 Feb 1927, Fayetteville, NC;

    iv.   JOYCE MARIE FAIRCLOTH, b. 16 Oct 1929

    v.   HELEN FAIRCLOTH, b. 16 Sep 1924;

    vi.   LOTTIE JUANITA FAIRCLOTH, b. 30 Oct 1932;

    vii.   JUDY ADLINE FAIRCLOTH, b. 27 Mar 1938, B St., Fayetteville, NC; d. 2005; .

    viii.   CARL HOUSTON FAIRCLOTH, b. 29 Oct 1920, Sampson Co., NC; d. 28 Dec 1971;

11.   STEPHEN PHILLIP^6 FAIRCLOTH *(ELIZABETH "LIZZIE"^{5} HALL, MOSES MCLAINE^4 FAIRCLOTH, SR., SOLOMON^3, BENJAMIN FRANKLIN^2, EDWARD^1 FARECLOTH)* was born 17 Oct 1888, and died 17 Jan 1958. He married (1) BETTY ELIZABETH SESSOMS in Married in the home of Diancy Sessoms, Sampson County, NC.

Children of STEPHEN FAIRCLOTH and BETTY SESSOMS are:

    i.   VAUGHN (HENRY^7 VON)FAIRCLOTH, b. 01 Jan 1916, Sampson Co., NC; d. 09 Jun 1982, Died of heart disease; m. RUBY FAIRCLOTH; b. 16 Jan 1924, Sampson Co., NC.

    ii.   PAUL M. FAIRCLOTH, b. Abt. 1911; d. 30 Jun 1988, Buried in Haney Family Cemetery by butler Funeral Home/Rev. Roger Jackson; m. LIZZIE GLENDON.

    iii.   RONIE ANN FAIRCLOTH, b. 25 Nov 1911; d. 19 May 1980, Died of diabetes and cancer, Sessoms Cemetery, Autryville, NC; m. JAMES K. OZZELL; b. 02 May 1905; d. 16 May 1977.

12.   LAMAR LALLISTER^6 FAIRCLOTH *(ELIZABETH "LIZZIE"^{5} HALL, MOSES MCLAINE^4 FAIRCLOTH, SR., SOLOMON^3, BENJAMIN FRANKLIN^2, EDWARD^1 FARECLOTH)* was born 30 Oct 1893, and died 07 Nov 1943 in Sampson Co., NC; buried 9 Nov in Johnson Family

Cemetery. He married BETTY FAIRCLOTH 03 Apr 1914, daughter of LUCIAN FAIRCLOTH and EMMA SESSOMS. Lamar was buried on 9 Nov 1943 in the Johnson Family Cemetery. Lamar Lallister Faircloth was a World War I Veteran who served as a Private in the 119th Infantry of the 30th Division. It is believed that he was wounded in the war and later in life had "spells" as a result of his injuries.

Children of LAMAR FAIRCLOTH and BETTY FAIRCLOTH are:
    i. SEPSIE[7] FAIRCLOTH, b. 15 Sep 1920, Sampson Co., NC.
       Date born 2: 15 Sep 1920
   ii. HOUSTON LEE FAIRCLOTH, b. 15 Dec 1921, Cumberland County, NC; d. 30 Apr 1981, Buried in Concord Baptist Church Cemetery in Stedman, NC; m. MARY BELLE HOWELL; b. 09 Sep 1917, Cumberland County, NC; d. 14 Apr 1967, Buried at Concord Baptist Church, Autryville, NC.
  iii. WILLIAM HOLT FAIRCLOTH, b. 02 Jan 1924, Cumberland County, NC.
   iv. ELVA FAIRCLOTH, b. 28 Jun 1927, Cumberland County, NC.
    v. HOOVER BRYANT FAIRCLOTH, b. 28 Feb 1929, Cumberland County, NC.
   vi. LELA FAIRCLOTH, b. 18 Oct 1933; m. UNKNOWN STRICKLAND.
  vii. LAMAR LALLISTER FAIRCLOTH, JR., b. 12 Jun 1937; d. 05 Jul 1981, Buried in Church of god Cemetery in Autryville, NC; m. NEVER MARRIED.
 viii. CHARLES EARL FAIRCLOTH, b. 06 Nov 1939, Sampson Co., NC.
   ix. JESSIE FAIRCLOTH, b. 26 Feb 1942, Sampson Co., NC.

13. SANTFORD ALLEN[6] FAIRCLOTH (*ELIZABETH "LIZZIE"[5] HALL, MOSES MCLAINE[4] FAIRCLOTH, SR., SOLOMON[3], BENJAMIN FRANKLIN[2], EDWARD[1] FARECLOTH*) was born 13 Mar 1900 in Sampson Co., NC, and died 18 Mar 1971 in Sampson Co., NC; He married ROSA FAIRCLOTH 10 Jan 1920and died 13 Dec 1980.

Children of SANTFORD FAIRCLOTH and ROSA FAIRCLOTH are:
    i. THELMA[7] FAIRCLOTH, b. 24 Nov 1920, Sampson Co., NC; m. ELMER BRAYTON COLLISTER, Aug 1941; b. 16 Mar 1920, Ohio.
   ii. JANEVA FAIRCLOTH, b. 06 Nov 1922, Sampson Co., NC; d. Died very young.
  iii. ROBERT J. FAIRCLOTH, b. Oct 1927, Cumberland County, NC.
   iv. AREY FAIRCLOTH, b. 31 Jul 1932, Sampson Co., NC.
    v. RAYMOND FAIRCLOTH, b. 19 May 1934, Sampson Co., NC; m. WANDA.
   vi. IRA FAIRCLOTH, m. UNKNOWN HALL.
  vii. RONIE NANCY FAIRCLOTH, b. 12 Sep 1924, Sampson Co., NC; d. 08 Feb 1925, Died of Pneumonia..

14. TROY[6] FAIRCLOTH (*ELIZABETH "LIZZIE"[5] HALL, MOSES MCLAINE[4] FAIRCLOTH, SR., SOLOMON[3], BENJAMIN FRANKLIN[2], EDWARD[1] FARECLOTH*) was born 13 Aug 1901 in Cumberland County, NC, and died 03 Sep 1966 in Buried 4 Sep in Salemburg Free Will Baptist Church Cemetery. He married PENNY FAIRCLOTH 26 Nov 1919 in Cumberland County, NC, daughter of ERVING FAIRCLOTH and MANDY NEW. She was born 07 Jun 1901 in Sampson Co., NC, and died 02 Jul 1973 in Buried at Salemburg Freewill Baptist Church. Troy buried 4 September 1966 in Salemburg Free Will Baptist Church Cemetery.

Children of TROY FAIRCLOTH and PENNY FAIRCLOTH are:
    i. LOUISA JANE[7] FAIRCLOTH, b. 19 Sep 1920, Sampson Co., NC; m. CLAUDIUM MCD. PETERSON, 07 Feb 1941; b. 1917.

ii. HUBERT FAIRCLOTH, b. 09 Sep 1923, Sampson Co., NC; m. PRISCILLA MAE AUTRY, 06 Apr 1956, Dillon, SC; b. 1926, South Autryville, NC.

iii. HOUSTON TROY FAIRCLOTH, b. 23 May 1926, Sampson Co., NC; d. Roseboro Cemetery, NC; m. (1) VENNIE FAIRCLOTH, 20 Jan 1946, Dillon, SC; b. 08 Jun 1923; d. 13 Mar 1975, Roseboro Cemetery, NC;   iv.   ROY   COSBY FAIRCLOTH, b. 15 Nov 1928, Sampson Co., NC; m. CHRISTINE, 22 Jun 1952; b. 04 Sep 1934; d. 07 Feb 1987.

v. LOYD FAIRCLOTH, b. 23 Nov 1932, Sampson Co., NC.

vi. MANDIE ELIZABETH FAIRCLOTH, b. 10 Aug 1935, Sampson Co., NC.

vii. TROY ABE FAIRCLOTH, b. 13 Sep 1939, Cumberland County, NC; d. 07 Apr 1974; m. CAROLYN MOTE.

15.   GEORGE WASHINGTON[6] FAIRCLOTH *(ELIZABETH "LIZZIE"[5] HALL, MOSES MCLAINE[4] FAIRCLOTH, SR., SOLOMON[3], BENJAMIN FRANKLIN[2], EDWARD[1] FARECLOTH)* was born 02 Apr 1892, and died 23 Jan 1971 in VA Hospital. buried in Sessoms Cemetery, Autryville, NC. He married (2) NANCY "NANNIE" SESSOMS 07 Feb 1911 in Married in the home of Hix "Hicks" Hall, in Sampson County, NC, daughter of DAWSON SESSOMS and EASTER FAIRCLOTH. She was born Abt. 1892.
George: Medical Information: died of a pulmonary emboli in the VA Hospital.

Child of GEORGE WASHINGTON FAIRCLOTH is:
i. RUBY[7] FAIRCLOTH, m. VON FAIRCLOTH; b. 01 Feb 1916; d. 09 Jun 1982, Buried in Brock Cemetery; died of heart disease, arteriosclerosis.

Children of GEORGE FAIRCLOTH and NANCY SESSOMS are:
ii. GEORGE THOMAS[7] FAIRCLOTH, b. 26 Jan 1916, Sampson Co., NC; d. 11 Nov 1972, Of myocardial arteriosclerosis; m. NELLIE ELIZABETH AUTRY; b. 11 Oct 1925.

iii. MARTHA HAZEL FAIRCLOTH, b. 26 Oct 1918, Sampson Co., NC; d. 26 Dec 1980; m. LUTHER TANNER.

iv. RUBY FAIRCLOTH, b. 16 Jan 1924, Sampson Co., NC; m. VAUGHN (HENRY VON)FAIRCLOTH; b. 01 Jan 1916, Sampson Co., NC; d. 09 Jun 1982, Died of heart disease.

v. ENICE FAIRCLOTH, b. 01 Jun 1926, Sampson Co., NC; m. LESTER HAYNIE, Abt. 03 Sep 1944; b. Abt. 1926.

vi. ROSIE ANNIE FAIRCLOTH, b. 10 Jun 1928, Sampson Co., NC; m. (1) OTIS HALL; b. 09 Jan 1925; m. (2) OTTIS BAILEY HALL; b. 09 Jan 1925.

vii. ROY CRAFTON "CLAXTON" FAIRCLOTH, b. 31 Jan 1920, Sampson Co., NC; m. EDNA EARL AUTRY; b. Abt. 1920.

viii. TATE FAIRCLOTH, b. 31 Aug 1930, Sampson Co., NC; d. 1967; m. FRANCES EMILY BICKER, 21 Jun 1958.

ix. FLEETIE "ADDIE FAIRCLOTH, b. 26 Nov 1920, Sampson Co., NC; m. EARNEST HALL, 19 Dec 1936; b. Abt. 1920.

16.   HANSON ASBERRY "BEAR"[6] FAIRCLOTH *(MOSES MCLAINE (MCLEWANEY)[5], MOSES MCLAINE[4], SOLOMON[3], BENJAMIN FRANKLIN[2], EDWARD[1] FARECLOTH)* was born 11 May 1862 in Sampson Co., NC, and died 27 Jan 1941 in Sampson Co., NC; He married ELIZABETH "LIZZIE" HALL Bet. 1887 - 1888, son of MOSES FAIRCLOTH and ELIZABETH HALL. He was born Abt. 1862, and died Bet. 1901 - 1911.

Children are listed above under (3) Elizabeth "Lizzie" Hall.

17. CHARLOTTE[6] FAIRCLOTH *(MOSES MCLAINE (MCLEWANEY)[5], MOSES MCLAINE[4], SOLOMON[3], BENJAMIN FRANKLIN[2], EDWARD[1] FARECLOTH)* was born Mar 1861, and died 1931 in Sampson Co., NC; buried by butler Funeral Home; 83 years old. Moses Cemetery, Sampson Co., NC. She married STANTLEY FAIRCLOTH in Certificate # 6794., son of PHILLIP FAIRCLOTH and JANE. He was born Dec 1859 in Sampson Co., NC, and died 1935 in Buried in the Moses Cemetery, Sampson County, NC. Charlotte: buried by Butler Funeral Home at 83 years old. This would put her birth date as 1848 if this is correct.
Stantley: Tombstone says he died at 85 years of age in 1935.

Children of CHARLOTTE FAIRCLOTH and STANTLEY FAIRCLOTH are:
    i. NANCY JANE[7] FAIRCLOTH, b. 07 Aug 1879, Sampson Co., NC; d. 06 Dec 1957, Sampson Co., NC; m. WILLIAM LLOYD NEW, 15 Jun 1902, Sampson Co., by S. J. Faircloth, Justice of Peace at E. Faircloth's residence; b. 1881, Cumberland County, NC.
    ii. GEORGIANNA FAIRCLOTH, b. Feb 1882, Sampson Co., NC; m. JORDAN HALL, 16 Jan 1904; b. 1882.
    iii. FLEET PITTMAN FAIRCLOTH, b. Oct 1891, Sampson Co., NC; m. NETA FAIRCLOTH, 22 Mar 1919, Marriage witnesses: Tate; First married John H. Hall, b. 1 Jan 1915 and died 23 Jul 1916..
    iv. MAMIE ELIZABETH FAIRCLOTH, b. Sep 1892; d. 07 Jun 1947.
    v. EVA CATHERINE "KATE" FAIRCLOTH, b. 30 Mar 1902; d. 08 Mar 1981, Sampson, Co., died of respiratory problems, buried 11 Mar 1981 in Roseboro, NC; m. UNKNOWN EVANS.
    vi. ALEXANDER FAIRCLOTH, b. 15 Sep 1898; d. 21 May 1960, Sampson, Co., committed suicide with 16 gauge shotgun; buried 23 May 1960;; m. MARY ETHEL TANNER, 24 Dec 1927; b. 29 Aug 1911, Sampson Co., NC; d. 28 Feb 1942, Sampson Co., NC, Moses Cemetery;.

18. PHILLIP[6] FAIRCLOTH *(MOSES MCLAINE (MCLEWANEY)[5], MOSES MCLAINE[4], SOLOMON[3], BENJAMIN FRANKLIN[2], EDWARD[1] FARECLOTH)* was born Aug 1869, and died 27 Feb 1967 in Died in Agnes Adcox Rest Home in Cumberland County, NC. He is buried in the Moses Cemetery, Sampson County, NC.. He married MOLLIE HALL. She was born 15 Jan 1872 in Cumberland County, NC. Phillip: Died from cerebral thrombosis.

Children of PHILLIP FAIRCLOTH and MOLLIE HALL are:
    i. MAXTON EUGENE "MACK"[7] FAIRCLOTH, b. 15 Feb 1897; d. 26 Aug 1953, Buried Brock Cemetery on 27 Aug 1953; Died of chronic pulmonary infection; m. MAMIE CLYDE FISHER, 15 Feb 1922; b. 1906.
    ii. BOB SHEPPARD FAIRCLOTH, b. 22 Dec 1909; d. 04 Jan 1989, Sampson Co., NC; buried in Moses Cemetery on 6 Jan by butler Funeral Home;.
    iii. VON FAIRCLOTH, b. 01 Feb 1916; d. 09 Jun 1982, Buried in Brock Cemetery; died of heart disease, arteriosclerosis; m. RUBY FAIRCLOTH.
    iv. JERUSHIA "RUSHIE" FAIRCLOTH, b. 27 Aug 1900; d. 12 Aug 1974; m. UNKNOWN TANNER.
    v. SARAH G. FAIRCLOTH, b. Aug 1899.

19. GEORGE W.[6] FAIRCLOTH *(SYLVANNIA C.[5], MOSES MCLAINE[4], SOLOMON[3], BENJAMIN FRANKLIN[2], EDWARD[1] FARECLOTH)* was born 10 Sep 1867, and died 14 Jul

1907. He married (1) LUCY R. WILLIAMS, daughter of REDDIN WILLIAMS and NANCY FAIRCLOTH. She was born 17 Apr 1867, and died 19 Jul 1902. He married (2) REPSIE Dec 1902. She was born 09 Dec 1881, and died 07 Aug 1952.

Children of GEORGE FAIRCLOTH and LUCY WILLIAMS are:
    i. BEULAH[7] FAIRCLOTH, b. Abt. 1902; m. THOMAS MASON SESSOMS; b. Abt. 1894.
    ii. MARION FAIRCLOTH.

20.   WRIGHT L.[6] FAIRCLOTH *(SYLVANNIA C.[5], MOSES MCLAINE[4], SOLOMON[3], BENJAMIN FRANKLIN[2], EDWARD[1] FARECLOTH)* was born 28 Apr 1857, and died 05 Jul 1918. He married (1) MARY LEE WILLIAMS. She was born 1858, and died 1893. He married (2) SARAH JANE SESSOMS.

Children of WRIGHT FAIRCLOTH and MARY WILLIAMS are:
    i. MARTHA L[7] FAIRCLOTH, b. May 1883; d. Bef. 1967.
    ii. WILLIAM P. FAIRCLOTH, b. Nov 1884.
    iii. THEODOCIA DOSHIE FAIRCLOTH, b. 20 Apr 1888; d. 25 Oct 1967; m. FRANKLIN JARVIS FAIRCLOTH; b. 25 Sep 1887, 7 Aug 1970.
    iv. HENRY GRADY FAIRCLOTH, b. 19 Nov 1890; d. 07 Mar 1973, Private in Co. E, 120th Inf. Reg in WW I.
    v. CLAUDIE FAIRCLOTH, b. 06 Jan 1893; d. 01 Jan 1943, Died in a sawmill accident..

21. HINTON KELLY CARR[6] FAIRCLOTH *(SAMPSON[5], MOSES MCLAINE[4], SOLOMON[3], BENJAMIN FRANKLIN[2], EDWARD[1] FARECLOTH)* was born 13 Aug 1853 in Sampson Co., NC, and died 11 Nov 1927 in Died of lobas pneumonia; Buried 14 Nov 1927 in the Joel Horne Cemetery, Sampson County.. He married (1) ALMIRA HORNE 1874, daughter of JOEL HORNE and BRINY HALL. She was born 1857, and died Abt. 1903. He married (2) MELISSA ADLINE MCDANIEL 08 Feb 1911, daughter of MACH MCDANIEL and MARIAH MCDANIEL. She was born 09 Aug 1878, and died 07 Mar 1936.

Children of HINTON FAIRCLOTH and ALMIRA HORNE are:
    i. HAYES SETTLES[7] FAIRCLOTH, b. 06 Jan 1878; d. 24 Nov 1952, Died of heart disease and uremia; Joel Horne Cemetery, Sampson County.; m. NEVER MARRIED.
    ii. WILLIAM "BILL" FAIRCLOTH, b. 1879; m. NEVER MARRIED.
    iii. DILLON ALLEN FAIRCLOTH, b. Dec 1880; d. Feb 1953; m. SYLVANNIA HALL; b. 20 Apr 1879; d. 18 Jul 1947, Buried 20 July.
    iv. SALLIE JANE FAIRCLOTH, b. 17 Jan 1883; d. 05 May 1937, Buried 8 May in Lucas Cemetery; died of cerebral hemorrhage;; m. GEORGE W. FAIRCLOTH; b. 1876.
    v. SION KELLY FAIRCLOTH, b. 20 Aug 1886; d. 14 Jun 1964, Buried 16 June in Horne Cemetery; died of diabetes, ulcers, heart disease; m. (1) HEATHER, 03 Aug 1907; b. Bet. 1889 - 1890; m. (2) PHEBIA AUTRY BROWN, 30 Oct 1935, 3rd wife.
    vi. ALMA WRIGHT FAIRCLOTH, b. 13 Jul 1888; d. 12 Jan 1936; m. LOVE ALLEN FAIRCLOTH, 26 Jul 1905; b. 29 Sep 1876; d. 13 Aug 1972.
    vii. ARTHUR MERLIN FAIRCLOTH, b. 26 Mar 1893; m. GAITHER BEULAH MCGHEE VANHOY; b. 26 Mar 1893, Sampson Co., NC.

viii. MOSES WATSON FAIRCLOTH, b. 03 Jan 1898; d. 24 Apr 1949.
ix. UNKNOWN FAIRCLOTH, d. Infant died in a fire.

22. WILLIAM BARNA[6] FAIRCLOTH (*SAMPSON[5], MOSES MCLAINE[4], SOLOMON[3], BENJAMIN FRANKLIN[2], EDWARD[1] FARECLOTH*) was born 02 Oct 1862, and died 01 Sep 1923 in Buried Horne Cemetery on 2 sep 1923; died from gallstones, TB & tumor in liver. He married SARAH SUSAN HORNE. She was born 1883 in Cumberland County, NC, and died 1884.

Children of WILLIAM FAIRCLOTH and SARAH HORNE are:
    i. ROZIE[7] FAIRCLOTH, b. 30 Oct 1914, Sampson Co., NC; d. Living in 1914.
    ii. GINSIE ELIZABETH FAIRCLOTH, b. 17 Apr 1916, Sampson Co., NC.
    iii. UNKNOWN FAIRCLOTH.

23. BLACKMON[6] FAIRCLOTH (*SAMPSON[5], MOSES MCLAINE[4], SOLOMON[3], BENJAMIN FRANKLIN[2], EDWARD[1] FARECLOTH*) was born 15 Oct 1848, and died 10 Mar 1924 in Buried in Rich Faircloth Cemetery; Buried 11 Mar 1924. He married RAINEY SESSOMS.

Children of BLACKMON FAIRCLOTH and RAINEY SESSOMS are:
    i. LUCIAN[7] FAIRCLOTH, b. 27 Sep 1870, Sampson Co., NC; d. 10 Dec 1927, Autryville, NC; possibly died Dec 12th, 1927.; m. EMMA SESSOMS; b. 15 Jun 1875; d. 09 Jul 1943, Died of TB in Sampson County, NC;.
    ii. BETTY FAIRCLOTH, b. 05 Aug 1919; m. LETT.
    iii. MILLARD FAIRCLOTH, m. LOU DEE CORE; b. Sep 1907; d. 1947, Died at 40 yrs old..

24. STANTLEY[6] FAIRCLOTH (*PHILLIP[5], MOSES MCLAINE[4], SOLOMON[3], BENJAMIN FRANKLIN[2], EDWARD[1] FARECLOTH*) was born Dec 1859 in Sampson Co., NC, and died 1935 in Buried in the Moses Cemetery, Sampson County, NC. He married CHARLOTTE FAIRCLOTH in Certificate # 6794., daughter of MOSES FAIRCLOTH and ANNIE HALL. She was born Mar 1861, and died 1931 in Sampson Co., NC; buried by butler Funeral Home; 83 years old. Moses Cemetery, Sampson Co., NC. Stantley: : Tombstone says he died at 85 years of age in 1935. Charlotte: Buried by Butler Funeral Home at 83 years old. This would put her birth date as 1848 if this is correct. Children are listed above under (17) Charlotte Faircloth.

25. SOLOMON (JONATHAN JAMES)[6] FAIRCLOTH (*JASPER JONATHAN[5], MOSES MCLAINE[4], SOLOMON[3], BENJAMIN FRANKLIN[2], EDWARD[1] FARECLOTH*) was born 28 Oct 1853 in Samson Co., NC, and died 08 Apr 1931 in Sampson Co., NC; of pneumonia;. He married RAENAH (RANIER?) DALLAS SPELL, daughter of CARLISLE SPELL and MARIAH AUTRY. She was born 18 Feb 1869 in Sampson Co., NC, and died 12 Feb 1931 in Cumberland County, NC; buried in Autryville Cemetery;.

Children of SOLOMON FAIRCLOTH and RAENAH SPELL are:
    i. BESSIE LEROY[7] FAIRCLOTH, b. 30 Mar 1888; d. 08 May 1920; m. WALTER TEACHEY NORRIS, SR.; b. 15 Jan 1881, Duplin County, NC; d. 15 Feb 1935.
    ii. CHARLIE SHEPARD FAIRCLOTH, b. 08 Nov 1889; d. 23 Oct 1961; m. KATIE JEWELL OATES; b. 11 Jan 1889, Sampson Co., NC; d. 11 Apr 1977, Junper, GA; buried in Parkhill Cemetery in Columbus, GA.

iii. EDGAR BYRON FAIRCLOTH, b. 27 Nov 1894; d. 11 Feb 1986; m. IDA LORENA AUTRY, 11 May 1918; b. 19 Sep 1901, Sampson Co., NC; d. 23 Aug 1961, Autryville, NC; buried 24 Aug; self inflicted gun shot wound; 20 gauge.
iv. IRA VAUGHN FAIRCLOTH, b. 13 Sep 1891; d. 05 May 1936, Buried at Autryville Federal Grave Marker, WW K, Sgt 318th, MG Bn; m. VARA MCWILLIAMS; b. 1909.
v. ROBERT FAIRCLOTH.
vi. INFANT FAIRCLOTH, b. 17 Sep 1898.

Descendants of Samuel Faircloth

Generation No. 1

```
  1     Samuel Faircloth      1760 - 1807
..    +Elizabeth 1763 - 1818
........    2      Nancy Faircloth
............               +Isaac Sessoms
........    2      Caleb Faircloth
........    2      Elizabeth Faircloth
........    2      Jonah Faircloth
```

Descendants of Benjamin Franklin Faircloth, Jr.

Generation No. 1

1. BENJAMIN FRANKLIN[3] FAIRCLOTH, JR.   *(BENJAMIN FRANKLIN[2], EDWARD[1] FARECLOTH)* was born Abt. 1780.

Descendants of William Faircloth

Generation No. 1

1. WILLIAM[3] FAIRCLOTH *(BENJAMIN FRANKLIN[2], EDWARD[1] FARECLOTH)* was born 1751. He married ELIZABETH SESSOMS. She was born 1750.

Descendants of Richard M. Faircloth

Generation No. 1

1. RICHARD M.[3] FAIRCLOTH *(BENJAMIN FRANKLIN[2], EDWARD[1] FARECLOTH)* was born Abt. 1780.

Descendants of Smithwick Faircloth

Generation No. 1

1. SMITHWICK[3] FAIRCLOTH *(BENJAMIN FRANKLIN[2], EDWARD[1] FARECLOTH)* was born Abt. 1780.

Descendants of Thomas Faircloth

Generation No. 1

1. THOMAS[3] FAIRCLOTH *(BENJAMIN FRANKLIN[2], EDWARD[1] FARECLOTH)* was born Abt. 1780.

Descendants of Robert Faircloth

Generation No. 1

1. ROBERT[3] FAIRCLOTH *(BENJAMIN FRANKLIN[2], EDWARD[1] FARECLOTH)* was born 1752. He married ELIZABETH LANE. She was born 1754.

Child of ROBERT FAIRCLOTH and ELIZABETH LANE is:
    i. ALLAN[4] FAIRCLOTH, b. 1770; d. Apr 1852.

Descendants of Moses McLaine Faircloth, Sr.

Moses F., died 1867, 82 yrs old.

Generation No. 1

1. MOSES MCLAINE[4] FAIRCLOTH, SR. *(SOLOMON[3], BENJAMIN FRANKLIN[2], EDWARD[1] FARECLOTH)* was born (as per headstone) 1785, and died 1867 at 82 yrs old. He married (1) ELIZABETH "LIZZIE" HALL. He married (2) PENELOPE. She was born Abt. 1799. Ages of Annie Nancy, Scott, Patience and Thomas J. are taken from the 1869 Sampson County Census. Moses, Sr. was born about 1801 according to the 1870 Census which lists him as 69 years old and living next to Samson Faircloth who lived next to Johnathan Faircloth in Sampson County, NC He died after 1870 as he is listed on the Census that year; his tombstone says he died in 1867, however, this must be an error. He is buried in the Moses Cemetery in Sampson County. He married Penny and she is listed in the 1870 Census as 73 years old.

Moses is listed on the 1870 Census as a farmer. Penelope is listed as 61 years old which puts her birth about 1799. Birth dates are really quite a puzzle. Consider the following: Moses age is listed as stable from 1840 through 1870 census years, b. 1801. Penelope's age varies. 1840 lists her as between 30 and 40 years which would put he birth between 1801 and 1809. In 1860 it is listed as 61 years old which would put the birth about 1799. In 1870, the age is listed as 73 which would put the birth date around 1797.

Macks' birth date stays the same throughout 1840, 1860 and 1870. One must remember that Moses and Penelope probably could not read or write, so written records of the family births were most likely not available to provide the census taker with accurate information. Whoever was at home at the time provided the information.

Census information can be confusing...in the 1830 Census, there are two Moses listed. Most likely the one which lists Moses as living near Evan, his brother, is the correct Moses. It lists Moses as owning 6 slaves and having the following household members:

    3 males under 5 (probably Moses, Barnabus, and Owen (b. 1825-30)
    1 male of 5 and under 1 (Jasper (b. 1820 - 25)
    1 MALE OF 30 and under 40 (Moses, Sr. (b. 1790 - 1800)
    1 female of 5 and under 10 (Sylvannia (b. 1820-25)
    1 female of 30 and under 40 (Penelope (b. 1790-1800)

Both Census's do not list Sampson in the year 1830. The second one does not list Barnabus which is also possible because his birth is placed between 1830-1837 and he could have been born after the census taker came to visit in 1830. Because of the flexibility of the time of year and whether each had a birthday or not, one year is flexible, such as Moses birth in 1801.

In addition, perhaps the family was visiting another family when the census was taken and added to that family OR moved while the census was being taken??
Name 2: Moses McLaine Faircloth, Sr. Date born 2: 1795 Died 2: Bet. 1860 - 1870, Died at 82 years old; Died 3: Aft. 1870

Considering the varying birth dates of Penelope, she must have married Moses sometime between 10 years old and 22 years old. Probably, more reasonable, considering the customs of the time, she would have been between 16 and 21 putting her birth about 1797-1803.

Child of MOSES FAIRCLOTH and ELIZABETH HALL is:
2.　i.　ELIZABETH "LIZZIE"[5] HALL

Children of MOSES FAIRCLOTH and PENELOPE are:
3.　　ii.　MOSES MCLAINE (MCLEWANEY)[5] FAIRCLOTH, JR., b. Abt. 1825; d. 22 Mar 1863, Died in SC of a fever in a local hospital..
4.　　iii.　SYLVANNIA C. FAIRCLOTH, b. 1826; d. Aft. 1880.
5.　　iv.　SAMPSON FAIRCLOTH, b. 23 Jan 1823; d. Aug 1906.
6.　　v.　OWEN FAIRCLOTH, b. 1837; d. Aft. 1905.
7.　　vi.　PHILLIP FAIRCLOTH, b. 1834; d. 01 Jan 1865, Civil War, of chronic dysentery.
　　vii.　BARNABUS FAIRCLOTH, b. 1837; d. 15 Apr 1864, Civil War; Died in MD at a POW Camp..Barnabus is listed as 5 and under 10 in the 1840 census putting his birth at 1837.

Barnabus was a Private in Company H. Regt., 20th Infantry. He was born in 1839 according to military records and enlisted on 10 June 1861 in Clinton, NC. He was captured 1-3 July 1863 at Gettysburg, PA and confined to Fort Delaware, Del and Point Lookout, MD where he died 15 April 1864 of diarrhea. He enlisted at age 21. He was transferred to point Lookout on October 15-18, 1863. He died in a hospital.
　　viii.　SARAH FAIRCLOTH, b. Abt. 1837.
Sarah is listed as 22 years old in 1860 and 30 years old in 1870 putting her birth year between 1838-40.
　　ix.　JANIE FAIRCLOTH, b. Abt. 1842.
Janie's age is listed as under 5 in 1850 and this puts her birth between 1845 and 1850.
More About JANIE FAIRCLOTH:
Date born 2: 1842
8.　　x.　JASPER JONATHAN FAIRCLOTH, b. Mar 1820, NC; d. Aft. 1900, Jasper and Sarah, his wife, buried at Autryville Baptist Church Cemetery;.
　　xi.　OWEN FAIRCLOTH, b. May 1830; d. Aft. 1905; m. MOLLIE FAIRCLOTH, 30 Nov 1865; b. 1832.
　　xii.　BARNABUS FAIRCLOTH, b. 1839; d. 15 Apr 1864, Died in Civil War.

Generation No. 2

2. HANSON ASBERRY FAIRCLOTH (*MOSES MCLAINE*[4] *FAIRCLOTH, SR., SOLOMON*[3], *BENJAMIN FRANKLIN*[2], *EDWARD*[1] *FARECLOTH*.. He was born 11 May 1862 in Sampson Co., NC, and died 27 Jan 1941 in Sampson Co., NC; buried in the Moses Cemetery in Sampson County, NC. His wife's name is presently unknown.

Children of HANSON FAIRCLOTH are:

9.   i.   LULA JANE[6] FAIRCLOTH, b. 16 Aug 1897, Sampson Co., NC; d. 23 Aug 1959, Cumberland County, NC; buried at Cross Creek Cemetery in Fayetteville, NC.

10.   ii.   STEPHEN PHILLIP FAIRCLOTH, b. 17 Oct 1888; d. 17 Jan 1958.

11.   iii. LAMAR LALLISTER FAIRCLOTH, b. 30 Oct 1893; d. 07 Nov 1943, Sampson Co., NC; buried 9 Nov in Johnson Family Cemetery.

       iv. UNKNOWN FAIRCLOTH, b. Bef. 1900.
          Notes for UNKNOWN FAIRCLOTH:
          Listed as a result of the 1900 Census records.

12.   v.   SANTFORD ALLEN FAIRCLOTH, b. 13 Mar 1900, Sampson Co., NC; d. 18 Mar 1971, Sampson Co., NC; Autryville Church of God Cemetery.

13.   vi.   TROY FAIRCLOTH, b. 13 Aug 1901, Cumberland County, NC; d. 03 Sep 1966, Buried 4 Sep in Salemburg Free Will Baptist Church Cemetery.

14.   vii. GEORGE WASHINGTON FAIRCLOTH, b. 02 Apr 1892; d. 23 Jan 1971, VA Hospital. buried in Sessoms Cemetery, Autryville, NC.

3.   MOSES MCLAINE (MCLEWANEY)[5] FAIRCLOTH, JR. *(MOSES MCLAINE[4], SOLOMON[3], BENJAMIN FRANKLIN[2], EDWARD[1] FARECLOTH)* was born Abt. 1825, and died 22 Mar 1863 in Died in SC of a fever in a local hospital.. He married (1) ANNIE NANCY HALL. She was born Abt. 1839, and died Bet. 1863 - 1868. He married (2) PATIENCE " PATIA" HALL. She was born 1845. Mother was Penelope.

Moses Jr. is listed as family #253 on the 1880 Census in Sampson County and listed as McLewaney. Patience Hall, the second wife of Moses Jr., was born in 1845 and had one child named Nancy Hall before she married McLewaney (Moses Jr.) McLewaney (Mack) adopted Nancy.

The 1880 Census shows Mack (Moses, Jr.), as 55 years of age and Patia as 35 on June 21-22, 1880. Military Records list Moses McLlvaine Faircloth as a private, born in 1825. He was a Sampson County farmer who enlisted on 4th of March 1862 in Fayetteville. He was discharged on the 26th of May 1862 as being over the age of 35. He reenlisted on the 16th of October 1862 in Cumberland County. He was assigned to C Company, Regiment 54, Infantry on the first enlistment. He was assigned to E Company, Regiment 8 on his second enlistment. He died on the 22nd of March 1863 of a fever in Charleston, SC during this enlistment. He was a cook.

I suspect that he left the first enlistment voluntarily, using his age as a legitimate reason because it was past time to put in the crops. Note that he returned to the service in October after the harvest time. Birth date according to Civil War Records.

Died in Charleston, SC in hospital of a fever. Listed as family #253 on the 1880 Census in Sampson County, NC and listed as McLewaney. Moses adopted Nancy's previous child, Patience Hall. Patience, his second wife, was born in 1845.

The 1880 Census shows Mack as 55 years of age and Patia as 35 on June 21-22, 1880. Military Records list Moses McLlvaine as a private, born in 1825. He was a Sampson County farmer who enlisted on 4th of March 1862 in Fayetteville. He was discharged on the 26th of May 1862 as being over the age of 35. He re-enlisted on the 16th of October 1862 in Cumberland County. He was assigned to C Company, Regiment 54, Infantry on the first enlistment. He was assigned to E Company, Regiment 8 on his second enlistment. He died on the 22nd of March 1863 of a fever in Charleston, SC during his enlistment. He was a cook.

He probably left the army the first time to put in the crops, and returned after the crops were harvested, taking care of his family back home.

Moses: Died 2: 22 Mar 1863, Charleston, SC

Patience was the second wife of Moses Faircloth, Jr.

Children of MOSES FAIRCLOTH and ANNIE HALL are:
15.   i.   HANSON ASBERRY "BEAR"[6] FAIRCLOTH, b. 11 May 1862, Sampson Co., NC;
            d. 27 Jan 1941, Sampson Co., NC; buried in the Moses Cemetery in Sampson
            County, NC.
16.   ii. CHARLOTTE FAIRCLOTH, b. Mar 1861; d. 1931, Sampson Co., NC; buried by
            butler Funeral Home; 83 years old. Moses Cemetery, Sampson Co., NC.
       iii. SCOTT FAIRCLOTH, b. Abt. 1849.
       iv. PATIENCE "PATRICIA"FAIRCLOTH, b. 1857.
       v.   THOMAS J. FAIRCLOTH, b. Jun 1859.
17.   vi. PHILLIP FAIRCLOTH, b. Aug 1869; d. 27 Feb 1967, Died in Agnes Adcox Rest
            Home in Cumberland County, NC. He is buried in the Moses Cemetery, Sampson
            County, NC..

Children of MOSES FAIRCLOTH and PATIENCE HALL are:
       vii. NANCY[6] HALL.
       viii. IDA E. FAIRCLOTH, b. Feb 1875, Sampson Co., NC; d. 09 Mar 1959, Sampson
            Co., NC; m. GRADY TANNER.
            Notes for IDA E. FAIRCLOTH:
            Buried in Moses Cemetery;
            Possibly born 1872.
            Date born 2: Feb 1875
            Medical Information: Died of a heart attack.
       ix. IRENE RENA FAIRCLOTH, b. 16 Jul 1879, Mother is Patience "Patia" Hall; m. M.
            O. MATTHEWS, 16 Dec 1903; b. 1876; d. 16 Dec 1903, Sampson Co., NC.
            Possibly born May 1877.
       x.   NANCY HALL FAIRCLOTH, b. adopted by Moses Jr..

4.   SYLVANNIA C.[5] FAIRCLOTH (MOSES MCLAINE[4], SOLOMON[3], BENJAMIN
FRANKLIN[2], EDWARD[1] FARECLOTH) was born 1826, and died Aft. 1880. She NEVER
MARRIED. Her birthdate fluctuates depending upon which census you are consulting. Living
with widowed mother in 1880.

Children of SYLVANNIA FAIRCLOTH and NEVER MARRIED are:
18.   i.   GEORGE W.[6] FAIRCLOTH, b. 10 Sep 1867; d. 14 Jul 1907.
19.   ii. WRIGHT L. FAIRCLOTH, b. 28 Apr 1857; d. 05 Jul 1918.

5.   SAMPSON[5] FAIRCLOTH (MOSES MCLAINE[4], SOLOMON[3], BENJAMIN FRANKLIN[2],
EDWARD[1] FARECLOTH) was born 23 Jan 1823, and died Aug 1906. He married (1) ANN
HALL. She was born Apr 1828, and died 1907. He married (2) NANNIE HOLLAND. She was
born in May be the same individual as Ann Hall, b. 1828. Sampson: Birth date established by
1840, 1960 and 1870 Census Records.
Resided in Sampson County, NC and enlisted in the Orange County Court House, VA on 1 Nov
1863 for the Civil War. He was present and accounted for until he deserted about 11 April 1864.
He returned to duty on 24 Sept 1864. He deserted again on 14 February 1865. He was captured
by the enemy in Sampson County on 16 March 1865 and confined at Hart's Island, new York
Harbor on 10 April 1865. He was released from Hart's Island on 19 June 1865 after taking the
Oath of allegiance. He was a member of C Company, 26th Regiment, NC State Troops. he
applied and was granted a soldiers pension on 27 July 1903 at 80 years of age.

At age 79, his widow, Annie, applied for a pension in Sampson county. She stated "My husband served all through the war." Sampson died in Sampson County in 1906.

Children of SAMPSON FAIRCLOTH and ANN HALL are:

      i. BARNEY[6] FAIRCLOTH, b. 1849; d. Bef. 1860.

20. ii. HINTON KELLY CARR FAIRCLOTH, b. 13 Aug 1853, Sampson Co., NC; d. 11 Nov 1927, Died of lobas pneumonia; Buried 14 Nov 1927 in the Joel Horne Cemetery, Sampson County.

     iii. MARY FAIRCLOTH, b. Abt. 1856; m. JAMES HALL.

21. iv. WILLIAM BARNA FAIRCLOTH, b. 02 Oct 1862; d. 01 Sep 1923, Buried Horne Cemetery on 2 sep 1923; died from gallstones, TB & tumor in liver.

22. v. BLACKMON FAIRCLOTH, b. 15 Oct 1848; d. 10 Mar 1924, Buried in Rich Faircloth Cemetery; Buried 11 Mar 1924.

6. OWEN[5] FAIRCLOTH (*MOSES MCLAINE[4], SOLOMON[3], BENJAMIN FRANKLIN[2], EDWARD[1] FARECLOTH*) was born 1837, and died Aft. 1905. He married MOLLIE 30 Nov 1865 in Sampson County, NC; married by J. c. Autry;. She was born 1832. Owen: Birth date is listed as 10 and under 15 in the 1840 Census putting his birth between 1830 and 1835. He is listed as 23 on the 1860 Census putting his birth at 1837. Owen was married by J. C. Autry, Justice of Peace in Sampson County, NC

Child of OWEN FAIRCLOTH and MOLLIE is:

      i. ABBIE[6] FAIRCLOTH, b. Sep 1881; m. D. MCK. HOWELL, 03 Sep 1905, Cumberland County, NC.

7. PHILLIP[5] FAIRCLOTH (*MOSES MCLAINE[4], SOLOMON[3], BENJAMIN FRANKLIN[2], EDWARD[1] FARECLOTH*) was born 1834, and died 01 Jan 1865 in Civil War, of chronic dysentery. He married JANE. Phillip is listed as of 5 and under 10 in the 1840 Census putting his birth at 1834. Phillip enlisted at the orange Court House, VA on November 1863 for the war. He was present or accounted for until he deserted on or about April 12, 1864. He returned to duty on September 24, 1864. He was present or accounted for until captured near Petersburg, VA on October 27, 1864 and confined at Point Lookout, Maryland where he died on Jan 1, 1865 of chronic dysentery

Child of PHILLIP FAIRCLOTH and JANE is:

23. i. STANTLEY[6] FAIRCLOTH, b. Dec 1859, Sampson Co., NC; d. 1935

8. JASPER JONATHAN[5] FAIRCLOTH (*MOSES MCLAINE[4], SOLOMON[3], BENJAMIN FRANKLIN[2], EDWARD[1] FARECLOTH*) was born Mar 1820 in NC, and died Aft. 1900 in Jasper and Sarah, his wife, buried at Autryville Baptist Church Cemetery;. He married (1) SARAH CAROLINE SESSOMS. She was born Bet. 1823 - 1828. He married (2) SARAH CAROLINA SESSOMS. Jasper possibly born March 1816.

Children of JASPER FAIRCLOTH and SARAH SESSOMS are:

      i. JASPER JONATHAN[6] FAIRCLOTH II, b. Feb 1861, Grave says he was born 1858.; d. 30 Dec 1950, Died of arteriosclosis & Pneumonia at 92 yrs of age.

     ii. SARAH M. FAIRCLOTH, b. 10 Mar 1859, NC; d. 16 Dec 1927, Buried Autryville Baptist Church Cemetery; died of heart disease; tombstone says born 12 Jan 1858..

     iii. WILLIAM FRANKLIN FAIRCLOTH, b. 1851.

24.   iv.   SOLOMON (JONATHAN JAMES) FAIRCLOTH, b. 28 Oct 1853, Samson Co., NC; d. 08 Apr 1931, Sampson Co., NC; of pneumonia;.
       v.   SHEPARD FAIRCLOTH, b. 1855.
       vi.   LOVE D. FAIRCLOTH, b. Abt. 1860, Possibly born between 1860-62.; d. 30 Dec 1950.

Generation No. 3

9.   LULA JANE[6] FAIRCLOTH *(ELIZABETH "LIZZIE"[5] HALL, MOSES MCLAINE[4] FAIRCLOTH, SR., SOLOMON[3], BENJAMIN FRANKLIN[2], EDWARD[1] FARECLOTH)* was born 16 Aug 1897 in Sampson Co., NC, and died 23 Aug 1959 in Cumberland County, NC; She married (1) SMITH.   She married (2) LAWRENCE C. FAIRCLOTH 10 Jan 1915 in Sampson County, NC, son of BENJAMIN FAIRCLOTH and ADLINE AUTRY.

Children of LULA FAIRCLOTH and LAWRENCE FAIRCLOTH are:
25.   i.   LILLIAN ELIZABETH[7] FAIRCLOTH, b. 15 Dec 1915, Sampson Co., NC; Little Coherie Township.; d. Fayetteville, NC;
26.   ii.   LEROY FAIRCLOTH, b. 05 May 1918, Hayne, NC.
27.   iii.   HERMAN REMUS FAIRCLOTH, b. 04 Feb 1927, Fayetteville, NC.
28.   iv.   JOYCE MARIE FAIRCLOTH, b. 16 Oct 1929.
29.   v.   HELEN FAIRCLOTH, b. 16 Sep 1924.
30.   vi.   LOTTIE JUANITA FAIRCLOTH, b. 30 Oct 1932.
31.   vii.   JUDY ADLINE FAIRCLOTH, b. 27 Mar 1938, B St., Fayetteville, NC; d. 2005.
32.   viii.   CARL HOUSTON FAIRCLOTH, b. 29 Oct 1920, Sampson Co., NC; d. 28 Dec 1971.

10.   STEPHEN PHILLIP[6] FAIRCLOTH *(ELIZABETH "LIZZIE"[5] HALL, MOSES MCLAINE[4] FAIRCLOTH, SR., SOLOMON[3], BENJAMIN FRANKLIN[2], EDWARD[1] FARECLOTH)* was born 17 Oct 1888, and died 17 Jan 1958. He married (1) BETTY ELIZABETH SESSOMS in Married in the home of Diancy Sessoms, Sampson County, NC.

Children of STEPHEN FAIRCLOTH and BETTY SESSOMS are:
33.   i.   VAUGHN (HENRY[7] VON)FAIRCLOTH, b. 01 Jan 1916, Sampson Co., NC; d. 09 Jun 1982, Died of heart disease.
34.   ii.   PAUL M. FAIRCLOTH, b. Abt. 1911; d. 30 Jun 1988, Buried in Haney Family Cemetery by butler Funeral Home/Rev. Roger Jackson.
35.   iii.   RONIE ANN FAIRCLOTH, b. 25 Nov 1911; d. 19 May 1980, Died of diabetes and cancer, Sessoms Cemetery, Autryville, NC.

11.   LAMAR LALLISTER[6] FAIRCLOTH *(ELIZABETH "LIZZIE"[5] HALL, MOSES MCLAINE[4] FAIRCLOTH, SR., SOLOMON[3], BENJAMIN FRANKLIN[2], EDWARD[1] FARECLOTH)* was born 30 Oct 1893, and died 07 Nov 1943 in Sampson Co., NC; buried 9 Nov in Johnson Family Cemetery. He married BETTY FAIRCLOTH 03 Apr 1914, daughter of LUCIAN FAIRCLOTH and EMMA SESSOMS. LAMAR buried on 9 Nov 1943 in the Johnson Family Cemetery. Lamar Lallister Faircloth was a World War I Veteran who served as a Private in the 119th Infantry of the 30th Division. It is believed that he was wounded in the war and later in life had "spells" as a result of his injuries.

Children of LAMAR FAIRCLOTH and BETTY FAIRCLOTH are:
       i.   SEPSIE[7] FAIRCLOTH, b. 15 Sep 1920, Sampson Co., NC.

36.   ii.   HOUSTON LEE FAIRCLOTH, b. 15 Dec 1921, Cumberland County, NC; d. 30 Apr 1981, Buried in Concord Baptist Church Cemetery in Stedman, NC.
      iii. WILLIAM HOLT FAIRCLOTH, b. 02 Jan 1924, Cumberland County, NC.
      iv.   ELVA FAIRCLOTH, b. 28 Jun 1927, Cumberland County, NC.
      v.   HOOVER BRYANT FAIRCLOTH, b. 28 Feb 1929, Cumberland County, NC.
      vi.   LELA FAIRCLOTH, b. 18 Oct 1933; m. UNKNOWN STRICKLAND.
      vii. LAMAR LALLISTER FAIRCLOTH, JR., b. 12 Jun 1937; d. 05 Jul 1981, Buried in Church of god Cemetery in Autryville, NC; m. NEVER MARRIED.
      viii. CHARLES EARL FAIRCLOTH, b. 06 Nov 1939, Sampson Co., NC.
      ix.   JESSIE FAIRCLOTH, b. 26 Feb 1942, Sampson Co., NC.

12. SANTFORD ALLEN[6] FAIRCLOTH (*ELIZABETH "LIZZIE"[5] HALL, MOSES MCLAINE[4] FAIRCLOTH, SR., SOLOMON[3], BENJAMIN FRANKLIN[2], EDWARD[1] FARECLOTH*) was born 13 Mar 1900 in Sampson Co., NC, and died 18 Mar 1971 in Sampson Co., NC; Autryville Church of God Cemetery. He married ROSA FAIRCLOTH 10 Jan 1920 in 67 Mile Post on ACL Railroad, Sampson County, NC, by J. E. Horne, Justice of the Peace, daughter of LUCIAN FAIRCLOTH and EMMA SESSOMS. She was born 22 Sep 1896 in Sampson Co., NC, and died 13 Dec 1980 in Buried Church of God Cemetery in Autryville, NC. Santford: Buried in the Church of God Cemetery in Autryville, NC.: Medical Information: Died of Cardiac Arrest. Rosa: Medical Information: died of Cancer and gallbladder problems.

Children of SANTFORD FAIRCLOTH and ROSA FAIRCLOTH are:
37.   i.   THELMA[7] FAIRCLOTH, b. 24 Nov 1920, Sampson Co., NC.
      ii.   JANEVA FAIRCLOTH, b. 06 Nov 1922, Sampson Co., NC; d. Died very young.
      iii. ROBERT J. FAIRCLOTH, b. Oct 1927, Cumberland County, NC.
      iv.   AREY FAIRCLOTH, b. 31 Jul 1932, Sampson Co., NC.
      v.   RAYMOND FAIRCLOTH, b. 19 May 1934, Sampson Co., NC; m. WANDA.
      vi.   IRA FAIRCLOTH, m. UNKNOWN HALL.
      vii. RONIE NANCY FAIRCLOTH, b. 12 Sep 1924, Sampson Co., NC; d. 08 Feb 1925, Died of Pneumonia..

13. TROY[6] FAIRCLOTH (*ELIZABETH "LIZZIE"[5] HALL, MOSES MCLAINE[4] FAIRCLOTH, SR., SOLOMON[3], BENJAMIN FRANKLIN[2], EDWARD[1] FARECLOTH*) was born 13 Aug 1901 in Cumberland County, NC, and died 03 Sep 1966 in Buried 4 Sep in Salemburg Free Will Baptist Church Cemetery. He married PENNY FAIRCLOTH 26 Nov 1919 in Cumberland County, NC, daughter of ERVING FAIRCLOTH and MANDY NEW. She was born 07 Jun 1901 in Sampson Co., NC, and died 02 Jul 1973 in Buried at Salemburg Freewill Baptist Church. Troy: Buried 4 September 1966 in Salemburg Free Will Baptist Church Cemetery.

Children of TROY FAIRCLOTH and PENNY FAIRCLOTH are:
      i.   LOUISA JANE[7] FAIRCLOTH, b. 19 Sep 1920, Sampson Co., NC; m. CLAUDIUM MCD. PETERSON, 07 Feb 1941; b. 1917.
      ii.   HUBERT FAIRCLOTH, b. 09 Sep 1923, Sampson Co., NC; m. PRISCILLA MAE AUTRY, 06 Apr 1956, Dillon, SC; b. 1926, South Autryville, NC.
38.   iii. HOUSTON TROY FAIRCLOTH, b. 23 May 1926, Sampson Co., NC; d. Roseboro Cemetery, NC.
      iv.   ROY COSBY FAIRCLOTH, b. 15 Nov 1928, Sampson Co., NC; m. CHRISTINE, 22 Jun 1952; b. 04 Sep 1934; d. 07 Feb 1987.
      v.   LOYD FAIRCLOTH, b. 23 Nov 1932, Sampson Co., NC.
      vi.   MANDIE ELIZABETH FAIRCLOTH, b. 10 Aug 1935, Sampson Co., NC.

39.   vii. TROY ABE FAIRCLOTH, b. 13 Sep 1939, Cumberland County, NC; d. 07 Apr 1974.

14.   GEORGE WASHINGTON[6] FAIRCLOTH *(ELIZABETH "LIZZIE"[5] HALL, MOSES MCLAINE[4] FAIRCLOTH, SR., SOLOMON[3], BENJAMIN FRANKLIN[2], EDWARD[1] FARECLOTH)* was born 02 Apr 1892, and died 23 Jan 1971 in VA Hospital. buried in Sessoms Cemetery, Autryville, NC. He married (2) NANCY "NANNIE" SESSOMS 07 Feb 1911 in Married in the home of Hix "Hicks" Hall, in Sampson County, NC, daughter of DAWSON SESSOMS and EASTER FAIRCLOTH. She was born Abt. 1892. George: Medical Information: Died of pulmonary emboli in the VA Hospital.

Child of GEORGE WASHINGTON FAIRCLOTH is:
        i.   RUBY[7] FAIRCLOTH, m. VON FAIRCLOTH; b. 01 Feb 1916; d. 09 Jun 1982, Buried in Brock Cemetery; died of heart disease, arteriosclerosis.

Children of GEORGE FAIRCLOTH and NANCY SESSOMS are:
40.   ii. GEORGE THOMAS[7] FAIRCLOTH, b. 26 Jan 1916, Sampson Co., NC; d. 11 Nov 1972, Of myocardial arteriosclerosis.
        iii. MARTHA HAZEL FAIRCLOTH, b. 26 Oct 1918, Sampson Co., NC; d. 26 Dec 1980; m. LUTHER TANNER.
41.   iv. RUBY FAIRCLOTH, b. 16 Jan 1924, Sampson Co., NC.
42.   v.   ENICE FAIRCLOTH, b. 01 Jun 1926, Sampson Co., NC.
43.   vi. ROSIE ANNIE FAIRCLOTH, b. 10 Jun 1928, Sampson Co., NC.
44.   vii. ROY CRAFTON "CLAXTON" FAIRCLOTH, b. 31 Jan 1920, Sampson Co., NC.
        viii. TATE FAIRCLOTH, b. 31 Aug 1930, Sampson Co., NC; d. 1967; m. FRANCES EMILY BICKER, 21 Jun 1958.
45.   ix. FLEETIE "ADDIE FAIRCLOTH, b. 26 Nov 1920, Sampson Co., NC.

15.   HANSON ASBERRY "BEAR"[6] FAIRCLOTH *(MOSES MCLAINE (MCLEWANEY)[5], MOSES MCLAINE[4], SOLOMON[3], BENJAMIN FRANKLIN[2], EDWARD[1] FARECLOTH)* was born 11 May 1862 in Sampson Co., NC, and died 27 Jan 1941 in Sampson Co., NC;. He married ELIZABETH "LIZZIE" HALL Bet. 1887 - 1888, son of MOSES FAIRCLOTH and ELIZABETH HALL. He was born Abt. 1862, and died Bet. 1901 - 1911.

16.   CHARLOTTE[6] FAIRCLOTH *(MOSES MCLAINE (MCLEWANEY)[5], MOSES MCLAINE[4], SOLOMON[3], BENJAMIN FRANKLIN[2], EDWARD[1] FARECLOTH)* was born Mar 1861, and died 1931 in Sampson Co., NC. She married STANTLEY FAIRCLOTH in Certificate # 6794., son of PHILLIP FAIRCLOTH and JANE

Children of CHARLOTTE FAIRCLOTH and STANTLEY FAIRCLOTH are:
        i.   NANCY JANE[7] FAIRCLOTH, b. 07 Aug 1879, Sampson Co., NC; d. 06 Dec 1957, Sampson Co., NC; m. WILLIAM LLOYD NEW, 15 Jun 1902, Sampson Co., by S. J. Faircloth, Justice of Peace at E. Faircloth's residence; b. 1881, Cumberland County, NC.
        ii. GEORGIANNA FAIRCLOTH, b. Feb 1882, Sampson Co., NC; m. JORDAN HALL, 16 Jan 1904; b. 1882.
46.   iii. FLEET PITTMAN FAIRCLOTH, b. Oct 1891, Sampson Co., NC.
        iv. MAMIE ELIZABETH FAIRCLOTH, b. Sep 1892; d. 07 Jun 1947.

47.   v.   EVA CATHERINE "KATE" FAIRCLOTH, b. 30 Mar 1902; d. 08 Mar 1981, Sampson, Co., died of respiratory problems, buried 11 Mar 1981 in Roseboro, NC.
48.   vi.   ALEXANDER FAIRCLOTH, b. 15 Sep 1898; d. 21 May 1960, Sampson, Co., committed suicide with 16 gauge shotgun; buried 23 May 1960;.

17.   PHILLIP[6] FAIRCLOTH (*MOSES MCLAINE (MCLEWANEY)[5], MOSES MCLAINE[4], SOLOMON[3], BENJAMIN FRANKLIN[2], EDWARD[1] FARECLOTH*) was born Aug 1869, and died 27 Feb 1967 in Died in Agnes Adcox Rest Home in Cumberland County, NC. He is buried in the Moses Cemetery, Sampson County, NC.. He married MOLLIE HALL. She was born 15 Jan 1872 in Cumberland County, NC.
Phillip: Died from cerebral thrombosis.

Children of PHILLIP FAIRCLOTH and MOLLIE HALL are:
49.   i.   MAXTON EUGENE "MACK"[7] FAIRCLOTH, b. 15 Feb 1897; d. 26 Aug 1953, Buried Brock Cemetery on 27 Aug 1953; Died of chronic pulmonary infection.
       ii.   BOB SHEPPARD FAIRCLOTH, b. 22 Dec 1909; d. 04 Jan 1989, Sampson Co., NC; buried in Moses Cemetery on 6 Jan by butler Funeral Home;.
       iii. VON FAIRCLOTH, b. 01 Feb 1916; d. 09 Jun 1982, Buried in Brock Cemetery; died of heart disease, arteriosclerosis; m. RUBY FAIRCLOTH.
       iv.   JERUSHIA "RUSHIE" FAIRCLOTH, b. 27 Aug 1900; d. 12 Aug 1974; m. UNKNOWN TANNER.
       v.   SARAH G. FAIRCLOTH, b. Aug 1899.

18.   GEORGE W.[6] FAIRCLOTH (*SYLVANNIA C.[5], MOSES MCLAINE[4], SOLOMON[3], BENJAMIN FRANKLIN[2], EDWARD[1] FARECLOTH*) was born 10 Sep 1867, and died 14 Jul 1907. He married (1) LUCY R. WILLIAMS, daughter of REDDIN WILLIAMS and NANCY FAIRCLOTH. She was born 17 Apr 1867, and died 19 Jul 1902. He married (2) REPSIE Dec 1902. She was born 09 Dec 1881, and died 07 Aug 1952.

Children of GEORGE FAIRCLOTH and LUCY WILLIAMS are:
       i.   BEULAH[7] FAIRCLOTH, b. Abt. 1902; m. THOMAS MASON SESSOMS; b. Abt. 1894.
       ii.   MARION FAIRCLOTH.

19.   WRIGHT L.[6] FAIRCLOTH (*SYLVANNIA C.[5], MOSES MCLAINE[4], SOLOMON[3], BENJAMIN FRANKLIN[2], EDWARD[1] FARECLOTH*) was born 28 Apr 1857, and died 05 Jul 1918. He married (1) MARY LEE WILLIAMS. She was born 1858, and died 1893. He married (2) SARAH JANE SESSOMS.

Children of WRIGHT FAIRCLOTH and MARY WILLIAMS are:
       i.   MARTHA L[7] FAIRCLOTH, b. May 1883; d. Bef. 1967.
       ii.   WILLIAM P. FAIRCLOTH, b. Nov 1884.
50.   iii. THEODOCIA DOSHIE FAIRCLOTH, b. 20 Apr 1888; d. 25 Oct 1967.
       iv.   HENRY GRADY FAIRCLOTH, b. 19 Nov 1890; d. 07 Mar 1973, Private in Co. E, 120th Inf. Reg in WW I.
       v.   CLAUDIE FAIRCLOTH, b. 06 Jan 1893; d. 01 Jan 1943, Died in a sawmill accident..

20. HINTON KELLY CARR[6] FAIRCLOTH *(SAMPSON[5], MOSES MCLAINE[4], SOLOMON[3], BENJAMIN FRANKLIN[2], EDWARD[1] FARECLOTH)* was born 13 Aug 1853 in Sampson Co., NC, and died 11 Nov 1927 in Died of lobas pneumonia; Buried 14 Nov 1927 in the Joel Horne Cemetery, Sampson County.. He married (1) ALMIRA HORNE 1874, daughter of JOEL HORNE and BRINY HALL. She was born 1857, and died Abt. 1903. He married (2) MELISSA ADLINE MCDANIEL 08 Feb 1911, daughter of MACH MCDANIEL and MARIAH MCDANIEL. She was born 09 Aug 1878, and died 07 Mar 1936.

Children of HINTON FAIRCLOTH and ALMIRA HORNE are:
- i. HAYES SETTLES[7] FAIRCLOTH, b. 06 Jan 1878; d. 24 Nov 1952, Died of heart disease and uremia; Joel Horne Cemetery, Sampson County.; m. NEVER MARRIED.
- ii. WILLIAM "BILL" FAIRCLOTH, b. 1879; m. NEVER MARRIED.
- 51. iii. DILLON ALLEN FAIRCLOTH, b. Dec 1880; d. Feb 1953.
- 52. iv. SALLIE JANE FAIRCLOTH, b. 17 Jan 1883; d. 05 May 1937, Buried 8 May in Lucas Cemetery; died of cerebral hemorrhage;.
- v. SION KELLY FAIRCLOTH, b. 20 Aug 1886; d. 14 Jun 1964, Buried 16 June in Horne Cemetery; died of diabetes, ulcers, heart disease; m. (1) HEATHER, 03 Aug 1907; b. Bet. 1889 - 1890; m. (2) PHEBIA AUTRY BROWN, 30 Oct 1935, 3rd wife.
- 53. vi. ALMA WRIGHT FAIRCLOTH, b. 13 Jul 1888; d. 12 Jan 1936.
- 54. vii. ARTHUR MERLIN FAIRCLOTH, b. 26 Mar 1893.
- viii. MOSES WATSON FAIRCLOTH, b. 03 Jan 1898; d. 24 Apr 1949.
- ix. UNKNOWN FAIRCLOTH, d. Infant died in a fire.

21. WILLIAM BARNA[6] FAIRCLOTH *(SAMPSON[5], MOSES MCLAINE[4], SOLOMON[3], BENJAMIN FRANKLIN[2], EDWARD[1] FARECLOTH)* was born 02 Oct 1862, and died 01 Sep 1923 in Buried Horne Cemetery on 2 sep 1923; died from gallstones, TB & tumor in liver. He married SARAH SUSAN HORNE. She was born 1883 in Cumberland County, NC, and died 1884.

Children of WILLIAM FAIRCLOTH and SARAH HORNE are:
- i. ROZIE[7] FAIRCLOTH, b. 30 Oct 1914, Sampson Co., NC; d. Living in 1914.
- ii. GINSIE ELIZABETH FAIRCLOTH, b. 17 Apr 1916, Sampson Co., NC.
- iii. UNKNOWN FAIRCLOTH.

22. BLACKMON[6] FAIRCLOTH *(SAMPSON[5], MOSES MCLAINE[4], SOLOMON[3], BENJAMIN FRANKLIN[2], EDWARD[1] FARECLOTH)* was born 15 Oct 1848, and died 10 Mar 1924 in Buried in Rich Faircloth Cemetery; Buried 11 Mar 1924. He married RAINEY SESSOMS.

Children of BLACKMON FAIRCLOTH and RAINEY SESSOMS are:
- 55. i. LUCIAN[7] FAIRCLOTH, b. 27 Sep 1870, Sampson Co., NC; d. 10 Dec 1927, Autryville, NC; possibly died Dec 12th, 1927..
- ii. BETTY FAIRCLOTH, b. 05 Aug 1919; m. LETT.
- 56. iii. MILLARD FAIRCLOTH.

23. STANTLEY[6] FAIRCLOTH *(PHILLIP[5], MOSES MCLAINE[4], SOLOMON[3], BENJAMIN FRANKLIN[2], EDWARD[1] FARECLOTH)* was born Dec 1859 in Sampson Co., NC, and died 1935. He married CHARLOTTE FAIRCLOTH in Certificate # 6794., daughter of MOSES

FAIRCLOTH and ANNIE HALL. She was born Mar 1861, and died 1931 in Sampson Co., Children are listed above under (16) Charlotte Faircloth.

24. SOLOMON (JONATHAN JAMES)[6] FAIRCLOTH (*JASPER JONATHAN[5], MOSES MCLAINE[4], SOLOMON[3], BENJAMIN FRANKLIN[2], EDWARD[1] FARECLOTH*) was born 28 Oct 1853 in Samson Co., NC, and died 08 Apr 1931 in Sampson Co., NC; of pneumonia;. He married RAENAH (RANIER?) DALLAS SPELL, daughter of CARLISLE SPELL and MARIAH AUTRY. She was born 18 Feb 1869 in Sampson Co., NC, and died 12 Feb 1931 in Cumberland County, NC; buried in Autryville Cemetery.

Children of SOLOMON FAIRCLOTH and RAENAH SPELL are:
57.   i.   BESSIE LEROY[7] FAIRCLOTH, b. 30 Mar 1888; d. 08 May 1920.
58.   ii. CHARLIE SHEPARD FAIRCLOTH, b. 08 Nov 1889; d. 23 Oct 1961.
59.   iii. EDGAR BYRON FAIRCLOTH, b. 27 Nov 1894; d. 11 Feb 1986.
60.   iv. IRA VAUGHN FAIRCLOTH, b. 13 Sep 1891; d. 05 May 1936, Buried at Autryville Federal Grave Marker, WW K, Sgt 318th, MG Bn.
      v.   ROBERT FAIRCLOTH.
      vi. INFANT FAIRCLOTH, b. 17 Sep 1898.

Generation No. 4

33. VAUGHN (HENRY[7] VON)FAIRCLOTH (*STEPHEN PHILLIP[7] FAIRCLOTH, HANSON ASBERRY "BEAR"[6], MOSES MCLAINE (MCLEWANEY)[5], MOSES MCLAINE[4], SOLOMON[3], BENJAMIN FRANKLIN[2], EDWARD[1] FARECLOTH*) was born 01 Jan 1916 in Sampson Co., NC, and died 09 Jun 1982 in Died of heart disease. He married RUBY FAIRCLOTH, daughter of GEORGE FAIRCLOTH and NANCY SESSOMS. She was born 16 Jan 1924 in Sampson Co., NC.

Children of VAUGHN VON)FAIRCLOTH and RUBY FAIRCLOTH are:
      i.   HENRY[8] VON FAIRCLOTH, b. 25 Dec 1943.
      ii.   GEORGE PHILLIP VON FAIRCLOTH, b. 22 Nov 1946.
      iii. BETTY LOU VON FAIRCLOTH, b. 02 Feb 1948.
      iv.   WILLARD ROY VON FAIRCLOTH, b. 12 Aug 1949.

34. PAUL M.[7] FAIRCLOTH (*STEPHEN PHILLIP[7], HANSON ASBERRY "BEAR"[6], MOSES MCLAINE (MCLEWANEY)[5], MOSES MCLAINE[4], SOLOMON[3], BENJAMIN FRANKLIN[2], EDWARD[1] FARECLOTH*) was born Abt. 1911, and died 30 Jun 1988 in Buried in Haney Family Cemetery by butler Funeral Home/Rev. Roger Jackson. He married LIZZIE GLENDON.

Children of PAUL FAIRCLOTH and LIZZIE GLENDON are:
      i.   CLARENCE S.[8] FAIRCLOTH.
      ii.   UNKNOWN FAIRCLOTH.
      iii. UNKNOWN FAIRCLOTH.
      iv.   UNKNOWN FAIRCLOTH.

35. RONIE ANN[7] FAIRCLOTH (*STEPHEN PHILLIP[7], HANSON ASBERRY "BEAR"[6], MOSES MCLAINE (MCLEWANEY)[5], MOSES MCLAINE[4], SOLOMON[3], BENJAMIN FRANKLIN[2], EDWARD[1] FARECLOTH*) was born 25 Nov 1911, and died 19 May 1980 in Died of diabetes and cancer, Sessoms Cemetery, Autryville, NC. She married JAMES K. OZZELL. He was born 02 May 1905, and died 16 May 1977.

Child of RONIE FAIRCLOTH and JAMES OZZELL is:
    i. JAMES WILBERT[8] OZZELL, b. 25 Jan 1927.

36. HOUSTON LEE[7] FAIRCLOTH (*LAMAR LALLISTER[7], HANSON ASBERRY "BEAR"[6], MOSES MCLAINE (MCLEWANEY)[5], MOSES MCLAINE[4], SOLOMON[3], BENJAMIN FRANKLIN[2], EDWARD[1] FARECLOTH*) was born 15 Dec 1921 in Cumberland County, NC, and died 30 Apr 1981 in Buried in Concord Baptist Church Cemetery in Stedman, NC. He married MARY BELLE HOWELL, daughter of GRAY HOWELL and SARAH RILEY. She was born 09 Sep 1917 in Cumberland County, NC, and died 14 Apr 1967 in Buried at Concord Baptist Church, Autryville, NC.

Children of HOUSTON FAIRCLOTH and MARY HOWELL are:
    i. ODIS LEE[8] FAIRCLOTH, b. 12 Feb 1942, Sampson Co., NC.
    ii. WILLARD HOUSTON FAIRCLOTH, b. 10 May 1943, Sampson Co., NC.
    iii. TOMMIE EARL FAIRCLOTH, b. 30 Dec 1945, Sampson Co., NC.

37. THELMA[7] FAIRCLOTH (*SANTFORD ALLEN[7], HANSON ASBERRY "BEAR"[6], MOSES MCLAINE (MCLEWANEY)[5], MOSES MCLAINE[4], SOLOMON[3], BENJAMIN FRANKLIN[2], EDWARD[1] FARECLOTH*) was born 24 Nov 1920 in Sampson Co., NC. She married ELMER BRAYTON COLLISTER Aug 1941, son of UNKNOWN COLLISTER and INA UNKNOWN. He was born 16 Mar 1920 in Ohio.

Children of THELMA FAIRCLOTH and ELMER COLLISTER are:
    i. ELMER BRAYTON[8] COLLISTER, JR., b. 12 Jul 1954, Sumter, SC; d. Died in an auto accident at 16 years old; Buried in Autryville Church of God Cemetery..
    ii. INA R.COLLISTER, b. 19 Oct 1957; m. UNKNOWN WHIPPLY.
    iii. MARY COLLISTER, b. 07 Aug 1952; m. UNKNOWN CONNLEY; b. 07 Aug 1952.
    iv. ELEANOR P. COLLISTER, b. 28 May 1942; m. UNKNOWN JOHNSON.
    v. JEWELL RAY COLLISTER, b. 29 Jan 1953; m. (1) UNKNOWN GAYE; m. (2) UNKNOWN CHALFANT.
    vi. EVA J. COLLISTER, b. 30 Sep 1962; m. UNKNOWN BRITT.
    vii. CAROL A. COLLISTER, b. 18 Feb 1947; m. UNKNOWN ARNETTE; b. Abt. 1947.
    viii. JAMES EARL COLLISTER, b. 06 Aug 1962.
    ix. BOBBIE JOYCE COLLISTER, b. 07 Nov 1943; d. 20 Apr 1990, Died at 46 yrs old. of cardiac pulmonary arrest and progressive breast cancer at Wayne Memorial Hospital in Goldsboro, NC; buried in Anderson Cemetery in Wayne Co., NC; m. DONALD R. ANDERSON.
    x. JUANITA COLLISTER, b. 13 Apr 1948; m. UNKNOWN LONG.

38. HOUSTON TROY[7] FAIRCLOTH (*TROY[7], HANSON ASBERRY "BEAR"[6], MOSES MCLAINE (MCLEWANEY)[5], MOSES MCLAINE[4], SOLOMON[3], BENJAMIN FRANKLIN[2], EDWARD[1] FARECLOTH*) was born 23 May 1926 in Sampson Co., NC, and died in Roseboro Cemetery, NC. He married (1) VENNIE FAIRCLOTH 20 Jan 1946 in Dillon, SC, daughter of ALLEN FAIRCLOTH and MISSOURI "ZUDE". She was born 08 Jun 1923, and died 13 Mar 1975 in Roseboro Cemetery, NC. He married (2) VENIE FAIRCLOTH 20 Jun 1946 in Dillon, SC, daughter of ALLEN FAIRCLOTH and MISSOURI HALL. She was born 08 Jun 1923, and died 13 Mar 1965 in Buried in Roseboro Cemetery..

Children of HOUSTON FAIRCLOTH and VENIE FAIRCLOTH are:
- i. FAYE[8] FAIRCLOTH, b. 05 Feb 1949.
- ii. DOROTHY FAIRCLOTH, b. 18 Sep 1947.
- iii. RUBEN ESTES FAIRCLOTH, b. 1951, Sampson Co., NC.
- iv. RICHARD " RICKY" HOUSTON FAIRCLOTH, b. 10 Oct 1955.
- v. LAWRENCE RAY FAIRCLOTH, b. 1952; d. Bef. 1984.
- vi. CATHY DIANE FAIRCLOTH, b. 10 Jan 1957.

39. TROY ABE[7] FAIRCLOTH (*TROY[7], HANSON ASBERRY "BEAR"[6], MOSES MCLAINE (MCLEWANEY)[5], MOSES MCLAINE[4], SOLOMON[3], BENJAMIN FRANKLIN[2], EDWARD[1] FARECLOTH*) was born 13 Sep 1939 in Cumberland County, NC, and died 07 Apr 1974. He married CAROLYN MOTE.

Children of TROY FAIRCLOTH and CAROLYN MOTE are:
- i. DEBBIE ANN[8] FAIRCLOTH, b. 16 Dec 1962.
- ii. FRANK TROY FAIRCLOTH, b. 19 Jun 1967.

40. GEORGE THOMAS[7] FAIRCLOTH (*GEORGE WASHINGTON[7], HANSON ASBERRY "BEAR"[6], MOSES MCLAINE (MCLEWANEY)[5], MOSES MCLAINE[4], SOLOMON[3], BENJAMIN FRANKLIN[2], EDWARD[1] FARECLOTH*) was born 26 Jan 1916 in Sampson Co., NC, and died 11 Nov 1972 in Of myocardial arteriosclerosis. He married NELLIE ELIZABETH AUTRY. She was born 11 Oct 1925.

Children of GEORGE FAIRCLOTH and NELLIE AUTRY are:
- i. RUBY AGNES[8] FAIRCLOTH, b. 22 Sep 1943; m. JACKIE BUTLER HORNE; b. 16 Jun 1940.
- ii. ELIZABETH NANNIE FAIRCLOTH, b. 13 Dec 1944, Sampson Co., NC; m. DICK SMITH SPORTS.
- iii. RUFFIN "RONNIE" FAIRCLOTH, b. 31 Dec 1946; m. DELORES FISHER; b. 03 Feb 1953.
- iv. JOYCE FAIRCLOTH, b. 05 Sep 1947; m. WILLIAM JESSUP HORNE, 16 May 1964; b. 04 Apr 1945.
- v. DAWSON HICKS FAIRCLOTH, b. 23 Nov 1948; m. MYRINDA RAY HILL.
- vi. BONNIE LOU FAIRCLOTH, b. 09 Feb 1950; m. (1) ROBERT CARTER; m. (2) CLARENCE MAXWELL.
- vii. FAYELENE FAIRCLOTH, b. 19 Mar 1952; m. HAROLD EUGENE HENDERSON; b. 09 May 1948.
- viii. JULIA FAIRCLOTH, b. 03 Sep 1953; m. RUBIN DANNY CASHWELL.
- ix. JUDY FAIRCLOTH, b. 03 Sep 1953; m. IRA FRANKIE BOLTON; b. 08 Nov 1952.
- x. STILLBORN FAIRCLOTH, b. 06 Mar 1955; d. 06 Mar 1955.

41. RUBY[7] FAIRCLOTH (*GEORGE WASHINGTON[7], HANSON ASBERRY "BEAR"[6], MOSES MCLAINE (MCLEWANEY)[5], MOSES MCLAINE[4], SOLOMON[3], BENJAMIN FRANKLIN[2], EDWARD[1] FARECLOTH*) was born 16 Jan 1924 in Sampson Co., NC. She married VAUGHN (HENRY VON)FAIRCLOTH, son of STEPHEN FAIRCLOTH and BETTY SESSOMS. He was born 01 Jan 1916 in Sampson Co., NC, and died 09 Jun 1982 in Died of heart disease.
    Children are listed above under (33) Vaughn (Henry Von)Faircloth.

42. ENICE[7] FAIRCLOTH (*GEORGE WASHINGTON[7], HANSON ASBERRY "BEAR"[6], MOSES MCLAINE (MCLEWANEY)[5], MOSES MCLAINE[4], SOLOMON[3], BENJAMIN FRANKLIN[2], EDWARD[1] FARECLOTH*) was born 01 Jun 1926 in Sampson Co., NC. She married LESTER HAYNIE Abt. 03 Sep 1944, son of MELVA HAYNIE. He was born Abt. 1926.

Children of ENICE FAIRCLOTH and LESTER HAYNIE are:
    i.   CAROLYN W.[8] HAYNIE, b. Abt. 1946; m. KENNETH WEST.
    ii.   SUSAN HAYNIE, b. Abt. 1946; m. UNKNOWN ADCOX.
    iii.   FRANCES HAYNIE, b. Abt. 1946; m. UNKNOWN HALES.
    iv.   MELVA HAYNIE, b. Abt. 1946.
    v.   GERALD HAYES HAYNIE, b. Abt. 1946; m. JUDAY SMITH.

43. ROSIE ANNIE[7] FAIRCLOTH (*GEORGE WASHINGTON[7], HANSON ASBERRY "BEAR"[6], MOSES MCLAINE (MCLEWANEY)[5], MOSES MCLAINE[4], SOLOMON[3], BENJAMIN FRANKLIN[2], EDWARD[1] FARECLOTH*) was born 10 Jun 1928 in Sampson Co., NC. She married (1) OTIS HALL. He was born 09 Jan 1925. She married (2) OTTIS BAILEY HALL, son of SOLOMON HALL and MARTHA CARTER. He was born 09 Jan 1925.

Children of ROSIE FAIRCLOTH and OTIS HALL are:
    i.   BRENDA ANN[8] HALL, b. 12 Aug 1946; m. MARSHALL BAILEY.
    ii.   OTTIS BAILEY HALL, JR., b. 07 Jul 1947; m. BETTY ROSE UNKNOWN.
    iii.   JOEL LAYTON "TOBY" HALL, b. 28 Jan 1950; m. JUDITY ANN HORNE.
    iv.   JERRY LEE HALL, b. 08 Nov 1957; d. Died as an infant in an auto accident.
    v.   UNKNOWN HALL, b. Abt. 1951; d. Died as an infant.
    vi.   UNKNOWN HALL, b. Abt. 1951; d. Died as an infant.

44. ROY CRAFTON "CLAXTON"[7] FAIRCLOTH (*GEORGE WASHINGTON[7], HANSON ASBERRY "BEAR"[6], MOSES MCLAINE (MCLEWANEY)[5], MOSES MCLAINE[4], SOLOMON[3], BENJAMIN FRANKLIN[2], EDWARD[1] FARECLOTH*) was born 31 Jan 1920 in Sampson Co., NC. He married EDNA EARL AUTRY. She was born Abt. 1920.

Child of ROY FAIRCLOTH and EDNA AUTRY is:
    i.   GEORGE WASHINTON[8] FAIRCLOTH.

45. FLEETIE "ADDIE[7] FAIRCLOTH (*GEORGE WASHINGTON[7], HANSON ASBERRY "BEAR"[6], MOSES MCLAINE (MCLEWANEY)[5], MOSES MCLAINE[4], SOLOMON[3], BENJAMIN FRANKLIN[2], EDWARD[1] FARECLOTH*) was born 26 Nov 1920 in Sampson Co., NC. She married EARNEST HALL 19 Dec 1936. He was born Abt. 1920.

Children of FLEETIE FAIRCLOTH and EARNEST HALL are:
    i.   ELWOOD[8] HALL, b. 27 Aug 1940; m. BETTY.
    ii.   JANICE HALL, b. 25 Oct 1942; m. SIDNEY SESSOMS; b. Abt. 1942.
    iii.   DALLAS HALL, b. 21 Aug 1944; m. JOYCE SMITH; b. Abt. 1944.
    iv.   WADE HALL, b. 29 May 1946.
    v.   BEATRICE HALL, b. 08 Aug 1953; m. ROBERT HALL.
    vi.   ANNETTE HALL, b. 29 Jan 1956; m. WADE SIMMONS.
    vii.   RONNIE HALL, b. 11 May 1963.

46. FLEET PITTMAN[7] FAIRCLOTH (*STANTLEY[6], PHILLIP[5], MOSES MCLAINE[4], SOLOMON[3], BENJAMIN FRANKLIN[2], EDWARD[1] FARECLOTH*) was born Oct 1891 in

Sampson Co., NC. He married NETA FAIRCLOTH 22 Mar 1919 in Marriage witnesses: Tate; First married John H. Hall, b. 1 Jan 1915 and died 23 Jul 1916..

Children of FLEET FAIRCLOTH and NETA FAIRCLOTH are:
    i.   RUBY[8] FAIRCLOTH.
    ii. TATE FAIRCLOTH.
    iii. RUFUS "TOBY" FAIRCLOTH.

47. EVA CATHERINE "KATE"[7] FAIRCLOTH (*STANTLEY[6], PHILLIP[5], MOSES MCLAINE[4], SOLOMON[3], BENJAMIN FRANKLIN[2], EDWARD[1] FARECLOTH*) was born 30 Mar 1902, and died 08 Mar 1981 in Sampson, Co., died of respiratory problems, buried 11 Mar 1981 in Roseboro, NC. She married UNKNOWN EVANS.

Children of EVA FAIRCLOTH and UNKNOWN EVANS are:
    i.   MARY JANE[8] EVANS, b. 19 Jun 1921; m. UNKNOWN JACKSON.
    ii. JACKSON EVANS.

48. ALEXANDER[7] FAIRCLOTH (*STANTLEY[6], PHILLIP[5], MOSES MCLAINE[4], SOLOMON[3], BENJAMIN FRANKLIN[2], EDWARD[1] FARECLOTH*) was born 15 Sep 1898, and died 21 May 1960 in Sampson, Co., committed suicide with 16 gauge shotgun; buried 23 May 1960;. He married MARY ETHEL TANNER 24 Dec 1927. She was born 29 Aug 1911 in Sampson Co., NC, and died 28 Feb 1942 in Sampson Co., NC, Moses Cemetery;. Name 2: Alexander Brance Faircloth

Children of ALEXANDER FAIRCLOTH and MARY TANNER are:
    i.   ELSIE[8] FAIRCLOTH, b. 20 Oct 1928, Sampson Co., NC; m. JAMES ALEX H------; b. 13 Mar 1931.
    ii. JAMES RANSON FAIRCLOTH, b. 14 Jun 1934, Sampson Co., NC; d. 22 Dec 1956.
    iii. MARY ALLICE FAIRCLOTH, b. 24 May 1939, Sampson Co., NC.
    iv. JONES ALEX FAIRCLOTH, b. 03 Mar 1930; m. ELVA MARIE FAIRCLOTH; b. 15 Mar 1933, Cumberland County, NC.

49. MAXTON EUGENE "MACK"[7] FAIRCLOTH (*PHILLIP[6], MOSES MCLAINE (MCLEWANEY)[5], MOSES MCLAINE[4], SOLOMON[3], BENJAMIN FRANKLIN[2], EDWARD[1] FARECLOTH*) was born 15 Feb 1897, and died 26 Aug 1953 in Buried Brock Cemetery on 27 Aug 1953; Died of chronic pulmonary infection. He married MAMIE CLYDE FISHER 15 Feb 1922. She was born 1906.

Children of MAXTON FAIRCLOTH and MAMIE FISHER are:
    i.   MAXTON EUGENE[8] FAIRCLOTH, JR., b. 19 Sep 1940.
    ii. MATTIE PEARL FAIRCLOTH, b. 31 Jul 1944.
    iii. JAMES ALLEN FAIRCLOTH, b. 22 Dec 1923.
    iv. DAVID FAIRCLOTH, b. 23 Apr 1925.
    v. EULA FAIRCLOTH, b. 30 Dec 1927.
    vi. HUBBART FAIRCLOTH, b. 09 Dec 1930.
    vii. ODIS FAIRCLOTH, b. 17 May 1934.
    viii. UNKNOWN FAIRCLOTH, b. Unknown.

50. THEODOCIA DOSHIE[7] FAIRCLOTH *(WRIGHT L.[6], SYLVANNIA C.[5], MOSES MCLAINE[4], SOLOMON[3], BENJAMIN FRANKLIN[2], EDWARD[1] FARECLOTH)* was born 20 Apr 1888, and died 25 Oct 1967. She married FRANKLIN JARVIS FAIRCLOTH, son of RAEFORD FAIRCLOTH and MARTHA PAGE. He was born 25 Sep 1887 in 7 Aug 1970.

Children of THEODOCIA FAIRCLOTH and FRANKLIN FAIRCLOTH are:
  i. MARY LEE[8] FAIRCLOTH, b. 17 Aug 1914; m. UNKNOWN FAIRCLOTH.
  ii. MAYBELL FAIRCLOTH, b. 27 Dec 1915; m. UNKNOWN AUTRY.

51. DILLON ALLEN[7] FAIRCLOTH *(HINTON KELLY CARR[6], SAMPSON[5], MOSES MCLAINE[4], SOLOMON[3], BENJAMIN FRANKLIN[2], EDWARD[1] FARECLOTH)* was born Dec 1880, and died Feb 1953. He married SYLVANNIA HALL, daughter of HENRY HALL and NANCY. She was born 20 Apr 1879, and died 18 Jul 1947 in Buried 20 July.

Children of DILLON FAIRCLOTH and SYLVANNIA HALL are:
  i. AARAN[8] FAIRCLOTH, b. 04 Oct 1914, Twin of Evelyn.
  ii. EVELYN FAIRCLOTH, b. 04 Oct 1914, Twin of Aaran.
  iii. RUBY FAIRCLOTH, b. 11 Sep 1919; d. Buried in Horne Cemetery, Sampson County; died of heart disease;.
  iv. UNKNOWN FAIRCLOTH.
  v. UNKNOWN FAIRCLOTH.
  vi. UNKNOWN FAIRCLOTH.
  vii. UNKNOWN FAIRCLOTH.
  viii. UNKNOWN FAIRCLOTH.
  ix. UNKNOWN FAIRCLOTH.

52. SALLIE JANE[7] FAIRCLOTH *(HINTON KELLY CARR[6], SAMPSON[5], MOSES MCLAINE[4], SOLOMON[3], BENJAMIN FRANKLIN[2], EDWARD[1] FARECLOTH)* was born 17 Jan 1883, and died 05 May 1937 in Buried 8 May in Lucas Cemetery; died of cerebral hemorrhage;. She married GEORGE W. FAIRCLOTH, son of WILSON FAIRCLOTH. He was born 1876.

Children of SALLIE FAIRCLOTH and GEORGE FAIRCLOTH are:
  i. UNKNOWN[8] FAIRCLOTH, m. THEOPHILUS HALL; b. 1902, Cumberland County, NC.
  ii. UNKNOWN FAIRCLOTH, d. Nov 1911.

53. ALMA WRIGHT[7] FAIRCLOTH *(HINTON KELLY CARR[6], SAMPSON[5], MOSES MCLAINE[4], SOLOMON[3], BENJAMIN FRANKLIN[2], EDWARD[1] FARECLOTH)* was born 13 Jul 1888, and died 12 Jan 1936. She married LOVE ALLEN FAIRCLOTH 26 Jul 1905, son of RAIFORD FAIRCLOTH and JARESTA FAIRCLOTH. He was born 29 Sep 1876, and died 13 Aug 1972.

Children of ALMA FAIRCLOTH and LOVE FAIRCLOTH are:
  i. MALISSIE JANE[8] FAIRCLOTH, b. Abt. 1909; m. THEOPHILUS HALL; b. 1902, Cumberland County, NC.
  ii. DASIE MAE FAIRCLOTH, b. Abt. May 1907; d. Nov 1911.
  iii. BUCK GILLIAM FAIRCLOTH, b. 06 Mar 1915; m. MALISSIE HALL, 03 Sep 1938; b. 25 Aug 1913.
  iv. CIMS S. FAIRCLOTH, b. 11 Dec 1924; d. 11 Dec 1924.

v. CALVIN OTTIS FAIRCLOTH, b. 07 Apr 1927; d. 23 Apr 1927.
vi. WILLIAM HARRISON FAIRCLOTH, b. 25 Jan 1931; d. 19 Mar 1946, Buried 20 Mar in Faircloth Cemetery; Shot self in heart;.
vii. MYRLENE FAIRCLOTH, b. 06 Sep 1928.
viii. ALLEN JUDSON FAIRCLOTH, m. NORA LEE HOBSON; b. 1921.

54. ARTHUR MERLIN[7] FAIRCLOTH (*HINTON KELLY CARR[6], SAMPSON[5], MOSES MCLAINE[4], SOLOMON[3], BENJAMIN FRANKLIN[2], EDWARD[1] FARECLOTH*) was born 26 Mar 1893. He married GAITHER BEULAH MCGHEE VANHOY. She was born 26 Mar 1893 in Sampson Co., NC.

Child of ARTHUR FAIRCLOTH and GAITHER VANHOY is:
i. WILLIS DELMA[8] FAIRCLOTH, m. MAXINE LORA SHAW.

55. LUCIAN[7] FAIRCLOTH (*BLACKMON[6], SAMPSON[5], MOSES MCLAINE[4], SOLOMON[3], BENJAMIN FRANKLIN[2], EDWARD[1] FARECLOTH*) was born 27 Sep 1870 in Sampson Co., NC, and died 10 Dec 1927 in Autryville, NC; possibly died Dec 12th, 1927.. He married EMMA SESSOMS, daughter of BLACKMON FAIRCLOTH and RAINEY SESSOMS. She was born 15 Jun 1875, and died 09 Jul 1943 in Died of TB in Sampson County, NC;.

Children of LUCIAN FAIRCLOTH and EMMA SESSOMS are:
i. ROSA[8] FAIRCLOTH, b. 22 Sep 1896, Sampson Co., NC; d. 13 Dec 1980, Buried Church of God Cemetery in Autryville, NC; Stepchild; m. SANTFORD ALLEN FAIRCLOTH, 10 Jan 1920, 67 Mile Post on ACL Railroad, Sampson County, NC, by J. E. Horne, Justice of the Peace; b. 13 Mar 1900, Sampson Co., NC; d. 18 Mar 1971, Sampson Co., NC; Autryville Church of God Cemetery. Rosa: gallbladder problems.
Sant buried in the Church of God Cemetery in Autryville, NC, Medical Information: Died of Cardiac Arrest.
ii. BETTY FAIRCLOTH, m. LAMAR LALLISTER FAIRCLOTH, 03 Apr 1914; b. 30 Oct 1893; d. 07 Nov 1943, Sampson Co., NC; buried 9 Nov in Johnson Family Cemetery. Buried on 9 Nov 1943 in the Johnson Family Cemetery.

56. MILLARD[7] FAIRCLOTH (*BLACKMON[6], SAMPSON[5], MOSES MCLAINE[4], SOLOMON[3], BENJAMIN FRANKLIN[2], EDWARD[1] FARECLOTH*) He married LOU DEE CORE. She was born Sep 1907, and died 1947 in Died at 40 yrs old..

Child of MILLARD FAIRCLOTH and LOU CORE is:
i. ELVA MARIE[8] FAIRCLOTH, b. 15 Mar 1933, Cumberland County, NC; m. JONES ALEX FAIRCLOTH; b. 03 Mar 1930.

57. BESSIE LEROY[7] FAIRCLOTH (*SOLOMON (JONATHAN JAMES)[6], JASPER JONATHAN[5], MOSES MCLAINE[4], SOLOMON[3], BENJAMIN FRANKLIN[2], EDWARD[1] FARECLOTH*) was born 30 Mar 1888, and died 08 May 1920. She married WALTER TEACHEY NORRIS, SR., son of WILLIAM NORRIS and NANCY UNKNOWN. He was born 15 Jan 1881 in Duplin County, NC, and died 15 Feb 1935.

Child of BESSIE FAIRCLOTH and WALTER NORRIS is:

i. WALTER[8] TEACHEY, JR., b. 27 Jul 1912, Sampson Co., NC; d. 31 May 1986; m. ALLIE RUTH SMITH, 15 Aug 1945, Roseboro, NC; b. 09 Dec 1914, Cumberland County, NC.

58.   CHARLIE SHEPARD[7] FAIRCLOTH *(SOLOMON (JONATHAN JAMES)[6], JASPER JONATHAN[5], MOSES MCLAINE[4], SOLOMON[3], BENJAMIN FRANKLIN[2], EDWARD[1] FARECLOTH)* was born 08 Nov 1889, and died 23 Oct 1961. He married KATIE JEWELL OATES, daughter of CLAUDE OATES and SUDIE MURRAY. She was born 11 Jan 1889 in Sampson Co., NC, and died 11 Apr 1977 in Junper, GA; buried in Parkhill Cemetery in Columbus, GA.

Children of CHARLIE FAIRCLOTH and KATIE OATES are:
    i. JEWELL OATES[8] FAIRCLOTH, b. 20 Mar 1917, DeFuniak Springs, FLA; d. Apr 1918.
    ii. CHARLES SHEPARD FAIRCLOTH, JR., b. 10 Feb 1919, DeFuniak Springs, FLA; m. (1) JUNE; m. (2) ALBERTA ANDREWS, 15 Jun 1940, Phenix City, ALA; b. 26 Jul 1919, Louisville, AL.
    iii. SYLVANNIA "SYLVIA" JANE FAIRCLOTH, b. 26 May 1923, Rentz, GA; Twin of Samuel; m. CHARLES ALFRED EDDINGS, 23 Dec 1947, Columbania, ALA; b. 10 Oct 1923, Alabama.
    iv. SAMUEL JUDSON FAIRCLOTH, b. 26 May 1923, Rentz, GA; Twin of Sylvannia.
    v. JACK FAIRCLOTH, b. 25 Feb 1926, Andalusia, AL; Twin of Jean; m. BIRDYE HOPE BORLAND, 01 Mar 1947, Trussiville, ALA; b. 11 Sep 1925.
    vi. JEAN FAIRCLOTH, b. 25 Feb 1926, Andalusia, AL; Twin of Jack; m. EDWARD HODGES.

59.   EDGAR BYRON[7] FAIRCLOTH *(SOLOMON (JONATHAN JAMES)[6], JASPER JONATHAN[5], MOSES MCLAINE[4], SOLOMON[3], BENJAMIN FRANKLIN[2], EDWARD[1] FARECLOTH)* was born 27 Nov 1894, and died 11 Feb 1986. He married IDA LORENA AUTRY 11 May 1918, daughter of FOY AUTRY and LILLIE HOLLINGWORTH. She was born 19 Sep 1901 in Sampson Co., NC, and died 23 Aug 1961 in Autryville, NC; buried 24 Aug; self inflicted gun shot wound; 20 gauge.

Children of EDGAR FAIRCLOTH and IDA AUTRY are:
    i. OSSIE VIRGINIA[8] FAIRCLOTH, b. 25 Apr 1919; m. ISHA THOMAS MCLAN.
    ii. UNKNOWN FAIRCLOTH, b. 07 Dec 1935, Stillborn.
    iii. UNKNOWN FAIRCLOTH, b. 28 Sep 1924, Stillborn.
    iv. HAROLD GIBSON FAIRCLOTH, b. 25 Feb 1926; d. 09 Sep 1984; m. MARIE SPELL.
    v. WAYNE MCNEIL FAIRCLOTH, b. 07 Nov 1927; m. RUBY KAY HORNE.
    vi. SOLOMON JAMES "S.J." FAIRCLOTH, b. 22 Sep 1930; m. VERNICE FAIRCLOTH; b. 30 Mar 1932.
    vii. BESSIE CAROLYN FAIRCLOTH, b. 28 Jul 1933.
    viii. SYLVIA JOAN FAIRCLOTH, b. 13 Sep 1935, Autryville, NC; buried 24 Aug; self inflicted gun shot wound; 20 gauge; m. TONY MOLETTIERE.

60.   IRA VAUGHN[7] FAIRCLOTH *(SOLOMON (JONATHAN JAMES)[6], JASPER JONATHAN[5], MOSES MCLAINE[4], SOLOMON[3], BENJAMIN FRANKLIN[2], EDWARD[1] FARECLOTH)* was born 13 Sep 1891, and died 05 May 1936 in Buried at Autryville Federal Grave Marker, WW K, Sgt 318th, MG Bn. He married VARA MCWILLIAMS. He was born 1909.

Children of IRA FAIRCLOTH and VARA MCWILLIAMS are:
    i.   IRA[8] VAUGHN, JR. FAIRCLOTH, b. 06 Nov 1932.
    ii. JAMES FRANKLIN VAUGHN, b. 05 Sep 1934.

Descendants of Nancy Faircloth

Generation No. 1

1. NANCY[4] FAIRCLOTH *(SAMUEL[3], BENJAMIN FRANKLIN[2], EDWARD[1] FARECLOTH)*
She married ISAAC SESSOMS.
More About ISAAC SESSOMS: Name 2: Isaac Sessums, Jr.

Descendants of Hanson Asberry Faircloth

Generation No. 1

1. **HANSON ASBERRY FAIRCLOTH** *(MOSES MCLAINE⁴ FAIRCLOTH, SR., SOLOMON³, BENJAMIN FRANKLIN², EDWARD¹ FARECLOTH).* He was born 11 May 1862 in Sampson Co., NC, and died 27 Jan 1941 in Sampson Co., NC; buried in the Moses Cemetery in Sampson County, NC. Hanson Asberry was known as "Bear" to the family. Bear usually wore a big, wide brim hat which was most fashionable at the time and resembled an over-sized Quaker hat. Hanson probably married Lizzie (Elizabeth Lizzie Hall) about 1887-88 as the 1900 Census in Sampson County states that they had been married for 12 years. Bear was about 24 when he married and Lizzie was about 16 years old. The 1900 Census lists Hanson Asberry Faircloth as born March 1863. Hanson's age is taken from the 1900 Census as of March 1863, aged 37, and the 1870 Census as 70 years old, both in Sampson County, NC

Children of ELIZABETH HALL and HANSON FAIRCLOTH are:

Generation No. 2

2. **LULA JANE⁶ FAIRCLOTH** *(ELIZABETH "LIZZIE"⁵ HALL, MOSES MCLAINE⁴ FAIRCLOTH, SR., SOLOMON³, BENJAMIN FRANKLIN², EDWARD¹ FARECLOTH)* was born 16 Aug 1897 in Sampson Co., NC, and died 23 Aug 1959 in Cumberland County, NC; She married LAWRENCE C. FAIRCLOTH 10 Jan 1915 in Sampson County, NC, son of BENJAMIN FAIRCLOTH and ADLINE AUTRY. He was born 13 Mar 1886 in Sampson Co., NC, and died 20 Oct 1952 in Fayetteville, NC;

Children of LULA FAIRCLOTH and LAWRENCE FAIRCLOTH are:
- 8.   i.   LILLIAN ELIZABETH⁷ FAIRCLOTH, b. 15 Dec 1915;
- 9.   ii.   LEROY FAIRCLOTH, b. 05 May 1918, Hayne, NC.
- 10.   iii. HERMAN REMUS FAIRCLOTH, b. 04 Feb 1927, Fayetteville, NC.
- 11.   iv.   JOYCE MARIE FAIRCLOTH, b. 16 Oct 1929.
- 12.   v.   HELEN FAIRCLOTH, b. 16 Sep 1924.
- 13.   vi.   LOTTIE JUANITA FAIRCLOTH, b. 30 Oct 1932.
- 14.   vii. JUDY ADLINE FAIRCLOTH, b. 27 Mar 1938, B St., Fayetteville, NC; d. 2005.
- 15.   viii. CARL HOUSTON FAIRCLOTH, b. 29 Oct 1920, Sampson Co., NC; d. 28 Dec 1971

3. **STEPHEN PHILLIP⁶ FAIRCLOTH** *(ELIZABETH "LIZZIE"⁵ HALL, MOSES MCLAINE⁴ FAIRCLOTH, SR., SOLOMON³, BENJAMIN FRANKLIN², EDWARD¹ FARECLOTH)* was born 17 Oct 1888, and died 17 Jan 1958. He married (1) BETTY ELIZABETH SESSOMS in Married in the home of Diancy Sessoms, Sampson County, NC.

Children of STEPHEN FAIRCLOTH and BETTY SESSOMS are:
- 16.   i.   VAUGHN (HENRY⁷ VON)FAIRCLOTH, b. 01 Jan 1916, Sampson Co., NC; d. 09 Jun 1982, Died of heart disease.

17.   ii.   PAUL M. FAIRCLOTH, b. Abt. 1911; d. 30 Jun 1988, Buried in Haney Family Cemetery by butler Funeral Home/Rev. Roger Jackson.

18.   iii.   RONIE ANN FAIRCLOTH, b. 25 Nov 1911; d. 19 May 1980, Died of diabetes and cancer, Sessoms Cemetery, Autryville, NC.

4. LAMAR LALLISTER[6] FAIRCLOTH *(ELIZABETH "LIZZIE"[5] HALL, MOSES MCLAINE[4] FAIRCLOTH, SR., SOLOMON[3], BENJAMIN FRANKLIN[2], EDWARD[1] FARECLOTH)* was born 30 Oct 1893, and died 07 Nov 1943 in Sampson Co., NC;

Children of LAMAR FAIRCLOTH and BETTY FAIRCLOTH are:
    i.   SEPSIE[7] FAIRCLOTH, b. 15 Sep 1920, Sampson Co., NC.
19.   ii.   HOUSTON LEE FAIRCLOTH, b. 15 Dec 1921, Cumberland County, NC; d. 30 Apr 1981, Buried in Concord Baptist Church Cemetery in Stedman, NC.
    iii.   WILLIAM HOLT FAIRCLOTH, b. 02 Jan 1924, Cumberland County, NC.
    iv.   ELVA FAIRCLOTH, b. 28 Jun 1927, Cumberland County, NC.
    v.   HOOVER BRYANT FAIRCLOTH, b. 28 Feb 1929, Cumberland County, NC.
    vi.   LELA FAIRCLOTH, b. 18 Oct 1933; m. UNKNOWN STRICKLAND.
    vii.   LAMAR LALLISTER FAIRCLOTH, JR., b. 12 Jun 1937; d. 05 Jul 1981, Buried in Church of god Cemetery in Autryville, NC; m. NEVER MARRIED.
    viii.   CHARLES EARL FAIRCLOTH, b. 06 Nov 1939, Sampson Co., NC.
    ix.   JESSIE FAIRCLOTH, b. 26 Feb 1942, Sampson Co., NC.

5. SANTFORD ALLEN[6] FAIRCLOTH *(ELIZABETH "LIZZIE"[5] HALL, MOSES MCLAINE[4] FAIRCLOTH, SR., SOLOMON[3], BENJAMIN FRANKLIN[2], EDWARD[1] FARECLOTH)* was born 13 Mar 1900 in Sampson Co., NC, and died 18 Mar 1971 in Sampson Co., NC; Autryville Church of God Cemetery. He married ROSA FAIRCLOTH 10 Jan 1920 in 67 Mile Post on ACL Railroad, Sampson County, NC, by J. E. Horne, Justice of the Peace, daughter of LUCIAN FAIRCLOTH and EMMA SESSOMS. She was born 22 Sep 1896 in Sampson Co., NC, and died 13 Dec 1980 in Buried Church of God Cemetery in Autryville, NC.

Children of SANTFORD FAIRCLOTH and ROSA FAIRCLOTH are:
20.   i.   THELMA[7] FAIRCLOTH, b. 24 Nov 1920, Sampson Co., NC.
    ii.   JANEVA FAIRCLOTH, b. 06 Nov 1922, Sampson Co., NC; d. Died very young.
    iii.   ROBERT J. FAIRCLOTH, b. Oct 1927, Cumberland County, NC.
    iv.   AREY FAIRCLOTH, b. 31 Jul 1932, Sampson Co., NC.
    v.   RAYMOND FAIRCLOTH, b. 19 May 1934, Sampson Co., NC; m. WANDA.
    vi.   IRA FAIRCLOTH, m. UNKNOWN HALL.
    vii.   RONIE NANCY FAIRCLOTH, b. 12 Sep 1924, Sampson Co., NC; d. 08 Feb 1925, Died of Pneumonia..

6. TROY[6] FAIRCLOTH *(ELIZABETH "LIZZIE"[5] HALL, MOSES MCLAINE[4] FAIRCLOTH, SR., SOLOMON[3], BENJAMIN FRANKLIN[2], EDWARD[1] FARECLOTH)* was born 13 Aug 1901 in Cumberland County, NC, and died 03 Sep 1966 in Buried 4 Sep in Salemburg Free Will Baptist Church Cemetery. He married PENNY FAIRCLOTH 26 Nov 1919 in Cumberland County, NC, daughter of ERVING FAIRCLOTH and MANDY NEW. She was born 07 Jun 1901 in Sampson Co., NC, and died 02 Jul 1973 in Buried at Salemburg Freewill Baptist Church.

Children of TROY FAIRCLOTH and PENNY FAIRCLOTH are:
    i.   LOUISA JANE[7] FAIRCLOTH, b. 19 Sep 1920, Sampson Co., NC; m. CLAUDIUM MCD. PETERSON, 07 Feb 1941; b. 1917.

ii. HUBERT FAIRCLOTH, b. 09 Sep 1923, Sampson Co., NC; m. PRISCILLA MAE AUTRY, 06 Apr 1956, Dillon, SC; b. 1926, South Autryville, NC.

21. iii. HOUSTON TROY FAIRCLOTH, b. 23 May 1926, Sampson Co., NC; d. Roseboro Cemetery, NC.

iv. ROY COSBY FAIRCLOTH, b. 15 Nov 1928, Sampson Co., NC; m. CHRISTINE, 22 Jun 1952; b. 04 Sep 1934; d. 07 Feb 1987.

v. LOYD FAIRCLOTH, b. 23 Nov 1932, Sampson Co., NC.

vi. MANDIE ELIZABETH FAIRCLOTH, b. 10 Aug 1935, Sampson Co., NC.

22. vii. TROY ABE FAIRCLOTH, b. 13 Sep 1939, Cumberland County, NC; d. 07 Apr 1974.

7. GEORGE WASHINGTON[6] FAIRCLOTH (*ELIZABETH "LIZZIE"[5] HALL, MOSES MCLAINE[4] FAIRCLOTH, SR., SOLOMON[3], BENJAMIN FRANKLIN[2], EDWARD[1] FARECLOTH*) was born 02 Apr 1892, and died 23 Jan 1971 in VA Hospital. buried in Sessoms Cemetery, Autryville, NC. He married (2) NANCY "NANNIE" SESSOMS 07 Feb 1911 in Married in the home of Hix "Hicks" Hall, in Sampson County, NC, daughter of DAWSON SESSOMS and EASTER FAIRCLOTH. She was born Abt. 1892.

Child of GEORGE WASHINGTON FAIRCLOTH is:

i. RUBY[7] FAIRCLOTH, m. VON FAIRCLOTH; b. 01 Feb 1916; d. 09 Jun 1982, Buried in Brock Cemetery; died of heart disease, arteriosclerosis.

Children of GEORGE FAIRCLOTH and NANCY SESSOMS are:

23. ii. GEORGE THOMAS[7] FAIRCLOTH, b. 26 Jan 1916, Sampson Co., NC; d. 11 Nov 1972, Of myocardial arteriosclerosis.

iii. MARTHA HAZEL FAIRCLOTH, b. 26 Oct 1918, Sampson Co., NC; d. 26 Dec 1980; m. LUTHER TANNER.

24. iv. RUBY FAIRCLOTH, b. 16 Jan 1924, Sampson Co., NC.

25. v. ENICE FAIRCLOTH, b. 01 Jun 1926, Sampson Co., NC.

26. vi. ROSIE ANNIE FAIRCLOTH, b. 10 Jun 1928, Sampson Co., NC.

27. vii. ROY CRAFTON "CLAXTON" FAIRCLOTH, b. 31 Jan 1920, Sampson Co., NC.

viii. TATE FAIRCLOTH, b. 31 Aug 1930, Sampson Co., NC; d. 1967; m. FRANCES EMILY BICKER, 21 Jun 1958.

28. ix. FLEETIE "ADDIE FAIRCLOTH, b. 26 Nov 1920, Sampson Co., NC.

Generation No. 3

16. VAUGHN (HENRY[7] VON)FAIRCLOTH (*STEPHEN PHILLIP[6] FAIRCLOTH, ELIZABETH "LIZZIE"[5] HALL, MOSES MCLAINE[4] FAIRCLOTH, SR., SOLOMON[3], BENJAMIN FRANKLIN[2], EDWARD[1] FARECLOTH*) was born 01 Jan 1916 in Sampson Co., NC, and died 09 Jun 1982 in Died of heart disease. He married RUBY FAIRCLOTH, daughter of GEORGE FAIRCLOTH and NANCY SESSOMS. She was born 16 Jan 1924 in Sampson Co., NC.

Children of VAUGHN VON)FAIRCLOTH and RUBY FAIRCLOTH are:

i. HENRY[8] VON FAIRCLOTH, b. 25 Dec 1943.

ii. GEORGE PHILLIP VON FAIRCLOTH, b. 22 Nov 1946.

iii. BETTY LOU VON FAIRCLOTH, b. 02 Feb 1948.

iv. WILLARD ROY VON FAIRCLOTH, b. 12 Aug 1949.

17. PAUL M.[7] FAIRCLOTH *(STEPHEN PHILLIP[6], ELIZABETH "LIZZIE"[5] HALL, MOSES MCLAINE[4] FAIRCLOTH, SR., SOLOMON[3], BENJAMIN FRANKLIN[2], EDWARD[1] FARECLOTH)* was born Abt. 1911, and died 30 Jun 1988 in Buried in Haney Family Cemetery by butler Funeral Home/Rev. Roger Jackson. He married LIZZIE GLENDON.

Children of PAUL FAIRCLOTH and LIZZIE GLENDON are:
  i.   CLARENCE S.[8] FAIRCLOTH.
  ii. UNKNOWN FAIRCLOTH.
  iii. UNKNOWN FAIRCLOTH.
  iv. UNKNOWN FAIRCLOTH.

18. RONIE ANN[7] FAIRCLOTH *(STEPHEN PHILLIP[6], ELIZABETH "LIZZIE"[5] HALL, MOSES MCLAINE[4] FAIRCLOTH, SR., SOLOMON[3], BENJAMIN FRANKLIN[2], EDWARD[1] FARECLOTH)* was born 25 Nov 1911, and died 19 May 1980 in Died of diabetes and cancer, Sessoms Cemetery, Autryville, NC. She married JAMES K. OZZELL. He was born 02 May 1905, and died 16 May 1977.

Child of RONIE FAIRCLOTH and JAMES OZZELL is:
  i.   JAMES WILBERT[8] OZZELL, b. 25 Jan 1927.

19. HOUSTON LEE[7] FAIRCLOTH *(LAMAR LALLISTER[6], ELIZABETH "LIZZIE"[5] HALL, MOSES MCLAINE[4] FAIRCLOTH, SR., SOLOMON[3], BENJAMIN FRANKLIN[2], EDWARD[1] FARECLOTH)* was born 15 Dec 1921 in Cumberland County, NC, and died 30 Apr 1981 in Buried in Concord Baptist Church Cemetery in Stedman, NC. He married MARY BELLE HOWELL, daughter of GRAY HOWELL and SARAH RILEY. She was born 09 Sep 1917 in Cumberland County, NC, and died 14 Apr 1967 in Buried at Concord Baptist Church, Autryville, NC.

Children of HOUSTON FAIRCLOTH and MARY HOWELL are:
  i.   ODIS LEE[8] FAIRCLOTH, b. 12 Feb 1942, Sampson Co., NC.
  ii. WILLARD HOUSTON FAIRCLOTH, b. 10 May 1943, Sampson Co., NC.
  iii. TOMMIE EARL FAIRCLOTH, b. 30 Dec 1945, Sampson Co., NC.

20. THELMA[7] FAIRCLOTH *(SANTFORD ALLEN[6], ELIZABETH "LIZZIE"[5] HALL, MOSES MCLAINE[4] FAIRCLOTH, SR., SOLOMON[3], BENJAMIN FRANKLIN[2], EDWARD[1] FARECLOTH)* was born 24 Nov 1920 in Sampson Co., NC. She married ELMER BRAYTON COLLISTER Aug 1941, son of UNKNOWN COLLISTER and INA UNKNOWN. He was born 16 Mar 1920 in Ohio.

Children of THELMA FAIRCLOTH and ELMER COLLISTER are:
  i.   ELMER BRAYTON[8] COLLISTER, JR., b. 12 Jul 1954, Sumter, SC; d. Died in an auto accident at 16 years old; Buried in Autryville Church of God Cemetery..
  ii. INA R.COLLISTER, b. 19 Oct 1957; m. UNKNOWN WHIPPLY.
  iii. MARY COLLISTER, b. 07 Aug 1952; m. UNKNOWN CONNLEY; b. 07 Aug 1952.
  iv. ELEANOR P. COLLISTER, b. 28 May 1942; m. UNKNOWN JOHNSON.
  v.   JEWELL RAY COLLISTER, b. 29 Jan 1953; m. (1) UNKNOWN GAYE; m. (2) UNKNOWN CHALFANT.
  vi. EVA J. COLLISTER, b. 30 Sep 1962; m. UNKNOWN BRITT.

vii. CAROL A. COLLISTER, b. 18 Feb 1947; m. UNKNOWN ARNETTE; b. Abt. 1947.

viii. JAMES EARL COLLISTER, b. 06 Aug 1962.

48.   ix. BOBBIE JOYCE COLLISTER, b. 07 Nov 1943; d. 20 Apr 1990, Died at 46 yrs old. of cardiac pulmonary arrest and progressive breast cancer at Wayne Memorial Hospital in Goldsboro, NC; buried in Anderson Cemetery in Wayne Co., NC.

x. JUANITA COLLISTER, b. 13 Apr 1948; m. UNKNOWN LONG.

21.   HOUSTON TROY[7] FAIRCLOTH *(TROY[6], ELIZABETH "LIZZIE"[5] HALL, MOSES MCLAINE[4] FAIRCLOTH, SR., SOLOMON[3], BENJAMIN FRANKLIN[2], EDWARD[1] FARECLOTH)* was born 23 May 1926 in Sampson Co., NC, and died in Roseboro Cemetery, NC. He married (1) VENNIE FAIRCLOTH 20 Jan 1946 in Dillon, SC, daughter of ALLEN FAIRCLOTH and MISSOURI "ZUDE". She was born 08 Jun 1923, and died 13 Mar 1975 in Roseboro Cemetery, NC. He married (2) VENIE FAIRCLOTH 20 Jun 1946 in Dillon, SC, daughter of ALLEN FAIRCLOTH and MISSOURI HALL. She was born 08 Jun 1923, and died 13 Mar 1965 in Buried in Roseboro Cemetery..

Children of HOUSTON FAIRCLOTH and VENIE FAIRCLOTH are:

i. FAYE[8] FAIRCLOTH, b. 05 Feb 1949.

ii. DOROTHY FAIRCLOTH, b. 18 Sep 1947.

iii. RUBEN ESTES FAIRCLOTH, b. 1951, Sampson Co., NC.

iv. RICHARD " RICKY" HOUSTON FAIRCLOTH, b. 10 Oct 1955.

v. LAWRENCE RAY FAIRCLOTH, b. 1952; d. Bef. 1984.

vi. CATHY DIANE FAIRCLOTH, b. 10 Jan 1957.

22.   TROY ABE[7] FAIRCLOTH *(TROY[6], ELIZABETH "LIZZIE"[5] HALL, MOSES MCLAINE[4] FAIRCLOTH, SR., SOLOMON[3], BENJAMIN FRANKLIN[2], EDWARD[1] FARECLOTH)* was born 13 Sep 1939 in Cumberland County, NC, and died 07 Apr 1974. He married CAROLYN MOTE.

Children of TROY FAIRCLOTH and CAROLYN MOTE are:

i. DEBBIE ANN[8] FAIRCLOTH, b. 16 Dec 1962.

ii. FRANK TROY FAIRCLOTH, b. 19 Jun 1967.

23.   GEORGE THOMAS[7] FAIRCLOTH *(GEORGE WASHINGTON[6], ELIZABETH "LIZZIE"[5] HALL, MOSES MCLAINE[4] FAIRCLOTH, SR., SOLOMON[3], BENJAMIN FRANKLIN[2], EDWARD[1] FARECLOTH)* was born 26 Jan 1916 in Sampson Co., NC, and died 11 Nov 1972 in Of myocardial arteriosclerosis. He married NELLIE ELIZABETH AUTRY. She was born 11 Oct 1925.

Children of GEORGE FAIRCLOTH and NELLIE AUTRY are:

49.   i. RUBY AGNES[8] FAIRCLOTH, b. 22 Sep 1943.

50.   ii. ELIZABETH NANNIE FAIRCLOTH, b. 13 Dec 1944, Sampson Co., NC.

51.   iii. RUFFIN "RONNIE" FAIRCLOTH, b. 31 Dec 1946.

52.   iv. JOYCE FAIRCLOTH, b. 05 Sep 1947.

53.   v. DAWSON HICKS FAIRCLOTH, b. 23 Nov 1948.

54.   vi. BONNIE LOU FAIRCLOTH, b. 09 Feb 1950.

55.   vii. FAYELENE FAIRCLOTH, b. 19 Mar 1952.

56.   viii. JULIA FAIRCLOTH, b. 03 Sep 1953.

57.   ix. JUDY FAIRCLOTH, b. 03 Sep 1953.

x. STILLBORN FAIRCLOTH, b. 06 Mar 1955; d. 06 Mar 1955.

24. RUBY[7] FAIRCLOTH (*GEORGE WASHINGTON[6], ELIZABETH "LIZZIE"[5] HALL, MOSES MCLAINE[4] FAIRCLOTH, SR., SOLOMON[3], BENJAMIN FRANKLIN[2], EDWARD[1] FARECLOTH*) was born 16 Jan 1924 in Sampson Co., NC. She married VAUGHN (HENRY VON)FAIRCLOTH, son of STEPHEN FAIRCLOTH and BETTY SESSOMS. He was born 01 Jan 1916 in Sampson Co., NC, and died 09 Jun 1982 in Died of heart disease. Children are listed above under (16) Vaughn (Henry Von)Faircloth.

25. ENICE[7] FAIRCLOTH (*GEORGE WASHINGTON[6], ELIZABETH "LIZZIE"[5] HALL, MOSES MCLAINE[4] FAIRCLOTH, SR., SOLOMON[3], BENJAMIN FRANKLIN[2], EDWARD[1] FARECLOTH*) was born 01 Jun 1926 in Sampson Co., NC. She married LESTER HAYNIE Abt. 03 Sep 1944, son of MELVA HAYNIE. He was born Abt. 1926.

Children of ENICE FAIRCLOTH and LESTER HAYNIE are:
58.   i.   CAROLYN W.[8] HAYNIE, b. Abt. 1946.
59.   ii.   SUSAN HAYNIE, b. Abt. 1946.
      iii.   FRANCES HAYNIE, b. Abt. 1946; m. UNKNOWN HALES.
      iv.   MELVA HAYNIE, b. Abt. 1946.
60.   v.   GERALD HAYES HAYNIE, b. Abt. 1946.

26. ROSIE ANNIE[7] FAIRCLOTH (*GEORGE WASHINGTON[6], ELIZABETH "LIZZIE"[5] HALL, MOSES MCLAINE[4] FAIRCLOTH, SR., SOLOMON[3], BENJAMIN FRANKLIN[2], EDWARD[1] FARECLOTH*) was born 10 Jun 1928 in Sampson Co., NC. She married (1) OTIS HALL. He was born 09 Jan 1925. She married (2) OTTIS BAILEY HALL, son of SOLOMON HALL and MARTHA CARTER. He was born 09 Jan 1925.

Children of ROSIE FAIRCLOTH and OTIS HALL are:
61.   i.   BRENDA ANN[8] HALL, b. 12 Aug 1946.
62.   ii.   OTTIS BAILEY HALL, JR., b. 07 Jul 1947.
63.   iii.   JOEL LAYTON "TOBY" HALL, b. 28 Jan 1950.
      iv.   JERRY LEE HALL, b. 08 Nov 1957; d. Died as an infant in an auto accident.
      v.   UNKNOWN HALL, b. Abt. 1951; d. Died as an infant.
      vi.   UNKNOWN HALL, b. Abt. 1951; d. Died as an infant.

27. ROY CRAFTON "CLAXTON"[7] FAIRCLOTH (*GEORGE WASHINGTON[6], ELIZABETH "LIZZIE"[5] HALL, MOSES MCLAINE[4] FAIRCLOTH, SR., SOLOMON[3], BENJAMIN FRANKLIN[2], EDWARD[1] FARECLOTH*) was born 31 Jan 1920 in Sampson Co., NC. He married EDNA EARL AUTRY. She was born Abt. 1920.

Child of ROY FAIRCLOTH and EDNA AUTRY is:
      i.   GEORGE WASHINTON[8] FAIRCLOTH.

28. FLEETIE "ADDIE[7] FAIRCLOTH (*GEORGE WASHINGTON[6], ELIZABETH "LIZZIE"[5] HALL, MOSES MCLAINE[4] FAIRCLOTH, SR., SOLOMON[3], BENJAMIN FRANKLIN[2], EDWARD[1] FARECLOTH*) was born 26 Nov 1920 in Sampson Co., NC. She married EARNEST HALL 19 Dec 1936. He was born Abt. 1920.

Children of FLEETIE FAIRCLOTH and EARNEST HALL are:
64.   i.   ELWOOD[8] HALL, b. 27 Aug 1940.

65.	ii.	JANICE HALL, b. 25 Oct 1942.
66.	iii.	DALLAS HALL, b. 21 Aug 1944.
67.	iv.	WADE HALL, b. 29 May 1946.
68.	v.	BEATRICE HALL, b. 08 Aug 1953.
69.	vi.	ANNETTE HALL, b. 29 Jan 1956.
	vii.	RONNIE HALL, b. 11 May 1963.

Generation No. 4

48. BOBBIE JOYCE[8] COLLISTER *(THELMA[7] FAIRCLOTH, SANTFORD ALLEN[6], ELIZABETH "LIZZIE"[5] HALL, MOSES MCLAINE[4] FAIRCLOTH, SR., SOLOMON[3], BENJAMIN FRANKLIN[2], EDWARD[1] FARECLOTH)* was born 07 Nov 1943, and died 20 Apr 1990 in Died at 46 yrs old. of cardiac pulmonary arrest and progressive breast cancer at Wayne Memorial Hospital in Goldsboro, NC; buried in Anderson Cemetery in Wayne Co., NC. She married DONALD R. ANDERSON.

Children of BOBBIE COLLISTER and DONALD ANDERSON are:
    i.   UNKNOWN[9] COLLISTER.
    ii. UNKNOWN COLLISTER.
    iii. UNKNOWN COLLISTER.
    iv. UNKNOWN COLLISTER.
    v.   UNKNOWN COLLISTER.

49. RUBY AGNES[8] FAIRCLOTH *(GEORGE THOMAS[7], GEORGE WASHINGTON[6], ELIZABETH "LIZZIE"[5] HALL, MOSES MCLAINE[4] FAIRCLOTH, SR., SOLOMON[3], BENJAMIN FRANKLIN[2], EDWARD[1] FARECLOTH)* was born 22 Sep 1943. She married JACKIE BUTLER HORNE. He was born 16 Jun 1940.

Child of RUBY FAIRCLOTH and JACKIE HORNE is:
    i.   JACKIE DARHYL[9] HORNE, b. 25 May 1966.

50. ELIZABETH NANNIE[8] FAIRCLOTH *(GEORGE THOMAS[7], GEORGE WASHINGTON[6], ELIZABETH "LIZZIE"[5] HALL, MOSES MCLAINE[4] FAIRCLOTH, SR., SOLOMON[3], BENJAMIN FRANKLIN[2], EDWARD[1] FARECLOTH)* was born 13 Dec 1944 in Sampson Co., NC. She married DICK SMITH SPORTS.

Children of ELIZABETH FAIRCLOTH and DICK SPORTS are:
    i.   KELLY[9] SPORTS, b. 06 Dec 1969.
    ii. WILLIAM SPORTS, b. 30 May 1971.

51. RUFFIN "RONNIE"[8] FAIRCLOTH *(GEORGE THOMAS[7], GEORGE WASHINGTON[6], ELIZABETH "LIZZIE"[5] HALL, MOSES MCLAINE[4] FAIRCLOTH, SR., SOLOMON[3], BENJAMIN FRANKLIN[2], EDWARD[1] FARECLOTH)* was born 31 Dec 1946. He married DELORES FISHER. She was born 03 Feb 1953.

Children of RUFFIN FAIRCLOTH and DELORES FISHER are:
    i.   TOMMIE LYNN[9] FAIRCLOTH, b. 25 Sep 1968.
    ii. RUFFIN CARL FAIRCLOTH, b. 10 Jan 1970.
    iii. JOHNNA DELORES FAIRCLOTH, b. 12 Jul 1972.

52.   JOYCE[8] FAIRCLOTH *(GEORGE THOMAS[7], GEORGE WASHINGTON[6], ELIZABETH "LIZZIE"[5] HALL, MOSES MCLAINE[4] FAIRCLOTH, SR., SOLOMON[3], BENJAMIN FRANKLIN[2], EDWARD[1] FARECLOTH)* was born 05 Sep 1947. She married WILLIAM JESSUP HORNE 16 May 1964. He was born 04 Apr 1945.

Children of JOYCE FAIRCLOTH and WILLIAM HORNE are:
   i.   WILLIAM JESSUP HORNE[9] HORNE III, b. 09 Sep 1965.
   ii. VICTORY TERRY HORNE HORNE, b. 27 May 1972.

53.   DAWSON HICKS[8] FAIRCLOTH *(GEORGE THOMAS[7], GEORGE WASHINGTON[6], ELIZABETH "LIZZIE"[5] HALL, MOSES MCLAINE[4] FAIRCLOTH, SR., SOLOMON[3], BENJAMIN FRANKLIN[2], EDWARD[1] FARECLOTH)* was born 23 Nov 1948. He married MYRINDA RAY HILL, daughter of ROBERT HILL and MABLE COTTLE.

Children of DAWSON FAIRCLOTH and MYRINDA HILL are:
   i.   CATINA LYNN[9] FAIRCLOTH, b. 09 Mar 1975.
   ii. JASON FAIRCLOTH, b. 07 Jan 1980.

54.   BONNIE LOU[8] FAIRCLOTH *(GEORGE THOMAS[7], GEORGE WASHINGTON[6], ELIZABETH "LIZZIE"[5] HALL, MOSES MCLAINE[4] FAIRCLOTH, SR., SOLOMON[3], BENJAMIN FRANKLIN[2], EDWARD[1] FARECLOTH)* was born 09 Feb 1950. She married (1) ROBERT CARTER.   She married (2) CLARENCE MAXWELL.

Children of BONNIE FAIRCLOTH and ROBERT CARTER are:
   i.   ROBIN ANN[9] CARTER, b. 11 Nov 1970.
   ii. CHRISTOPHER MICHAEL CARTER, b. 27 Jul 1978.

55.   FAYELENE[8] FAIRCLOTH *(GEORGE THOMAS[7], GEORGE WASHINGTON[6], ELIZABETH "LIZZIE"[5] HALL, MOSES MCLAINE[4] FAIRCLOTH, SR., SOLOMON[3], BENJAMIN FRANKLIN[2], EDWARD[1] FARECLOTH)* was born 19 Mar 1952. She married HAROLD EUGENE HENDERSON, son of DEWEY HENDERSON and NANNY LEARY. He was born 09 May 1948.

Children of FAYELENE FAIRCLOTH and HAROLD HENDERSON are:
   i.   LISA CAROL[9] HENDERSON, b. 08 Nov 1968.
   ii.   HAROLD EUGENE HENDERSON, JR., b. 07 Oct 1971.
   iii. TAMMIE FAITH HENDERSON, b. 10 Feb 1975.

56.   JULIA[8] FAIRCLOTH *(GEORGE THOMAS[7], GEORGE WASHINGTON[6], ELIZABETH "LIZZIE"[5] HALL, MOSES MCLAINE[4] FAIRCLOTH, SR., SOLOMON[3], BENJAMIN FRANKLIN[2], EDWARD[1] FARECLOTH)* was born 03 Sep 1953. She married RUBIN DANNY CASHWELL, son of RUBIN CASHWELL and MARSHA HORNE.

Child of JULIA FAIRCLOTH and RUBIN CASHWELL is:
   i.   ELIZABETH DONELL[9] CASHWELL.

57.   JUDY[8] FAIRCLOTH *(GEORGE THOMAS[7], GEORGE WASHINGTON[6], ELIZABETH "LIZZIE"[5] HALL, MOSES MCLAINE[4] FAIRCLOTH, SR., SOLOMON[3], BENJAMIN*

FRANKLIN[2], EDWARD[1] FARECLOTH) was born 03 Sep 1953. She married IRA FRANKIE BOLTON. He was born 08 Nov 1952.

Child of JUDY FAIRCLOTH and IRA BOLTON is:
    i. UNKNOWN[9] BOLTON.

58. CAROLYN W.[8] HAYNIE (ENICE[7] FAIRCLOTH, GEORGE WASHINGTON[6], ELIZABETH "LIZZIE"[5] HALL, MOSES MCLAINE[4] FAIRCLOTH, SR., SOLOMON[3], BENJAMIN FRANKLIN[2], EDWARD[1] FARECLOTH) was born Abt. 1946. She married KENNETH WEST.

Child of CAROLYN HAYNIE and KENNETH WEST is:
    i. AMY[9] WEST.

59. SUSAN[8] HAYNIE (ENICE[7] FAIRCLOTH, GEORGE WASHINGTON[6], ELIZABETH "LIZZIE"[5] HALL, MOSES MCLAINE[4] FAIRCLOTH, SR., SOLOMON[3], BENJAMIN FRANKLIN[2], EDWARD[1] FARECLOTH) was born Abt. 1946. She married UNKNOWN ADCOX.

Child of SUSAN HAYNIE and UNKNOWN ADCOX is:
    i. LINDSEY[9] ADCOX.

60. GERALD HAYES[8] HAYNIE (ENICE[7] FAIRCLOTH, GEORGE WASHINGTON[6], ELIZABETH "LIZZIE"[5] HALL, MOSES MCLAINE[4] FAIRCLOTH, SR., SOLOMON[3], BENJAMIN FRANKLIN[2], EDWARD[1] FARECLOTH) was born Abt. 1946. He married JUDAY SMITH.

Children of GERALD HAYNIE and JUDAY SMITH are:
    i. DONNIE[9] HANIE, Jr.
    ii. CARIE HANIE.

61. BRENDA ANN[8] HALL (ROSIE ANNIE[7] FAIRCLOTH, GEORGE WASHINGTON[6], ELIZABETH "LIZZIE"[5] HALL, MOSES MCLAINE[4] FAIRCLOTH, SR., SOLOMON[3], BENJAMIN FRANKLIN[2], EDWARD[1] FARECLOTH) was born 12 Aug 1946. She married MARSHALL BAILEY.

Children of BRENDA HALL and MARSHALL BAILEY are:
    i. KENNETH[9] BAILEY.
    ii. MARSHA ANN BAILEY.

62. OTTIS BAILEY[8] HALL, JR. (ROSIE ANNIE[7] FAIRCLOTH, GEORGE WASHINGTON[6], ELIZABETH "LIZZIE"[5] HALL, MOSES MCLAINE[4] FAIRCLOTH, SR., SOLOMON[3], BENJAMIN FRANKLIN[2], EDWARD[1] FARECLOTH) was born 07 Jul 1947. He married BETTY ROSE UNKNOWN.

Children of OTTIS HALL and BETTY UNKNOWN are:
    i. BRYAN[9] HALL, b. 04 Jun 1976.
    ii. STEVEN M. HALL, b. 09 Dec 1979.

63. JOEL LAYTON "TOBY"[8] HALL (ROSIE ANNIE[7] FAIRCLOTH, GEORGE WASHINGTON[6], ELIZABETH "LIZZIE"[5] HALL, MOSES MCLAINE[4] FAIRCLOTH, SR.,

SOLOMON[3], BENJAMIN FRANKLIN[2], EDWARD[1] FARECLOTH) was born 28 Jan 1950. He married JUDITY ANN HORNE, daughter of WILLIAM HORNE and ESTHER GRIFFIN.

Children of JOEL HALL and JUDITY HORNE are:
    i. KRISTY ANN[9] HALL, b. 20 Jan 1977.
   ii. JERRY D. HALL, b. 09 Sep 1979; d. Died in an auto accident..

64.   ELWOOD[8] HALL *(FLEETIE "ADDIE[7] FAIRCLOTH, GEORGE WASHINGTON[6], ELIZABETH "LIZZIE"[5] HALL, MOSES MCLAINE[4] FAIRCLOTH, SR., SOLOMON[3], BENJAMIN FRANKLIN[2], EDWARD[1] FARECLOTH)* was born 27 Aug 1940. He married BETTY.

Children of ELWOOD HALL and BETTY are:
    i. ELWOOD[9] HALL, JR..
   ii. KELLY HALL.
  iii. KIM HALL.

65.   JANICE[8] HALL *(FLEETIE "ADDIE[7] FAIRCLOTH, GEORGE WASHINGTON[6], ELIZABETH "LIZZIE"[5] HALL, MOSES MCLAINE[4] FAIRCLOTH, SR., SOLOMON[3], BENJAMIN FRANKLIN[2], EDWARD[1] FARECLOTH)* was born 25 Oct 1942. She married SIDNEY SESSOMS. He was born Abt. 1942.

Children of JANICE HALL and SIDNEY SESSOMS are:
    i. DONALD[9] HALL, b. Abt. 1962.
   ii. EDDIE HALL, b. Abt. 1962.
  iii. TEDDIE HALL, b. Abt. 1962.

66.   DALLAS[8] HALL *(FLEETIE "ADDIE[7] FAIRCLOTH, GEORGE WASHINGTON[6], ELIZABETH "LIZZIE"[5] HALL, MOSES MCLAINE[4] FAIRCLOTH, SR., SOLOMON[3], BENJAMIN FRANKLIN[2], EDWARD[1] FARECLOTH)* was born 21 Aug 1944. He married JOYCE SMITH. She was born Abt. 1944.

Child of DALLAS HALL and JOYCE SMITH is:
    i. TAMMY[9] HALL, b. Abt. 1964.

67.   WADE[8] HALL *(FLEETIE "ADDIE[7] FAIRCLOTH, GEORGE WASHINGTON[6], ELIZABETH "LIZZIE"[5] HALL, MOSES MCLAINE[4] FAIRCLOTH, SR., SOLOMON[3], BENJAMIN FRANKLIN[2], EDWARD[1] FARECLOTH)* was born 29 May 1946.

Child of WADE HALL is:
    i. ANGEL[9] HALL.

68.   BEATRICE[8] HALL *(FLEETIE "ADDIE[7] FAIRCLOTH, GEORGE WASHINGTON[6], ELIZABETH "LIZZIE"[5] HALL, MOSES MCLAINE[4] FAIRCLOTH, SR., SOLOMON[3], BENJAMIN FRANKLIN[2], EDWARD[1] FARECLOTH)* was born 08 Aug 1953. She married ROBERT HALL.

Child of BEATRICE HALL and ROBERT HALL is:
    i. JASON[9] HALL.

69. ANNETTE[8] HALL *(FLEETIE "ADDIE[7] FAIRCLOTH, GEORGE WASHINGTON[6], ELIZABETH "LIZZIE"[5] HALL, MOSES MCLAINE[4] FAIRCLOTH, SR., SOLOMON[3], BENJAMIN FRANKLIN[2], EDWARD[1] FARECLOTH)* was born 29 Jan 1956. She married WADE SIMMONS.

Child of ANNETTE HALL and WADE SIMMONS is:
　　　i. LISA[9] SIMMONS.

Descendants of
*Moses M*cLaine *(McLewaney)* *F*aircloth, *Jr.*

Generation No. 1

1. MOSES MCLAINE (MCLEWANEY)[5] FAIRCLOTH, JR. *(MOSES MCLAINE[4], SOLOMON[3], BENJAMIN FRANKLIN[2], EDWARD[1] FARECLOTH)* was born Abt. 1825, and died 22 Mar 1863 in Died in SC of a fever in a local hospital.. He married (1) ANNIE NANCY HALL. She was born Abt. 1839, and died Bet. 1863 - 1868. He married (2) PATIENCE " PATIA" HALL. She was born 1845. Moses' mother was Penelope.

Moses Jr. is listed as family #253 on the 1880 Census in Sampson County and listed as McLewaney. Patience Hall, the second wife of Moses Jr., was born in 1845 and had one child named Nancy Hall before she married McLewaney (Moses Jr.) McLewaney (Mack) adopted Nancy.

The 1880 Census shows Mack (Moses, Jr.), as 55 years of age and Patia as 35 on June 21-22, 1880. Military Records list Moses McLlvaine Faircloth as a private, born in 1825. He was a Sampson County farmer who enlisted on 4th of March 1862 in Fayetteville. He was discharged on the 26th of May 1862 as being over the age of 35. He reenlisted on the 16th of October 1862 in Cumberland County. He was assigned to C Company, Regiment 54, Infantry on the first enlistment. He was assigned to E Company, Regiment 8 on his second enlistment. He died on the 22nd of March 1863 of a fever in Charleston, SC during this enlistment. He was a cook.

I suspect that he left the first enlistment voluntarily, using his age as a legitimate reason because it was past time to put in the crops. Note that he returned to the service in October after the harvest time. Birth date according to Civil War Records.

Listed as family #253 on the 1880 Census in Sampson County, NC and listed as McLewaney. Moses adopted Nancy's previous child, Patience Hall.

He probably left the army the first time to put in the crops, and returned after the crops were harvested, taking care of his family back home.

Children of MOSES FAIRCLOTH and ANNIE HALL are:
2.   i.   HANSON ASBERRY "BEAR"[6] FAIRCLOTH, b. 11 May 1862
3.   ii. CHARLOTTE FAIRCLOTH, b. Mar 1861; d. 1931
     iii. SCOTT FAIRCLOTH, b. Abt. 1849.
     iv. PATIENCE "PATRICIA"FAIRCLOTH, b. 1857.
     v.   THOMAS J. FAIRCLOTH, b. Jun 1859.
4.   vi. PHILLIP FAIRCLOTH, b. Aug 1869; d. 27 Feb 1967

Children of MOSES FAIRCLOTH and PATIENCE HALL are:
     vii. NANCY[6] HALL.
     viii. IDA E. FAIRCLOTH, b. 2 Feb 1875, Sampson Co., NC; d. 09 Mar 1959, Sampson Co., NC; m. GRADY TANNER. Ida buried in Moses Cemetery; Possibly born 1872. Medical Information: Died of a heart attack.

ix. IRENE RENA FAIRCLOTH, b. 16 Jul 1879, Mother is Patience "Patia" Hall; m. M. O. MATTHEWS, 16 Dec 1903; b. 1876; d. 16 Dec 1903, Sampson Co., NC. Irene possibly born May 1877.

x. NANCY HALL FAIRCLOTH, b. adopted by Moses Jr..

(Note: Generations of Hanson Asberry are included under the descendents of Handson Asberry Faircloth)

23. VAUGHN (HENRY[8] VON)FAIRCLOTH *(STEPHEN PHILLIP[7] FAIRCLOTH, HANSON ASBERRY "BEAR"[6], MOSES MCLAINE (MCLEWANEY)[5], MOSES MCLAINE[4], SOLOMON[3], BENJAMIN FRANKLIN[2], EDWARD[1] FARECLOTH)* was born 01 Jan 1916 in Sampson Co., NC, and died 09 Jun 1982 in Died of heart disease. He married RUBY FAIRCLOTH, daughter of GEORGE FAIRCLOTH and NANCY SESSOMS. She was born 16 Jan 1924 in Sampson Co., NC.

Children of VAUGHN VON)FAIRCLOTH and RUBY FAIRCLOTH are:
i. HENRY[9] VON FAIRCLOTH, b. 25 Dec 1943.
ii. GEORGE PHILLIP VON FAIRCLOTH, b. 22 Nov 1946.
iii. BETTY LOU VON FAIRCLOTH, b. 02 Feb 1948.
iv. WILLARD ROY VON FAIRCLOTH, b. 12 Aug 1949.

24. PAUL M.[8] FAIRCLOTH *(STEPHEN PHILLIP[7], HANSON ASBERRY "BEAR"[6], MOSES MCLAINE (MCLEWANEY)[5], MOSES MCLAINE[4], SOLOMON[3], BENJAMIN FRANKLIN[2], EDWARD[1] FARECLOTH)* was born Abt. 1911, and died 30 Jun 1988 in Buried in Haney Family Cemetery by butler Funeral Home/Rev. Roger Jackson. He married LIZZIE GLENDON.

Children of PAUL FAIRCLOTH and LIZZIE GLENDON are:
i. CLARENCE S.[9] FAIRCLOTH.
ii. UNKNOWN FAIRCLOTH.
iii. UNKNOWN FAIRCLOTH.
iv. UNKNOWN FAIRCLOTH.

25. RONIE ANN[8] FAIRCLOTH *(STEPHEN PHILLIP[7], HANSON ASBERRY "BEAR"[6], MOSES MCLAINE (MCLEWANEY)[5], MOSES MCLAINE[4], SOLOMON[3], BENJAMIN FRANKLIN[2], EDWARD[1] FARECLOTH)* was born 25 Nov 1911, and died 19 May 1980 in Died of diabetes and cancer, Sessoms Cemetery, Autryville, NC. She married JAMES K. OZZELL. He was born 02 May 1905, and died 16 May 1977.

Child of RONIE FAIRCLOTH and JAMES OZZELL is:
i. JAMES WILBERT[9] OZZELL, b. 25 Jan 1927.

26. HOUSTON LEE[8] FAIRCLOTH *(LAMAR LALLISTER[7], HANSON ASBERRY "BEAR"[6], MOSES MCLAINE (MCLEWANEY)[5], MOSES MCLAINE[4], SOLOMON[3], BENJAMIN FRANKLIN[2], EDWARD[1] FARECLOTH)* was born 15 Dec 1921 in Cumberland County, NC, and died 30 Apr 1981 in Buried in Concord Baptist Church Cemetery in Stedman, NC. He married MARY BELLE HOWELL, daughter of GRAY HOWELL and SARAH RILEY. She was born 09 Sep 1917 in Cumberland County, NC, and died 14 Apr 1967 in Buried at Concord Baptist Church, Autryville, NC.

Children of HOUSTON FAIRCLOTH and MARY HOWELL are:

i. ODIS LEE[9] FAIRCLOTH, b. 12 Feb 1942, Sampson Co., NC.
ii. WILLARD HOUSTON FAIRCLOTH, b. 10 May 1943, Sampson Co., NC.
iii. TOMMIE EARL FAIRCLOTH, b. 30 Dec 1945, Sampson Co., NC.

27. THELMA[8] FAIRCLOTH *(SANTFORD ALLEN[7], HANSON ASBERRY "BEAR"[6], MOSES MCLAINE (MCLEWANEY)[5], MOSES MCLAINE[4], SOLOMON[3], BENJAMIN FRANKLIN[2], EDWARD[1] FARECLOTH)* was born 24 Nov 1920 in Sampson Co., NC. She married ELMER BRAYTON COLLISTER Aug 1941, son of UNKNOWN COLLISTER and INA UNKNOWN. He was born 16 Mar 1920 in Ohio.

Children of THELMA FAIRCLOTH and ELMER COLLISTER are:
i. ELMER BRAYTON[9] COLLISTER, JR., b. 12 Jul 1954, Sumter, SC; d. Died in an auto accident at 16 years old; Buried in Autryville Church of God Cemetery..
ii. INA R. COLLISTER, b. 19 Oct 1957; m. UNKNOWN WHIPPLY.
iii. MARY COLLISTER, b. 07 Aug 1952; m. UNKNOWN CONNLEY; b. 07 Aug 1952.
iv. ELEANOR P. COLLISTER, b. 28 May 1942; m. UNKNOWN JOHNSON.
v. JEWELL RAY COLLISTER, b. 29 Jan 1953; m. (1) UNKNOWN GAYE; m. (2) UNKNOWN CHALFANT.
vi. EVA J. COLLISTER, b. 30 Sep 1962; m. UNKNOWN BRITT.
vii. CAROL A. COLLISTER, b. 18 Feb 1947; m. UNKNOWN ARNETTE; b. Abt. 1947.
viii. JAMES EARL COLLISTER, b. 06 Aug 1962.
ix. BOBBIE JOYCE COLLISTER, b. 07 Nov 1943; d. 20 Apr 1990, Died at 46 yrs old. of cardiac pulmonary arrest and progressive breast cancer at Wayne Memorial Hospital in Goldsboro, NC; buried in Anderson Cemetery in Wayne Co., NC; m. DONALD R. ANDERSON.
x. JUANITA COLLISTER, b. 13 Apr 1948; m. UNKNOWN LONG.

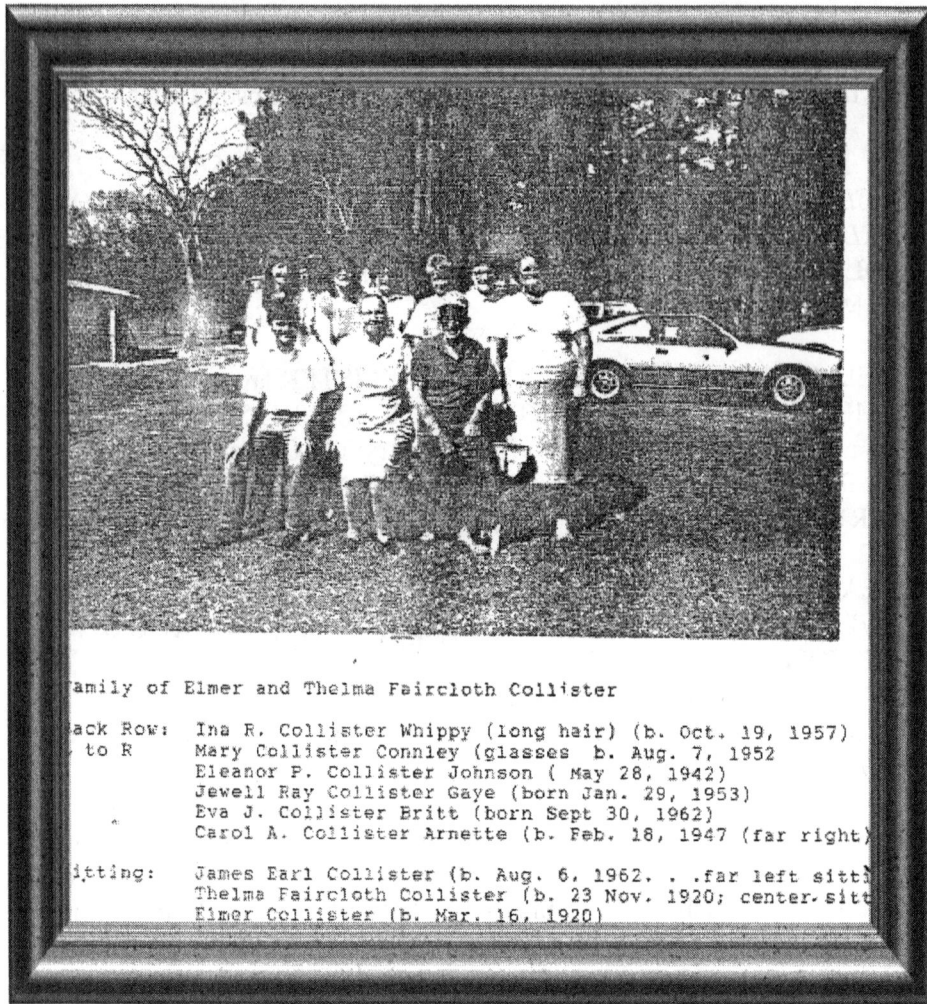

Family of Elmer and Themla Faircloth Collister:
Back Row left to right: Ina R. eollister Whippy (long hair) (b. Oct 19, 1957), Mary Collister Connley (glasses, b. Aug 7, 1852, Eleanor P. Collister Johnson b. May 28, 1942, Jewell Ray Collister Gaye, b. Jan 29, 1953, Eva J. Collister Britt, b. Sep 30, 1962, Carol A. Collister Arnette, b. Feb 18, 1947 (far right)

Sitting: James Earl Collister, b aug 6, 19662, far left sitting
Thelma Faircloth Collister, b Nov 23, 1920 sitting in center
Elmer Collister, b. Mar 16, 1920/

28.   HOUSTON TROY[8] FAIRCLOTH *(TROY[7], HANSON ASBERRY "BEAR"[6], MOSES MCLAINE (MCLEWANEY)[5], MOSES MCLAINE[4], SOLOMON[3], BENJAMIN FRANKLIN[2], EDWARD[1] FARECLOTH)* was born 23 May 1926 in Sampson Co., NC, and died in Roseboro Cemetery, NC. He married (1) VENNIE FAIRCLOTH 20 Jan 1946 in Dillon, SC, daughter of ALLEN FAIRCLOTH and MISSOURI "ZUDE". She was born 08 Jun 1923, and died 13 Mar 1975 in Roseboro Cemetery, NC.

Children of HOUSTON FAIRCLOTH and VENIE FAIRCLOTH are:

    i.   FAYE[9] FAIRCLOTH, b. 05 Feb 1949.
   ii.   DOROTHY FAIRCLOTH, b. 18 Sep 1947.
  iii.   RUBEN ESTES FAIRCLOTH, b. 1951, Sampson Co., NC.
   iv.   RICHARD " RICKY" HOUSTON FAIRCLOTH, b. 10 Oct 1955.
    v.   LAWRENCE RAY FAIRCLOTH, b. 1952; d. Bef. 1984.
   vi.   CATHY DIANE FAIRCLOTH, b. 10 Jan 1957.

29. TROY ABE[8] FAIRCLOTH *(TROY[7], HANSON ASBERRY "BEAR"[6], MOSES MCLAINE (MCLEWANEY)[5], MOSES MCLAINE[4], SOLOMON[3], BENJAMIN FRANKLIN[2], EDWARD[1] FARECLOTH)* was born 13 Sep 1939 in Cumberland County, NC, and died 07 Apr 1974. He married CAROLYN MOTE.

Children of TROY FAIRCLOTH and CAROLYN MOTE are:
    i.   DEBBIE ANN[9] FAIRCLOTH, b. 16 Dec 1962.
   ii.   FRANK TROY FAIRCLOTH, b. 19 Jun 1967.

30. GEORGE THOMAS[8] FAIRCLOTH *(GEORGE WASHINGTON[7], HANSON ASBERRY "BEAR"[6], MOSES MCLAINE (MCLEWANEY)[5], MOSES MCLAINE[4], SOLOMON[3], BENJAMIN FRANKLIN[2], EDWARD[1] FARECLOTH)* was born 26 Jan 1916 in Sampson Co., NC, and died 11 Nov 1972 in Of myocardial arteriosclerosis. He married NELLIE ELIZABETH AUTRY. She was born 11 Oct 1925.

Children of GEORGE FAIRCLOTH and NELLIE AUTRY are:
     i.   RUBY AGNES[9] FAIRCLOTH, b. 22 Sep 1943; m. JACKIE BUTLER HORNE; b. 16 Jun 1940.
    ii.   ELIZABETH NANNIE FAIRCLOTH, b. 13 Dec 1944, Sampson Co., NC; m. DICK SMITH SPORTS.
   iii.   RUFFIN "RONNIE" FAIRCLOTH, b. 31 Dec 1946; m. DELORES FISHER; b. 03 Feb 1953.
   iv.   JOYCE FAIRCLOTH, b. 05 Sep 1947; m. WILLIAM JESSUP HORNE, 16 May 1964; b. 04 Apr 1945.
    v.   DAWSON HICKS FAIRCLOTH, b. 23 Nov 1948; m. MYRINDA RAY HILL.
   vi.   BONNIE LOU FAIRCLOTH, b. 09 Feb 1950; m. (1) ROBERT CARTER; m. (2) CLARENCE MAXWELL.
   vii.   FAYELENE FAIRCLOTH, b. 19 Mar 1952; m. HAROLD EUGENE HENDERSON; b. 09 May 1948.
  viii.   JULIA FAIRCLOTH, b. 03 Sep 1953; m. RUBIN DANNY CASHWELL.
   ix.   JUDY FAIRCLOTH, b. 03 Sep 1953; m. IRA FRANKIE BOLTON; b. 08 Nov 1952.
    x.   STILLBORN FAIRCLOTH, b. 06 Mar 1955; d. 06 Mar 1955.

31. RUBY[8] FAIRCLOTH *(GEORGE WASHINGTON[7], HANSON ASBERRY "BEAR"[6], MOSES MCLAINE (MCLEWANEY)[5], MOSES MCLAINE[4], SOLOMON[3], BENJAMIN FRANKLIN[2], EDWARD[1] FARECLOTH)* was born 16 Jan 1924 in Sampson Co., NC. She married VAUGHN (HENRY VON) FAIRCLOTH, son of STEPHEN FAIRCLOTH and BETTY SESSOMS. He was born 01 Jan 1916 in Sampson Co., NC, and died 09 Jun 1982 in Died of heart disease.

Children are listed above under (23) Vaughn (Henry Von) Faircloth.

32. ENICE[8] FAIRCLOTH *(GEORGE WASHINGTON[7], HANSON ASBERRY "BEAR"[6], MOSES MCLAINE (MCLEWANEY)[5], MOSES MCLAINE[4], SOLOMON[3], BENJAMIN FRANKLIN[2], EDWARD[1] FARECLOTH)* was born 01 Jun 1926 in Sampson Co., NC. She married LESTER HAYNIE Abt. 03 Sep 1944, son of MELVA HAYNIE. He was born Abt. 1926.

Children of ENICE FAIRCLOTH and LESTER HAYNIE are:
    i.   CAROLYN W.[9] HAYNIE, b. Abt. 1946; m. KENNETH WEST.

    ii. SUSAN HAYNIE, b. Abt. 1946; m. UNKNOWN ADCOX.
   iii. FRANCES HAYNIE, b. Abt. 1946; m. UNKNOWN HALES.
   iv. MELVA HAYNIE, b. Abt. 1946.
    v. GERALD HAYES HAYNIE, b. Abt. 1946; m. JUDAY SMITH.

33. ROSIE ANNIE[8] FAIRCLOTH (*GEORGE WASHINGTON*[7], *HANSON ASBERRY "BEAR"*[6], *MOSES MCLAINE (MCLEWANEY)*[5], *MOSES MCLAINE*[4], *SOLOMON*[3], *BENJAMIN FRANKLIN*[2], *EDWARD*[1] *FARECLOTH*) was born 10 Jun 1928 in Sampson Co., NC. She married (1) OTIS HALL. He was born 09 Jan 1925. She married (2) OTTIS BAILEY HALL, son of SOLOMON HALL and MARTHA CARTER. He was born 09 Jan 1925.

Children of ROSIE FAIRCLOTH and OTIS HALL are:
    i. BRENDA ANN[9] HALL, b. 12 Aug 1946; m. MARSHALL BAILEY.
   ii. OTTIS BAILEY HALL, JR., b. 07 Jul 1947; m. BETTY ROSE UNKNOWN.
  iii. JOEL LAYTON "TOBY" HALL, b. 28 Jan 1950; m. JUDITY ANN HORNE.
   iv. JERRY LEE HALL, b. 08 Nov 1957; d. Died as an infant in an auto accident.
    v. UNKNOWN HALL, b. Abt. 1951; d. Died as an infant.
   vi. UNKNOWN HALL, b. Abt. 1951; d. Died as an infant.

34. ROY CRAFTON "CLAXTON"[8] FAIRCLOTH (*GEORGE WASHINGTON*[7], *HANSON ASBERRY "BEAR"*[6], *MOSES MCLAINE (MCLEWANEY)*[5], *MOSES MCLAINE*[4], *SOLOMON*[3], *BENJAMIN FRANKLIN*[2], *EDWARD*[1] *FARECLOTH*) was born 31 Jan 1920 in Sampson Co., NC. He married EDNA EARL AUTRY. She was born Abt. 1920.

Child of ROY FAIRCLOTH and EDNA AUTRY is:
    i. GEORGE WASHINTON[9] FAIRCLOTH.

35. FLEETIE "ADDIE[8] FAIRCLOTH (*GEORGE WASHINGTON*[7], *HANSON ASBERRY "BEAR"*[6], *MOSES MCLAINE (MCLEWANEY)*[5], *MOSES MCLAINE*[4], *SOLOMON*[3], *BENJAMIN FRANKLIN*[2], *EDWARD*[1] *FARECLOTH*) was born 26 Nov 1920 in Sampson Co., NC. She married EARNEST HALL 19 Dec 1936. He was born Abt. 1920.

Children of FLEETIE FAIRCLOTH and EARNEST HALL are:
    i. ELWOOD[9] HALL, b. 27 Aug 1940; m. BETTY.
   ii. JANICE HALL, b. 25 Oct 1942; m. SIDNEY SESSOMS; b. Abt. 1942.
  iii. DALLAS HALL, b. 21 Aug 1944; m. JOYCE SMITH; b. Abt. 1944.
   iv. WADE HALL, b. 29 May 1946.
    v. BEATRICE HALL, b. 08 Aug 1953; m. ROBERT HALL.
   vi. ANNETTE HALL, b. 29 Jan 1956; m. WADE SIMMONS.
  vii. RONNIE HALL, b. 11 May 1963.

36. ELSIE[8] FAIRCLOTH (*ALEXANDER*[7], *CHARLOTTE*[6], *MOSES MCLAINE (MCLEWANEY)*[5], *MOSES MCLAINE*[4], *SOLOMON*[3], *BENJAMIN FRANKLIN*[2], *EDWARD*[1] *FARECLOTH*) was born 20 Oct 1928 in Sampson Co., NC. She married JAMES ALEX H------. He was born 13 Mar 1931.

Child of ELSIE FAIRCLOTH and JAMES H------ is:
    i. MARY ALLICE[9] H??????, b. 24 May 1939.

37.   JONES ALEX[8] FAIRCLOTH *(ALEXANDER[7], CHARLOTTE[6], MOSES MCLAINE (MCLEWANEY)[5], MOSES MCLAINE[4], SOLOMON[3], BENJAMIN FRANKLIN[2], EDWARD[1] FARECLOTH)* was born 03 Mar 1930. He married ELVA MARIE FAIRCLOTH, daughter of MILLARD FAIRCLOTH and LOU CORE. She was born 15 Mar 1933 in Cumberland County, NC.

Children of JONES FAIRCLOTH and ELVA FAIRCLOTH are:
   i.   DORIS MARIE[9] FAIRCLOTH, b. 12 Nov 1951; m. JOE SMITH.
   ii. GAIL DIAN FAIRCLOTH, b. 22 Mar 1954; m. EWEN TANNER.
   iii. MARY LOUISE FAIRCLOTH, b. 09 Feb 1955; m. REX CASHWELL.
   iv. BRIDGET JOAN FAIRCLOTH, b. 14 Apr 1968; m. DALE LUIS.

Descendants of Hanson Asberry "Bear" Faircloth

Generation No. 1

1. HANSON ASBERRY "BEAR"[6] FAIRCLOTH   *(MOSES MCLAINE (MCLEWANEY)*[5], *MOSES MCLAINE*[4], *SOLOMON*[3], *BENJAMIN FRANKLIN*[2], *EDWARD*[1] *FARECLOTH)* was born 11 May 1862 in Sampson Co., NC, and died 27 Jan 1941 in Sampson Co., NC; buried in the Moses Cemetery in Sampson County, NC. He married ELIZABETH "LIZZIE" HALL Bet. 1887 – 1888. She was born Abt. 1862, and died Bet. 1901 - 1911. Hanson's age is taken from the 1900 Census as of March 1863, aged 37, and the 1870 Census as 70 years old, both in Sampson County, NC.

Hanson Asberry was known as "Bear" to the family. Bear usually wore a big, wide brim hat which was most fashionable at the time and resembled an over-sized Quaker hat. Hanson probably married Lizzie about 1887-88 as the 1900 Census in Sampson County states that they had been married for 12 years. Bear was about 24 when he married and Lizzie was about 16 years old.

Joyce Faircloth Taylor remembers that "bear would come to the house (Lula and Lawrence's home on B Street in Fayetteville, NC) every Christmas, alone. he would catch the bus from Hayne, where he lived, and walk to the house which was several blocks from the bus station. he walked with a cane. He had a very long beard (down to the middle of his chest) and would take home a bag of fruit containing apples, oranges, and tangerines, which Lula had prepared for him. This was a Christmas tradition for Grandpa Bear to come and spend Christmas with the family.

Birth dates of his children were listed as identified on the 1900 Sampson County Census. Census records do not always match death certificates but it is more likely that the parents would know if a child was two months old on the census date than the loved one would know the birth year at the death (as is the case with Sanford and Lamar).

Joyce remembers that Grandpa Bear died in his home in Hayne. As was the custom of the time, all of the curtains were drawn so he could die in darkness. His body was taken to the Butler's Funeral Home in Roseboro, NC, Sampson County, NC, and buried in the Moses Cemetery on 28 January 1941.

The 1900 Census lists Hanson Asberry Faircloth as born March 1863.

Children of HANSON FAIRCLOTH and ELIZABETH HALL are:

2.   i.   LULA JANE[7] FAIRCLOTH, b. 16 Aug 1897, Sampson Co., NC; d. 23 Aug 1959, Cumberland County, NC;
3.   ii. STEPHEN PHILLIP FAIRCLOTH, b. 17 Oct 1888; d. 17 Jan 1958.
4.   iii. LAMAR LALLISTER FAIRCLOTH, b. 30 Oct 1893; d. 07 Nov 1943, Sampson Co., NC;
      iv. UNKNOWN FAIRCLOTH, b. Bef. 1900. Listed as a result of the 1900 Census records.
5.   v.   SANTFORD ALLEN FAIRCLOTH, b. 13 Mar 1900, Sampson Co., NC; d. 18 Mar 1971, Sampson Co., NC; Autryville Church of God Cemetery.
6.   vi. TROY FAIRCLOTH, b. 13 Aug 1901, Cumberland County, NC; d. 03 Sep 1966, Buried 4 Sep in Salemburg Free Will Baptist Church Cemetery.
7.   vii. GEORGE WASHINGTON FAIRCLOTH, b. 02 Apr 1892; d. 23 Jan 1971, VA Hospital. buried in Sessoms Cemetery, Autryville, NC.

Generation No. 2

2.   LULA JANE[7] FAIRCLOTH *(HANSON ASBERRY "BEAR"[6], MOSES MCLAINE (MCLEWANEY)[5], MOSES MCLAINE[4], SOLOMON[3], BENJAMIN FRANKLIN[2], EDWARD[1] FARECLOTH)* was born 16 Aug 1897 in Sampson Co., NC, and died 23 Aug 1959 in Cumberland County, NC; buried at Cross Creek Cemetery in Fayetteville, NC. She married (1) SMITH.   She married (2) LAWRENCE C. FAIRCLOTH 10 Jan 1915 in Sampson County, NC, son of BENJAMIN FAIRCLOTH and ADLINE AUTRY. He was born 13 Mar 1886 in Sampson Co., NC, and died 20 Oct 1952 in Fayetteville, NC; buried in Cross Creek Cemetery, Fayetteville, NC. Lawrence: Cause of Death: Apoplexy (hardening of the arteries)

Children of LULA FAIRCLOTH and LAWRENCE FAIRCLOTH are:
8.   i.   LILLIAN ELIZABETH[8] FAIRCLOTH, b. 15 Dec 1915 d. Fayetteville, NC.
9.   ii.   LEROY FAIRCLOTH, b. 05 May 1918, Hayne, NC.
10.   iii. HERMAN REMUS FAIRCLOTH, b. 04 Feb 1927, Fayetteville, NC.
11.   iv.   JOYCE MARIE FAIRCLOTH, b. 16 Oct 1929.
12.   v.   HELEN FAIRCLOTH, b. 16 Sep 1924.
13.   vi.   LOTTIE JUANITA FAIRCLOTH, b. 30 Oct 1932.
14.   vii. JUDY ADLINE FAIRCLOTH, b. 27 Mar 1938, B St., Fayetteville, NC; d. 2005.
15.   viii. CARL HOUSTON FAIRCLOTH, b. 29 Oct 1920, Sampson Co., NC; d. 28 Dec 1971

3.   STEPHEN PHILLIP[7] FAIRCLOTH *(HANSON ASBERRY "BEAR"[6], MOSES MCLAINE (MCLEWANEY)[5], MOSES MCLAINE[4], SOLOMON[3], BENJAMIN FRANKLIN[2], EDWARD[1] FARECLOTH)* was born 17 Oct 1888, and died 17 Jan 1958. He married (1) BETTY ELIZABETH SESSOMS in Married in the home of Diancy Sessoms, Sampson County, NC.

Children of STEPHEN FAIRCLOTH and BETTY SESSOMS are:
16.   i.   VAUGHN (HENRY[8] VON)FAIRCLOTH, b. 01 Jan 1916, Sampson Co., NC; d. 09 Jun 1982, Died of heart disease.
17.   ii.   PAUL M. FAIRCLOTH, b. Abt. 1911; d. 30 Jun 1988, Buried in Haney Family Cemetery by butler Funeral Home/Rev. Roger Jackson.
18.   iii. RONIE ANN FAIRCLOTH, b. 25 Nov 1911; d. 19 May 1980, Died of diabetes and cancer, Sessoms Cemetery, Autryville, NC.

4.   LAMAR LALLISTER[7] FAIRCLOTH *(HANSON ASBERRY "BEAR"[6], MOSES MCLAINE (MCLEWANEY)[5], MOSES MCLAINE[4], SOLOMON[3], BENJAMIN FRANKLIN[2], EDWARD[1] FARECLOTH)* was born 30 Oct 1893, and died 07 Nov 1943 in Sampson Co., NC; buried 9 Nov in Johnson Family Cemetery. He married BETTY FAIRCLOTH 03 Apr 1914, daughter of LUCIAN FAIRCLOTH and EMMA SESSOMS. Lamar was buried on 9 Nov 1943 in the Johnson Family Cemetery.
    Lamar Lallister Faircloth was a World War I Veteran who served as a Private in the 119th Infantry of the 30th Division.

Children of LAMAR FAIRCLOTH and BETTY FAIRCLOTH are:
        i.   SEPSIE[8] FAIRCLOTH, b. 15 Sep 1920, Sampson Co., NC.
19.   ii.   HOUSTON LEE FAIRCLOTH, b. 15 Dec 1921, Cumberland County, NC; d. 30 Apr 1981, Buried in Concord Baptist Church Cemetery in Stedman, NC.
        iii. WILLIAM HOLT FAIRCLOTH, b. 02 Jan 1924, Cumberland County, NC.

    iv.   ELVA FAIRCLOTH, b. 28 Jun 1927, Cumberland County, NC.
    v.   HOOVER BRYANT FAIRCLOTH, b. 28 Feb 1929, Cumberland County, NC.
    vi.   LELA FAIRCLOTH, b. 18 Oct 1933; m. UNKNOWN STRICKLAND.
    vii.   LAMAR LALLISTER FAIRCLOTH, JR., b. 12 Jun 1937; d. 05 Jul 1981, Buried in Church of god Cemetery in Autryville, NC; m. NEVER MARRIED.
    viii.   CHARLES EARL FAIRCLOTH, b. 06 Nov 1939, Sampson Co., NC.
    ix.   JESSIE FAIRCLOTH, b. 26 Feb 1942, Sampson Co., NC.

5.   SANTFORD ALLEN[7] FAIRCLOTH (*HANSON ASBERRY "BEAR"[6], MOSES MCLAINE (MCLEWANEY)[5], MOSES MCLAINE[4], SOLOMON[3], BENJAMIN FRANKLIN[2], EDWARD[1] FARECLOTH*) was born 13 Mar 1900 in Sampson Co., NC, and died 18 Mar 1971 in Sampson Co., NC; Autryville Church of God Cemetery. He married ROSA FAIRCLOTH 10 Jan 1920 in 67 Mile Post on ACL Railroad, Sampson County, NC, by J. E. Horne, Justice of the Peace, daughter of LUCIAN FAIRCLOTH and EMMA SESSOMS. She was born 22 Sep 1896 in Sampson Co., NC, and died 13 Dec 1980 in Buried Church of God Cemetery in Autryville, NC.

Sant and Rosa Faircloth

Sant is buried in the Church of God Cemetery in Autryville, NC. He died of Cardiac Arrest. Rosa died of Cancer and gallbladder problems.

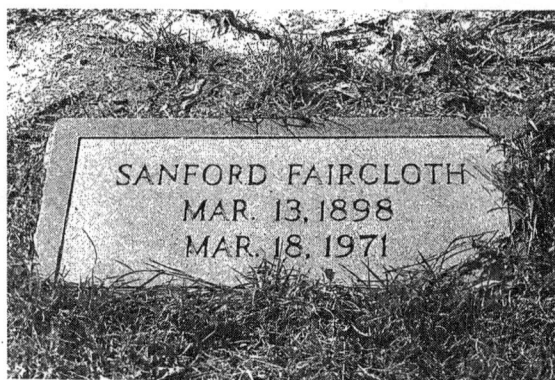

Children of SANTFORD FAIRCLOTH and ROSA FAIRCLOTH are:

20.   i.   THELMA[8] FAIRCLOTH, b. 24 Nov 1920, Sampson Co., NC.

      ii. JANEVA FAIRCLOTH, b. 06 Nov 1922, Sampson Co., NC; d. Died very young.

     iii. ROBERT J. FAIRCLOTH, b. Oct 1927, Cumberland County, NC.

     iv. AREY FAIRCLOTH, b. 31 Jul 1932, Sampson Co., NC.

      v. RAYMOND FAIRCLOTH, b. 19 May 1934, Sampson Co., NC; m. WANDA.

     vi. IRA FAIRCLOTH, m. UNKNOWN HALL.

    vii. RONIE NANCY FAIRCLOTH, b. 12 Sep 1924, Sampson Co., NC; d. 08 Feb 1925, Died of Pneumonia..

6. TROY[7] FAIRCLOTH (*HANSON ASBERRY "BEAR"[6], MOSES MCLAINE (MCLEWANEY)[5], MOSES MCLAINE[4], SOLOMON[3], BENJAMIN FRANKLIN[2], EDWARD[1] FARECLOTH*) was born 13 Aug 1901 in Cumberland County, NC, and died 03 Sep 1966 in Buried 4 Sep in Salemburg Free Will Baptist Church Cemetery. He married PENNY FAIRCLOTH 26 Nov 1919 in Cumberland County, NC, daughter of ERVING FAIRCLOTH and MANDY NEW. She was born 07 Jun 1901 in Sampson Co., NC, and died 02 Jul 1973 in Buried at Salemburg Freewill Baptist Church. Troy: Buried 4 September 1966 in Salemburg Free Will Baptist Church Cemetery.

Children of TROY FAIRCLOTH and PENNY FAIRCLOTH are:

      i. LOUISA JANE[8] FAIRCLOTH, b. 19 Sep 1920, Sampson Co., NC; m. CLAUDIUM MCD. PETERSON, 07 Feb 1941; b. 1917.

      ii. HUBERT FAIRCLOTH, b. 09 Sep 1923, Sampson Co., NC; m. PRISCILLA MAE AUTRY, 06 Apr 1956, Dillon, SC; b. 1926, South Autryville, NC.

21.   iii. HOUSTON TROY FAIRCLOTH, b. 23 May 1926, Sampson Co., NC; d. Roseboro Cemetery, NC.

iv. ROY COSBY FAIRCLOTH, b. 15 Nov 1928, Sampson Co., NC; m. CHRISTINE, 22 Jun 1952; b. 04 Sep 1934; d. 07 Feb 1987.
v. LOYD FAIRCLOTH, b. 23 Nov 1932, Sampson Co., NC.
vi. MANDIE ELIZABETH FAIRCLOTH, b. 10 Aug 1935, Sampson Co., NC.
22. vii. TROY ABE FAIRCLOTH, b. 13 Sep 1939, Cumberland County, NC; d. 07 Apr 1974.

7. GEORGE WASHINGTON[7] FAIRCLOTH *(HANSON ASBERRY "BEAR"[6], MOSES MCLAINE (MCLEWANEY)[5], MOSES MCLAINE[4], SOLOMON[3], BENJAMIN FRANKLIN[2], EDWARD[1] FARECLOTH)* was born 02 Apr 1892, and died 23 Jan 1971 in VA Hospital. buried in Sessoms Cemetery, Autryville, NC. He married (2) NANCY "NANNIE" SESSOMS 07 Feb 1911 in Married in the home of Hix "Hicks" Hall, in Sampson County, NC, daughter of DAWSON SESSOMS and EASTER FAIRCLOTH. She was born Abt. 1892. George: Medical Information: Died of a pulmonary emboli in the VA Hospital.

Child of GEORGE WASHINGTON FAIRCLOTH is:
i. RUBY[8] FAIRCLOTH, m. VON FAIRCLOTH; b. 01 Feb 1916; d. 09 Jun 1982, Buried in Brock Cemetery; died of heart disease, arteriosclerosis.

Children of GEORGE FAIRCLOTH and NANCY SESSOMS are:
23. ii. GEORGE THOMAS[8] FAIRCLOTH, b. 26 Jan 1916, Sampson Co., NC; d. 11 Nov 1972, Of myocardial arteriosclerosis.
iii. MARTHA HAZEL FAIRCLOTH, b. 26 Oct 1918, Sampson Co., NC; d. 26 Dec 1980; m. LUTHER TANNER.
24. iv. RUBY FAIRCLOTH, b. 16 Jan 1924, Sampson Co., NC.
25. v. ENICE FAIRCLOTH, b. 01 Jun 1926, Sampson Co., NC.
26. vi. ROSIE ANNIE FAIRCLOTH, b. 10 Jun 1928, Sampson Co., NC.
27. vii. ROY CRAFTON "CLAXTON" FAIRCLOTH, b. 31 Jan 1920, Sampson Co., NC.
viii. TATE FAIRCLOTH, b. 31 Aug 1930, Sampson Co., NC; d. 1967; m. FRANCES EMILY BICKER, 21 Jun 1958.
28. ix. FLEETIE "ADDIE FAIRCLOTH, b. 26 Nov 1920, Sampson Co., NC.

Generation No. 3

16. VAUGHN (HENRY[8] VON)FAIRCLOTH *(STEPHEN PHILLIP[7] FAIRCLOTH, HANSON ASBERRY "BEAR"[6], MOSES MCLAINE (MCLEWANEY)[5], MOSES MCLAINE[4], SOLOMON[3], BENJAMIN FRANKLIN[2], EDWARD[1] FARECLOTH)* was born 01 Jan 1916 in Sampson Co., NC, and died 09 Jun 1982 in Died of heart disease. He married RUBY FAIRCLOTH, daughter of GEORGE FAIRCLOTH and NANCY SESSOMS. She was born 16 Jan 1924 in Sampson Co., NC.

Children of VAUGHN VON)FAIRCLOTH and RUBY FAIRCLOTH are:
i. HENRY[9] VON FAIRCLOTH, b. 25 Dec 1943.
ii. GEORGE PHILLIP VON FAIRCLOTH, b. 22 Nov 1946.
iii. BETTY LOU VON FAIRCLOTH, b. 02 Feb 1948.
iv. WILLARD ROY VON FAIRCLOTH, b. 12 Aug 1949.

17.   PAUL M.[8] FAIRCLOTH *(STEPHEN PHILLIP[7], HANSON ASBERRY "BEAR"[6], MOSES MCLAINE (MCLEWANEY)[5], MOSES MCLAINE[4], SOLOMON[3], BENJAMIN FRANKLIN[2], EDWARD[1] FARECLOTH)* was born Abt. 1911, and died 30 Jun 1988 in Buried in Haney Family Cemetery by butler Funeral Home/Rev. Roger Jackson. He married LIZZIE GLENDON.

Children of PAUL FAIRCLOTH and LIZZIE GLENDON are:
   i.   CLARENCE S.[9] FAIRCLOTH.
   ii. UNKNOWN FAIRCLOTH.
   iii. UNKNOWN FAIRCLOTH.
   iv. UNKNOWN FAIRCLOTH.

18.   RONIE ANN[8] FAIRCLOTH *(STEPHEN PHILLIP[7], HANSON ASBERRY "BEAR"[6], MOSES MCLAINE (MCLEWANEY)[5], MOSES MCLAINE[4], SOLOMON[3], BENJAMIN FRANKLIN[2], EDWARD[1] FARECLOTH)* was born 25 Nov 1911, and died 19 May 1980 in Died of diabetes and cancer, Sessoms Cemetery, Autryville, NC. She married JAMES K. OZZELL. He was born 02 May 1905, and died 16 May 1977.

Child of RONIE FAIRCLOTH and JAMES OZZELL is:
   i.   JAMES WILBERT[9] OZZELL, b. 25 Jan 1927.

19.   HOUSTON LEE[8] FAIRCLOTH *(LAMAR LALLISTER[7], HANSON ASBERRY "BEAR"[6], MOSES MCLAINE (MCLEWANEY)[5], MOSES MCLAINE[4], SOLOMON[3], BENJAMIN FRANKLIN[2], EDWARD[1] FARECLOTH)* was born 15 Dec 1921 in Cumberland County, NC, and died 30 Apr 1981 in Buried in Concord Baptist Church Cemetery in Stedman, NC. He married MARY BELLE HOWELL, daughter of GRAY HOWELL and SARAH RILEY. She was born 09 Sep 1917 in Cumberland County, NC, and died 14 Apr 1967 in Buried at Concord Baptist Church, Autryville, NC.

Children of HOUSTON FAIRCLOTH and MARY HOWELL are:
   i.   ODIS LEE[9] FAIRCLOTH, b. 12 Feb 1942, Sampson Co., NC.
   ii. WILLARD HOUSTON FAIRCLOTH, b. 10 May 1943, Sampson Co., NC.
   iii. TOMMIE EARL FAIRCLOTH, b. 30 Dec 1945, Sampson Co., NC.

27.   ROY CRAFTON "CLAXTON"[8] FAIRCLOTH *(GEORGE WASHINGTON[7], HANSON ASBERRY "BEAR"[6], MOSES MCLAINE (MCLEWANEY)[5], MOSES MCLAINE[4], SOLOMON[3], BENJAMIN FRANKLIN[2], EDWARD[1] FARECLOTH)* was born 31 Jan 1920 in Sampson Co., NC. He married EDNA EARL AUTRY. She was born Abt. 1920.

Child of ROY FAIRCLOTH and EDNA AUTRY is:
   i.   GEORGE WASHINTON[9] FAIRCLOTH.

28.   FLEETIE "ADDIE[8] FAIRCLOTH *(GEORGE WASHINGTON[7], HANSON ASBERRY "BEAR"[6], MOSES MCLAINE (MCLEWANEY)[5], MOSES MCLAINE[4], SOLOMON[3], BENJAMIN FRANKLIN[2], EDWARD[1] FARECLOTH)* was born 26 Nov 1920 in Sampson Co., NC. She married EARNEST HALL 19 Dec 1936. He was born Abt. 1920.

Children of FLEETIE FAIRCLOTH and EARNEST HALL are:
64.   i.   ELWOOD[9] HALL, b. 27 Aug 1940.
65.   ii. JANICE HALL, b. 25 Oct 1942.

66.   iii.   DALLAS HALL, b. 21 Aug 1944.
67.   iv.   WADE HALL, b. 29 May 1946.
68.   v.   BEATRICE HALL, b. 08 Aug 1953.
69.   vi.   ANNETTE HALL, b. 29 Jan 1956.
      vii.   RONNIE HALL, b. 11 May 1963.

48.   BOBBIE JOYCE[9] COLLISTER *(THELMA[8] FAIRCLOTH, SANTFORD ALLEN[7], HANSON ASBERRY "BEAR"[6], MOSES MCLAINE (MCLEWANEY)[5], MOSES MCLAINE[4], SOLOMON[3], BENJAMIN FRANKLIN[2], EDWARD[1] FARECLOTH)* was born 07 Nov 1943, and died 20 Apr 1990 in Died at 46 yrs old. of cardiac pulmonary arrest and progressive breast cancer at Wayne Memorial Hospital in Goldsboro, NC; buried in Anderson Cemetery in Wayne Co., NC. She married DONALD R. ANDERSON.

Children of BOBBIE COLLISTER and DONALD ANDERSON are:
     i.   UNKNOWN[10] COLLISTER.
     ii.   UNKNOWN COLLISTER.
     iii.   UNKNOWN COLLISTER.
     iv.   UNKNOWN COLLISTER.
     v.   UNKNOWN COLLISTER.

49.   RUBY AGNES[9] FAIRCLOTH *(GEORGE THOMAS[8], GEORGE WASHINGTON[7], HANSON ASBERRY "BEAR"[6], MOSES MCLAINE (MCLEWANEY)[5], MOSES MCLAINE[4], SOLOMON[3], BENJAMIN FRANKLIN[2], EDWARD[1] FARECLOTH)* was born 22 Sep 1943. She married JACKIE BUTLER HORNE. He was born 16 Jun 1940.

Child of RUBY FAIRCLOTH and JACKIE HORNE is:
     i.   JACKIE DARHYL[10] HORNE, b. 25 May 1966.

50.   ELIZABETH NANNIE[9] FAIRCLOTH *(GEORGE THOMAS[8], GEORGE WASHINGTON[7], HANSON ASBERRY "BEAR"[6], MOSES MCLAINE (MCLEWANEY)[5], MOSES MCLAINE[4], SOLOMON[3], BENJAMIN FRANKLIN[2], EDWARD[1] FARECLOTH)* was born 13 Dec 1944 in Sampson Co., NC. She married DICK SMITH SPORTS.

Children of ELIZABETH FAIRCLOTH and DICK SPORTS are:
     i.   KELLY[10] SPORTS, b. 06 Dec 1969.
     ii.   WILLIAM SPORTS, b. 30 May 1971.

51.   RUFFIN "RONNIE"[9] FAIRCLOTH *(GEORGE THOMAS[8], GEORGE WASHINGTON[7], HANSON ASBERRY "BEAR"[6], MOSES MCLAINE (MCLEWANEY)[5], MOSES MCLAINE[4], SOLOMON[3], BENJAMIN FRANKLIN[2], EDWARD[1] FARECLOTH)* was born 31 Dec 1946. He married DELORES FISHER. She was born 03 Feb 1953.

Children of RUFFIN FAIRCLOTH and DELORES FISHER are:
     i.   TOMMIE LYNN[10] FAIRCLOTH, b. 25 Sep 1968.
     ii.   RUFFIN CARL FAIRCLOTH, b. 10 Jan 1970.
     iii.   JOHNNA DELORES FAIRCLOTH, b. 12 Jul 1972.

52.   JOYCE[9] FAIRCLOTH *(GEORGE THOMAS[8], GEORGE WASHINGTON[7], HANSON ASBERRY "BEAR"[6], MOSES MCLAINE (MCLEWANEY)[5], MOSES MCLAINE[4], SOLOMON[3],*

BENJAMIN FRANKLIN², EDWARD¹ FARECLOTH) was born 05 Sep 1947. She married WILLIAM JESSUP HORNE 16 May 1964. He was born 04 Apr 1945.

Children of JOYCE FAIRCLOTH and WILLIAM HORNE are:
   i. WILLIAM JESSUP HORNE¹⁰ HORNE III, b. 09 Sep 1965.
   ii. VICTORY TERRY HORNE, b. 27 May 1972.

53. DAWSON HICKS⁹ FAIRCLOTH *(GEORGE THOMAS⁸, GEORGE WASHINGTON⁷, HANSON ASBERRY "BEAR"⁶, MOSES MCLAINE (MCLEWANEY)⁵, MOSES MCLAINE⁴, SOLOMON³, BENJAMIN FRANKLIN², EDWARD¹ FARECLOTH)* was born 23 Nov 1948. He married MYRINDA RAY HILL, daughter of ROBERT HILL and MABLE COTTLE.

Children of DAWSON FAIRCLOTH and MYRINDA HILL are:
   i. CATINA LYNN¹⁰ FAIRCLOTH, b. 09 Mar 1975.
   ii. JASON FAIRCLOTH, b. 07 Jan 1980.

54. BONNIE LOU⁹ FAIRCLOTH *(GEORGE THOMAS⁸, GEORGE WASHINGTON⁷, HANSON ASBERRY "BEAR"⁶, MOSES MCLAINE (MCLEWANEY)⁵, MOSES MCLAINE⁴, SOLOMON³, BENJAMIN FRANKLIN², EDWARD¹ FARECLOTH)* was born 09 Feb 1950. She married (1) ROBERT CARTER. She married (2) CLARENCE MAXWELL.

Children of BONNIE FAIRCLOTH and ROBERT CARTER are:
   i. ROBIN ANN¹⁰ CARTER, b. 11 Nov 1970.
   ii. CHRISTOPHER MICHAEL CARTER, b. 27 Jul 1978.

55. FAYELENE⁹ FAIRCLOTH *(GEORGE THOMAS⁸, GEORGE WASHINGTON⁷, HANSON ASBERRY "BEAR"⁶, MOSES MCLAINE (MCLEWANEY)⁵, MOSES MCLAINE⁴, SOLOMON³, BENJAMIN FRANKLIN², EDWARD¹ FARECLOTH)* was born 19 Mar 1952. She married HAROLD EUGENE HENDERSON, son of DEWEY HENDERSON and NANNY LEARY. He was born 09 May 1948.

Children of FAYELENE FAIRCLOTH and HAROLD HENDERSON are:
   i. LISA CAROL¹⁰ HENDERSON, b. 08 Nov 1968.
   ii. HAROLD EUGENE HENDERSON, JR., b. 07 Oct 1971.
   iii. TAMMIE FAITH HENDERSON, b. 10 Feb 1975.

56. JULIA⁹ FAIRCLOTH *(GEORGE THOMAS⁸, GEORGE WASHINGTON⁷, HANSON ASBERRY "BEAR"⁶, MOSES MCLAINE (MCLEWANEY)⁵, MOSES MCLAINE⁴, SOLOMON³, BENJAMIN FRANKLIN², EDWARD¹ FARECLOTH)* was born 03 Sep 1953. She married RUBIN DANNY CASHWELL, son of RUBIN CASHWELL and MARSHA HORNE.

Child of JULIA FAIRCLOTH and RUBIN CASHWELL is:
   i. ELIZABETH DONELL¹⁰ CASHWELL.

57. JUDY⁹ FAIRCLOTH *(GEORGE THOMAS⁸, GEORGE WASHINGTON⁷, HANSON ASBERRY "BEAR"⁶, MOSES MCLAINE (MCLEWANEY)⁵, MOSES MCLAINE⁴, SOLOMON³, BENJAMIN FRANKLIN², EDWARD¹ FARECLOTH)* was born 03 Sep 1953. She married IRA FRANKIE BOLTON. He was born 08 Nov 1952.

Child of JUDY FAIRCLOTH and IRA BOLTON is:
    i. UNKNOWN[10] BOLTON.

58. CAROLYN W.[9] HAYNIE (*ENICE[8] FAIRCLOTH, GEORGE WASHINGTON[7], HANSON ASBERRY "BEAR"[6], MOSES MCLAINE (MCLEWANEY)[5], MOSES MCLAINE[4], SOLOMON[3], BENJAMIN FRANKLIN[2], EDWARD[1] FARECLOTH*) was born Abt. 1946. She married KENNETH WEST.

Child of CAROLYN HAYNIE and KENNETH WEST is:
    i. AMY[10] WEST.

59. SUSAN[9] HAYNIE (*ENICE[8] FAIRCLOTH, GEORGE WASHINGTON[7], HANSON ASBERRY "BEAR"[6], MOSES MCLAINE (MCLEWANEY)[5], MOSES MCLAINE[4], SOLOMON[3], BENJAMIN FRANKLIN[2], EDWARD[1] FARECLOTH*) was born Abt. 1946. She married UNKNOWN ADCOX.

Child of SUSAN HAYNIE and UNKNOWN ADCOX is:
    i. LINDSEY[10] ADCOX.

60. GERALD HAYES[9] HAYNIE (*ENICE[8] FAIRCLOTH, GEORGE WASHINGTON[7], HANSON ASBERRY "BEAR"[6], MOSES MCLAINE (MCLEWANEY)[5], MOSES MCLAINE[4], SOLOMON[3], BENJAMIN FRANKLIN[2], EDWARD[1] FARECLOTH*) was born Abt. 1946. He married JUDAY SMITH.

Children of GERALD HAYNIE and JUDAY SMITH are:
    i. DONNIE[10] HANIE, JR..
    ii. CARIE HANIE.

61. BRENDA ANN[9] HALL (*ROSIE ANNIE[8] FAIRCLOTH, GEORGE WASHINGTON[7], HANSON ASBERRY "BEAR"[6], MOSES MCLAINE (MCLEWANEY)[5], MOSES MCLAINE[4], SOLOMON[3], BENJAMIN FRANKLIN[2], EDWARD[1] FARECLOTH*) was born 12 Aug 1946. She married MARSHALL BAILEY.

Children of BRENDA HALL and MARSHALL BAILEY are:
    i. KENNETH[10] BAILEY.
    ii. MARSHA ANN BAILEY.

62. OTTIS BAILEY[9] HALL, JR. (*ROSIE ANNIE[8] FAIRCLOTH, GEORGE WASHINGTON[7], HANSON ASBERRY "BEAR"[6], MOSES MCLAINE (MCLEWANEY)[5], MOSES MCLAINE[4], SOLOMON[3], BENJAMIN FRANKLIN[2], EDWARD[1] FARECLOTH*) was born 07 Jul 1947. He married BETTY ROSE UNKNOWN.

Children of OTTIS HALL and BETTY UNKNOWN are:
    i. BRYAN[10] HALL, b. 04 Jun 1976.
    ii. STEVEN M. HALL, b. 09 Dec 1979.

63. JOEL LAYTON "TOBY"[9] HALL (*ROSIE ANNIE[8] FAIRCLOTH, GEORGE WASHINGTON[7], HANSON ASBERRY "BEAR"[6], MOSES MCLAINE (MCLEWANEY)[5], MOSES MCLAINE[4], SOLOMON[3], BENJAMIN FRANKLIN[2], EDWARD[1] FARECLOTH*) was born 28 Jan

1950. He married JUDITY ANN HORNE, daughter of WILLIAM HORNE and ESTHER GRIFFIN.

Children of JOEL HALL and JUDITY HORNE are:
    i.   KRISTY ANN[10] HALL, b. 20 Jan 1977.
    ii. JERRY D. HALL, b. 09 Sep 1979; d. Died in an auto accident..

64.   ELWOOD[9] HALL *(FLEETIE "ADDIE[8] FAIRCLOTH, GEORGE WASHINGTON[7], HANSON ASBERRY "BEAR"[6], MOSES MCLAINE (MCLEWANEY)[5], MOSES MCLAINE[4], SOLOMON[3], BENJAMIN FRANKLIN[2], EDWARD[1] FARECLOTH)* was born 27 Aug 1940. He married BETTY.

Children of ELWOOD HALL and BETTY are:
    i.   ELWOOD[10] HALL, JR..
    ii. KELLY HALL.
    iii. KIM HALL.

65.   JANICE[9] HALL *(FLEETIE "ADDIE[8] FAIRCLOTH, GEORGE WASHINGTON[7], HANSON ASBERRY "BEAR"[6], MOSES MCLAINE (MCLEWANEY)[5], MOSES MCLAINE[4], SOLOMON[3], BENJAMIN FRANKLIN[2], EDWARD[1] FARECLOTH)* was born 25 Oct 1942. She married SIDNEY SESSOMS. He was born Abt. 1942.

Children of JANICE HALL and SIDNEY SESSOMS are:
    i.   DONALD[10] HALL, b. Abt. 1962.
    ii. EDDIE HALL, b. Abt. 1962.
    iii. TEDDIE HALL, b. Abt. 1962.

66.   DALLAS[9] HALL *(FLEETIE "ADDIE[8] FAIRCLOTH, GEORGE WASHINGTON[7], HANSON ASBERRY "BEAR"[6], MOSES MCLAINE (MCLEWANEY)[5], MOSES MCLAINE[4], SOLOMON[3], BENJAMIN FRANKLIN[2], EDWARD[1] FARECLOTH)* was born 21 Aug 1944. He married JOYCE SMITH. She was born Abt. 1944.

Child of DALLAS HALL and JOYCE SMITH is:
    i.   TAMMY[10] HALL, b. Abt. 1964.

67.   WADE[9] HALL *(FLEETIE "ADDIE[8] FAIRCLOTH, GEORGE WASHINGTON[7], HANSON ASBERRY "BEAR"[6], MOSES MCLAINE (MCLEWANEY)[5], MOSES MCLAINE[4], SOLOMON[3], BENJAMIN FRANKLIN[2], EDWARD[1] FARECLOTH)* was born 29 May 1946.

Child of WADE HALL is:
    i.   ANGEL[10] HALL.

68.   BEATRICE[9] HALL *(FLEETIE "ADDIE[8] FAIRCLOTH, GEORGE WASHINGTON[7], HANSON ASBERRY "BEAR"[6], MOSES MCLAINE (MCLEWANEY)[5], MOSES MCLAINE[4], SOLOMON[3], BENJAMIN FRANKLIN[2], EDWARD[1] FARECLOTH)* was born 08 Aug 1953. She married ROBERT HALL.

Child of BEATRICE HALL and ROBERT HALL is:
    i.   JASON[10] HALL.

69.   ANNETTE[9] HALL *(FLEETIE "ADDIE[8] FAIRCLOTH, GEORGE WASHINGTON[7], HANSON ASBERRY "BEAR"[6], MOSES MCLAINE (MCLEWANEY)[5], MOSES MCLAINE[4], SOLOMON[3], BENJAMIN FRANKLIN[2], EDWARD[1] FARECLOTH)* was born 29 Jan 1956. She married WADE SIMMONS.

Child of ANNETTE HALL and WADE SIMMONS is:
   i.   LISA[10] SIMMONS.

Descendants of Charlotte Faircloth

Generation No. 1

1.   CHARLOTTE[6] FAIRCLOTH *(MOSES MCLAINE (MCLEWANEY)[5], MOSES MCLAINE[4], SOLOMON[3], BENJAMIN FRANKLIN[2], EDWARD[1] FARECLOTH)* was born Mar 1861, and died 1931 in Sampson Co., NC; buried by butler Funeral Home; 83 years old. Moses Cemetery, Sampson Co., NC.   She married STANTLEY FAIRCLOTH in Certificate # 6794., son of PHILLIP FAIRCLOTH and JANE. He was born Dec 1859 in Sampson Co., NC, and died 1935 in Buried in the Moses Cemetery, Sampson County, NC.   Charlotte was buried by Butler Funeral Home at 83 years old. This would put her birth date as 1848 if this is correct. Stantley tombstone says he died at 85 years of age in 1935.

Children of CHARLOTTE FAIRCLOTH and STANTLEY FAIRCLOTH are:
   i.   NANCY JANE[7] FAIRCLOTH, b. 07 Aug 1879, Sampson Co., NC; d. 06 Dec 1957, Sampson Co., NC; m. WILLIAM LLOYD NEW, 15 Jun 1902, Sampson Co., by S. J. Faircloth, Justice of Peace at E. Faircloth's residence; b. 1881, Cumberland County, NC.

ii. GEORGIANNA FAIRCLOTH, b. Feb 1882, Sampson Co., NC; m. JORDAN HALL, 16 Jan 1904; b. 1882.

2. iii. FLEET PITTMAN FAIRCLOTH, b. Oct 1891, Sampson Co., NC.

iv. MAMIE ELIZABETH FAIRCLOTH, b. Sep 1892; d. 07 Jun 1947.

3. v. EVA CATHERINE "KATE" FAIRCLOTH, b. 30 Mar 1902; d. 08 Mar 1981, Sampson, Co., died of respiratory problems, buried 11 Mar 1981 in Roseboro, NC.

4. vi. ALEXANDER FAIRCLOTH, b. 15 Sep 1898; d. 21 May 1960, Sampson, Co., committed suicide with 16 gauge shotgun; buried 23 May 1960;.

Generation No. 2

2. FLEET PITTMAN^7 FAIRCLOTH *(CHARLOTTE^6, MOSES MCLAINE (MCLEWANEY)^5, MOSES MCLAINE^4, SOLOMON^3, BENJAMIN FRANKLIN^2, EDWARD^1 FARECLOTH)* was born Oct 1891 in Sampson Co., NC. He married NETA FAIRCLOTH 22 Mar 1919 in Marriage witnesses: Tate; First married John H. Hall, b. 1 Jan 1915 and died 23 Jul 1916..

Children of FLEET FAIRCLOTH and NETA FAIRCLOTH are:
i. RUBY^8 FAIRCLOTH.
ii. TATE FAIRCLOTH.
iii. RUFUS "TOBY" FAIRCLOTH.

3. EVA CATHERINE "KATE"^{7} FAIRCLOTH *(CHARLOTTE^6, MOSES MCLAINE (MCLEWANEY)^5, MOSES MCLAINE^4, SOLOMON^3, BENJAMIN FRANKLIN^2, EDWARD^1 FARECLOTH)* was born 30 Mar 1902, and died 08 Mar 1981 She married UNKNOWN EVANS.

Children of EVA FAIRCLOTH and UNKNOWN EVANS are:
i. MARY JANE^8 EVANS, b. 19 Jun 1921; m. UNKNOWN JACKSON.
ii. JACKSON EVANS.

4. ALEXANDER^7 FAIRCLOTH *(CHARLOTTE^6, MOSES MCLAINE (MCLEWANEY)^5, MOSES MCLAINE^4, SOLOMON^3, BENJAMIN FRANKLIN^2, EDWARD^1 FARECLOTH)* was born 15 Sep 1898, and died 21 May

Children of ALEXANDER FAIRCLOTH and MARY TANNER are:
5. i. ELSIE^8 FAIRCLOTH, b. 20 Oct 1928, Sampson Co., NC.
ii. JAMES RANSON FAIRCLOTH, b. 14 Jun 1934, Sampson Co., NC; d. 22 Dec 1956.
iii. MARY ALLICE FAIRCLOTH, b. 24 May 1939, Sampson Co., NC.
6. iv. JONES ALEX FAIRCLOTH, b. 03 Mar 1930.

Generation No. 3

5. ELSIE^8 FAIRCLOTH *(ALEXANDER^7, CHARLOTTE^6, MOSES MCLAINE (MCLEWANEY)^5, MOSES MCLAINE^4, SOLOMON^3, BENJAMIN FRANKLIN^2, EDWARD^1 FARECLOTH)* was born 20 Oct 1928 in Sampson Co., NC. She married JAMES ALEX H------. He was born 13 Mar 1931.

Child of ELSIE FAIRCLOTH and JAMES H------ is:
i. MARY ALLICE^9 H??????, b. 24 May 1939.

6. JONES ALEX[8] FAIRCLOTH *(ALEXANDER[7], CHARLOTTE[6], MOSES MCLAINE (MCLEWANEY)[5], MOSES MCLAINE[4], SOLOMON[3], BENJAMIN FRANKLIN[2], EDWARD[1] FARECLOTH)* was born 03 Mar 1930. He married ELVA MARIE FAIRCLOTH, daughter of MILLARD FAIRCLOTH and LOU CORE. She was born 15 Mar 1933 in Cumberland County, NC.

Children of JONES FAIRCLOTH and ELVA FAIRCLOTH are:
7. i.   DORIS MARIE[9] FAIRCLOTH, b. 12 Nov 1951.
8. ii.   GAIL DIAN FAIRCLOTH, b. 22 Mar 1954.
9. iii. MARY LOUISE FAIRCLOTH, b. 09 Feb 1955.
    iv.   BRIDGET JOAN FAIRCLOTH, b. 14 Apr 1968; m. DALE LUIS.

Generation No. 4

7. DORIS MARIE[9] FAIRCLOTH *(JONES ALEX[8], ALEXANDER[7], CHARLOTTE[6], MOSES MCLAINE (MCLEWANEY)[5], MOSES MCLAINE[4], SOLOMON[3], BENJAMIN FRANKLIN[2], EDWARD[1] FARECLOTH)* was born 12 Nov 1951. She married JOE SMITH.

Children of DORIS FAIRCLOTH and JOE SMITH are:
    i.   ELIZABETH[10] SMITH, m. CHRIS DENNING.
    ii.   JOETTE SMITH.

8. GAIL DIAN[9] FAIRCLOTH *(JONES ALEX[8], ALEXANDER[7], CHARLOTTE[6], MOSES MCLAINE (MCLEWANEY)[5], MOSES MCLAINE[4], SOLOMON[3], BENJAMIN FRANKLIN[2], EDWARD[1] FARECLOTH)* was born 22 Mar 1954. She married EWEN TANNER.

Children of GAIL FAIRCLOTH and EWEN TANNER are:
    i.   DALE EWEN[10] TANNER, b. 27 Sep 1977.
    ii.   HEATHER TANNER.

9. MARY LOUISE[9] FAIRCLOTH *(JONES ALEX[8], ALEXANDER[7], CHARLOTTE[6], MOSES MCLAINE (MCLEWANEY)[5], MOSES MCLAINE[4], SOLOMON[3], BENJAMIN FRANKLIN[2], EDWARD[1] FARECLOTH)* was born 09 Feb 1955. She married REX CASHWELL.

Children of MARY FAIRCLOTH and REX CASHWELL are:
    i.   STEPHEN[10] CASHWELL, b. 03 Oct 1977.
    ii.   CASSIE CASHWELL, b. 15 Oct 1981.

Descendants of Neta Faircloth

Generation No. 1

1. NETA[1] FAIRCLOTH She married (1) JOHN J. HALL. He was born 26 Jan 1887, and died 23 Jul 1916. She married (2) FLEET PITTMAN FAIRCLOTH 22 Mar 1919 in Marriage

witnesses: Tate;   First married John H. Hall, b. 1 Jan 1915 and died 23 Jul 1916., son of STANTLEY FAIRCLOTH and CHARLOTTE FAIRCLOTH.   He was born Oct 1891 in Sampson Co., NC.

Children of NETA FAIRCLOTH and FLEET FAIRCLOTH are:
    i.   RUBY[2] FAIRCLOTH.
   ii.   TATE FAIRCLOTH.
  iii.   RUFUS "TOBY" FAIRCLOTH.

Descendants of Eva Catherine "Kate" Faircloth

Generation No. 1

1. EVA CATHERINE "KATE"[7] FAIRCLOTH *(STANTLEY[6], PHILLIP[5], MOSES MCLAINE[4], SOLOMON[3], BENJAMIN FRANKLIN[2], EDWARD[1] FARECLOTH)* was born 30 Mar 1902, and died 08 Mar 1981 in Sampson, Co., died of respiratory problems, buried 11 Mar 1981 in Roseboro, NC. She married UNKNOWN EVANS.

Children of EVA FAIRCLOTH and UNKNOWN EVANS are:
    i.   MARY JANE[8] EVANS, b. 19 Jun 1921; m. UNKNOWN JACKSON.
   ii.   JACKSON EVANS.

Descendants of Alexander Faircloth

Generation No. 1

1. ALEXANDER[7] FAIRCLOTH *(STANTLEY[6], PHILLIP[5], MOSES MCLAINE[4], SOLOMON[3], BENJAMIN FRANKLIN[2], EDWARD[1] FARECLOTH)* was born 15 Sep 1898, and died 21 May 1960 in Sampson, Co., committed suicide with 16 gauge shotgun; buried 23 May 1960;. He married MARY ETHEL TANNER 24 Dec 1927. She was born 29 Aug 1911 in Sampson Co., NC, and died 28 Feb 1942 in Sampson Co., NC, Moses Cemetery;. Name 2: Alexander Brance Faircloth

Children of ALEXANDER FAIRCLOTH and MARY TANNER are:
2.   i.   ELSIE[8] FAIRCLOTH, b. 20 Oct 1928, Sampson Co., NC.
       ii.   JAMES RANSON FAIRCLOTH, b. 14 Jun 1934, Sampson Co., NC; d. 22 Dec 1956.
     iii.   MARY ALLICE FAIRCLOTH, b. 24 May 1939, Sampson Co., NC.
3.   iv.   JONES ALEX FAIRCLOTH, b. 03 Mar 1930.

Generation No. 2

2.   ELSIE[8] FAIRCLOTH *(ALEXANDER[7], STANTLEY[6], PHILLIP[5], MOSES MCLAINE[4], SOLOMON[3], BENJAMIN FRANKLIN[2], EDWARD[1] FARECLOTH)* was born 20 Oct 1928 in Sampson Co., NC. She married JAMES ALEX H------. He was born 13 Mar 1931.

Child of ELSIE FAIRCLOTH and JAMES H------ is:
>   i.   MARY ALLICE[9] H??????, b. 24 May 1939.

3.   JONES ALEX[8] FAIRCLOTH *(ALEXANDER[7], STANTLEY[6], PHILLIP[5], MOSES MCLAINE[4], SOLOMON[3], BENJAMIN FRANKLIN[2], EDWARD[1] FARECLOTH)* was born 03 Mar 1930. He married ELVA MARIE FAIRCLOTH, daughter of MILLARD FAIRCLOTH and LOU CORE. She was born 15 Mar 1933 in Cumberland County, NC.

Children of JONES FAIRCLOTH and ELVA FAIRCLOTH are:
4.   i.   DORIS MARIE[9] FAIRCLOTH, b. 12 Nov 1951.
5.   ii. GAIL DIAN FAIRCLOTH, b. 22 Mar 1954.
6.   iii. MARY LOUISE FAIRCLOTH, b. 09 Feb 1955.
>   iv. BRIDGET JOAN FAIRCLOTH, b. 14 Apr 1968; m. DALE LUIS.

Generation No. 3

4.   DORIS MARIE[9] FAIRCLOTH *(JONES ALEX[8], ALEXANDER[7], STANTLEY[6], PHILLIP[5], MOSES MCLAINE[4], SOLOMON[3], BENJAMIN FRANKLIN[2], EDWARD[1] FARECLOTH)* was born 12 Nov 1951. She married JOE SMITH.

Children of DORIS FAIRCLOTH and JOE SMITH are:
>   i.   ELIZABETH[10] SMITH, m. CHRIS DENNING.
>   ii. JOETTE SMITH.

5.   GAIL DIAN[9] FAIRCLOTH *(JONES ALEX[8], ALEXANDER[7], STANTLEY[6], PHILLIP[5], MOSES MCLAINE[4], SOLOMON[3], BENJAMIN FRANKLIN[2], EDWARD[1] FARECLOTH)* was born 22 Mar 1954. She married EWEN TANNER.

Children of GAIL FAIRCLOTH and EWEN TANNER are:
>   i.   DALE EWEN[10] TANNER, b. 27 Sep 1977.
>   ii. HEATHER TANNER.

6.   MARY LOUISE[9] FAIRCLOTH *(JONES ALEX[8], ALEXANDER[7], STANTLEY[6], PHILLIP[5], MOSES MCLAINE[4], SOLOMON[3], BENJAMIN FRANKLIN[2], EDWARD[1] FARECLOTH)* was born 09 Feb 1955. She married REX CASHWELL.

Children of MARY FAIRCLOTH and REX CASHWELL are:
>   i.   STEPHEN[10] CASHWELL, b. 03 Oct 1977.
>   ii. CASSIE CASHWELL, b. 15 Oct 1981.

Descendants of Phillip Faircloth

Generation No. 1

1.   PHILLIP[6] FAIRCLOTH   *(MOSES MCLAINE (MCLEWANEY)[5], MOSES MCLAINE[4], SOLOMON[3], BENJAMIN FRANKLIN[2], EDWARD[1] FARECLOTH)* was born Aug 1869, and died 27 Feb 1967 in Died in Agnes Adcox Rest Home in Cumberland County, NC. He is buried in the Moses Cemetery, Sampson County, NC.. He married MOLLIE HALL. She was born 15 Jan 1872 in Cumberland County, NC. Phillip died from cerebral thrombosis.

Children of PHILLIP FAIRCLOTH and MOLLIE HALL are:
2.   i.   MAXTON EUGENE "MACK"[7] FAIRCLOTH, b. 15 Feb 1897; d. 26 Aug 1953
       ii.   BOB SHEPPARD FAIRCLOTH, b. 22 Dec 1909; d. 04 Jan 1989, Sampson Co., NC;
      iii.   VON FAIRCLOTH, b. 01 Feb 1916; d. 09 Jun 1982 m. RUBY FAIRCLOTH.
       iv.   JERUSHIA "RUSHIE" FAIRCLOTH, b. 27 Aug 1900; d. 12 Aug 1974; m. UNKNOWN TANNER.
        v.   SARAH G. FAIRCLOTH, b. Aug 1899.

Generation No. 2

2.   MAXTON EUGENE "MACK"[7] FAIRCLOTH *(PHILLIP[6], MOSES MCLAINE (MCLEWANEY)[5], MOSES MCLAINE[4], SOLOMON[3], BENJAMIN FRANKLIN[2], EDWARD[1] FARECLOTH)* was born 15 Feb 1897, and died 26 Aug 1953 in Buried Brock Cemetery on 27 Aug 1953; Died of chronic pulmonary infection. He married MAMIE CLYDE FISHER 15 Feb 1922. She was born 1906.

Children of MAXTON FAIRCLOTH and MAMIE FISHER are:
        i.   MAXTON EUGENE[8] FAIRCLOTH, JR., b. 19 Sep 1940.
       ii.   MATTIE PEARL FAIRCLOTH, b. 31 Jul 1944.
      iii.   JAMES ALLEN FAIRCLOTH, b. 22 Dec 1923.
       iv.   DAVID FAIRCLOTH, b. 23 Apr 1925.
        v.   EULA FAIRCLOTH, b. 30 Dec 1927.
       vi.   HUBBART FAIRCLOTH, b. 09 Dec 1930.
      vii.   ODIS FAIRCLOTH, b. 17 May 1934.
     viii.   UNKNOWN FAIRCLOTH, b. Unknown.

Generation No. 1

1.   LULA JANE⁷ FAIRCLOTH   *(HANSON ASBERRY "BEAR"⁶, MOSES MCLAINE (MCLEWANEY)⁵, MOSES MCLAINE⁴, SOLOMON³, BENJAMIN FRANKLIN², EDWARD¹ FARECLOTH)* was born 16 Aug 1897 in Sampson Co., NC, and died 23 Aug 1959 in Cumberland County, NC; buried at Cross Creek Cemetery in Fayetteville, NC. She married (1) SMITH.   She married (2) LAWRENCE C. FAIRCLOTH 10 Jan 1915 in Sampson County, NC, son of BENJAMIN FAIRCLOTH and ADLINE AUTRY. He was born 13 Mar 1886 in Sampson Co., NC, and died 20 Oct 1952 in Fayetteville, NC; buried in Cross Creek Cemetery, Fayetteville, NC.

Lawrence cause of Death: Apoplexy (hardening of the arteries)

Children of LULA FAIRCLOTH and LAWRENCE FAIRCLOTH are:
2.   i.   LILLIAN ELIZABETH⁸ FAIRCLOTH, b. 15 Dec 1915; d. Fayetteville, NC;
3.   ii. LEROY FAIRCLOTH, b. 05 May 1918, Hayne, NC.
4.   iii. HERMAN REMUS FAIRCLOTH, b. 04 Feb 1927, Fayetteville, NC.
5.   iv. JOYCE MARIE FAIRCLOTH, b. 16 Oct 1929.
6.   v.   HELEN FAIRCLOTH, b. 16 Sep 1924.
7.   vi. LOTTIE JUANITA FAIRCLOTH, b. 30 Oct 1932.
8.   vii. JUDY ADLINE FAIRCLOTH, b. 27 Mar 1938, B St., Fayetteville, NC; d. 2005.
9.   viii. CARL HOUSTON FAIRCLOTH, b. 29 Oct 1920, Sampson Co., NC; d. 28 Dec 1971

Joyce   Helen   Roy   Herman   Lottie   Judy

Joyce Christine, Erika, Lula, Judy

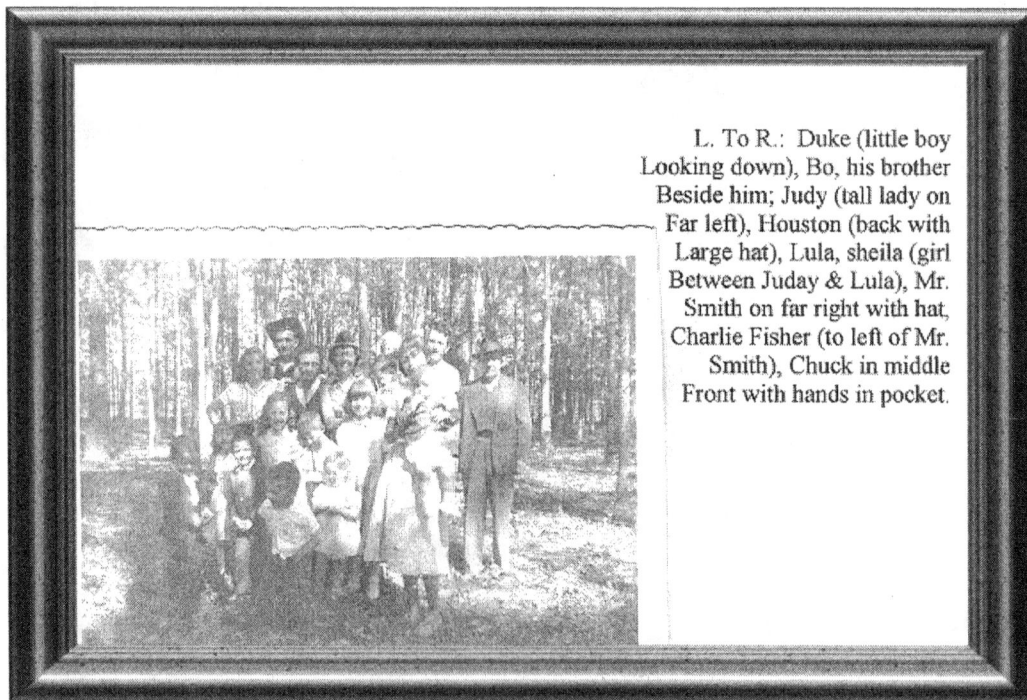

L. To R.: Duke (little boy Looking down), Bo, his brother Beside him; Judy (tall lady on Far left), Houston (back with Large hat), Lula, sheila (girl Between Juday & Lula), Mr. Smith on far right with hat, Charlie Fisher (to left of Mr. Smith), Chuck in middle Front with hands in pocket.

L to R: Duke (little boy looking down), Bo, his brother. Beside him: J udy (tall lady on far left; Houseton (back with large hat), Lula, Sheila (girl between Judy and Lula), Mr. Smith on far right with hat; Charlie Fisher (to left of Mr. Smith), Chuck in middle front with hand in pocket.

238

Notes:

Generation No. 1

1.   HERMAN REMUS[10] FAIRCLOTH *(LAWRENCE C.[9], BENJAMIN F.[8], THEOPHELES "AFFIE"[7], ARTHUR[6], HARDWICK[5], WILLIAM[4], WILLIAM[3], WILLIAM[2], WILLIAM[1])* was born 04 Feb 1927 in Fayetteville, NC.   He married ERIKA ELSE KREISLER 07 May 1950 in Germany, daughter of ARTHUR KREISLER and ELSE KUNNERT.   She was born 05 Aug 1929 in Stollenwasser, Germany (Jannusk, Poland).

Herman & Erika Faircloth

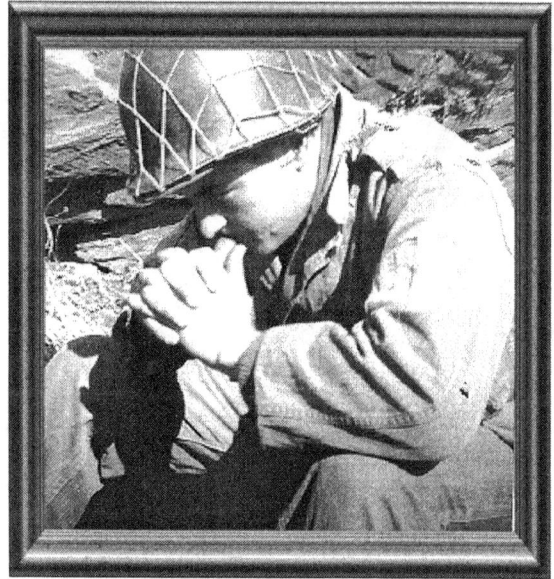

Herman as a sniper in Korea

RZECZPOSPOLITA POLSKA
Województwo Śląsko Dąbrowskie
Powiat Gliwice
Urząd Stanu Cywilnego
Tworog
Nr 26   1929

Odpis skrócony aktu urodzenia

Zaświadczam, że   Kreisler Eryka Else - - - - - - - - - -
urodził się dnia   piątego sierpnia - - - - - - - - - - 5.8. - - -
tysiąc   dziewięćset dwudziestego dziewiątego roku 1929 roku
w   Hanusku gmin. Tworog pow. Gliwice
z ojca   Artur Kreisler kupiec - - - - - - - - zamieszkałego
                (imię i nazwisko)   (zawód)
w   Hanusku gmina Tworog pow. Gliwice
i matki   Else Kreisler z domu Kunert bez zawodu
        (imię i nazwisko)   (nazwisko rodowe)   (zawód)
zamieszkałej w   Hanusku gmina Tworog pow. Gliwice
                                                . 49r.
                                            Stanu Cywilnego:

Erika Else Kreisler Faircloth

Lula, Herman and Chrystal

Notes:

North Carolina State Board of Health
BUREAU OF VITAL STATISTICS
STANDARD CERTIFICATE OF BIRTH

Registration District No. *No-2489*

72
Certificate No. 425

1. *Cumberland* OF BIRTH

City *Fayetteville NC* or Village _____ (No. _____ St.; _____ Ward)
(If birth occurred in hospital or institution, give its name instead of street and number)

2. FULL NAME OF CHILD *Unnamed* *Herman Pierce Faircloth* (If child is not yet named, make supplemental report, as directed)

3. Sex of child *Male* | To be answered only in event of plural births. | 4. Twin, triplet, or other _____ | 6. Parents married? *Yes* | 7. Date of birth *Feb 4* — *27*
5. Number, in order of birth _____ | | | (Name of Month) (Day) (Year)

FATHER	MOTHER
8. Full name *Lawrence C Faircloth*	14. Full maiden name *Lula Faircloth*
9. Residence (Usual place of abode) If nonresident, give place and State *NC*	15. Residence (Usual place of abode) If nonresident, give place and State *NC*
10. Color or race *White*	11. Age at last birthday *39* (Years)	16. Color or race *White*	17. Age at last birthday *27* (Years)
12. Birthplace (city or place) (State or country) *NC*	18. Birthplace (city or place) (State or country) *NC*
13. Occupation	19. Occupation
Nature of industry	Nature of industry *House wife*

20. Number of children of this mother (Taken as of time of birth of child herein certified and including this child.) (a) Born alive and now living *5* (b) Born alive, but now dead *0* (c) Stillborn *0*

21. Did you use drops in baby's eyes at birth to prevent blindness? *Yes* If not, why not? _____

CERTIFICATE OF ATTENDING PHYSICIAN OR MIDWIFE*

I hereby certify that I attended the birth of this child, who was *Born Alive* at *9:45* on the date above stated.
(Born alive or stillborn) (Hour, a.m. or p.m.)

23. (Signature) *A. Allred M.D.* (State whether physician or midwife)

24. P. O. _____

Given name added from supplemental report

2-7-1944

J. W. Johnson Registrar

25. Witness _____ (Signature of witness necessary only when 23 is signed by mark)

26. Filed *3-5-27* 27. *Hm Faulk* Local Registrar

28. P. O. *Fayetteville NC*

*When there was no attending physician or midwife, then the father, householder, etc., should make this return. If a child breathes even once, it must not be reported as stillborn. No report is desired of stillbirths before the fifth month of pregnancy.

151

Herman had open heart surgery in 2005 to repair several blocked arteries. He recovered wonderfully after several months of rehabilitation.

Children of HERMAN FAIRCLOTH and ERIKA KREISLER are:
2.   i.   JOYCE CHRISTINE[11] FAIRCLOTH, b. 18 Sep 1951, Ft. Benning, GA (Columbus).
3.   ii. JAMES ARTHUR LAWRENCE FAIRCLOTH, b. 21 Aug 1953, Baltimore, MD.
4.   iii. PHILLIP HERMAN FAIRCLOTH, b. 23 Oct 1958, Ft. Benning, GA.

Notes:

2.   JOYCE   CHRISTINE[11]   FAIRCLOTH   *(HERMAN   REMUS[10],* *LAWRENCE C.[9], BENJAMIN F.[8], THEOPHELES "AFFIE"[7], ARTHUR[6], HARDWICK[5], WILLIAM[4], WILLIAM[3], WILLIAM[2], WILLIAM[1])* was born 18 Sep 1951 in Ft. Benning, GA (Columbus). Christy earned a Bachelors Degree from Pembroke State University and a Master's degree from Campbell University. She married MICHAEL EDWARD JUDAH 03 Aug 1974 in Clarksville, TN, son of KENNETH JUDAH and CERISE HUDSON Michael died 2006.

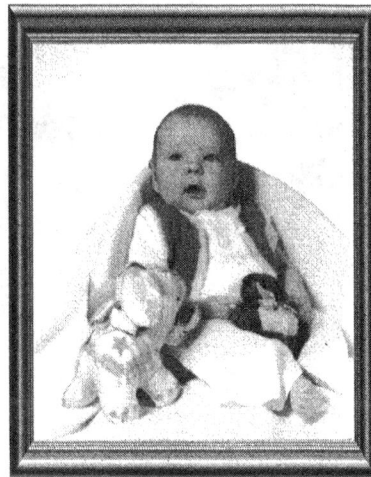

Joyce Christine Faircloth

Christy and Gypsy

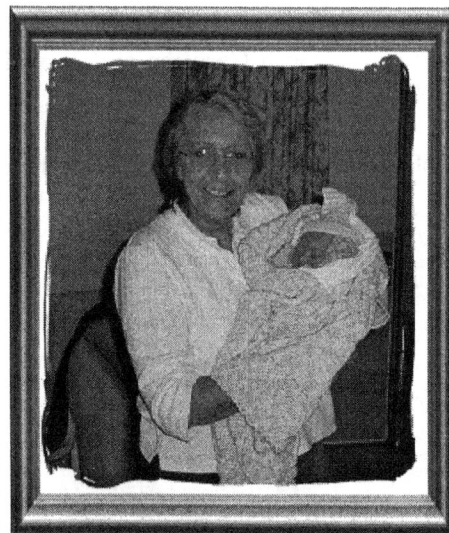

Christy and Grandson, Isaih Dale Fisher

Child of JOYCE FAIRCLOTH and MICHAEL JUDAH is:

5.　　i.　JENNIFER HEATHER BROOKE[12] JUDAH, b. 25 Jul 1975, Wurzburg, Germany. Jenny was very athletic and excelled in Tennis and Softball, pitching for various softball teams throughout her life. She earned a Bachelor's Degree from the University of Wilmington, NC and is presently working on her Master's Degree in Criminal Justice from East Carolina University which she expects to complete later this year. (2007)

Jennifer Judah Fisher

Christy and Jenny raised English Springer Spaniels for most of their adult life. Among them is her prized Bailey, a black/white springer who works as a search and rescue dog. Bailey has recovered multiple individuals in his career with the Brunswick Search and Resuce Team, Brunswick County, NC. Both Christy and Jenny are members of the team and have participated in many searches throughout North and South Carolina and served as officers of the team from it's inception in 1999.

Bailey, the English Springer Spaniel which Christy worked in Search and Rescue.

3.   JAMES ARTHUR LAWRENCE[11] FAIRCLOTH *(HERMAN REMUS[10]*, *LAWRENCE C.[9]*, *BENJAMIN F.[8]*, *THEOPHELES "AFFIE"[7]*, *ARTHUR[6]*, *HARDWICK[5]*, *WILLIAM[4]*, *WILLIAM[3]*, *WILLIAM[2]*, *WILLIAM[1]*) was born 21 Aug 1953 in Baltimore, MD. He married (1) RACHEL SHERI FULFORD.   He married (2) REBECCA OLIVER in Columbus, NC. Jamie and Becky currently reside in Columbus, NC.

James (Jamie) Faircloth

Becky Oliver Faircloth

Children of JAMES FAIRCLOTH and RACHEL FULFORD are Brandice Cane and James Cary Faircloth.

Notes:

i. BRANDICE CANE[12] FAIRCLOTH, b. April 7, 1975, Wilmington, NC; New Hanover Hospital. Cane is presently engaged to be married to Brea Chenille Stanley on May 5, 2007 in Supply, NC. Brea was born on 14 Oct 1975. her mother is Cathy Brown. Her grandparents are Otis and Katherine Causey.

Cane in a pipeline

Cane and Brea

Cane has always been an avid surfer and has surfed worldwide.

ii. JAMES CARY FAIRCLOTH, b. December 10, 1979 in Wilmington, NC; New Hanover Hospital. Cary has enjoyed playing bashetball with the Wilmington Wheelchair Team and has traveled across the states as far as California.

Cary Faircloth

Notes:

4. PHILLIP HERMAN[11] FAIRCLOTH (*HERMAN REMUS*[10], *LAWRENCE C.*[9], *BENJAMIN F.*[8],

4. PHILLIP HERMAN[11] FAIRCLOTH (*HERMAN REMUS*[10], *LAWRENCE C.*[9], *BENJAMIN F.*[8], *THEOPHELES "AFFIE"*[7], *ARTHUR*[6], *HARDWICK*[5], *WILLIAM*[4], *WILLIAM*[3], *WILLIAM*[2], *WILLIAM*[1]) was born 23 Oct 1958 in Ft. Benning, GA. He married BEVERLY ANNETTE PUTOFF in Supply, NC;. Beverly was born 10 Dec 1959.

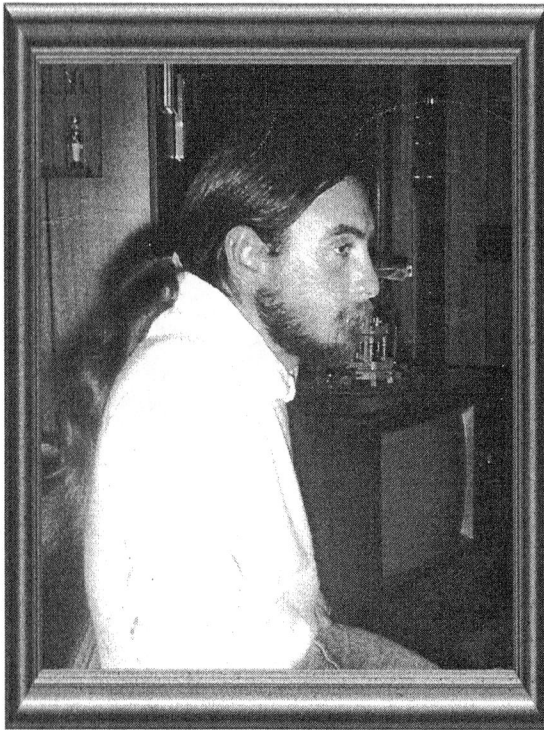

Children of PHILLIP FAIRCLOTH and BEVERLY PUTOFF are:
6.   i.   JESSIE AMBER NICOLE[12] FAIRCLOTH, b. 02 May 1981, Wilmington, NC; New Hanover Hospital.
7.   ii.   ERIKA HUNTER FAIRCLOTH, b. 26 Dec 1986, Wilmington, NC; New Hanover Hospital.

Front: Hunter and Beverly; Back: Phillip and Nicole.

Notes:

5. JENNIFER HEATHER BROOKE[12] JUDAH *(JOYCE CHRISTINE*[11] *FAIRCLOTH, HERMAN REMUS*[10]*, LAWRENCE C.*[9]*, BENJAMIN F.*[8]*, THEOPHELES "AFFIE"*[7]*, ARTHUR*[6]*, HARDWICK*[5]*, WILLIAM*[4]*, WILLIAM*[3]*, WILLIAM*[2]*, WILLIAM*[1]*)* was born 25 Jul 1975 in Wurzburg, Germany. She married JONATHAN DALE FISHER, son of GARY FISHER and PAULA HUGHES. He was born 28 Nov 1977 in New Hanover Hospital, Wilmington, NC.

She married JONATHAN DALE FISHER   **Jon as a Baby**

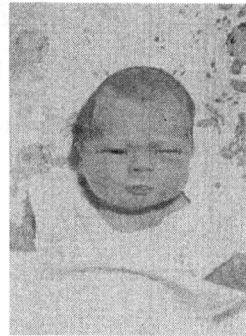

Jonathan and Jennifer Fisher

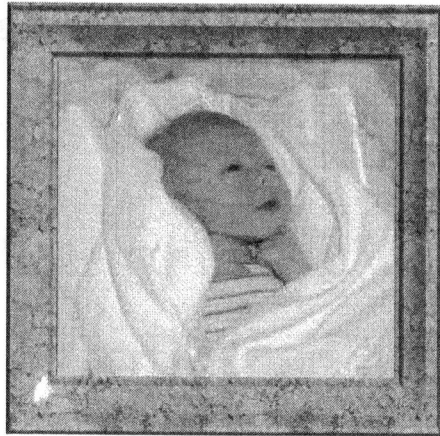

Isaih at Seven Days Old

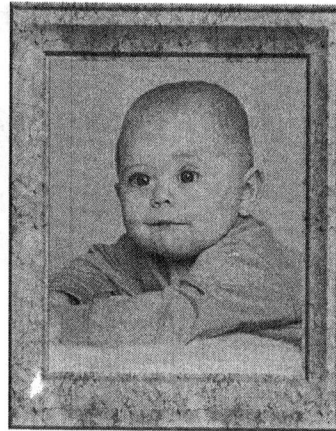

Isaih at Seven Months Old

Notes:

Interjection of Family History of Jonathan Fisher, husband of Jennifer Heather Brooke Judah Fisher and father of Isaih Dale Fisher

Descendants of Orie Fisher

Generation No. 1

1. ORIE[1] FISHER He married GERTRUDE CROW.

Children of ORIE FISHER and GERTRUDE CROW are:
2.   i.   GARY NEIL[2] FISHER, b. 02 Feb.
3.   ii. DONNA KAYE FISHER, d. Bet. 1995 - 1996, Kinston, NC.

Generation No. 2

2. GARY NEIL[2] FISHER (*ORIE[1]*) was born 02 Feb. He married PAULA DIANE HUGHES, daughter of ROBERT HUGHES and ANNIE FULLERTON. She was born 08 Apr 1955.

Child of GARY FISHER and PAULA HUGHES is:
4.   i.   JONATHAN DALE[3] FISHER, b. 28 Nov 1977, New Hanover Hospital, Wilmington, NC.

3. DONNA KAYE[2] FISHER (*ORIE[1]*) died Bet. 1995 - 1996 in Kinston, NC.

Child of DONNA KAYE FISHER is:
      i.   MARK ALLEN[3] FISHER, b. 27 Jan 1972.

Generation No. 3

4. JONATHAN DALE[3] FISHER (*GARY NEIL[2], ORIE[1]*) was born 28 Nov 1977 in New Hanover Hospital, Wilmington, NC. He married JENNIFER HEATHER BROOKE JUDAH, daughter of MICHAEL JUDAH and JOYCE FAIRCLOTH. Jonathan is currently working on his Associate Degree in Turf Management at Brunswick Community College and expected to complete that degree later this year (2007). He then plans to pursue his Bachelor's Degree

Children of JONATHAN FISHER and JENNIFER JUDAH are:
      i.   ISAIH DALE[4] FISHER, b. 17 Mar 2005, Wilmington, NC; New Hanover Hospital..
      ii. EXPECTED FISHER, b. Apr 2006, Not yet born.

Descendants of Robert C. Hughes

Generation No. 1

1. ROBERT C.[1] HUGHES He married ANNIE BELL FULLERTON. She was born 01 Nov.

Children of ROBERT HUGHES and ANNIE FULLERTON are:
2. i. PAULA DIANE[2] HUGHES, b. 08 Apr 1955.
  ii. ROBERT C. HUGHES, JR., m. DONNA UNKNOWN.
  iii. WALTER OLEN HUGHES, m. IMOGENE UNKNOWN.
  iv. JIMMY DALE HUGHES, d. Died in auto accident; Struck by a vehicle;; m. BRENDA UNKNOWN.
  v. EDDIE ALLEN HUGHES, d. Deceased; never married;.

Generation No. 2

2. PAULA DIANE[2] HUGHES *(ROBERT C.[1])* was born 08 Apr 1955. She married (1) GARY NEIL FISHER, son of ORIE FISHER and GERTRUDE CROW. He was born 02 Feb. She married (2) RICHARD COPE.

Child of PAULA HUGHES and GARY FISHER is:
3. i. JONATHAN DALE[3] FISHER, b. 28 Nov 1977, New Hanover Hospital, Wilmington, NC. Married Jennifer Heather Brooke Judah, b. 25 Jul 1975.
  ii. ROBIN VANESSA FISHER, b. 23 June 1973; married Christopher Russ, b. 12 Sep 1973
  iii. MARK ALLEN FISHER, b. 27 January 1973.

Generation No. 3

3. JONATHAN DALE[3] FISHER *(PAULA DIANE[2] HUGHES, ROBERT C.[1])* was born 28 Nov 1977 in New Hanover Hospital, Wilmington, NC. He married JENNIFER HEATHER BROOKE JUDAH

Children of JONATHAN FISHER and JENNIFER JUDAH are:
  i. ISAIH DALE[4] FISHER, b. 17 Mar 2005, Wilmington, NC; New Hanover Hospital..
  ii. EXPECTED FISHER, b. Apr 2007, Not yet born; male.

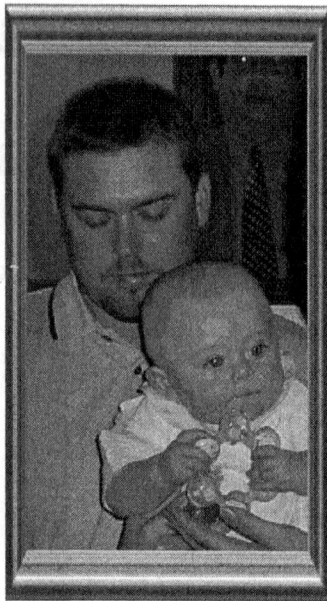

Jonathan & Isaih

Isaih and Jennifer

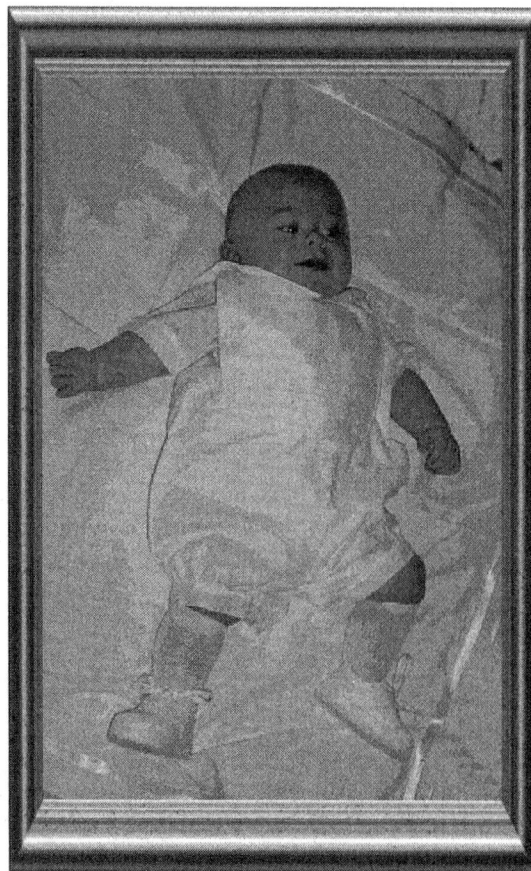

Christening Day for Isaih at Sabbath Home Church

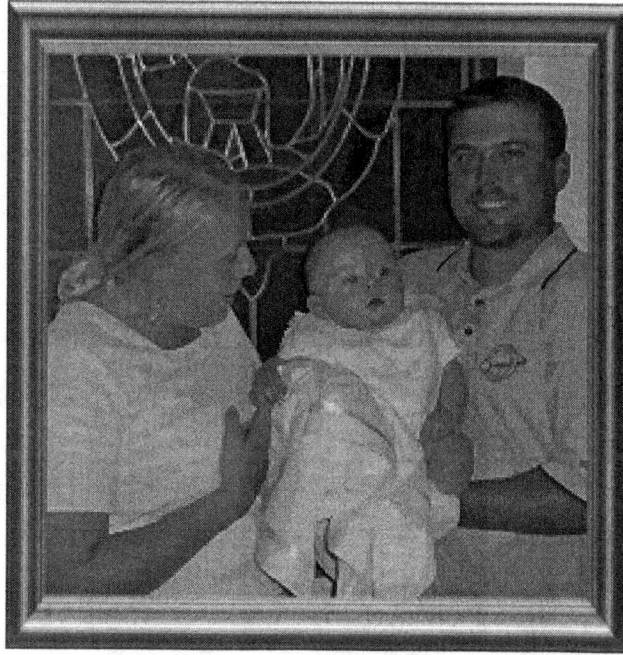

Jennifer, Isaih and Jonathan

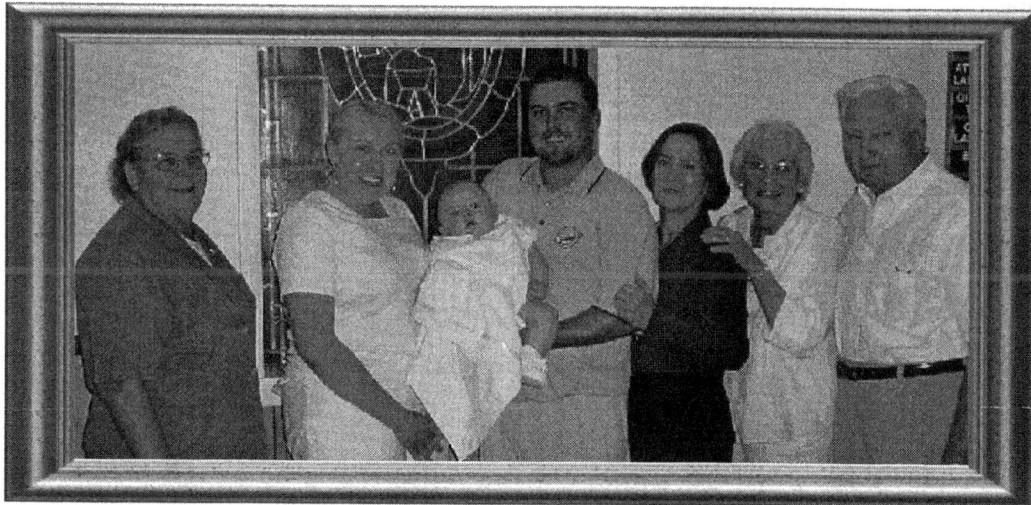

Annie Belle Hughes, Jennifer Fisher, Isiah Fisher, Jonathan Fisher, Paula Cope,
Erika Faircloth, Herman Faircloth

Great-Grandmother, Erika Great-Grandfather, Herman and Isaih   Mother, Jennifer

 **And their dog, Carolina's Wedding Rings…"Ringo"..
Scully, and Kaitlynn, all English Springer Spaniels.**

Children of JENNIFER JUDAH and JONATHAN FISHER are:

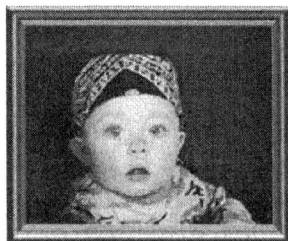

ISAIH DALE[13] FISHER, b. 17 Mar 2005, Wilmington, NC; New Hanover Hospital.

ii. EXPECTED FISHER, b. Apr 2006, Not yet born. Male.

Notes:

6. JESSIE AMBER NICOLE[12] FAIRCLOTH (*PHILLIP HERMAN*[11], *HERMAN REMUS*[10], *LAWRENCE C.*[9], *BENJAMIN F.*[8], *THEOPHELES "AFFIE"*[7], *ARTHUR*[6], *HARDWICK*[5], *WILLIAM*[4], *WILLIAM*[3], *WILLIAM*[2], *WILLIAM*[1]) was born 02 May 1981 in Wilmington, NC; New Hanover Hospital. She married DAVID CARTER. David was born August 20, _____.

Children of NICOLE FAIRCLOTH and DAVID CARTER are:
   i. MADISON LAYLA[13] ELIZABETH CARTER, born January 6, 2000
   ii. ERIKA HAYLEY CARTER, born November 10, 2001.

Layla   Hayley   David and Nicole

7. ERIKA HUNTER[12] FAIRCLOTH *(PHILLIP HERMAN[11], HERMAN REMUS[10], LAWRENCE C.[9], BENJAMIN F.[8], THEOPHELES "AFFIE"[7], ARTHUR[6], HARDWICK[5], WILLIAM[4], WILLIAM[3], WILLIAM[2], WILLIAM[1])* was born 26 Dec 1986 in Wilmington, NC; New Hanover Hospital.

Hunter

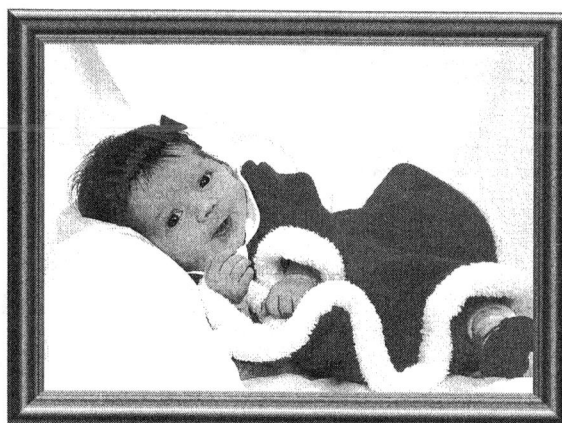

Adrian and Audrianna

Children of ERIKA HUNTER FAIRCLOTH are:
  i. ADRIAN[13] ANSON LEE FAIRCLOTH, b. January 16, 2004.
  ii. ERIKA AUDREANNA ELSE FAIRCLOTH, b. November 13, 2006.

261

Else, Erika, Arthur and Wolfgang Kreisler

Descendants of Walter Krajczi

Generation No. 1

1. WALTER[1] KRAJCZI He married GERTRUD.
Child of WALTER KRAJCZI and GERTRUD is:
2.　　i.　HEINRICH[2] KRAJCZI.

Generation No. 2
2. HEINRICH[2] KRAJCZI (*WALTER[1]*) He married ALMA ERICH.
Child of HEINRICH KRAJCZI and ALMA ERICH is:
3.　　i.　OSCAR[3] KRAJCZI.

Generation No. 3
3. OSCAR[3] KRAJCZI (*HEINRICH[2], WALTER[1]*)
Child of OSCAR KRAJCZI is:
4.　　i.　JOSEF[4] KRAJCZI, b. 29 Jan 1866, Friedruchsgratz, Poland; d. Jan 1945, Mechtal, Poland.

Generation No. 4

4.   JOSEF⁴ KRAJCZI *(OSCAR³, HEINRICH², WALTER¹)* was born 29 Jan 1866 in Friedruchsgratz, Poland, and died Jan 1945 in Mechtal, Poland.   He married AUGUSTA JANETZEK. She was born 07 Oct 1868 in Friedrichshutte, Poland, and died 1932.

Children of JOSEF KRAJCZI and AUGUSTA JANETZEK are:

    i.   ARTHUR ROBERT⁵ KREISLER, b. 11 Feb 1894, Hanussek Piassetzna; d. 20 Jun 1975, Coburg, Germany; m. ELSE KUNNERT, 25 Oct 1920, Koingshutte, Poland; b. 28 Jun 1895, Bismarchutte, Poland; d. 25 Jan 1977, Coburg, Germany.
   ii.   OSKAR KREISLER, b. 05 Aug 1889.
  iii.   HEINRICH KREISLER, b. 30 Mar 1891; d. Died in World War I..
   iv.   ALMA KREISLER, b. 07 Jun 1896.
    v.   ERICH KREISLER, b. 04 Aug 1898.
   vi.   WALTER KREISLER, b. 01 Sep 1900.
  vii.   GERTRUD KREISLER, b. 10 Mar 1902.

Back, standing: Unknown Janetzek. Back row sitting: Marie Kunert, Augusta Krajczi, Josef Krajczi, Georg Kunert, Unknown Jantzek in chair on right. Front row: Else Krajczi Kreisler holding baby Erika Else Kreisler, Heinz Kreisler, Lotte Janetzek, Wolfgang Kreisler (young boy), Hertha Slawik (with musical instrument). Photo circa 1929.

Descendants of Augusta Janetzek

Generation No. 1

1. AUGUSTA[1] JANETZEK was born 07 Oct 1868 in Friedrichshutte, Poland, and died 1932. She married JOSEF KRAJCZI, son of OSCAR KRAJCZI. He was born 29 Jan 1866 in Friedruchsgratz, Poland, and died Jan 1945 in Mechtal, Poland.

Children of AUGUSTA JANETZEK and JOSEF KRAJCZI are:

2.   i.   ARTHUR ROBERT[2] KREISLER, b. 11 Feb 1894, Hanussek Piassetzna; d. 20 Jun 1975, Coburg, Germany.
        ii.   OSKAR KREISLER, b. 05 Aug 1889.
      iii.   HEINRICH KREISLER, b. 30 Mar 1891; d. Died in World War I..
      iv.   ALMA KREISLER, b. 07 Jun 1896.
       v.   ERICH KREISLER, b. 04 Aug 1898.
      vi.   WALTER KREISLER, b. 01 Sep 1900.
     vii.   GERTRUD KREISLER, b. 10 Mar 1902.

Generation No. 2

2. ARTHUR ROBERT[2] KREISLER *(AUGUSTA[1] JANETZEK)* was born 11 Feb 1894 in Hanussek Piassetzna, and died 20 Jun 1975 in Coburg, Germany. He married ELSE KUNNERT 25 Oct 1920 in Koingshutte, Poland, daughter of GEORGE KUNERT and MARIE WENDE. She was born 28 Jun 1895 in Bismarchutte, Poland, and died 25 Jan 1977 in Coburg, Germany.

Wolfgang Kreisler, Chrystal Faircloth, Arthur and Else Kreisler

Children of ARTHUR KREISLER and ELSE KUNNERT (pictured above) are:
3.   i.   ERIKA ELSE[3] KREISLER, b. 05 Aug 1929, Stollenwasser, Germany (Jannusk, Poland).
        ii. WOLFGANG JOSEF KREISLER, b. 30 Oct 1927.
4.   iii. HEINZ ARTHUR KREISLER, b. 15 Dec 1921, Boruschowitz.

Heinz Kreisler

Wolfgang Kreisler

Heinz, Erika, and Renate

Generation No. 3

3. ERIKA ELSE³ KREISLER *(ARTHUR ROBERT², AUGUSTA¹ JANETZEK)* was born 05 Aug 1929 in Stollenwasser, Germany (Jannusk, Poland). She married HERMAN REMUS FAIRCLOTH 07 May 1950 in Germany, son of LAWRENCE FAIRCLOTH and LULA FAIRCLOTH. He was born 04 Feb 1927 in Fayetteville, NC.

Erika Kreisler

epublic Poland.
rovince Upper-Silesia.
istrict Gleiwitz.
egistrar's Office Tworog.
.26 / 1929.

Shortened copy of the certificate of birth.

It is certified that K r e i s l e r, Erika, Else, was born on the fifth August - 5th VIII.- nineteenhundredandtwentynine - 1929 - in H a n u s k, commune Tworog, district Gleiwitz ...... from the father Artur K r e i s l e r, merchant ...... residing in Hanusk, commune Tworog, district Gleiwitz ....and from the mother Else K r e i s l e r, née Kunert, without profession, residing in Hanusk, commune Tworog, district Gleiwitz.

T w o r o g, the 31st March, 1949.

The Registrar of the Registrar's Office:

signed: name.

Seal:
Registrar's Office
Tworog, district
Gleiwitz.

True translation from Polish into English is certified:
Coburg 1st November, 1949.

F.D. ... HOFF

v. Centralverband der ...

Children of ERIKA KREISLER and HERMAN FAIRCLOTH are:

5. i. JOYCE CHRISTINE[4] FAIRCLOTH, b. 18 Sep 1951, Ft. Benning, GA (Columbus).
6. ii. JAMES ARTHUR LAWRENCE FAIRCLOTH, b. 21 Aug 1953, Baltimore, MD.
7. iii. PHILLIP HERMAN FAIRCLOTH, b. 23 Oct 1958, GA.

4. HEINZ ARTHUR[3] KREISLER *(ARTHUR ROBERT[2], AUGUSTA[1] JANETZEK)* was born 15 Dec 1921 in Boruschowitz. He married RENATE ELFRIEDE HELENE SEIDLER. She was born 04 Sep 1928.

Heinz Kreisler

Children of HEINZ KREISLER and RENATE SEIDLER are:

8.   i.   MATTHIAS HEINZ^4 KREISLER, b. 25 Jan 1952, Coburg, Germany.
9.   ii.   THOMAS KREISLER, b. 08 Sep 1955, Coburg, Germany.
      iii.   SYBI RENATE KREISLER, b. 06 Aug 1957, Coburg, Germany.
      iv.   YUTTA ANGELIKA KREISLER, b. 22 Mar 1971, Coburg, Germany.

Dr. Matthias Kreisler, 2005

8.   MATTHIAS HEINZ[4] KREISLER *(HEINZ ARTHUR[3], ARTHUR ROBERT[2], AUGUSTA[1] JANETZEK)* was born 25 Jan 1952 in Coburg, Germany. He married DAGMAR HESS 23 Nov 1986. She was born 26 Aug 1962. Matthis is a practicing dentist.

Child of MATTHIAS KREISLER and DAGMAR HESS is:
     i.   HELEN LISA[5] KREISLER, b. 23 Feb 1987.

9.   THOMAS[4] KREISLER *(HEINZ ARTHUR[3], ARTHUR ROBERT[2], AUGUSTA[1] JANETZEK)* was born 08 Sep 1955 in Coburg, Germany. He married BETTINA LINDEMANN 05 Apr 1985. She was born 23 Dec 1959.

Dr. Thomas Kreisler

Children of THOMAS KREISLER and BETTINA LINDEMANN are:
Thomas is a practicing medical physician specializing in homeopathic medicine.

     i.   FEDERICK[5] KREISLER, b. 08 May 1987.
    ii.   PAUL KREISLER, b. 09 Jul 1985; d. 10 Mar 1986, Crib Death.

****

In 2005, Erika dictated a description of her experiences during World War I, when she was about 14 years old.

Tworok, Poland

We are Slavs by heritage. Our genealogical roots were deep into Yugoslavia and Czechoslovakia. We lived in a small town called Tworok, Poland. My father was the town mayor, and we owned a small store in Tworok. I attended private schools and generally life was good.....until January 7th, 1945.

It was the bitterest day, very cold. On January 7, 1945 I first left my home in Tworok. We had heard the bombing in the past weeks. Now it was getting closer and closer, louder and louder. We had been told of the Russian approach to our area and the stories of the Russians raping and killing, especially young girls. My Tanta Hauta "aunt" was most concerned and said "we can't let that happen to Erika...she cannot stay here". She was fearful of my fate. I kept cleaning house, just daily chores. Tante Hauta asked me "why are you cleaning? Are you cleaning for the Russians?". We all stopped and began to pack our suitcase. My Aunt and I were going to leave. My brothers were away, members of the German military, Heinz and Wolfgang. My mother planned to stay in the surrounding woods for a few days, then return to the home. Since my father was the Burgemeister, and owned his own store, we hesitated to leave all of our possessions unattended. I cried at the thought of leaving my mother. I was but 14 years old.

We went to the train station...there were no more tickets for sale. There were also NOmore trains to run. Actually, no more train conductors...they had left also. We did find one man who said he could drive a train...everyone crowded onto the train sitting silent on the tracks. As we were boarding, my mother appeared with a bundle under her arm. "The Russians are in town....we must leave immediately. We can't hide in the woods because it is too cold.. She said that father would stay behind and take care of the house. He would get as many of the town records as possible, load them and some furniture onto a horse and wagon and meet us somewhere at a later time. We had agreed to meet at my aunt's house in Germany, if we could get there...

The Trip to Czechoslovakia

We boarded the train. The driver had no conductor/driving a train experience. He managed to start the train but had no idea how to turn on the heat in the cars. Our toes were frozen. The train shot by the Russian bombers...This was to be the "last train out". People panicked, crowded on board and we were off.

We traveled toward Czechoslovakia. By the third day, the heat was on in the passenger cars. But at such a high level, we were very, very hot!! We had to walk part of the way...on the right side of the road were the people going east...some Russian prisoners. Some with no shoes. On the left side of the road we went west...long lines of travelers. Just before we left home, my father gave us a whole bag of ration cards so we could buy bread. When we passed Russian soldiers, my Aunt would slip them some bread. We didn't have much either. Russians were under German guard, but we slipped them some anyway. My Aunt was like that. We worried that my Aunt would end up getting us all put into a concentration camp.

I also had a ration card good for ONE dress, one handkerchief, and one pair of shoes. As refugees, my Aunt took my card and changed the handkerchief to a "dress". This was not allowed and definitely punishable, but Erika got two dresses. We bought that brown dress. "I can still see her sitting at the kitchen table erasing the handkerchief and forging the extra dress. But we got away with it. No one could have been poorer than us."

We finally reached Czechoslovakia. My brother, Heinz was stationed in Prague. We were delighted to be closer to him. We lived in a school for about a month. This school was set up for the refugees with nowhere else to go. We remained there till February 13th. My father arrived and found us at the school. One aunt in Germany was kept abreast of our location and able to relay this information to my father. My father told us we can't stay here in Prague...the Russians are fast approaching this area.

Everyone had talked of returning home...this was after all just a temporary evasion until the Russians left the area. We planned to return home within days. This didn't appear to be the fate in store for us. We wanted to return to our home in Poland. So we went to the train station. The trains were again full...so we waited in the cellar till our name was called, indicating that our train was ready to go. Millions were waiting for their names to be called and waited a long time. Our destination this time was Germany, my aunt's house.

The Trip to Germany

My mother and I managed to board the train...but my father couldn't push through the crowd. I started to cry. A nearby person asked me why I was crying...and I explained because my father can't get through the crowds. This person began helping us and everyone moved aside so my father could board the train. The people were hanging on to the bumpers. In Dresden, my father got in and we were on the train to Grimma. I was tired. Part of the way we went by foot, stayed in empty schools overnight. At one of these places, while I slept, someone stole my boots...there were black leather, laying on the floor. We had no blankets in January. It was cold. Without my boats I had to wear my "other" pair of shoes, my summer shoes. It was soooo cold and I was soooo tired, it really got to me emotionally.

We ended up at my Aunt's home in Germany. The Americans came into Germany and our area, very peacefully. The River was dividing the town....on the right side the Russians occupied the area. On the left side, the Americans held firm. Just as I crawled into bed, with thenight air chilling me, the sirens went off. The bombing had started again. I told my Aunt that "I don't want to get up. " But the adults insisted that we go into the cellar. The sky towards Dresden was firey red, the entire sky. Dresden was being bombed. We hear the next afternoon that they bombed the train station...the same one where we were at the day before was now rubble. It was only grace that allowed me to get over the sights I saw and heard. Many adults and even my parents had a very difficult time blocking out those images throughout their life. As a young person, I could more easily block out the images I had seen.

People threw fire bombs...people were on fire. People running through the streets heading toward the river...jumping into the river while on fire. The entire town was bombed.

A few days later, my brother, Heinz, was captured by the Russians in Czecholslavakia , close to Prague. He could speak Russian and Polish, so he was used as an interpreter. This was to his advantage at that time. There were so many prisoners at the time, the Russians would let some of the prisoners go. Some were sent to Russia to work as "slave labor". Others were given papers and just released. Heinz wrote out his own release papers with a pass to Poland, hoping we were still in our home town in Poland. He learned we were now in Germany . Some of the released soldiers who were in Germany and wanted to get to Poland traded orders/papers with

Heinz. Both soldiers headed towards their families. He totally changed his identity and made it to my Aunt's house. He had as his goal to be back home with his family on my mother's birthday in June.

My brother, Wolfe, was captured by the United States soldiers and shot in the chest by Russian soldiers…all at seventeen years old. He left the front to come to my Aunt's house…the family predetermined location in case it was impossible to stay at home in Polant. My relatives, Heidi's family, and many other relatives all came to this one Aunt's home. The Americans came and lived in her house too. The Americans allowed us to stay in the kitchen during the daytime, but we must leave the house at night. My Aunt would wash their clothes and in return the Americans gave us food.

We found another place to live at a 'wealthy ladies' home. Her brother owned an aluminum factory in England. She was crippled and lived alone in her beautiful home. She took people "in" like us because she was afraid to live alone during this time.

Directly across the street from this home lived the American Commandant. This was a very exclusive portion of town…in the town of Grimma, Germany. You could look into the Commandant's yard from this house and we watched them closely. We didn't have much else to do from February through June.

Heinz arrived in Grimma and joined us at the wealthy ladies home. He had been with us just two days when he say something. Heinz was still in the area under his "false" passport with his younger brother, Wolf, wounded and bedridden. Once in a while the Americans would come to the house an steal things like the alarm clock. Once of those trips, I was in the kitchen and the American asked me if there were any German soldiers in the house? Some neighbors had told him that there were soldiers at this residence. I explained that "yes, my brother was wounded and in bed and only 17 years old." The US solders were in uniforms and had guns and entered Wolfe's room. Wolfe jumped up, quite alarmed. The solders said, "no, lay back down and when you feel like it, go to the hospital and get papers and you won't have to go to prison.".

Heinz had noticed that the US Commander and Russian officers were going into the same house. The US was packing up. The Russians were moving in. Heinz knew that if the US was leaving and the Russians moving in….we needed to move. He knew someone in Bamberg and vowed not to stay in this place with the Russians. This was a Saturday with the US pulling out. ON Sunday the 21st of June, we left Grimma on the train to Leipzig. The Leipzig train station was now in total rubble so we kept going to Dresden…the end of the line.

We started walking. We slept in old barns and for supper the farmer brought us boiled potatoes—a luxury. Hundreds of other refugees were on this road to Bayreuth. While walking we arrived at a "border patrol" area and there was a man with a two wheel pushcart. He offered us his cart. Oh, yes, we felt like we had a limosene. Now we didn't have to carry our suitcases and took turns pushing the cart over the hills. Other people walked with us and shared our cart. One perons helped the other.

Finally a truck came and we were able to ride the rest of the way to Bamburg.
Soon after arrival to Bamburg, I began working for the RED Cross and took classes in nursing school. Then I met your Daddy (Herman R. Faircloth). This was the beginning of a love affair that would never end. This was a chance in a trillion to meet your Daddy. As of 2005, Momma is 75 years old and Daddy just turned 78 on Feb 4, 2005. The love affair continues.

(This account as told to Joyce Christine Faircloth Judah, daughter of Herman R. and Erika E. Faircloth) on February 5, 2005 at Holden Beach, NC by Erika E. Faircloth at age 75).

Gasthaus zum Silberblick in Friedrichshütte/OS., Kr. Tarnowitz. Inh. Karl Zuber

Gasthaus (Guesthouse) in Friedrichschutte (the name of the town after 1939) Tarnowitz is the neighboring town/area. This guesthouse was owned by Josep Krajczi great-great-grandfather of Isaih Dale Fisher, great grandfather of Joyce Christine Faircloth Judah and grandfather of Erika Else (Krajczi) Kreisler Faircloth.

Generation No. 1

1. LILLIAN ELIZABETH[10] FAIRCLOTH *(LAWRENCE C.[9], BENJAMIN F.[8], THEOPHELES "AFFIE"[7], ARTHUR[6], HARDWICK[5], WILLIAM[4], WILLIAM[3], WILLIAM[2], WILLIAM[1])* was born 15 Dec 1915 in Sampson Co., NC; Little Coherie Township., and died in Fayetteville, NC; buried in Bear Creek, NC next to George, her husband. She married GEORGE OZMENT.

Children of LILLIAN FAIRCLOTH and GEORGE OZMENT are:
2.   i. JACK LAWRENCE[11] OZMENT, b. 02 May 1937.
         ii. BOBBIE OZMENT.
        iii. FAYE LUNETTE OZMENT, m. JACK N. JONES.
Notes:

Birth certificate — North Carolina State Board of Health, Bureau of Vital Statistics, Certificate of Birth

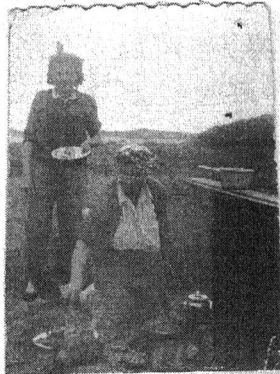

Lizzie Lillie standing and Lula Faircloth, kneeling at an outing at Fort Fisher.

Generation No. 2

2. JACK LAWRENCE[11] OZMENT *(LILLIAN ELIZABETH[10] FAIRCLOTH, LAWRENCE C.[9], BENJAMIN F.[8], THEOPHELES "AFFIE"[7], ARTHUR[6], HARDWICK[5], WILLIAM[4], WILLIAM[3], WILLIAM[2], WILLIAM[1])* was born 02 May 1937. He married BETTY LOU JOINER. She was born 27 Jan 1939.

Children of JACK OZMENT and BETTY JOINER are:
3.   i. SUSAN DENISE[12] OZMENT, b. 22 Feb, Fayetteville, NC.
       ii. JACK LAWRENCE OZMENT II, b. 20 Dec 1960, Fayetteville, NC.

Generation No. 3

3. SUSAN DENISE[12] OZMENT *(JACK LAWRENCE[11], LILLIAN ELIZABETH[10] FAIRCLOTH, LAWRENCE C.[9], BENJAMIN F.[8], THEOPHELES "AFFIE"[7], ARTHUR[6], HARDWICK[5], WILLIAM[4], WILLIAM[3], WILLIAM[2], WILLIAM[1])* was born 22 Feb in Fayetteville, NC. She married CHARLES LATTIMORE May 1982, son of CHARLES LATTIMORE and SUSAN OZMENT.

Children of SUSAN OZMENT and CHARLES LATTIMORE are:
     i. WILLIAM DOUGLAS[13] LATTIMORE, b. 16 Dec 1983, Raleigh, NC.
     ii. LORA LEIGH LATTIMORE, b. 26 Aug 1964; m. GEORGE BUTLER.

Notes:

Generation No. 1

1. LEROY[10] FAIRCLOTH *(LAWRENCE C.[9], BENJAMIN F.[8], THEOPHELES "AFFIE"[7], ARTHUR[6], HARDWICK[5], WILLIAM[4], WILLIAM[3], WILLIAM[2], WILLIAM[1])* was born 05 May 1918 in Hayne, NC. He married (1) ADDIE MAE CHEEK.   He married (2) ALICE TAYLOR.

Child of LEROY FAIRCLOTH and ADDIE CHEEK is:
    i. BONNIE[11] FAIRCLOTH.

Roy   Bonnie   Roy's Granddaughter/
                         Bonnie's Daughter

North Carolina State Board of Health

BUREAU OF VITAL STATISTICS

CERTIFICATE OF BIRTH

1 PLACE OF BIRTH	
County	Sampson
Township or Town or City	Little Coharie
Registration District No.	82 7008
Certificate No.	27
(If birth occurs in hospital or other institution, give name of same instead of street number)	
2 FULL NAME OF CHILD	Fairchild
3 Boy or Girl	Boy
4 Twin, triplet, or other?	
5 Number in order of birth	
6 Parents married?	Yes
7 Date of birth	May 3, 1918

FATHER		MOTHER	
8 FULL NAME	Lawrence Fairchild	14 NAME BEFORE MARRIAGE	Lula Cath Fairchild
9 POSTOFFICE ADDRESS	Hayne N.C.	15 POSTOFFICE ADDRESS	Hayne N.C.
10 COLOR	White	16 COLOR	White
11 AGE AT LAST BIRTHDAY		17 AGE AT LAST BIRTHDAY	
12 BIRTHPLACE	Hayne N.C.	18 BIRTHPLACE	Hayne N.C.
13 OCCUPATION	Farmer	19 OCCUPATION	Farm Labor

20 Number of children born to this mother, including present birth... 3

21 Number of children of this mother now living... 3

CERTIFICATE OF ATTENDING PHYSICIAN OR MIDWIFE

22 I hereby certify that I attended the birth of this child, who was Alive at 7:20 A.M. on the date above stated.

23 (Signature) William Tanner McCooke (State whether physician or midwife)

24 P.O. Hayne N.C.

Given name added from supplemental report

8-1-79 NWS

25 Witness (Signature of witness necessary only when 23 is signed by mark)

26 Filed May 19 18

27 J. W. Quinn Local Registrar

28 P.O. Richmond

*When there was no attending physician or midwife, then the father, householder, etc., should make this return. If a child breathes even once, it must not be reported as stillborn. No report is desired of stillbirths before the fifth month of pregnancy.

Generation No. 1

1.   JOYCE MARIE[10] FAIRCLOTH   (*LAWRENCE C.[9], BENJAMIN F.[8], THEOPHELES "AFFIE"[7], ARTHUR[6], HARDWICK[5], WILLIAM[4], WILLIAM[3], WILLIAM[2], WILLIAM[1]*) was born 16 Oct 1929. She married (1) DONALD TAYLOR, son of WILLIAM TAYLOR and LULA CURRIE.   She married (2) CHARLIE FLOYD FISHER. He was born 04 Nov 1926, and died 28 Apr 1956.

Joyce and Don Taylor

Joyce lived most of her life with her husband, Donald, on Camelot Drive in Fayetteville, NC. Her young pixie look, and her cheerful attitude made her one of my favorite aunts. Her home was her castle and was tastefully decorated with the country look. It contained many beautiful antiques including her own cross stitch pictures and her antique doll collection. Her basket collection was her pride. Joyce worked at Belks Department Store for many years till her retirement. She sang in the church choir and had a voice like an angel. Joyce is a great conversationalist and anyone could go to her home and feel most welcomed at any time.

Children of JOYCE FAIRCLOTH and DONALD TAYLOR are:
2.   i.   DONALD LAYLON[11] TAYLOR, b. 13 Mar 1959.
3.   ii. LISA MARIE TAYLORR, b. 19 Nov 1960.

Children of JOYCE FAIRCLOTH and CHARLIE FISHER are:
4.   iii. CHARLIE FLOYD[11] FISHER, b. 04 Nov 1949, Fayetteville, NC.
5.   iv. LINNIE LOU FISHER, b. 03 Nov 1947, Fayetteville, NC.
6.   v.   BRENDA SUE FISHER, b. 07 Nov 1951.

Generation No. 2

2.   DONALD LAYLON[11] TAYLOR *(JOYCE MARIE[10] FAIRCLOTH, LAWRENCE C.[9], BENJAMIN F.[8], THEOPHELES "AFFIE"[7], ARTHUR[6], HARDWICK[5], WILLIAM[4], WILLIAM[3], WILLIAM[2], WILLIAM[1])* was born 13 Mar 1959. He married MARCIE ANN YOUNG. She died Mar 1999 in Duke Hospital; died of Leukemia;.
Donald and his sister, Lisa, both moved to the Grays Creek area and have a far-like home setting with their respective families. Both Donnie and Lisa loved animals and seemed to always surround themselves with plenty of them.

Children of DONALD TAYLOR and MARCIE YOUNG are:
        i.   CHASITY ANN[12] TAYLOR, b. 11 Aug 1983.
        ii. LEIGHTON TAYLOR, b. 31 Oct 1991.

3.   LISA MARIE[11] TAYLORR *(JOYCE MARIE[10] FAIRCLOTH, LAWRENCE C.[9], BENJAMIN F.[8], THEOPHELES "AFFIE"[7], ARTHUR[6], HARDWICK[5], WILLIAM[4], WILLIAM[3], WILLIAM[2], WILLIAM[1])* was born 19 Nov 1960. She married JAMES EDWARD PHILLIPS 06 Apr 1979.

Child of LISA TAYLOR and JAMES PHILLIPS is:
        i.   TINA MARIE[12] PHILLIPS, b. 06 Sep 1984.

4.   CHARLIE FLOYD[11] FISHER *(JOYCE MARIE[10] FAIRCLOTH, LAWRENCE C.[9], BENJAMIN F.[8], THEOPHELES "AFFIE"[7], ARTHUR[6], HARDWICK[5], WILLIAM[4], WILLIAM[3], WILLIAM[2], WILLIAM[1])* was born 04 Nov 1949 in Fayetteville, NC. He married JENNIFER MCLAUREN.

Children of CHARLIE FISHER and JENNIFER MCLAUREN are:
        i.   CHARLIE FLOYD[12] FISHER, b. 25 Aug 1968; m. COLLEEN.
7.   ii. HEATHER SUZANNE FISHER, b. 18 Apr 1970.

5.   LINNIE LOU[11] FISHER *(JOYCE MARIE[10] FAIRCLOTH, LAWRENCE C.[9], BENJAMIN F.[8], THEOPHELES "AFFIE"[7], ARTHUR[6], HARDWICK[5], WILLIAM[4], WILLIAM[3], WILLIAM[2], WILLIAM[1])* was born 03 Nov 1947 in Fayetteville, NC. She married GARY TIERNEY.

Children of LINNIE FISHER and GARY TIERNEY are:
        i.   KIM[12] TIERNEY, b. 15 Jan; m. JOSEPH DAIGEL.
        ii. GARY TIERNEY, b. 28 Mar 1973; m. CHRISTY.

6. BRENDA SUE[11] FISHER *(JOYCE MARIE[10] FAIRCLOTH, LAWRENCE C.[9], BENJAMIN F.[8], THEOPHELES "AFFIE"[7], ARTHUR[6], HARDWICK[5], WILLIAM[4], WILLIAM[3], WILLIAM[2], WILLIAM[1])* was born 07 Nov 1951. She married (2) TERRY BARBER. She married (1)LARRY CASHWELL.

Child of BRENDA FISHER and TERRY BARBER is:
> i. TERYY LYNDELL[12] BARBER.

Child of BRENDA FISHER and LARRY CASHWELL is:
8.   ii. LARRY GRANT[12] CASHWELL, JR., b. 03 Mar 1973.

Generation No. 3

7. HEATHER SUZANNE[12] FISHER *(CHARLIE FLOYD[11], JOYCE MARIE[10] FAIRCLOTH, LAWRENCE C.[9], BENJAMIN F.[8], THEOPHELES "AFFIE"[7], ARTHUR[6], HARDWICK[5], WILLIAM[4], WILLIAM[3], WILLIAM[2], WILLIAM[1])* was born 18 Apr 1970. She married (1) JOE. He died in Died prior to Heather marrying Joe. She married (2) UNKNOWN.

Children of HEATHER FISHER and JOE are:
> i. WHITNEY[13], b. Abt. 1997.
> ii. JEREMY WHITNEY, b. Abt. 1992.

8. LARRY GRANT[12] CASHWELL, JR. *(BRENDA SUE[11] FISHER, JOYCE MARIE[10] FAIRCLOTH, LAWRENCE C.[9], BENJAMIN F.[8], THEOPHELES "AFFIE"[7], ARTHUR[6], HARDWICK[5], WILLIAM[4], WILLIAM[3], WILLIAM[2], WILLIAM[1])* was born 03 Mar 1973. He married ANGIE LAUDENCLAWS (SPELLING?). She was born Abt. 1973.

Children of LARRY CASHWELL and ANGIE (SPELLING?) are:
> i. LARRY GRANT[13] CASHWELL III, b. 13 Feb 1995.
> ii. ASHLEY BLAKE CASHWELL, b. 09 Apr 1999.

Notes:

Descendants of Helen Faircloth

Generation No. 1

1. HELEN[10] FAIRCLOTH *(LAWRENCE C.*[9]*, BENJAMIN F.*[8]*, THEOPHELES "AFFIE"*[7]*, ARTHUR*[6]*, HARDWICK*[5]*, WILLIAM*[4]*, WILLIAM*[3]*, WILLIAM*[2]*, WILLIAM*[1]*)* was born 16 Sep 1924. She married WINFRED PAUL SAUNDERS 06 Mar 1947 in Raeford, NC, son of WILLIAM SAUNDERS and BERTIE HOLD. He was born 08 Dec 1921, and died 06 Jul 1999.

283

Paul and Helen Saunders   **Helen Saunders**

Children of HELEN FAIRCLOTH and WINFRED SAUNDERS are:

2.   i.   WILLIAM LAWRENCE[11] SAUNDERS, b. 17 Jun 1948, Fayetteville, NC.

3.   ii. PAUL WINFORD SAUNDERS, b. 10 Sep 1951.

4.   iii. STEVEN ANTHONY SAUNDERS, b. 22 May 1959, Fayetteville, NC.

Generation No. 2

2. WILLIAM LAWRENCE[11] SAUNDERS *(HELEN[10] FAIRCLOTH, LAWRENCE C.[9], BENJAMIN F.[8], THEOPHELES "AFFIE"[7], ARTHUR[6], HARDWICK[5], WILLIAM[4], WILLIAM[3], WILLIAM[2], WILLIAM[1])* was born 17 Jun 1948 in Fayetteville, NC. He married (1) KATHY. He married (2) BOBBIE.

Larry and Bobbie

Child of WILLIAM SAUNDERS and KATHY is:
    i. TRACY[12] SAUNDERS, b. 28 Mar 1974.

3.   PAUL WINFORD[11] SAUNDERS *(HELEN[10] FAIRCLOTH, LAWRENCE C.[9], BENJAMIN F.[8], THEOPHELES "AFFIE"[7], ARTHUR[6], HARDWICK[5], WILLIAM[4], WILLIAM[3], WILLIAM[2], WILLIAM[1])* was born 10 Sep 1951. He married CAROLYN FUQUA 27 Jun 1971. She was born 17 Aug 1953.

Windy and Carolyn Saunders

Children of PAUL SAUNDERS and CAROLYN FUQUA are:
    i. KARA[12] SAUNDERS, b. 03 Oct 1982.
   ii. DANA SAUNDERS, b. 18 Sep 1971.

4. STEVEN ANTHONY[11] SAUNDERS *(HELEN[10] FAIRCLOTH, LAWRENCE C.[9], BENJAMIN F.[8], THEOPHELES "AFFIE"[7], ARTHUR[6], HARDWICK[5], WILLIAM[4], WILLIAM[3], WILLIAM[2], WILLIAM[1])* was born 22 May 1959 in Fayetteville, NC. He married (1) KARYL MCKEE. He married (2) JACKIE PARADISE.

Children of STEVEN SAUNDERS and KARYL MCKEE are:
    i. JASON[12] SAUNDERS.
   ii. MALE SAUNDERS.

Descendants of Lottie Juanita Faircloth

Generation No. 1

1. LOTTIE JUANITA[10] FAIRCLOTH *(LAWRENCE C.[9], BENJAMIN F.[8], THEOPHELES "AFFIE"[7], ARTHUR[6], HARDWICK[5], WILLIAM[4], WILLIAM[3], WILLIAM[2], WILLIAM[1])* was born 30 Oct 1932. She married ARWOOD HAMMOND 25 Nov. He was born Abt. 1930, and died in Buried in Legion Road Cemetery, Hope, Mills, NC. Arwood died of a heart attack while at home and enroute to the hospital.

Children of LOTTIE FAIRCLOTH and ARWOOD HAMMOND are:
2.   i.   KATHY ANN[11] HAMMOND, b. 19 Oct 1951, Fayetteville, NC.
        ii.   ARWOOD HAMMOND, b. 28 Apr; m. (1) TERESA MILAN; m. (2) VALERIE TONNETT.
       iii.   MELISSA SUE HAMMOND, b. 21 May.
        iv.   BOBBY HAMMOND, b. 14 Jun.

Bobby Hammond

Woody Hammond

2. KATHY ANN[11] HAMMOND *(LOTTIE JUANITA[10] FAIRCLOTH, LAWRENCE C.[9], BENJAMIN F.[8], THEOPHELES "AFFIE"[7], ARTHUR[6], HARDWICK[5], WILLIAM[4], WILLIAM[3], WILLIAM[2], WILLIAM[1])* was born 19 Oct 1951 in Fayetteville, NC. She married THOMAS DAVID DAUGHTRY.

David and Kathy Daughtry

Children of KATHY HAMMOND and THOMAS DAUGHTRY are:
    i. THOMAS DAVID[12] DAUGHTRY.
    ii. ADAM WOOD DAUGHTRY.

Descendants of Judy Adline Faircloth

Generation No. 1

1.   JUDY ADLINE[10] FAIRCLOTH *(LAWRENCE C.[9], BENJAMIN F.[8], THEOPHELES "AFFIE"[7], ARTHUR[6], HARDWICK[5], WILLIAM[4], WILLIAM[3], WILLIAM[2], WILLIAM[1])* was born 27 Mar 1938 in B St., Fayetteville, NC, and died 2005. She married RAEFORD SMITH.

Children of JUDY FAIRCLOTH and RAEFORD SMITH are:
- i.   JULIE[11] SMITH, d. Abt. 1993, Died of cancer;.
- ii.   MICHAEL SMITH.
- iii. DONNA SMITH.
- iv. DONNIE SMITH.
2. v.   GINA SMITH, b. 07 Jun 1962.
- vi. TINA SMITH, b. 07 Jun 1962.
- vii. SHANE SMITH.
- viii. UNKNOWN SMITH, b. Abt. 1989.
- ix. JOHN SMITH.

Generation No. 2

2.   GINA[11] SMITH *(JUDY ADLINE[10] FAIRCLOTH, LAWRENCE C.[9], BENJAMIN F.[8], THEOPHELES "AFFIE"[7], ARTHUR[6], HARDWICK[5], WILLIAM[4], WILLIAM[3], WILLIAM[2], WILLIAM[1])* was born 07 Jun 1962.

Child of GINA SMITH is:
          i.   LENA MELISSA[12] SMITH, b. 18 Jan 1983.

Notes:

Generation No. 1

1.   CARL HOUSTON[10] FAIRCLOTH   *(LAWRENCE C.[9], BENJAMIN F.[8], THEOPHELES "AFFIE"[7], ARTHUR[6], HARDWICK[5], WILLIAM[4], WILLIAM[3], WILLIAM[2], WILLIAM[1])* was born 29 Oct 1920 in Sampson Co., NC, and died 28 Dec 1971 in Died in Chapel Hill Hospital during open heart surgery. Buried in Cross Creek Cemetery. Fayetteville, NC. He married (1) LILLIAN BERNICE BROWN, daughter of HOWARD B. BROWN. He married (2) LENA MAE BEARD 27 Jan 1948 in Dillon, SC, daughter of ALBERT BEARD and JENNY MCDONALD.

Houston and Lena Faircloth

Notes:

North Carolina State Board of Health

BUREAU OF VITAL STATISTICS

CERTIFICATE OF BIRTH

942

1 PLACE OF BIRTH

County Sampson

Township Little Coharie

or Town

or City

Registration District No. 82-7008

Certificate No. 103

(No.) (If birth occurs in hospital, or other institution, give name of same instead of street number) St.; Ward

2 FULL NAME OF CHILD Carl Houston Faircloth

3 Boy Girl Boy

4 Twin, triplet, or other?

5 Number in order of birth (To be answered only in event of plural births)

6 Parents married? yes

7 Date of birth Oct. 29 1920 (Name of Month) (Day) (Year)

FATHER	MOTHER
8 FULL NAME Lawrence Faircloth	14 NAME BEFORE MARRIAGE Lula J. Faircloth
9 POSTOFFICE ADDRESS Hoyne N.C.	15 POSTOFFICE ADDRESS Hoyne N.C.
10 COLOR White 11 AGE AT LAST BIRTHDAY 34 (Years)	16 COLOR White 17 AGE AT LAST BIRTHDAY 22 (Years)
12 BIRTHPLACE Sampson Co. N.C.	18 BIRTHPLACE Sampson Co. N.C.
13 OCCUPATION Day Laborer	19 OCCUPATION Housewife

20 Number of children born to this mother, including present birth 3

21 Number of children of this mother now living 3

CERTIFICATE OF ATTENDING PHYSICIAN OR MIDWIFE*

22 I hereby certify that I attended the birth of this child, who was born alive (Born alive or stillborn) at 9 A.M. (Hour, a. m. or p. m.) on the date above stated.

23 (Signature) G. L. Sikes M. D. (State whether physician or midwife)

24 P.O. Salemburg N.C.

Given name added from supplemental report

25 Witness (Signature of witness necessary only when 23 is signed by mark)

26 Filed Nov. 1 1920 27 L. M. White Local Registrar

28 P.O. Roseboro N.C.

Given name added from supplemental report ____, 19

Registrar

*When there was no attending physician or midwife, then the father, householder, etc., should make this return. If a child breathes even once, it must not be reported as stillborn. No report is desired of stillbirths before the fifth month of pregnancy.

Medical Information: Lillian died of Meningitis and neck trouble.

Houston and Lillian

Child of CARL FAIRCLOTH and LILLIAN BROWN is:

2.   i.   SHEILA RUBY[11] FAIRCLOTH, b. 05 Oct 1945.

Children of CARL FAIRCLOTH and LENA BEARD are:

3.   ii.   RONNIE DEVON[11] BEARD, b. 20 Mar 1946.

      iii.   CARL LEONDIOUS "BO" BEARD, b. 12 Jun 1948, Cumberland County, NC.

4.   iv.   HOUSTON DEARLD FAIRCLOTH, b. 21 Sep 1949.

5.   v.   KAREN ANN FAIRCLOTH, b. 30 Jul 1951.

6.   vi.   JUDY LORETTA FAIRCLOTH, b. 09 Dec 1952, Cumberland County, NC.

Generation No. 2

2.   SHEILA RUBY[11] FAIRCLOTH (*CARL HOUSTON[10], LAWRENCE C.[9], BENJAMIN F.[8], THEOPHELES "AFFIE"[7], ARTHUR[6], HARDWICK[5], WILLIAM[4], WILLIAM[3], WILLIAM[2], WILLIAM[1]*) was born 05 Oct 1945. She married DAVID MCKAY.

Sheila and David McKay

Children of SHEILA FAIRCLOTH and DAVID MCKAY are:
- i. KELLY PICKETT[12] MCKAY, b. 04 Jun, Kenansville, NC.
- ii. WILLIAM DAVID MCKAY, b. 15 Nov 1976, Kenansville, NC.

3. RONNIE DEVON[11] BEARD *(CARL HOUSTON[10] FAIRCLOTH, LAWRENCE C.[9], BENJAMIN F.[8], THEOPHELES "AFFIE"[7], ARTHUR[6], HARDWICK[5], WILLIAM[4], WILLIAM[3], WILLIAM[2], WILLIAM[1])* was born 20 Mar 1946. He married FAYE BUIE.

Children of RONNIE BEARD and FAYE BUIE are:
- i. EDDIE[12] BEARD, b. 1965.
- ii. DONNA RENEE BEARD, b. Sep 1970.
- iii. RONNIE DEVON, JR. BEARD, b. Aug.

4. HOUSTON DEARLD[11] FAIRCLOTH *(CARL HOUSTON[10], LAWRENCE C.[9], BENJAMIN F.[8], THEOPHELES "AFFIE"[7], ARTHUR[6], HARDWICK[5], WILLIAM[4], WILLIAM[3], WILLIAM[2], WILLIAM[1])* was born 21 Sep 1949. He married CHERRY L. GODWIN.

Children of HOUSTON FAIRCLOTH and CHERRY GODWIN are:
- i. KIMBERLY ANN[12] BEARD, b. 25 May 1968.
- ii. HOUSTON DEARLD FAIRCLOTH, JR., b. 17 Apr 1971.

5. KAREN ANN[11] FAIRCLOTH *(CARL HOUSTON[10], LAWRENCE C.[9], BENJAMIN F.[8], THEOPHELES "AFFIE"[7], ARTHUR[6], HARDWICK[5], WILLIAM[4], WILLIAM[3], WILLIAM[2], WILLIAM[1])* was born 30 Jul 1951. She married JOHNNY FAIRCLOTH Jan.

Child of KAREN FAIRCLOTH and JOHNNY FAIRCLOTH is:
- i. JOHNNY NELSON[12] FAIRCLOTH, JR., b. 21 Mar 1975.

6. JUDY LORETTA[11] FAIRCLOTH *(CARL HOUSTON[10], LAWRENCE C.[9], BENJAMIN F.[8], THEOPHELES "AFFIE"[7], ARTHUR[6], HARDWICK[5], WILLIAM[4], WILLIAM[3], WILLIAM[2], WILLIAM[1])* was born 09 Dec 1952 in Cumberland County, NC. She married DAVID TAYLOR.

Children of JUDY FAIRCLOTH and DAVID TAYLOR are:
- i. DAVID CARL TAYLOR[12] TAYLOR, b. 12 Jul 1970.
- ii. ZACHARY ANTHONY TAYLOR, b. 23 Mar 1979.

Notes:

End of Descendents of Lawrence C. and Lula J. Faircloth

PEDIGREE CHARTS OF THE FAMILY OF
EDWARD FARECLOTH

Standard Pedigree Tree

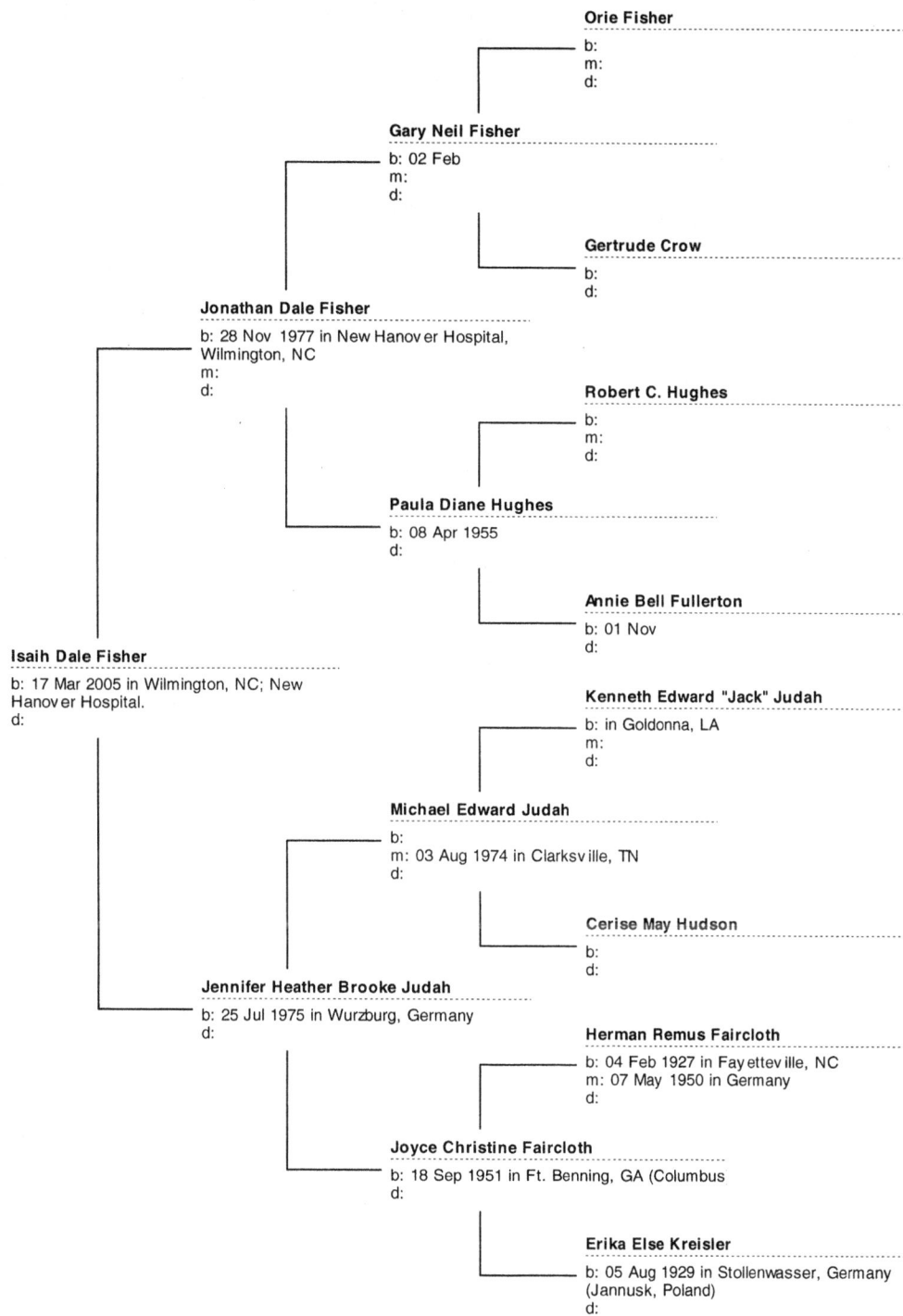

Orie Fisher
b:
m:
d:

Gary Neil Fisher
b: 02 Feb
m:
d:

Gertrude Crow
b:
d:

Jonathan Dale Fisher
b: 28 Nov 1977 in New Hanover Hospital,
Wilmington, NC
m:
d:

Robert C. Hughes
b:
m:
d:

Paula Diane Hughes
b: 08 Apr 1955
d:

Annie Bell Fullerton
b: 01 Nov
d:

Isaih Dale Fisher
b: 17 Mar 2005 in Wilmington, NC; New
Hanover Hospital.
d:

Kenneth Edward "Jack" Judah
b: in Goldonna, LA
m:
d:

Michael Edward Judah
b:
m: 03 Aug 1974 in Clarksville, TN
d:

Cerise May Hudson
b:
d:

Jennifer Heather Brooke Judah
b: 25 Jul 1975 in Wurzburg, Germany
d:

Herman Remus Faircloth
b: 04 Feb 1927 in Fayetteville, NC
m: 07 May 1950 in Germany
d:

Joyce Christine Faircloth
b: 18 Sep 1951 in Ft. Benning, GA (Columbus
d:

Erika Else Kreisler
b: 05 Aug 1929 in Stollenwasser, Germany
(Jannusk, Poland)
d:

Notes:

Standard Pedigree Tree

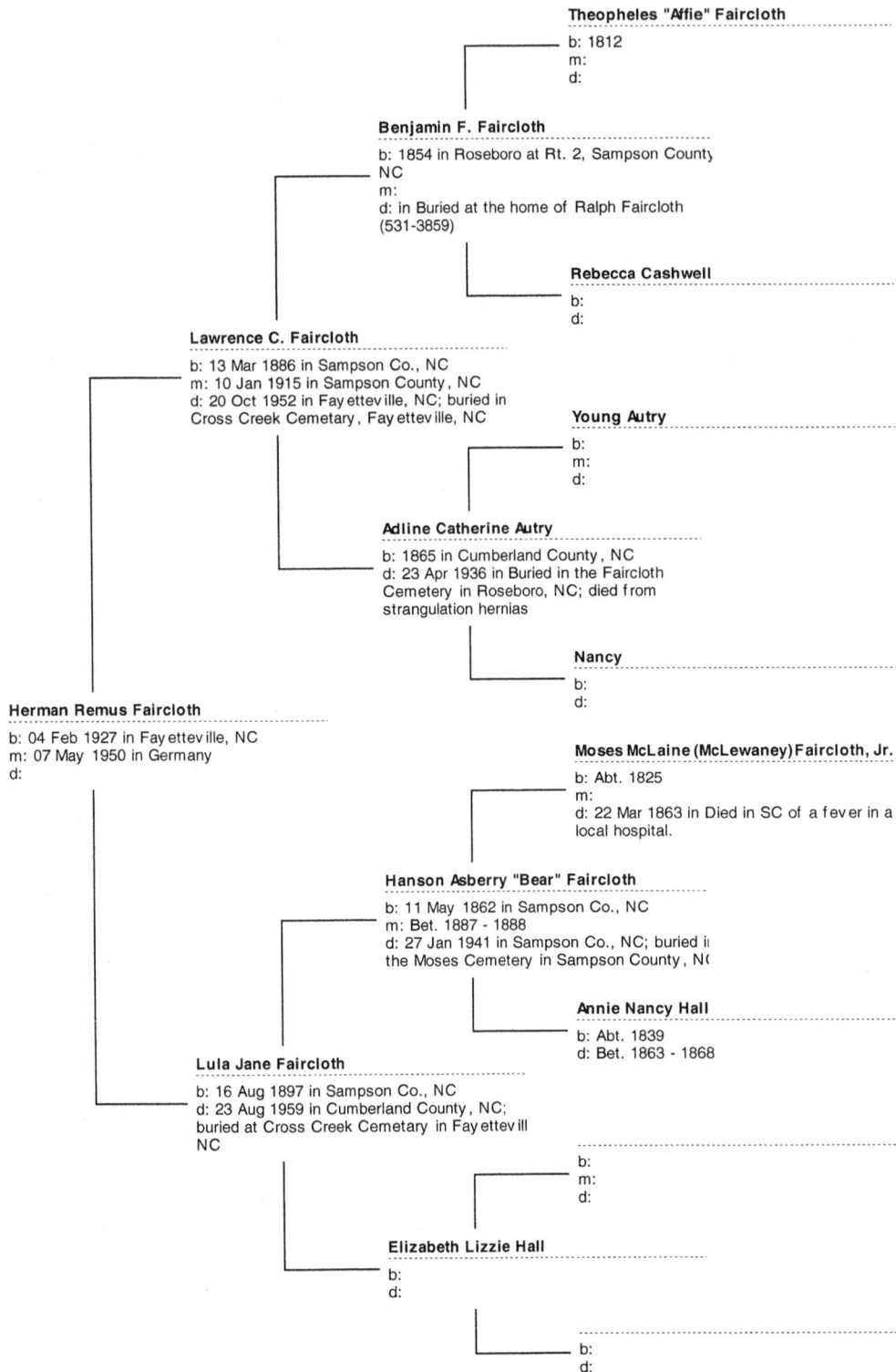

Theopheles "Affie" Faircloth
b: 1812
m:
d:

Benjamin F. Faircloth
b: 1854 in Roseboro at Rt. 2, Sampson County
NC
m:
d: in Buried at the home of Ralph Faircloth
(531-3859)

Rebecca Cashwell
b:
d:

Lawrence C. Faircloth
b: 13 Mar 1886 in Sampson Co., NC
m: 10 Jan 1915 in Sampson County, NC
d: 20 Oct 1952 in Fayetteville, NC; buried in
Cross Creek Cemetary, Fayetteville, NC

Young Autry
b:
m:
d:

Adline Catherine Autry
b: 1865 in Cumberland County, NC
d: 23 Apr 1936 in Buried in the Faircloth
Cemetery in Roseboro, NC; died from
strangulation hernias

Nancy
b:
d:

Herman Remus Faircloth
b: 04 Feb 1927 in Fayetteville, NC
m: 07 May 1950 in Germany
d:

Moses McLaine (McLewaney) Faircloth, Jr.
b: Abt. 1825
m:
d: 22 Mar 1863 in Died in SC of a fever in a
local hospital.

Hanson Asberry "Bear" Faircloth
b: 11 May 1862 in Sampson Co., NC
m: Bet. 1887 - 1888
d: 27 Jan 1941 in Sampson Co., NC; buried in
the Moses Cemetery in Sampson County, NC

Annie Nancy Hall
b: Abt. 1839
d: Bet. 1863 - 1868

Lula Jane Faircloth
b: 16 Aug 1897 in Sampson Co., NC
d: 23 Aug 1959 in Cumberland County, NC;
buried at Cross Creek Cemetary in Fayettevill
NC

b:
m:
d:

Elizabeth Lizzie Hall
b:
d:

b:
d:

Notes:

298

Standard Pedigree Tree

Edward Farecloth
b: Bet. 1700 - 1710
m:
d:

Benjamin Franklin Faircloth, Sr.
b: 1735
m:
d:

Sarah Unknown
b: Bet. 1700 - 1710
d: Aft. 1774

Solomon Faircloth
b: Abt. 1765
m:
d:

b:
m:
d:

Letitia "Leddy" GARNER
b: 1735
d:

b:
d:

Moses McLaine Faircloth, Sr.
b: Bet. 1795 - 1801
m:
d: Bet. 1860 - 1870 in 82 y rs old when died
about 1860-70. Charleston, SC

b:
m:
d:

b:
m:
d:

b:
d:

b:
d:

b:
d:

b:
m:
d:

b:
d:

b:
d:

Notes:

Pedigree Charts of the Family of

William Faircloth, I

Standard Pedigree Tree

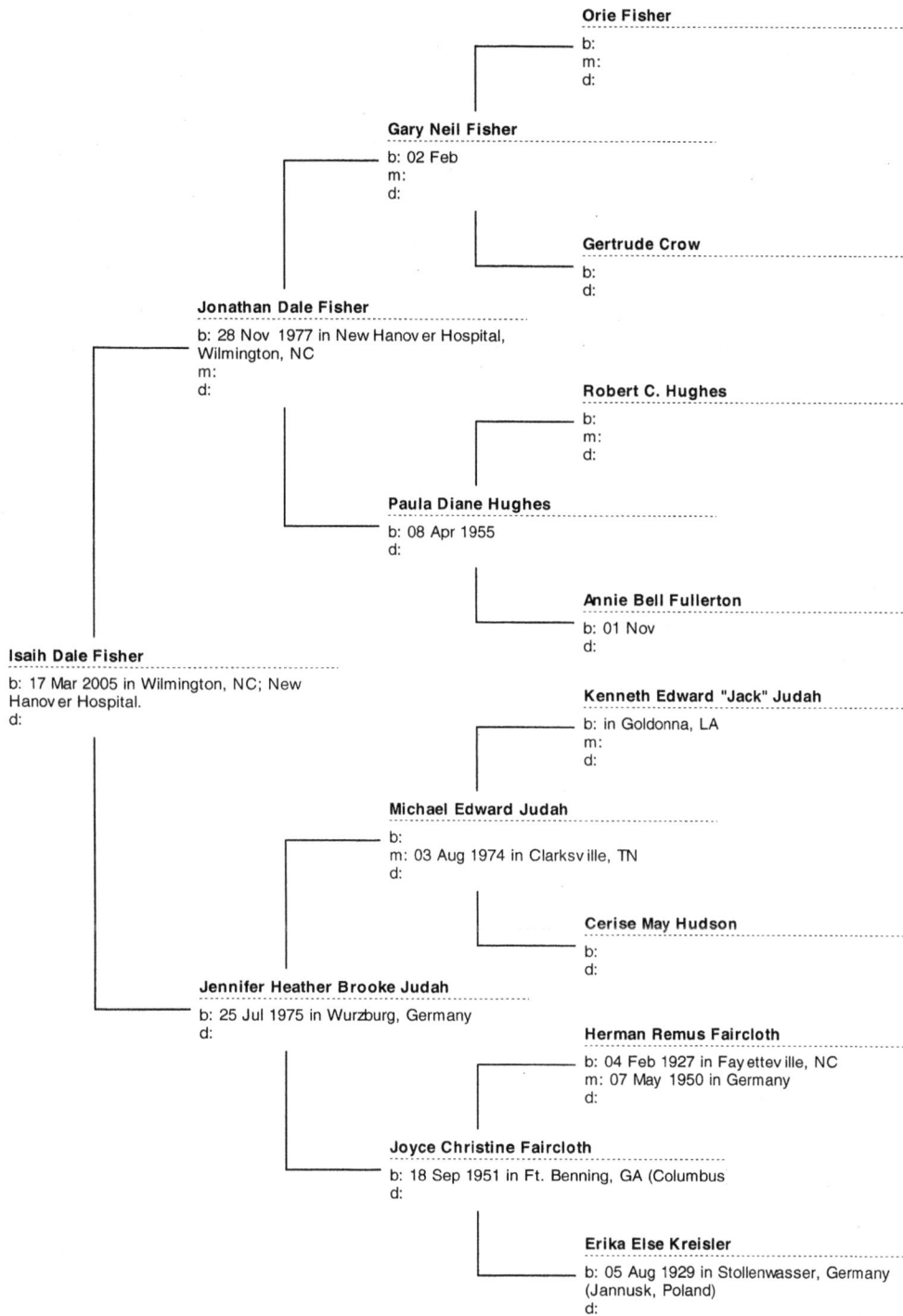

Orie Fisher
b:
m:
d:

Gary Neil Fisher
b: 02 Feb
m:
d:

Gertrude Crow
b:
d:

Jonathan Dale Fisher
b: 28 Nov 1977 in New Hanover Hospital,
Wilmington, NC
m:
d:

Robert C. Hughes
b:
m:
d:

Paula Diane Hughes
b: 08 Apr 1955
d:

Annie Bell Fullerton
b: 01 Nov
d:

Isaih Dale Fisher
b: 17 Mar 2005 in Wilmington, NC; New
Hanover Hospital.
d:

Kenneth Edward "Jack" Judah
b: in Goldonna, LA
m:
d:

Michael Edward Judah
b:
m: 03 Aug 1974 in Clarksville, TN
d:

Cerise May Hudson
b:
d:

Jennifer Heather Brooke Judah
b: 25 Jul 1975 in Wurzburg, Germany
d:

Herman Remus Faircloth
b: 04 Feb 1927 in Fayetteville, NC
m: 07 May 1950 in Germany
d:

Joyce Christine Faircloth
b: 18 Sep 1951 in Ft. Benning, GA (Columbus
d:

Erika Else Kreisler
b: 05 Aug 1929 in Stollenwasser, Germany
(Jannusk, Poland)
d:

Notes:

301

Standard Pedigree Tree

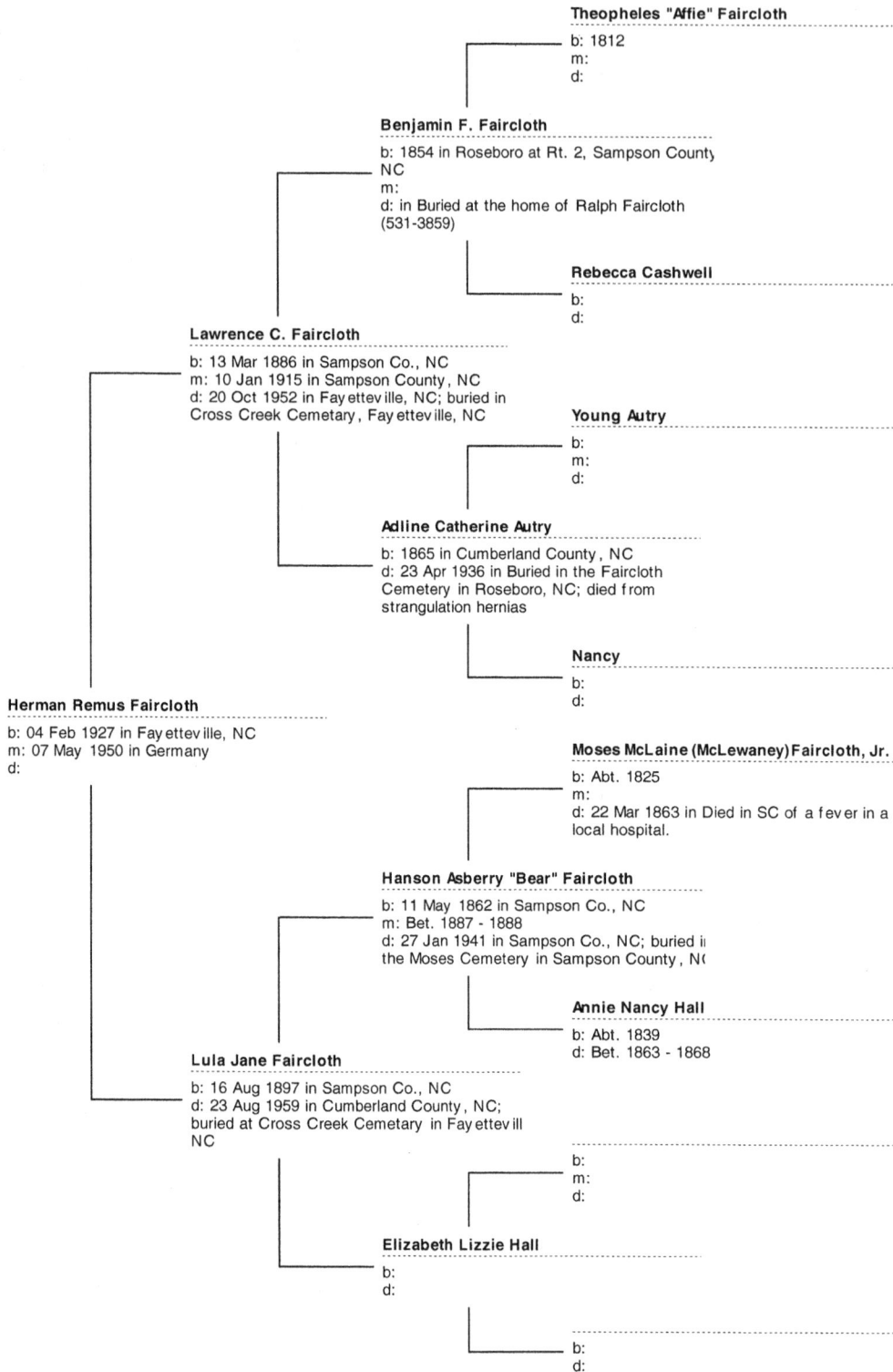

Theopheles "Affie" Faircloth
b: 1812
m:
d:

Benjamin F. Faircloth
b: 1854 in Roseboro at Rt. 2, Sampson County, NC
m:
d: in Buried at the home of Ralph Faircloth (531-3859)

Rebecca Cashwell
b:
d:

Lawrence C. Faircloth
b: 13 Mar 1886 in Sampson Co., NC
m: 10 Jan 1915 in Sampson County, NC
d: 20 Oct 1952 in Fayetteville, NC; buried in Cross Creek Cemetary, Fayetteville, NC

Young Autry
b:
m:
d:

Adline Catherine Autry
b: 1865 in Cumberland County, NC
d: 23 Apr 1936 in Buried in the Faircloth Cemetery in Roseboro, NC; died from strangulation hernias

Nancy
b:
d:

Herman Remus Faircloth
b: 04 Feb 1927 in Fayetteville, NC
m: 07 May 1950 in Germany
d:

Moses McLaine (McLewaney) Faircloth, Jr.
b: Abt. 1825
m:
d: 22 Mar 1863 in Died in SC of a fever in a local hospital.

Hanson Asberry "Bear" Faircloth
b: 11 May 1862 in Sampson Co., NC
m: Bet. 1887 - 1888
d: 27 Jan 1941 in Sampson Co., NC; buried in the Moses Cemetery in Sampson County, NC

Annie Nancy Hall
b: Abt. 1839
d: Bet. 1863 - 1868

Lula Jane Faircloth
b: 16 Aug 1897 in Sampson Co., NC
d: 23 Aug 1959 in Cumberland County, NC; buried at Cross Creek Cemetary in Fayetteville NC

b:
m:
d:

Elizabeth Lizzie Hall
b:
d:

b:
d:

Notes:

302

Standard Pedigree Tree

William Faircloth IV
b: Bet. 1740 - 1749
m:
d: 1765

Hardwick Faircloth
b: 1754 in Edgecombe Co., NC or Sampson County, NC
m:
d: Abt. 1810 in Sampson County, NC?

Sarah
b: Abt. 1730
d: Abt. 1727

Arthur Faircloth
b: 1775 in Sampson Co., NC; possible child c Samuel;
m:
d: Aft. 1840 in Bladen Co., NC

b:
m:
d:

Sarah Suggs
b:
d:

b:
d:

Theopheles "Affie" Faircloth
b: 1812
m:
d:

b:
m:
d:

Archibald McDaniel
b: Abt. 1860
m:
d:

b:
d:

Mary Ann McDaniel "Dicey Ann"
b: Bet. 1880 - 1890
d:

b:
m:
d:

Mary
b: Abt. 1860
d:

b:
d:

Notes:

Standard Pedigree Tree

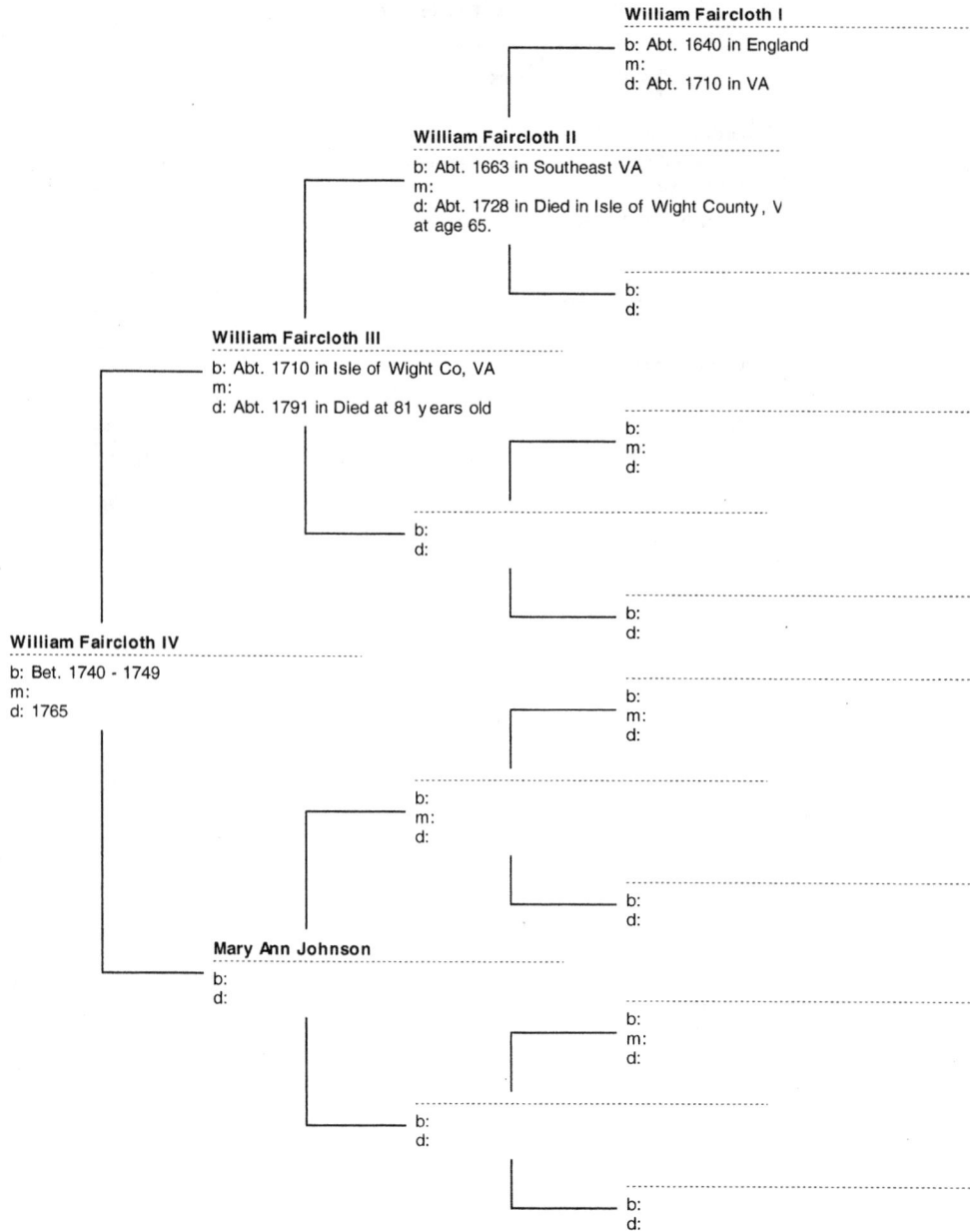

William Faircloth I
....
b: Abt. 1640 in England
m:
d: Abt. 1710 in VA

William Faircloth II
....
b: Abt. 1663 in Southeast VA
m:
d: Abt. 1728 in Died in Isle of Wight County, V
at age 65.

....
b:
d:

William Faircloth III
....
b: Abt. 1710 in Isle of Wight Co, VA
m:
d: Abt. 1791 in Died at 81 years old

....
b:
m:
d:

....
b:
d:

....
b:
d:

William Faircloth IV
....
b: Bet. 1740 - 1749
m:
d: 1765

....
b:
m:
d:

....
b:
m:
d:

....
b:
d:

....
b:
d:

Mary Ann Johnson
....
b:
d:

....
b:
m:
d:

....
b:
m:
d:

....
b:
d:

....
b:
d:

Notes:

Note: All records listed are not guaranteed for accuracy or data input errors. All information is presumed accurate, but no liability exists for its accuracy. When doubts of accuracy or documentation to prove accuracy is known, that information is noted. It is well known that others may interpret data differently or re-assign children to different parents. Every courtesy has been taken to present other known views.

And to the spirit which sat on my left shoulder throughout the editing of this book....you were welcome

Herman R. Faircloth and Great-Grandson, Isaih Dale Fisher

THE BEGINNING......

INDEX

317

318

320

330

Family Notes:

Family Notes:

Family Notes:

Family Notes:

Family Notes:

_____

_____

_____

_____

_____

_____

_____

_____

_____

_____

_____

_____

_____

_____

_____

_____

_____

_____

_____

_____

_____

_____

_____

_____

_____

_____

_____

_____

_____

* 9 7 8 0 7 8 8 4 4 4 7 2 2 *